CITY OF GOD

Other books by Robert C. Linthicum:

Christian Revolution for Church Renewal (1972)
Choose You This Day: Creating the Future for Your Church (1975)
The People Who Met God (1980)
The People Who Turned the World Upside Down (1982)
A Transformacao da Cidade (1990, Brazil)
Empowering the Poor: Community Organizing Among the "Rag, Tag and Bobtail" (1991)

CITY OF GOD
CITY OF SATAN

A Biblical Theology
of the Urban Church

Robert C. Linthicum

ZondervanPublishingHouse
Academic and Professional Books
Grand Rapids, Michigan

A Division of HarperCollins*Publishers*

Requests for information should be addressed to:
Zondervan Publishing House
Academic and Professional Books
Grand Rapids, Michigan 49530

All royalties from this book support World Vision's "Urban Advance" ministry in major cities of Asia, Africa, and Latin America.

Cover Design by Rachel Hostetter
Cover Illustration by Paul Klee. Auserwählte Stätte. *1927.*

Library of Congress Cataloging-in-Publication Data
Linthicum, Robert C.
    City of God, city of Satan : a biblical theology for the urban church / Robert C. Linthicum.
        p. cm.
    Includes bibliographical references and index.
    ISBN 0-310-53141-1
    1. Cities and towns—Religious aspects—Christianity. 2. Cities and towns—Biblical teaching. 3. City churches. 4. Evangelistic work. 5. Church renewal. I. Title.
BR115.C45L55   1991   90-24199
250'.9173'2—dc20   CIP

Printed in the United States of America

94 95 96 / CH / 10 9 8 7 6 5 4

To the members of
Edgewater Presbyterian Church in Chicago and
Grosse Pointe Woods Presbyterian Church near Detroit,
this book is affectionately dedicated.

For seventeen years between them,
these congregations welcomed
my family and me into their hearts,
reached out in compassion to their communities,
and lived before us that urban theology
that I struggle here to place into words.

CONTENTS

PREFACE

The first day of the four-day urban workshop had ended, and those attending the largest gathering of evangelical pastors in the history of Bogota, Colombia, were preparing to leave. Someone had turned off the television lights; people had stopped their video and audio recorders. It was time to go home after a busy day together.

But no one was leaving! Suddenly I became aware that the workshop's participants were all standing around the room, arms waving, voices rising, in animated conversation.

I turned to Hector Pardo, the pastor who heads the evangelical coalition in Colombia. "What's happening, Hector?" I asked. "Why are people staying? What is exciting them so?"

"Brother Bob," Hector replied, "it is what you presented today. These pastors have been trying to minister in a city they can barely cope with, much less understand. What has happened today is that you have provided a way for them to biblically understand their city and their ministry in this city. And they don't want to let this moment pass!"

It has been my privilege as the director of World Vision's Office of Urban Advance to see this scene repeated often over the past four years. Part of my responsibilities for World Vision is to lead workshops for urban pastors and Christian leaders throughout the world. Several thousand pastors from thirty-eight pivotal cities in Australia, Bangladesh, Brazil, Colombia, Great Britain, Hong Kong, India, Japan, Kenya, Malawi, Mexico, the Philippines, Singapore, Taiwan, Thailand, Zimbabwe, and the United States have thus far participated in these urban workshops.

Particularly in "two-thirds world" countries (often referred to as the third world), pastors have insisted that the praxis of urban ministry be grounded in biblical reflection. This in turn has accelerated a long-time intention of mine to write the urban biblical theology that I had been slowly formulating over previous years. The result has been the World Vision curriculum, "City of Yahweh; City of Ba'al," which I developed and have since taught in the thirty-eight cities referred to. The reactions and responses of my urban third world brothers and sisters in the faith—

ranging from enthusiastic support to penetrating criticism—have in turn matured and shaped that material.

The book you are about to read is the result of that reflective interaction with third world and first world urban pastors over the past four years. But it has developed primarily out of my continuing efforts to integrate my biblical reflection and my practice of ministry as an urban pastor and community organizer over the previous twenty-five years. In that quarter of a century I had pastored churches successively in Chicago, in Milwaukee, in Rockford, Illinois, back in Chicago, and in Detroit. During the last three pastorates I had also engaged in community organizing. I will share in this book some of the events that made me realize that I needed a theology adequate to the challenge of urban ministry. But suffice it to say here that I discovered that the practical work of ministering in the midst of urban human need could not be carried on for very long without the biblical framework that would place meaning upon the city's injustice and confusion.

It is the purpose of this study to develop from the Scriptures a systematic, internally consistent theology of the city. It is my desire to present an analysis of the city that is sociologically sound and provides a biblical explanation for the nature, extent, and structures of power in a city. In addition, this analysis will seek to present a biblical exposition of the purpose and mission of the church in the city. Finally, this study will examine biblical insights for the purpose of spiritual sustenance of God's people in the work of the church in the city. In short, this study is an attempt to develop a biblical urban theology—a theology that seeks to be visionary in scope yet intensely practical in its applicability to urban churches and pastors.

Because World Vision has played such a significant supportive role in the development of this book, I have assigned all royalties from the book to support the Urban Advance of World Vision International in the great cities of Asia, Africa, and Latin America.

Of course, no theology comes solely from the person who writes it. All of us are greatly influenced by our brothers and sisters in the faith, and I am no exception. Those familiar with Walter Wink's work on the principalities and powers and Walter Brueggeman's work on systems and structures will note that both men have influenced my theology profoundly. So, too, has the work of community organizer Saul Alinsky, revolutionary educator Paulo Freire (Brazil), biblical scholars Segundo Galilea (Chile) and Albert Nolan (South Africa), and the servant-oriented people at Washington's Church of the Savior—especially N. Gordon Cosby, Elizabeth O'Connor, and Don McClanen.

Some of World Vision's best theologians have stimulated my theology of the city with their critiques and contributions. I am particularly grateful to former president Tom Houston (Scotland), vice-presidents

Manfred Grellert (Brazil), Sam Kamaleson (India), and Bryant Myers, to Tom McAlpine of MARC, and to my colleague in the Office of Urban Advance, Ken Luscombe (Australia). Finally, I would be remiss if I didn't express my gratitude to Graeme Irvine (Australia), president of World Vision International, for his encouragement and to Dayton Roberts (Costa Rica), editor of MARC Publications, who urged me to convert my curriculum into this book.

Of course, I stated earlier the profound influence those who have taken the course "City of Yahweh, City of Ba'al" have had. Of the thousands who have shared with me in this experience, there are those whose insights, evaluations, and critiques have been particularly helpful. I want to give recognition especially to Viju Abraham (India), Mariano Avila (Mexico), Jose Borges (Brazil), Jerry Chang (Taiwan), Peter Chao (Singapore), Jose Chuquin (Colombia), Saul Cruz (Mexico), Darci Dusilek (Brazil), Michael Eastman (Great Britain), Stephen Githumbi (Kenya), Goh Eng Kee (Singapore), Winfred Jeyaraj and the other urban staff of World Vision India, Ravikant Kant (India), Vladimir Korotkov (Australia), Colin Marchant (Great Britain), Yasuo Masuda (Japan), Ruben Medina (Mexico), Joseph M'Ikunyua (Kenya), Peter Mkolesia (Malawi), Moffat Ndou (Zimbabwe), David Ngai (Hong Kong), Hector Pardo (Colombia), Kathy and Andrew Purves (United States), Zacarias Salas (Colombia), Elizabeth Steele (United States), Jim Stobaugh (United States), Ray Swartzback (United States), Sam Thanaseelan (India), and Jan Willette (United States).

Finally, my deepest appreciation and gratitude goes to my best friend, closest companion, lover and wife, Marlene, who has always been willing to share me with the church and the city and who has been prayer warrior, advocate, encourager, and my best critic for over thirty years. All these sisters and brothers in the faith from all over the world have, through their lives, ministries, and insights, helped to write *City of God, City of Satan*. For them all, I praise the Lord!

Robert C. Linthicum
Los Angeles, California

ACKNOWLEDGMENTS

Bible versions cited in addition to the New International Version are the following:

JB, *Jerusalem Bible* (Garden City, N.Y.: Doubleday, 1966). Used by permission of the publisher.

KJV, *The Holy Bible, King James Version.*

LB, *The Living Bible* (Wheaton, Ill.: Tyndale House, 1972).

MOFFATT, *The Holy Bible, a New Translation by James Moffatt* (New York: Harper, 1950).

NEB, *The New English Bible* (Oxford and Cambridge: Oxford University Press and Cambridge University Press, 1970).

NRSV, *The New Revised Standard Version* (New York: Division of Christian Education of the National Council of the Churches of Christ in the United States of America, 1989).

PHILLIPS, *The New Testament in Modern English*, J. B. Phillips, trans. (New York: Macmillan, 1960).

TEV, *The Holy Bible, Today's English Version* (New York: American Bible Society, 1976).

The author is grateful for permission to use quotations from the following publications:

Athol Gill, "From Down Under: Biblical Perspectives on Poverty and the Poor" (Melbourne: Victorian Council of Christian Education, 1986). Used by permission of the author.

Anne Keegan, "A Neighborhood Misses Jack and His Bike," *Chicago Tribune* (1983). Copyright © by Chicago Tribune Company, all rights reserved. Used with permission.

Ross Langmead, "Pilgrim Song" and "In God's Family," from the album *On the Road*. Used by permission of the composer.

Robert Linthicum, *The People Who Turned the World Upside Down: Leader's Guide* (Tucker, Ga.: Lay Renewal Publications, 1982). Used by permission of the publisher.

Robert Linthicum, "Networking: Hope for the Church in the City," *Urban Mission* (January 1987). Used by permission.

Colin Marchant, *Signs in the City* (London: Hodder & Stoughton, 1985). Used by permission of the author.

Caryl Micklem, *Contemporary Prayers for Public Worship* (London: SCM Press, 1967). Used by permission of the publisher.

Excerpts from Lewis Mumford, *The City in History* (London: Harcourt, Brace, 1961; renewed 1989 by Lewis Mumford). Reprinted by permission of the publisher.

Eugene H. Peterson, *Run with the Horses* (Downers Grove, Ill.: InterVarsity Press, 1983). Used by permission of the author.

William Skudlarek, "A Most Transparent Life: An Interview with Dom Helder Camara," *Sojourners* (December 1987). Used by permission of the publisher.

PART I

THE CITY: BATTLEGROUND

Chapter One

OUR CITY: GOD'S CREATION

He has set his foundation on the holy mountain;
    the LORD loves the gates of Zion
    more than all the dwellings of Jacob.
Glorious things are said of you, O city of God:
    "I will record [Egypt] and Babylon
    among those who acknowledge me—
    Philistia too, and Tyre, along with Cush—
    and will say, 'This one was born in Zion.' "
Indeed, of Zion it will be said,
    "This one and that one were born in her,
    and the Most High himself will establish her."
The LORD will write in the register of the peoples:
    "This one was born in Zion."
As they make music they will sing,
    "All my fountains are in you" (Psalm 87).

THE CHALLENGE OF THE CITY

> In about 19 years, the world will undergo a momentous change: for the
> first time in recorded history a majority of the world's people will live
> in cities—primarily the cities of Asia, Africa and Latin America. These
> cities will be of enormous size and will be plagued by unemployment,
> overcrowding and disease, where services such as power, water,
> sanitation or refuse disposal will be strained to the breaking point.[1]

So said Rafael Salas, the late executive director of the United Nations Fund
for Population Activities, when he spoke in Madras in 1986.

Cities all over the world are facing an unprecedented growth
explosion. As Salas has indicated, sometime close to the turn of the
century there will be more people living in cities than will be living in
towns or villages, on farms, in tribes, or in any other human habitation.

For the first time in its history, the world will be more urban than rural. Countries in the northern hemisphere will appear more urbanized than southern countries. By C.E. 2000, 94 percent of the population of Canada and the United States will live in cities, as will 82 percent of all Europeans and 80 percent of all Russians.[2] In contrast, only 36 percent of all Asians and 45 percent of all Africans will live in cities (Latin America provides the one third world exception—73 percent of its people will live in its cities).[3]

Such statistics are misleading, however. They do not reflect the tremendous number of people already concentrated in southern hemisphere cities or the tremendous growth occurring in those cities. The 36 percent of the population gathered in Asia's cities, for example, is numerically greater than the entire combined urban population of the developed countries.

Growth in third world cities is phenomenal. It is estimated that in the years between 1975 and 2000 the increase in the urban population of Latin America will be 216 percent, of China 224 percent, of the rest of Asia 269 percent, of the Middle East 302 percent, and of Africa 347 percent.[4]

Cities in the third world are not the only ones growing. Although the cities in the developed world are growing more slowly than in the third world, their metropolitan areas continue to expand. The greater Los Angeles metropolis, for example, numbered 4,000,000 in 1950 and is now 9,500,000. By the turn of the century, its population will be nearly 14,000,000. Paris, at 5,500,000 in 1950, is projected to reach 10,000,000 by the year 2000. Although economically it appears a part of the first world, Tokyo's growth compares with any third world metropolis. In 1950 the population was 6,700,000; by 2000 it will grow to be 23,800,000.[5]

We can best see the growth in the world's cities in this simple fact. In 1950 only seven cities in the world had a population of more than 5,000,000. Thirty-five years later, the number of such giant cities had swollen to thirty-four. In another thirty-five years, there will be ninety-three cities on our globe with populations in excess of 5,000,000.[6]

Even more obvious is the growth in third world giant cities. Of the seven cities in 1950 with populations exceeding 5,000,000, only two were located in Asia, Africa, or Latin America. By 1985, twenty-two of the thirty-four giant cities were in the third world. By 2020 it is projected that the third world will be home to eighty of the ninety-three cities.[7]

Cities in Crisis

But what's wrong with growth? People who have lived their lives in the first world have grown up believing in growth. But in the third world—and among the first world's poor—growth is terrible news. Even a healthy city's infrastructure cannot cope with a significant increase in population. And when a city like Mexico City receives more than half a million new people each year (as it presently does), its sanitation system, refuse disposal, provision of power and water, and capacity to house, feed, and employ these people is overwhelmed.

The results of such rapid and worldwide growth are evident everywhere. Fifty thousand homeless people live on New York City streets. Another 27,000 people live in temporary shelters, and an estimated 100,000 households are doubled up in apartments of friends and relatives.[8] Sixty percent of the entire population of Guayaquil, Ecuador, lives in shantytowns amid garbage-strewn mud flats and polluted water.[9] In Bombay, India, 1,000,000 people live in a slum built on a giant garbage dump.[10]

In Detroit, seventy-two percent of all the young employable adults in that city's poorest census tract can't find work—and will probably never find it.[11] Seventy-five percent of the families who live in Lagos, Nigeria, live in one-room shacks.[12] Half a million people will live their entire lives on the streets of Calcutta and will never have a roof over their heads.[13] In São Paulo, Brazil, 700,000 children have been abandoned by their parents to live by their wits on its streets.[14]

This is the city—for God's sake! This is the city God loves and for which Christ died. And this is the city where Christ's church is and where it is called to minister.

Called to a City

It is incumbent upon Christians today to recognize and enthusiastically enter into the challenge of the new, emerging world. God is calling the church into the city. Our world is becoming an urban world—and this is an inevitable and irreversible trend. Only our Lord's return or humanity's destruction of itself in a mushroom cloud will prevent the urbanization of the world. But we are not only faced with the mind-boggling growth of the world's existing cities—even the most rural and isolated areas of the world will be exposed to urbanization. It was apparent that a new age had dawned when, for two weeks in 1988, the entire world could "sit" in the stadiums and "walk" the streets of Seoul, Korea, because television brought the city into the home during live telecasts of the Olympics. There is no doubt that this is an increasingly urban world.

No previous generation has had to face human problems of this magnitude or had to wield urban power on this scale. This means that the church has unprecedented potential for ministry and world evangelization. The world is coming to the city—and we can be there to greet it in Christ's name.

The most insightful of the church's prophetic thinkers recognize the potential of the "open door that no one can shut" (Rev. 3:8). The church is rediscovering the city—in both the developed and the developing worlds. Emerging from that rediscovery is a profoundly new methodology for doing urban ministry—a collective wisdom evolving from theologians and urban ministry practitioners alike. New words are entering the ministry vocabulary—words like *networking, urban exegesis, community organization*—all symbolic of the changing style of ministry adapted to an urban world.

While we are rediscovering the city's mission field and introducing an urban methodology, our biblical and theological reflection is limited. We enter the city equipped with an urban sociology and urban tools for ministry, but we carry with us the baggage of a theology designed in rural Europe. Even the very way we formulate theological questions and the frameworks we use to construct our theological thought have been forged from our rural past. What we are in need of is a theology as urban as our sociology and missiology—a theology, as Ray Bakke puts it, "as big as the city itself"!

I entered urban ministry in 1955 by working with Afro-American youth and children in a Chicago slum. I have been at it ever since. As the years passed, I became increasingly aware that my theology was inadequate for my inner-city pastorates and community organizing.

Incident after incident reminded me that I suffered from a theology gap. A theology that would be adequate for a rural world or Western culture was not adequate for the city. Manifestations of raw corporate evil, almost beyond the power even of its perpetrators to control, made nonsense of a doctrine of sin perceived as individual acts of wrongdoing. My confrontation with economic and political exploiters of the poor who were also faithful communicants in their churches made a mockery of the church as the body of Christ. My experiences increased my frustration with a theology learned in college and seminary's halls of ivy. I will share some of those experiences with you in this book in the hope that they will aid you in reflecting on comparable incidents in your own life.

As a result of this frustration, in 1969 I began an intentional search for an urban theology that would work for me. I have been caught up in biblical research on this issue ever since; for the past eleven years I have devoted one hour a day to the task. This "movable feast" has gone with me throughout the world wherever I have worked. I continue to delve into Scripture to formulate a theology that realistically and accurately understands the city in all its complexity and uncovers biblical principles for ministering within that complexity.

I began my biblical research in order to bring theological sense to my city ministries. I continued it as a way of supporting my congregations and my own self in the midst of ministering to and defending the urban poor and powerless around us. This theology sustained my congregations and me, for we had become spiritually exhausted as a result of such draining and demanding ministry.

As this biblical theology gradually matured, so did my ministry and my congregations' capacity to deal in redeeming and healing ways with both the powerful and the powerless. What both my congregations and I discovered was how relevant and how urban a book the Bible really is.

The Bible: An Urban Book

It comes as a surprise to all of us: the Bible actually is an urban book! It is hard for us to appreciate that the world of Moses and David and Daniel and Jesus was an urban world. But it was—their world was probably more urban than any civilization before it or any after it for the next fifteen hundred years.

The world in which the Bible was written was dominated by its cities. By 2000 B.C.E., Abraham's city of Ur numbered 250,000.[15] Ancient Nineveh was so large that it took three days to cross it on foot (Jonah 3:3 NRSV). Babylon at the time of Nebuchadnezzar was an amazing city with eleven miles of walls and a water and irrigation system (perhaps even including flush toilets) not equaled again until the end of the nineteenth century.[16] In New Testament times Ephesus had street lighting along its famed Arcadius Street, of which Ammianus wrote, "The brilliancy of the lamps at night often equaled the light of day."[17] Antioch had sixteen miles of colonnaded streets. And Rome? Well, there was no city to equal Rome.

The Rome of the apostle Paul's day numbered more than one million people—the first city in human history to exceed that number. Its streets were so crowded that wheeled traffic had to be banned from its center during the day. The rich lived in large, private mansions, the middle class in sophisticated apartment buildings. But the poor—the great mass of the residents of Rome—lived in 46,000 tenement houses, many eight to ten stories high.[18] The first high-rise apartment buildings were built not in Chicago, but in ancient Rome nearly two thousand years ago!

We can begin to understand the sheer immensity of the city when we consider Lanciana's list of public works between C.E. 312 and 315:

> 1,790 palaces, 926 baths, 8 commons, 30 parks and gardens, 700 public pools and 500 fountains fed by 130 reservoirs, 254 bakehouses, 290 warehouses, 37 gates, 36 marble arches, 2 circuses, 2 amphitheaters, 3 theaters, 28 libraries, 4 gladiatorial schools, 5 nautical spectacles for sea fights, 6 obelisks, 8 bridges, 19 "water channels," 3,785 bronze statues and 10,000 carved figures.[19]

Rome, Alexandria, Athens, Corinth, Susa, Persepolis, Babylon, Nineveh, Thebes, Memphis—we can only understand the great civilizations of the Near East by appreciating the power and influence of these primary cities. These were urban civilizations, their great cities dominating the culture, art, religion, politics, economics, education, and social systems of their day.

The biblical people of God were themselves urban people. David was king of Jerusalem as well as of an empire. Isaiah and Jeremiah were both prophets committed to Jerusalem. The Scriptures tell us that Daniel was appointed mayor of the city of Babylon by King Nebuchadnezzar. Nehemiah was a city planner, a community organizer, and governor over Jerusalem.

Paul was Christianity's premier evangelist to the major cities of the Roman Empire. John envisioned God's ultimate intentions for humanity as an indescribable city. Jesus' redemptive act of crucifixion could only happen in a city where the political power of Rome and the religious influence of the Jewish priesthood acted in concert to kill the Son of God.

Most of Paul's letters were written to city churches as primers on how the church can effectively carry on ministry in a city. The Psalter is filled with city psalms; note how often they speak of Jerusalem or Mount Zion (Mount Zion, incidentally, is not some rural snow-capped peak; it's the hill upon which Jerusalem was built!). Paul's doctrine of the principalities and powers opens one up to an understanding of the nature of power in the city.

If the Bible is such an urban book, why do we not see it that way? It is simply because we approach the Bible from an essentially rural theological perspective. When we read the Bible, we are thinking "country" instead of "city." We see what we read through "rural glasses."

When the Roman Empire fell in the fifth century C.E., the Western world entered the Dark Ages—so called because the culture and knowledge of the previous seven hundred years were lost to European and Arab alike, except for those monks who preserved them in their monasteries. The population of Rome, which stood at one million at the time of Christ, fell by the fifth century to only twenty-five thousand. Yet it was still the largest city in Europe!

It was not until the twelfth century that European cities began to grow significantly. Even then they were small in comparison to biblical cities—Paris at 100,000, Florence at 45,000, Venice at 90,000.[20] After Rome's decline, it would take Europe nearly thirteen hundred years to produce its next city of a million people. That would be London in 1820. (It should be pointed out, however, that during the Dark Ages the Far East continued to produce million-population cities—Changan [modern Xian] in the eighth century, Peking [Beijing] and Tokyo in the eighteenth.)

The Bible was written in an urban Near East, but the main theological formulations of the faith of the church developed in a rural Europe. Consider the formative theologians of the early, medieval, and Reformation churches: St. Paul, John of Damascus, Augustine, Anselm,

Aquinas, Luther, Calvin. Only the first three wrote in an urban culture and from an urban perspective; their theological contributions come to us from before C.E. 400. Only Calvin, among later theologians, attempted theological formulation for an urban environment—and the Geneva of his day numbered only sixteen thousand! Not until the nineteenth and twentieth centuries did theologians consciously begin to allow city environments to influence their application of the Bible to urban life.

I discovered that, as a pastor called to serve the poor, the lost, and the churched in the city, I had to allow the scales to fall away from my eyes and begin to read the Bible as an urban book. When I did, I found a fascinating urban world there—with an urban Gospel to proclaim!

When I was a seminary student thirty years ago, I was impressed by a professor who defined theological inquiry in a way that has influenced me ever since. He said, "Students, always remember that theology is a verb, not a noun!" Now of course the word *theology* is a noun. But what the professor communicated that day was a valuable lesson: theology is primarily meant to be a process, not a product. It is faith in search of understanding.

As I have theologized about the city over these past nineteen years, what I have developed is not the final word—not even *my* final word. Instead, I have developed a biblical theology that serves me presently as I continue in urban ministry. Others have worked out and are creating significant urban biblical theologies for our time.[21] But the subject of this book is the theology that works for me right now, one that has grown with me as I have matured over thirty years of city ministry. It is simply a brief pause, a moment of reflection I wish to share with you. Perhaps it will be of help as you seek to develop an urban biblical theology that will inform, support, and encourage you in your work for Christ's kingdom.

HOW DOES SCRIPTURE VIEW MY CITY?

I believe the starting place for a Christian, when considering the city, is with the question, "How does Scripture view my city?" We can state the essential biblical assumption as follows:

> The city is the locus of a great and continuing battle between the God of Israel and/or the church and the god of the world.

In the Old Testament the God of Israel may be called "Yahweh"; in the New Testament, "the God of our Lord and Savior, Jesus Christ." In the Old Testament the god of the world may be named "Baal"; in the New Testament, "Satan." But whether God is Yahweh or the Father of Jesus Christ, whether the Evil One is called Baal or Satan, the overarching message is the same. This world is a battlefield. The greatest battle goes on inside our cities: the battle between God and Satan.

One place in Scripture where this continuing theme surfaces is in Jeremiah 9:11–14. The Lord Yahweh says through the prophet,

> "I will make Jerusalem a heap of ruins,
>   a haunt of jackals;
> and I will lay waste the towns of Judah
>   so no one can live there."

> What man is wise enough to understand this? Who has been instructed by the LORD and can explain it? Why has the land been ruined and laid waste like a desert that no one can cross?

> The LORD said, "It is because they have forsaken my law, which I set before them; they have not obeyed me or followed my law. Instead, they have followed the stubbornness of their hearts; they have followed the Baals, as their fathers taught them."

"I will make Jerusalem a heap of ruins," God says. And for what reason? "Because they have forsaken my law . . . they have followed the Baals." Jeremiah is in essence saying, "Israel could have made Jerusalem the City of Yahweh; instead the people have allowed their city to become the city of Baal."

The continuing battle between God and Satan for control of a city is expressed throughout Scripture. But here are two particularly intriguing ways in which that battle manifests itself: the comparison drawn between the cities of Babylon and Jerusalem, and the very name the Israelites chose for their idealized city—Jerusalem. Let's look briefly at each.

Babylon Versus Jerusalem

Babylon is used throughout Scripture as a symbol of a city fully given over to Satan. The city is first introduced in Genesis 11 in humanity's decision to build a Tower of Babel (the Plain of Shinar, mentioned in the text as the city of the ziggurat, was later the location of Babylon). God confused their languages because the people declared, "Come, let us build ourselves a city, with a tower that reaches to the heavens, so that we may make a name for ourselves" (Gen. 11:4).

Babylon receives its final attention in Revelation 16 to 18, where it is portrayed as the epitome of evil, a city totally given over to evil and to the Evil One. "Babylon the Great, the Mother of Prostitutes and of the Abominations of the Earth" (Rev. 17:5) is the city's epitaph as every detail of it is removed from the face of the earth (see chapter 12 for a full examination of the apocalyptic end of Babylon).

In between the first and last books of the Bible, the city of Babylon is synonymous with all that is dark and evil in a city. Babylon is painted in Scripture as a bureaucratic, self-serving, and dehumanizing social system with economics geared to benefit its privileged and exploit its poor, with politics of oppression and with a religion that ignores covenant with God and deifies power and wealth (Isa. 14:5–21; Jer. 50:2–17; 51:6–10; Dan. 3:1–7; Rev. 17:1–6; 18:2–19, 24). Much of what is dark and evil in Babylon is replicated in cities (even Jerusalem) throughout the biblical story.

Jerusalem, by contrast, is seen in its idealized form as the city of God. It, too, is introduced in Genesis (14:17–24) in the figure of Melchizedek, king of Salem (Salem is a former name of Jerusalem). The entire biblical drama concludes in the last chapters of the book of Revelation with the vision of "the Holy City, the new Jerusalem, coming down out of heaven from God" (Rev. 21:2; see chapter 12 of this book for a full exploration of the new Jerusalem).

In between the beginning and the end of the Bible, an idealized Jerusalem is celebrated as city as it was meant to be—a city belonging to God. As a social system, it is called to witness to God's shalom (Ps. 122:6–9; 147:2). As an economic entity, it is meant to practice equitable stewardship, and in its politics, a communal and just existence (Exod. 25–40; 1 Sam. 8:4, 20, among other passages. The 1 Samuel passage is an example of community action, but one that rejected God. See chapter 2 of this book for a further explanation). Finally, Jerusalem is portrayed as the spiritual center of the world, a model city living in trust and faith under the lordship of God (Isa. 8:18; Mic. 4:1; Deut. 17:14–20).

The idealized Jerusalem (which, of course, never existed) and the dark and evil Babylon are types—cities pressed to their logical extremes as a continual reminder to the biblical reader that every city includes both elements. Every city has both Babylon and Jerusalem in it, for every city is the battleground between the god of Babylon (Baal, Satan) and the God of Jerusalem (Yahweh, the Lord) for domination and control.

Babylon in Jerusalem

An even more graphic portrayal of this urban biblical theme is expressed in the etymology of the word *Jerusalem*. The traditional interpretation given to the name is "city of peace." But biblical scholars such as Millar Burrows have pointed out that the name actually means "foundation of Shalem."[22] The traditional interpretation, "city of peace," is etymologically unfounded.

The first references to Jerusalem in the Bible are found in Genesis 14:18 and Psalm 76:2, where it is called in Hebrew *Shalem* (in English, "Salem"). Melchizedek is referred to in Genesis 14:18 as "king of Salem" and "priest of God Most High." In this story Abraham obviously considers Melchizedek a superior, for he receives a blessing from the priest and gives him "a tithe of everything." Christians have always assumed that Melchizedek was superior because he was the conveyor of God's peace (and thus his attributes are assigned to the city of which he was king). But there is nothing to support that contention in Scripture itself. Both in Genesis 14 and in Psalm 110 he is called simply a priest, and in the former, "king of Salem."

The earliest known names for Jerusalem were Urushalim (the Egyptian Execration Texts, c. 1850 B.C.E.) or Shalem. Apparently the city received the name *Jerusalem* only after King David annexed it to Israel and made it his capital (2 Sam. 5:6–12).

Since the root name for Jerusalem is Urushalim or Shalem, we have to ask the question, "Who or what is Shalem?" Shalem was the local god of pre-Israelite Canaan. It was the god symbolized in the planet Venus, the evening star. After the Israelite conquest, Shalem was identified with the Canaanite gods Ashtar and Molech. These gods were in reality the Canaanite manifestations of the "international" deity—Baal.[23]

Does the name Jerusalem have anything to do with peace? Obviously the Hebrew words *shalem* and *shalom* ("peace") are virtually identical. Is there a relationship? Apparently there is. In the Canaanite language, the god's name *Shalem* actually meant "completion." This meaning evolved from the Canaanites' perception of Shalem as Venus, the evening star— which completed the day. Therefore, as time went on and language evolved, the word *shalem* came to be identified with a place—Jerushalem—and with the concept of "completion" or "fulfillment." This became the base for the later Israelite word *shalom* or "peace."[24] But one should not then make the mistake of assuming that the name of David's city was Jeru*shalom*.It was not: It was Jeru*shalem*.

If the city Urushalim or Shalem means "foundation of Shalem," or the city of Shalem, what, then, does the prefix *Je* mean? It is the anglicized version of the Hebrew word *Yah* and thus an abbreviation for the word *Yahweh!* When King David conquered Jerusalem, he added the name of his and Israel's God to the name of a city that previously had been named for the god Shalem. The name Yahweh was not substituted for the name of Shalem; it was added to it!

In the very name *Jerusalem* is expressed the tension of every city. It is *Je*-rusalem—the city of Yahweh, of God. It is Jeru-*salem* —the city of Baal (or Satan). Jerusalem is the city of Yahweh. Jerusalem is the city of Baal. It is a city that contains the power and influence of both forces within its walls. The very name of Israel's primary (and idealized) city expresses the foundational urban message of the Bible. Jerusalem—and every city—is the battleground between God and Satan for domination of its people and their structures.

Yahweh and Baal

The essential Old Testament assumption about the city is that it is the battleground between Yahweh and Baal. The essential New Testament urban assumption is that the city struggles between God and Satan. If that is so, then it is important that we clearly understand the foundational beliefs about Yahweh and Baal upon which this assumption is based. Who was Baal to the ancient Israelites? Who was Yahweh?

Yahweh was Israel's cosmic deity, the God of Abraham, Isaac, and Jacob, the God of the burning bush, the God of the Exodus. The name by which God is called in the Old Testament is introduced in Exodus 3:14 as "I AM WHO I AM." The third-person form of that formula (speaking grammatically) is "Yahweh." But the Hebrew word cannot simply be translated "He is" (the English third person of "I am"). The actual Hebrew word has a more causal sense to it. "I become what I become" or "I will cause to be what I will cause to be" might be more accurate.

By telling Moses the holy name, God identified his essential nature. By using this name, God proclaimed that he was neither a regional deity (to be confined to one country over which God had exclusive sovereignty) or a nature deity (controlling the cycles of nature). Yahweh—by the very fact that he was named Yahweh—was the God who was sovereign over history.

As creator and controller of history, Yahweh could call a people out of Egypt and could defeat the Egyptians who would seek to resist God. Yahweh could lead his people through a barren land to give them a land "flowing with milk and honey." The God who causes everything and everyone to be is the God who could liberate Israel from bondage, save them from their own worst selves, and liberate them to be God's people.

But the God who could free could also demand. The God who could liberate a body of slaves would demand they become a nation. And the God of the Old Testament demanded of the Israelites both individual responsibility and social justice. How magnificently God's expectations for Israel are stated by the prophet Micah: "And what does the LORD require of you? To act justly and to love mercy and to walk humbly with your God" (Mic. 6:8).

Baal was the other primary cosmic deity for much of the Old Testament era. Baal was the god of all the nations of the Near East except for Egypt (Egyptians worshiped Amon-Re) and Israel (Israelites worshiped Yahweh). Baal might have local names (e.g., Marduk, Molech) in order to express some local cultic connection. But the worship by whatever name was the worship of Baal.

The question of whether Israel's prophets, priests, and most astute leaders believed in gods other than Yahweh remains a subject of continuing debate. But there is no question that many ordinary people as well as leaders like Kings Ahab and Manasseh did believe in other gods. The battle that occupied centuries of Israelite history was the battle best stated by the prophet Elijah: "How long will you waver between two opinions? If the LORD is God, follow him; but if Baal is God, follow him" (1 Kings 18:21).

Baal began, in his mythological development, as a god of fire and water and then evolved into the god of procreation. As he became a god worshiped by many nations, Baal became the god of cult prostitution and sexual license. The "high places" and "groves" against which the Israelite prophets railed were the gathering places for the worship of Baal; such worship was expressed, not through liturgy, but through public sex, both with prostitutes (priestesses of Baal) and with other worshipers, male or female. Thus Baal became a very popular god—every person's excuse for licentiousness.

Yahweh was seen in the Old Testament as a God of covenant and responsibility. Baal was seen in the ancient Near East as the god of debauchery and license. Since their respective followers claimed their god as the only authentic cosmic deity, it was inevitable that there would be constant confrontation between Yahweh and Baal. That confrontation makes up much of the Old Testament ("If Yahweh is God . . ."). And that same confrontation underlies the Scripture's evaluation of the city.

"Because they have forsaken my law . . . they have followed the Baals" (Jer. 9:13–14)—because you have chosen to be Jerus*alem* rather than *Je*rusalem: this is the battle of the Bible. Whether it is put in terms of Yahweh and Baal, God and Satan, or Christ and Caesar, every city is a city of conflict. It is a city of conflict between the "Yahwehs" and the "Baals" of life—between the forces of freedom and the forces of license, between the forces of justice and the forces of exploitation, between the forces of love and the forces of lust, between the forces of God and the forces of Satan.

These forces lie at the heart and soul of every city. These forces permeate every structure and system of the city—from courtroom to classroom, from politician's podium to preacher's pulpit. And these forces battle within every one of us, too! This is the battle of the city—the essential biblical context for understanding our city.

THE CITY AS GOD'S CREATION

At this point I suspect that the reader is beginning to ask, "Is this man falling into the cult of Zoroastrianism? Is he suggesting that there are two equal forces caught up in a cosmic war—God and Satan? Is the battle of the city a battle between two equals?"

No, it is not. God is Yahweh—the One who causes to be what is caused to be. Scripture repeatedly exposes us to a God who triumphs.

Pharaoh, the personification of the Egyptian god Amon-Re, is forced to let God's people go (Exod. 12:35–42). Nebuchadnezzar, the personal representative of Marduk-Baal, is forced to proclaim, "Praise be to the God of Shadrach, Meshach and Abednego . . . for no other god can save in this way" (Dan. 3:28–29). In the book of Revelation, the "second Roman" emperor and his cult of emperor worship are destroyed by God, and the crowds sing, "Salvation and glory and power belong to our God!" (Rev. 19:1). The god Amon-Re is conquered in his capital city, Rameses. The god Baal is humbled in Babylon. The ultimate Caesar is destroyed in the final and most bestial Rome. God is more powerful than Amon-Re, than Baal, than Caesar, than Satan.

Although the Bible is uncompromising in the preeminence of God, it also wants us to take sin seriously. We will not take sin seriously if we do not honestly examine it, understand it, and expose it at work within us, within our structures and systems, throughout the warp and woof of our cities, and in all its demonic capacity to possess and to seek control.

Urban ministry needs to celebrate the city! It needs to take seriously the evil in the city as well. In this section we would seek to celebrate the city. That celebration begins with the discovery that the city is an act of God's creation just as much as is all of nature! We need to celebrate because God deeply loves the city, both because he created it and because it is his abode. Let us examine together some Scripture that will enable us to enter into the heart of God, a heart that loves the city he has created.

City Psalms

Of the 150 psalms in the Psalter, 49 are city psalms. Most, of course, deal with Jerusalem, but some deal with other cities (most notably Babylon). Most are psalms that express God's creative love for the city. We do not have the space here to explore these psalms comprehensively, but I would like us to consider three psalms that are in one quire—Psalms 42, 46, and 48.

Psalm 42 is the lament of an Israelite in exile. It is built around the mocking question, "Where is your God?" Today we would answer that question, "God is wherever God's people are." But not so this Israelite. His response to the question is quite instructive to us who are seeking an urban biblical theology.

This psalmist longs for fellowship with God.

> As the deer pants for streams of water,
>   so my soul pants for you, O God.
> My soul thirsts for God, for the living God.
>   When can I go and meet with God? (vv. 1–2).

It is intriguing that the psalmist does not ask the question, *"Where* can I go to meet with God?"* but *"When* can I go?" The psalmist knows where God is to be found. His concern is when he can go to that place, for he is being forced by his exile to live where God is absent.

Where, then, is God to be found?

- "When can I go and meet with God?" It is made clear (Deut. 31:11; Ps. 27:4, 8; Exod. 33:20) that God's "face" or presence is to be found in God's sanctuary or home, a reference to the tabernacle and, later, the temple.

- "How I used to go with the multitude, leading the procession to the house of God" (Ps. 42:4). When the psalmist remembers when he has been with God, he recalls his participation in joyous, triumphal processions to the Holy City and to its temple.

So what is the answer to the question, "Where is your God?" The answer is, "God is in God's holy city, Jerusalem." The psalmist in exile is bereft of God's presence. He is downcast because God will not come to him. He must go to Jerusalem where God is enthroned if he wishes to be in fellowship with God. But he is prevented from making that pilgrimage because he is a captive in Babylon. So he can do nothing but grieve in God's absence.

But there is hope. The psalm ends on that faint, feeble glimmer of hope—a hope that, by the very way it is presented, reveals the psalmist's inability to perceive any other way of dealing with God's presence except to understand that he must go to God and not have God come to him:

> Why are you downcast, O my soul?
> Why so disturbed within me?
> Put your hope in God,
> for I will yet praise him,
> my Savior and my God (v. 11).

Somehow the psalmist will be set free from exile so that he might make his way to Jerusalem where he can again stand before the face of God. He will praise God in Jerusalem. That is his only hope!

Psalm 46 is set in three sections, divided by the refrain:

> The Lord Almighty is with us;
> the God of Jacob is our fortress.

(The refrain is found in verses 7 and 11; biblical scholars believe the refrain was originally also found between verses 3 and 4, and it is so restored in the Jerusalem Bible.)

God's presence in the temple safeguards and sanctifies the city of Jerusalem, even in the midst of unprecedented chaos and violence (vv. 1–3, 5–6). The city is watered by God's purified waters (v. 4). Because of that city's presence in the world, nation lives at peace with nation and

humanity can be still and silent before God, worshiping and working in
fellowship and reconciliation with God (vv. 8–10).

The strongest city references are found in verses 4–5, where the
psalmist makes a very bold assertion:

> There is a river whose streams make
> glad the city of God,
> the holy place where the Most High dwells.
> God is within her, she will not fall;
> God will help her at break of day.

In contrast to Psalm 42, which taught that God's abode is in the
city—that we have to go to the city if we are to find God—the author of
Psalm 46 goes a step further. Not only is God to be found inside the city,
not only is the city God's primary dwelling place, but God also sanctifies
and blesses the city. He therefore protects the city against all harm. The
city is made holy by God's presence in it! It is kept from chaos, collapse,
and evil domination by God's presence. That is how much God loves the
city.

Psalm 48, "the urban-dweller's Twenty-third Psalm," begins by
reminding us that God is found primarily in *the* city—Jerusalem. God is
"most worthy of praise, in the city of our God" (v. 1). God's presence in
the city makes it "beautiful in its loftiness, the joy of the whole earth," this
"city of the Great King" (v. 2).

Why is Jerusalem to be celebrated in this way as the abode of God? It
is because "God is in her citadels; he has shown himself to be her fortress"
(v. 3). God became Jerusalem's fortress when Israel's political order
learned to trust God rather than its own defense. God defeated an enemy
whom Israel's army could not defeat. God, this passage is stating, can
enter into the political process and transform it. God can change the
premises and the actions of the political order and can "convert" it from
defense to acceptance and trust. Even in such a pragmatic science as
politics, God can act as Savior and Lord—if people allow him to do so.

What was the event that caused Israel to put such trust in God? The
second section of this psalm, verses 4–7, gives us only the vaguest
intimation. It could have been the unsuccessful campaign of Syria and
Israel against Ahaz, king of Judah, in 735 B.C.E. (2 Kings 16:5–6). Or it
could have been the famed siege of Jerusalem by Sennacherib of Assyria,
recorded in both 2 Kings 19 and Isaiah 36–37. Or it could have been a
third event with which we are not familiar.

Whichever event it was, the point is that God protected Jerusalem in
the midst of its vulnerability. That protection affirmed what Israel had
long proclaimed—that God protected the city in which he dwelt. There is
something deeply thrilling about the way verse 8 is translated in the
Jerusalem Bible:

> What we had heard we saw for ourselves
> in the city of our God,
> the city of Yahweh Sabaoth,
> God-protected for ever.

Here the children of Israel experience for themselves what they have always been taught: that God loves the city, protects it, and invests himself in it. We can believe that truth as well—and be open and perceptive to experience it for ourselves!

The third section of Psalm 48 begins with a prayer of thanksgiving for God's defense of the city. The reputation of God's love for and protection of his city, the psalmist writes, has gone to the very ends of the earth. Not only God's people, but even those in the suburbs and towns around Jerusalem exult in God's commitment to the city.

Then the psalm moves in a most unpredictable and striking direction. One expects that the psalmist would now launch into a celebration of God's power and love. Instead he begins to celebrate the city! The psalmist writes,

> Walk about Zion, go around her,
> count her towers,
> consider well her ramparts,
> view her citadels,
> that you may tell of them to the next generation (vv. 12–13).

I can envision the psalmist walking—perhaps even skipping—down Jerusalem's streets, effusively pointing first with one hand and then the other as he directs the eyes of the people he escorts. "Look over there," he says. "Look at that magnificent building—its height, the detail of its stone work, the exquisitely carved doorway! And look, look on the other side of the street. Note that enormous wall—one hundred and twenty feet high, it is! And it is anchored on bedrock twelve feet below! And notice the enclosed bridge that arches over the street and connects the wall with the building! Isn't that a truly beautiful and symmetrical arch? And as we pass the arch, look to your left between the two buildings. Do you now see the little courtyard nestled between them? Look at its inviting fountain and the shade of its trees. Just imagine sitting there in the cool of late afternoon, shielded from the noise of the street, and quietly reading the Torah. *God made all that!*"

"God made all that!" How would we feel about our city if we began walking its streets, admiring its buildings, and reviewing its exquisite architecture? And what a difference it would make if we could begin viewing our city, not through eyes that saw only its dirt and deprivation, but through eyes that could recognize the handiwork of the Creator. God created the city even as he created the mountains and hills and trees and brooks. In the countryside God has used the forces of nature to carve and shape and mold. In the city God has used the creativity of human beings to carve and shape and mold! The city is to be celebrated and admired, not simply for itself, but because the city is the creation and primary abode of God.

As Psalm 48 closes, the Jerusalem Bible translates its closing sentence in a way that I find particularly meaningful:

> Tell the next generation
> that God is here,
> our God and leader
> for ever and ever (v. 14).

This is the psalmist's instruction to God's people: celebrate the city in order to keep reminding its occupants that this is a city of God, that God is here "for ever and ever." It is precisely because the church has failed over the centuries to "tell the next generation that God is here" that God's people have come to emphasize what is dark and evil about the city and have missed the concrete truth that God is there. Many of the church have fled the city to more "conducive" climes of suburb and countryside, seeking God in woods and mountains and peaceful places. As a result, the church has unconsciously moved in a pantheistic direction and has largely abandoned God's primary abode—the city. The issue is not that God has abandoned the Jerusalems of the world as much as it is that God's people have abandoned the cities and have taken their household gods with them.

If we have eyes to see, we can still look around the city and there "count her towers, consider well her ramparts, view her citadels" and discover that what we had heard we now see for ourselves, that

> this God is our God for ever and ever;
> he will be our guide even to the end (Ps. 48:14).

Jerusalem the Bride: Part 1

Ezekiel 16:1–14 gives us the most moving glimpse into God's deep love for the city. Jerusalem is likened to an unclaimed baby, born and abandoned in the open fields. But God, happening upon that baby, speaks the living word that enables the baby to live and to grow. Then Ezekiel very tenderly writes,

> "You grew up and developed and became the most beautiful of jewels. Your breasts were formed and your hair grew, you who were naked and bare. Later I passed by, and when I looked at you and saw that you were old enough for love, I spread the corner of my garment over you and covered your nakedness. I gave you my solemn oath and entered into a covenant with you, declares the Sovereign LORD, and you became mine" (Ezek. 16:7–8).

God, Ezekiel is telling us, fell in love with Jerusalem! The city, unloved, unclaimed, abandoned, and apparently undesirable, was in fact desired. "You were old enough for love." And God, seeing the city in all its nakedness and vulnerability, in all its great potential to be both loving and beautiful, fell in love with it. So, Ezekiel tells us, God married the city; it became his wife.

> "I bathed you with water and washed the blood from you and put ointments on you. I clothed you with an embroidered dress and put leather sandals on you. I dressed you in fine linen and covered you with costly garments. I adorned you with jewelry. . . . Your food was fine flour, honey and olive oil. You became very beautiful and rose to be a queen. And your fame spread among the nations on account of your beauty, because the splendor I had given you made your beauty perfect, declares the Sovereign LORD" (Ezek. 16:9–11, 13–14).

The story, of course, turns tragic. Jerusalem, God's deeply loved wife, turns to other lovers and becomes a whore. But that portion of the story is for another chapter of this book. Here I wish to focus on God's great love for the city.

Note the kind of love suggested in this passage. It is the love of a man for a woman; it is a possessing love, a jealous love, a sexual love. It is the kind of love that two lovers feel in the early stages of their relationship, a love so all-encompassing, so overwhelming, so completely focused in each other that to come across one's old love letters thirty years later both awakens happy memories and makes one feel, well, slightly embarrassed at such intensity. That is how God loves your city! Are you willing to be embarrassed by God's love?

Potpourri of Loving Scripture

Isaiah 60:1–5, 14–21, like the Psalms, also develops the theme of God's creation of the city of Jerusalem (and consequently of all cities). But this passage explores why God creates cities. Speaking to the city, the prophet declares:

> "Arise, shine, for your light has come,
>   and the glory of the LORD rises upon you.
> See, darkness covers the earth
>   and thick darkness is over the peoples,
> but the LORD rises upon you
>   and his glory appears over you" (vv. 1–2).

To God, the city is a lighthouse in a world of darkness, the creation of God to which the earth is drawn.

> "The sons of your oppressors will come
>   bowing before you;

> all who despise you will bow down
>   at your feet
> and will call you the City of the LORD,
>   Zion of the Holy One of Israel.
> Although you have been forsaken and hated,
>   with no one traveling through,
> I will make you the everlasting pride
>   and the joy of all generations" (vv. 14–15).

Why does God treat the city with such favor? Why does he transform with pride what has been hated and shunned and abandoned by generations past? For what purpose has God created the city? The prophet tells us,

> "Then will all your people be righteous
>   and they will possess the land forever.
> They are the shoot I have planted,
>   the work of my hands,
>   for the display of my splendor" (v. 21).

God has created, loved, preserved, and redeemed the city so that it can be transformed into the city God intends it to be. And as that transformed community, the city becomes a lighthouse to the world, the manifestation of God's handiwork to the nation and the world.

Deuteronomy 6:10–14, like Ezekiel 16, is an expression of covenantal love. It is God's instructions to the Israelites on the eve of their entrance into the Promised Land. For forty years they have wandered in the wilderness as God prepared them for their new life in Canaan. As they stand on the far side of the Jordan River, waiting to cross it into Canaan, Moses speaks on God's behalf.

> When the LORD your God brings you into the land he swore to your fathers, to Abraham, Isaac and Jacob, to give you—a land with large, flourishing cities you did not build, houses filled with all kinds of good things you did not provide, wells you did not dig, and vineyards and olive groves you did not plant—then when you eat and are satisfied, be careful that you do not forget the LORD, who brought you out of Egypt, out of the land of slavery (Deut. 6:10–12).

The essential message is twofold: (1) all you have is God's gift to you, and (2) be faithful stewards of that gift. God has invested in Canaan. Over the centuries God has built its economy (wells, vineyards, olive groves), its infrastructure (houses), and its source of wealth and joy ("large, flourishing cities"). This investment is for one purpose: to give these cities as God's gift to God's own people someday. God invests the city in us. All God asks of us is what he asked of ancient Israel—that we receive God's gift of our cities, celebrate that gift, and then use that gift "to glorify God and to enjoy him forever."

Jonah 3:1—4:11 provides a different view of God's love. "Go to the great city of Nineveh and proclaim to it the message I give you," God commands a reluctant Jonah (3:2). First, note the city. It is not Jerusalem, but Nineveh. Second, note what God wants Jonah to preach: "Go to the great city of Nineveh and preach against it, because its wickedness has come up before me" (1:2). Jonah, finally persuaded through his encounter with a fish, does so. And the king of Nineveh says, "Let everyone call urgently on God. Let them give up their evil ways and their violence. Who knows? God may yet relent and with compassion turn from his fierce anger so that we will not perish" (3:8–9).

The story tells us that God does relent. There are few passages in Scripture more revealing of God's love than God's response to a complaining Jonah:

> But the LORD said, "You have been concerned about this vine, though you did not tend it or make it grow. It sprang up overnight and died overnight. But Nineveh has more than a hundred and twenty thousand people who cannot tell their right hand from their left, and many cattle as well. Should I not be concerned about that great city?" (Jonah 4:10–11).

Here again love is expressed that is as profound as that in Ezekiel. Here is God as concerned for a wicked, pagan city as he is for his own city, Jerusalem. God feels sorrowful over the plight of the 120,000 adults and children of Nineveh as well as their animals, all of whom God created. And God feels forgiveness for a wicked king and wicked people who don sackcloth and ashes and repent of the wicked things they have done. God loves Nineveh, just as God loves Jerusalem. God grieves over the city's sin and quickly offers it forgiveness!

Luke 13:34–35 and *19:41–44* present an even more poignant example of God's deep love for the city. In these similar passages Jesus gazes upon the city, and from the very depths of his heart well up these words:

> "O Jerusalem, Jerusalem, you who kill the prophets and stone those
> sent to you, how often I have longed to gather your children together,
> as a hen gathers her chicks under her wings, but you were not
> willing!" (Luke 13:34).

Here is not the rejected lover, but the abandoned mother. Here is God as the loving mother, seeking to gather her children to her and seeing them not only refuse her love, but scatter from her, rejecting her. Here are tears; here is compassion. There is only one word to express what Jesus is feeling here: hurt!—the deepest, the most profound hurt. Such transparent hurt, such openly expressed hurt, such vulnerability can only come from the most profound love. And for whom? "Jerusalem, Jerusalem"—a city! God's city! Our city!

Isaiah 62:1–5 is a most fitting passage with which to conclude our exploration of God's feelings for the city. This passage is greatly misinterpreted, for normally it is applied either to the Christian or to the church. Both are illegitimate interpretations, however, that indicate how deeply our anti-urban bias really runs. The prophet makes it quite clear about whom he is writing when he begins this chapter with the words, "For Zion's sake I will not keep silent, for Jerusalem's sake I will not remain quiet" (v. 1). The passage that follows (vv. 2–5) is addressed to Jerusalem and written in the second person. To enable us to truly appreciate what God is saying here through the prophet, I have changed it to the third person.

> The nations will see Jerusalem's righteousness,
>> and all kings its glory;
> The city will be called by a new name
>> that the mouth of the LORD will bestow.
> Jerusalem will be a crown of splendor in the LORD's hand,
>> a royal diadem in the hand of its God.
> No longer will they call the city Deserted,
>> or name its land Desolate.
> But the city will be called My Delight
>> and its land Married;
> for the LORD will take delight in his city,
>> and its land will be married.
> As a young man marries a maiden,
>> so will its Builder wed the city;
> as a bridegroom rejoices over his bride,
>> so will God rejoice over the city (Adapted from NIV).

Thus does God love the city he created!

Living into God's Love for Our City

It is easy for us to study the Scriptures about God's love for the city, reflect on that study, and even talk to our colleagues about it. But how can we give ourselves permission to truly feel with God his love for our city? How can we experience that divine city-love firsthand? Here is a spiritual exercise I suggest you try in order to give yourself the opportunity to feel God's love for your city.

In a favorite room (your study or office, den, dining room, or bedroom) place a large map of your city. Spend time in silence and in an open, prayerful spirit before that map. Ask God to reveal to you seven sites in the city that are particularly precious to him. Wait for God to show you those places. Those seven sites might come to you in one sitting; it may take several days. But wait on God with openness and receptivity. When the seven places have been given to you, you are ready for the most exciting stage of this spiritual exercise.

Take a full day off from your normal activities (do not worry; the world will still somehow survive!). Visit every one of those sites. Here is how I suggest you visit them:

If it is possible, walk to each site. If the sites are too far from each other for walking, then drive or take public transportation to within a few blocks of the next site. But do not drive all the way to the site! Instead, park the car or end the ride several blocks away. Walk to the site slowly, reflectively, in a relaxed manner. Look around you. Take it all in. Let your eyes see and your ears hear and your nostrils smell. Enjoy the city God has created.

When you get to the site, stand before it. Remain in silence. If it is convenient to sit there, do so. Linger awhile. Again, let your eyes and ears and nostrils and feet and hands observe and touch and feel for you. Imbibe the reality of that site. Then, when it is time, ask God why it is so precious to him.

Open your Bible (you did remember to bring it along with you on the trip, didn't you?). Read one of the Scripture passages on God's love that we examined earlier in this chapter. Read one passage for each site, so that you have read the seven passages by the time you have finished your pilgrimage. After you have read the first passage at the first site, be silent and listen for God's answer. Slowly God will tell you why this spot in your city is so precious to him. Write down your impressions in a notebook. Stay awhile in quiet, receptive prayer.

Move on to the second site. Repeat the same liturgy. By the time your day and spiritual pilgrimage have ended, you will have begun to see the city in a new and more appreciative way. You will be seeing your city through new eyes—God's eyes!

In the closing words of the book of Isaiah, the prophet writes,

"Before she goes into labor,
      she gives birth;
before the pains come upon her,
      she delivers a son.
Who has ever heard of such a thing?
      Who has ever seen such things?
Can a country be born in a day
      or a nation be brought forth in a moment?
Yet no sooner is Zion in labor
      than she gives birth to her children.
Do I bring to the moment of birth
      and not give delivery?" says the LORD.
"Do I close up the womb
      when I bring to delivery?" says your God.
"Rejoice with Jerusalem and be glad for her,
      all you who love her;

rejoice greatly with her,
    all you who mourn over her.
For you will nurse and be satisfied
    at her comforting breasts;
you will drink deeply
    and delight in her overflowing abundance" (Isa. 66:7–10).

The whole world belongs to God—including the city. It was made by God's hand, for God placed in humanity the capacity to create the city. And no matter how big it may be or how overwhelming its needs—even though it may have to absorb ten thousand new refugees every day as does Bombay, even though it may have grown from nine million to nineteen million people in just seven years as has Mexico City, even though it may have the largest Asian population of any city outside Asia as does Los Angeles—God is bigger than that city and its needs. That city cannot contain God, and God is in control!

But what God wants most for the city is that God's people—the church—will be humble of heart, contrite, and cognizant of their own sins and therefore not condemning of those in the city who are marginalized, who are poor or powerless or without hope. God wants a people who can tremble in awe both at the work God would do in that city and at the recognition that they are called to be a part of that great work.

God has begun a good work in every city. Will the God who opens the womb not bring the infant to birth? The city and the Christians of the city can rejoice, for God is at work in that city through God's people. And no matter how immense those problems may be, no matter how great the needs of its inhabitants may be, God will make of each city what God has designed and intended the city to become. God will accomplish his purpose—and, praise God, we are privileged to be an instrument of that purpose!

Chapter Two

OUR CITY AS THE ABODE OF PERSONAL AND SYSTEMIC EVIL

In 1988 I visited Medellín, Colombia, where I spent an afternoon in a slum of beggars and thieves, where as many as twenty-five families occupy a single house. One pregnant woman invited me into an apartment just large enough for a bed and boxes piled in the corners. On a bed lay the woman's one-and-a-half-year-old child and her nine-month-old baby.

"Every day," she said, "I carry my babies into downtown Medellín. I lay my two babies out on a blanket, sit next to them and open my coat so everyone can see how pregnant I am. And then I beg for money. All the money I have to raise these babies I get from begging this way."

The only power many of the poor wield is over their own bodies. In desperation, they will sell even that for pennies. I recently walked down Falkland Road, Bombay's infamous red-light district. As far as I could see, the street was lined with alcoves equipped with curtains and a bed. Outside each one was a prostitute—there were hundreds of them, block after block, scarcely seven feet apart.

What made it worse was that at least a third of them were little girls. All but one looked under sixteen. And around their feet and on their laps played swarms of even younger children—the next generation of male and female prostitutes.[1]

These are stories of powerlessness. And herein is the evil of the city!

In the previous chapter we studied the bright side of the city—the city as the abode of God's love and creative energy. In this chapter we turn to the dark side of the city and begin examining the biblical message of the city as the abode of evil. For only in understanding both the nature of a city's goodness and its evil can we truly hope to understand the city into which God has called us, his people, to minister.

WHAT IS EVIL ABOUT THE CITY?

Scripture provides us with a number of indicators concerning the evil of a city. First, it stresses that much of a city's evil is personal. When such sin accumulates among its people (as it did in Sodom [Gen. 19]), the city itself becomes overwhelmed by and possessed by such sin. Thus, in a profound sense the sin takes on corporate dimensions because it is being very slavishly indulged in by a vast number of that city's citizens. Perhaps the people who most carefully analyzed the dimensions of such sin were Israel's prophets.

Isaiah and Jeremiah

The books of Isaiah and Jeremiah are both essentially explorations of the nature, breadth, and depth of Israel's sin. Since both prophets were city prophets, both living in and having a deep commitment to Jerusalem, their analysis of Israel's sin was inevitably an analysis of Jerusalem's sin.

Isaiah the prophet, in chapter 58, asks the question: What is true worship (or fasting)? The people ask:

> " 'Why have we fasted,' they say,
>   'and you have not seen it?
> Why have we humbled ourselves,
>   and you [God] have not noticed?' " (v. 3).

God answers:

> "On the day of your fasting, you do as you please
>   and exploit all your workers.
> Your fasting ends in quarreling and strife,
>   and in striking each other with wicked fists.
> You cannot fast as you do today
>   and expect your voice to be heard on high" (vv. 3–4).

What, then, is true worship? God declares:

> "Is not this the kind of fasting I have chosen:
> to loose the chains of injustice
>   and untie the cords of the yoke,
> to set the oppressed free
>   and break every yoke?
> Is it not to share your food with the hungry
>   and to provide the poor wanderer with shelter—
> when you see the naked, to clothe him,
>   and not to turn away from your own flesh and blood?" (vv. 6–7).

On behalf of his people, the prophet confesses the nature of Israel's and Jerusalem's evil:

> For our offenses are many in your sight,
>   and our sins testify against us.
> Our offenses are ever with us,
>   and we acknowledge our iniquities:
> rebellion and treachery against the LORD,
>   turning our backs on our God,
> fomenting oppression and revolt,
>   uttering lies our hearts have conceived.
> So justice is driven back,
>   and righteousness stands at a distance;
> truth has stumbled in the streets,
>   honesty cannot enter (Isa. 59:12–14).

Through these repeated themes the Isaiah passages express the nature of the sin of Jerusalem's residents: injustice toward the powerless, oppression of the poor, exploitation of workers. All these, Isaiah suggests, cause God's people to turn their backs on God so that "truth has stumbled" on Jerusalem's streets and "honesty cannot enter" there.

Jeremiah takes it a step further. Neither economic, political, and social irresponsibility toward the poor, nor the powerless and the marginalized of the city are in themselves the problem, Jeremiah suggests. Rather, such are manifestations of the underlying sin of the city's people: idolatry.

> "Hear the word of the LORD, O kings of Judah and people of Jerusalem. This is what the LORD Almighty, the God of Israel, says: Listen! I am going to bring a disaster on this place that will make the ears of everyone who hears of it tingle. For they have forsaken me and made this a place of foreign gods; they have burned sacrifices in it to gods that neither they nor their fathers nor the kings of Judah ever knew, and they have filled this place with the blood of the innocent. They have built the high places of Baal to burn their sons in the fire as offerings to Baal—something I did not command or mention, nor did it enter my mind" (Jer. 19:3–5).

> "People from many nations will pass by this city and will ask one another, 'Why has the LORD done such a thing to this great city?' And the answer will be: 'Because they have forsaken the covenant of the LORD their God and have worshiped and served other gods'" (Jer. 22:8–9).

The sins of a city's people include self-indulgence, economic injustice, exploitation, and the oppression of those less powerful than the oppressor (we see it even in the class bully in an elementary school). But all such social sins, the prophets declare, are the inevitable manifestations of people who have given themselves over to the service of other gods (money, power, prestige, or commitment to their own group) rather than centering their city's life in the worship of the Lord God.

Jerusalem the Bride: Part 2

Perhaps the most dramatic and vivid presentation of this understanding of a city's sin is given by Ezekiel in the continuation of his figure of Jerusalem as the bride of God.

In Ezekiel 16, God's love for Jerusalem is portrayed as a liberating, sexual love that manifests itself in the Lord's marriage to the city. But whereas verses 1–14 deal with Jerusalem as the bride of God, verses 15–34 deal with her fall from grace.

That fall does not come suddenly. It is a process: a slow, steadily developing unfaithfulness to God and his covenant with the city. She first becomes infatuated with her own beauty, impressed by herself and the status she has apparently won in the world. Then she increasingly prostitutes herself: "You lavished your favors on anyone who passed by and your beauty became his" (v. 15). Jerusalem's people increasingly succumb to idolatry and thus adulterate the covenant. The bride then begins offering her sons and daughters in human sacrifice to the gods of Canaan and the nations around Israel. Finally, the bride disseminates the worship of false gods throughout the land: "In addition to all your other wickedness, you built a mound for yourself and made a lofty shrine in every public square" (vv. 23–24).

Why? It is not for political gain or the making of allegiances to other nations, Ezekiel states. That could at least be understood, even if not condoned. It is not for economic advantage, especially in doing business with other nations. No, the bride Israel gives "gifts to all your lovers, bribing them to come to you from everywhere for your illicit favors. So in your prostitution you are the opposite of others; no one runs after you for your favors. You are the very opposite, for you give payment and none is given to you" (vv. 33–34).

This is a picture of the decline and destruction of a soul—not simply the souls of the individuals who make up Jerusalem, but of the city herself. It is a reminder that a city can abandon God. And it does so, not so much by one awful decision, but little by little as it pursues wealth, prestige, and power to the exclusion of responsibility toward humanity and obedience toward God.

Such disloyalty toward God, Ezekiel points out, will not benefit Jerusalem in the end. Her "lovers"—the other nations of the Near East—will eventually conquer Jerusalem, destroy her temple, raze the city, seize Israel's wealth as booty, and take the city's leaders into captivity. What is the advantage, then, of being disloyal to God and rejecting him? The people have lost out to absolutely everyone, have gained no long-term political advantage, and have rejected their only potential source of salvation and liberation. They have alienated the only One who could actually save them.

Ezekiel poignantly describes the seriousness of this crime as he compares Jerusalem's crime with the sins of her sister cities Sodom and Samaria. He writes:

> "Now this was the sin of your sister Sodom: She and her daughters were arrogant, overfed and unconcerned; they did not help the poor and needy. They were haughty and did detestable things before me. Therefore I did away with them as you have seen. Samaria did not commit half the sins you did. You have done more detestable things than they, and have made your sisters seem righteous by all these things you have done" (Ezek. 16:49–51).

Social injustice (especially toward a city's own poor), exploitation, sexual perversity, pride, gluttony, arrogance, complacency are all terrible sins. Combined, they are capable of destroying the soul of a city. Nothing, however, is as evil as idolatry. To worship something other than God as god is to reject the only One who can actually bring salvation. This was Jerusalem's sin, for the city placed national security ahead of God; the city was willing to sacrifice God in order to worship security.

WHAT ARE THE ROOTS OF A CITY'S EVIL?

A city's evil is made up of personal aggrandizement, self-indulgence, social injustice, and idolatry. But such—while extremely grave—do not get at the heart of a city's sin.

What are the roots of a city's evil? There is no more critical question for urban Christians to ask than this one, because we Christians as individuals and the church as the body of Christ are hopelessly naive about the nature and extent of evil in the city. That is why the church has been essentially ineffective in urban ministry.

We are told that the first rule of warfare is to know the enemy. As long as we hold to an inadequate and naive understanding of a city's evil, we will never appreciate the full scope and power of the enemy we face. It is imperative that we have an adequate biblical understanding of the nature of urban evil. Only then can we, as God's people, hope to have any significant impact on that city.

Evil: Individual or Corporate?

Evangelical Protestantism has tended to center its theology in God's work of salvation. Particularly in its more popular, nonreflective forms, the evangel has historically been proclaimed in terms of individual salvation—the calling of the sinner to Christ. Because of this emphasis on individual salvation, evangelicals have been inclined to approach evil as individual. If Christ's atoning work is sufficient to cover all sin, and if salvation is understood as individual, then the sin that salvation covers must be individual as well. Otherwise, Christ's death is insufficient to cover our sins. Because it is sufficient and because salvation is seen as the redemption of the individual, the evangelical preacher is forced into an examination of sin that is individual. The danger with such an approach is that those who stress exclusively the individual dimensions of salvation can neither understand the full extent of evil nor appreciate the full salvific work of Christ.

It is instructive to note that three major theologies of Christendom— Calvinism, Roman Catholicism, and Orthodoxy—have avoided this problem. Calvinism centers its theologizing in the sovereignty of God, Roman Catholicism in the efficacy of church and sacrament, and Orthodoxy in God as creator. With these theologies, all three traditions have developed a strong sense of corporate and societal sin, which is reflected in each church's historical involvement in the social, economic, and political issues of society.

It is the contention of this book that Scripture presents salvation as both individual and corporate. The biblical writers understood evil this way. Note the broad use of corporate images to describe the saved condition—covenant people, the nation Israel, the people of God, the remnant, the kingdom of God, the church, the New Jerusalem.

I came face-to-face with the evil of a city early in my ministry. Although it was a grim and most painful experience, I thank God that I was brought to an early awareness of the corporate dimensions of a city's evil. Glimpsing the depth of evil of that city transformed my entire ministry. I learned the truth while I was still a college student. It was an overwhelming and bitter truth to learn. But it taught me that city evil was far greater than my limited biblical understanding. And that insight changed my ministry.

I was working among black teenagers in a government project (in which the poor were warehoused in high-rise buildings) in a United States city. Our youth ministry included a spectrum of recreational and athletic activities centered around Bible studies. A fourteen-year-old girl (whom I will call Eva) began to attend one of these Bible study groups.

Eva was an exceptionally beautiful teenager, physically mature for her age. She became even more radiant when she received Christ as her Lord and Savior. I began discipling Eva, building her up in the "nurture and admonition" of the Lord.

My academic year was drawing to a close and I was looking forward to returning home for summer vacation. Just before I was to leave my teenage "parish," Eva came to me greatly troubled.

"Bob," she said, "I am under terrible pressure and I don't know what to do. There is a very large gang in this project that recruits girls to be prostitutes for wealthy white men in the suburbs. They are trying to force me to join them. I know it's wrong. But what should I do?"

I gave Eva all the appropriate advice I had learned in church and college about how if she resisted evil, it would flee from her. I urged her to stick with her Bible study group and not to give in to this gang's demands.

Then I left for my summer vacation.

Three months later, I returned to school and to the ministry in which I was engaged in that city. Eva was nowhere to be found. When I asked about her at the Bible study, the other youth told me she had stopped coming about a month after I had left.

I went to Eva's apartment in one of the project buildings to talk with her. Eva answered to my knock on the door. As soon as she saw me, she burst into tears.

"They got to me, Bob," she said. "I've become a whore!"

"Eva, how could you give in like that?" I unsympathetically responded. "Why didn't you resist?"

"I didn't give in," she responded. "I was forced." Then she told me a story of terror.

"First, they told me they would beat my father if I didn't become one of their prostitutes. I refused, and they beat him—bad. Then they said my brother was to be next. He ended up in the hospital. Then they told me that if I didn't yield, they would gang-rape my mother. I knew they meant it, and I had no alternative. So I gave in and became one of their whores."

"But, Eva," I said, "why didn't you get some protection? Why didn't you go to the police?"

"Bob, you white honkey," Eva responded. "Who do you think *they* are?"

I had come face-to-face with evil in that city. I was introduced to the corporate, systemic nature of urban evil. I suddenly realized that the police were the gang operating the prostitution ring and recruiting young girls like Eva out of that slum. The police in that precinct—the very people entrusted with the task of protecting and defending the people—were the worst exploiters of the people. I eventually discovered that what the police were doing in that one precinct was only the tip of the iceberg of what was happening all over that city, because the entire legal and political system was arrayed to protect those who were betraying the people in order to enrich themselves.

It was in this encounter in 1957 that I first realized that a city's evil is far greater than the sum of the sin of its individuals. The very systems of a city could become corrupt, grasping, oppressive, and exploitative. Sin in the city could be systemic and corporate. And it little mattered even if all the Evas among a city's poor were to be converted, because the evil in the systems could destroy them through the corrupting corporate power. We cannot simply save individuals in the city and expect that the city will get saved. If the church does not deal with the systems and structures of evil in the city, then it will not effectively transform the lives of that city's individuals.

I still grieve over what happened to Eva. I have often repented of the inadequate support I gave to her in the greatest crisis of her young life. But I also thank God for what I learned from this experience. This event forced me to take a look at my theology and to recognize that my understanding of the city and its evil was inadequate for ministering there in a truly effective way. So began my lifetime quest for a biblical theology as big as the city itself. This book and twenty-nine years of urban ministry are the result.

The Systems of a City

Understanding the nature of evil in the city requires examining the primary systems that make a city function and then analyzing these systems biblically.

What are the classic systems of a city—that is, the systems any city *must* have in order to function? It is widely suggested that the systems that order the life of a city are economic, political, and religious. By "religious" I mean the system that gives the city its reason for existence (the word's original sense, from the Latin *religio*, means "to bind fast" or "to structure"). A religion is that which structures or brings ordered meaning to life. With such a definition, we can readily see that even the most secular and materialistic city has a religion, because it uses a commitment to modernity to bring order and structure to its existence.

All other social institutions (education, health care, culture and the arts, social services) are subsystems of the economic, political, and religious systems of a city. In fact, until several hundred years ago, each of these subsystems was regarded as a part of the religious system, for it was the responsibility of the church to carry out these services and to be patron of the city's art and culture.

What insights can we gain from Scripture to help us make these urban systems godly and beneficial instead of corrupt and evil?

GODLY POLITICAL, ECONOMIC, AND RELIGIOUS SYSTEMS

The clearest exposition of the development of the systems of Israel's corporate life may be found in the book of Deuteronomy. This book, especially chapter 6, lays out the principles and laws that provided order and structure to the nation.

Chapter 6 is part of Moses' final speech to his people. For forty years he led them through the wilderness, taking a ragtag, rebellious band of former slaves and building them into a nation. But the time finally arrived when Israel could no longer remain in the wilderness and had to get on with their national life and enter the Promised Land.

Before they crossed over the Jordan River, the narrative tells us, Moses gathered the children of Israel to speak to them one more time. He said he would not go with them, but would return to the desert to die; his disciple, Joshua, would lead them.

Infinitely wiser than they, Moses knew that the difficulties and trials of the desert were as nothing compared with the difficulties and trials of life in the Promised Land. The trials of the wilderness had disciplined and strengthened Israel; the trials of the Promised Land would erode and weaken the nation. Moses had to warn the people against the temptations of wealth, power, and prestige that awaited them in their land.

In his final speech Moses reminded Israel that he had dreamed a great dream about a new nation, a kingdom lived under God. That new society had been carefully constructed and practiced in the desert. But now, Moses told the people in Deuteronomy 6, you are to go into a new land to possess it. It will be a land of pagans who will not accept or even appreciate your way of life; instead, they will oppose it. The new land will be filled with cities of great wealth, which you will appropriate; that wealth may erode your way of life. That new land will bring you much prosperity so that you will think you have made yourself strong rather than perceiving all as a gift from God; that power will undermine your dependence on God. This is what you will face in the new land—people who will oppose, wealth that will erode, power that will undermine your way of life.

What do you need to do, Moses asked, to establish the kingdom of God in a pagan land? The answer to that question is what Deuteronomy, especially the sixth chapter, is all about.

A Religion of Relationship

According to the text, Moses proclaimed,

> Hear, O Israel: The LORD our God, the LORD is one. Love the LORD your God with all your heart and with all your soul and with all your strength. These commandments that I give you today are to be upon your hearts (Deut. 6:4–6).

> Do not follow other gods, the gods of the peoples around you; for the LORD your God, who is among you, is a jealous God and his anger will burn against you, and he will destroy you from the face of the land. Do not test the LORD your God as you did at Massah (vv. 14–16).

The foundation for the building of a nation or of a city, the author of Deuteronomy tells us, is relationship with God. True religion is not the observance of liturgies, laws, and rituals, but an active, growing relationship with God. Moses called Israel to love God "with all your heart and with all your soul and with all your strength." Commandments were not rules to be obeyed, but conditions of relationship engraved on one's heart. To follow other gods, therefore, was the cruelest possible thing an Israelite could do—it would be striking at the very heart of the human society God wished to create in Palestine. Moses wanted Israel to build the systems of its cities and nation on relationship with God.

A Politics of Justice

In light of his call to relationship with God, Moses commanded Israel,

> These commandments that I give you today are to be upon your hearts. Impress them on your children. Talk about them when you sit at home and when you walk along the road, when you lie down and when you get up. Tie them as symbols on your hands and bind them on your foreheads. Write them on the doorframes of your houses and on your gates (Deut. 6:6–9).

> Be sure to keep the commands of the LORD your God and the stipulations and decrees he has given you. Do what is right and good in the LORD's sight, so that it may go well with you and you may go in and take over the good land that the LORD promised on oath to your forefathers, thrusting out all your enemies before you, as the LORD said (Deut. 6:17–19).

Authentic corporate relationship with God inevitably leads to a politics of justice. Moses instructed Israel to be sure to "keep the commands of the LORD your God," to engrave them "upon your hearts," "impress them on your children," and be consumed with reflecting on them and obeying them in every activity.

But what are these commandments and stipulations and decrees that Israel was to obey?

Whether the blueprint was Plato's *Republic* or Thomas More's *Utopia* or Karl Marx's *Communist Manifesto*, every creator of a new order for humanity has made a fatal mistake. All such dreams of a perfect society have failed because humans are not perfect. The new society that Moses prepared the Israelites to inaugurate in the Promised Land was not, however, a utopian state. The commandments, stipulations, and decrees that formed the fiber of that new society were all laws and covenants, not of perfection, but of justice!

When we read the commandments and regulations that follow Moses' speech in Deuteronomy, we are amazed to discover that they deal mostly with issues of justice. They deal with such concerns as the redistribution of wealth to the poor, protection of the widow, liberation of the enslaved, limitations on the power of rulers, justice in warfare, safeguarding the welfare of wives and unmarried women in adjudication and cases of homicide, and protection of the divorcée, the orphan, the stranger, the sick, the visitor, and the enfeebled. To fulfill the kingdom of God successfully in a pagan city, according to Moses, Israel was to develop and maintain a politics of justice.

It now becomes clear why Moses' first command to the Israelites was to "love the LORD your God with all your heart and with all your soul and with all your strength." It would have been insufficient to build a nation by practicing individual justice. The people needed to recognize the authentic origin of justice, namely, a righteous God, and just actions as a grateful response to him. People are truly motivated to practice the Golden Rule when the source of that motivation is a love relationship with God. Those who are at peace with God will wish to be at peace with their neighbor. When we see that all the good in life has not been deserved but has been given by God, we will desire to share that good with others. The foundation for a just order, therefore, is a personal, active relationship with God. Israel was able to maintain God's just kingdom in the Promised Land and in her cities to the degree that she was able to maintain a vital, personal faith in God.

An Economics of Stewardship

Finally, Moses taught Israel,

> When the LORD your God brings you into the land he swore to your fathers, to Abraham, Isaac and Jacob, to give you—a land with large, flourishing cities you did not build, houses filled with all kinds of good things you did not provide, wells you did not dig, and vineyards and olive groves you did not plant—then when you eat and are satisfied, be careful that you do not forget the LORD, who brought you out of Egypt, out of the land of slavery (Deut. 6:10–12).

To maintain God's kingdom successfully in the cities of a pagan land, Moses said, Israel would have to adopt an economics of stewardship. And here is exposed the radically different perception of ownership under which Israel ordered its national and urban life.

The people of Israel did not believe that a person could own land; they believed he could only have temporary custody. God was the owner, and both the nation in general and each Israelite were given temporary trust over some of God's possessions. Thus the Promised Land was given to Israel by God, and with it, the valleys and hills and rivers and wheat and fig trees, its iron and copper and its great and flourishing cities. This was all gift—given to Israel by the land's owner, God. And those in whom God had invested the land were to be responsible and good stewards of this trust, for they would one day be held accountable for their custodianship of that land.

That is why it was so horrible for an Israelite to say, "My power and the strength of my hands have produced this wealth for me" (Deut. 8:17). That boast was not simply arrogance; it was blasphemy, for it denied that God had freely given the land to him, had placed the riches in the land for him to mine and grow, so that he could care for, cultivate, and protect that land as God's trustee.

The new kingdom of God that Moses had prepared Israel to institute in the land of Canaan, therefore, was to be the land and city of God, the place God owned. Because God owned this land and freely and graciously offered it and its cities to Israel, the people were to be responsible stewards of it. They were to treat each other and all people around them justly—for they were all sojourners on God's land (Deut. 6:20–25). They were to eliminate poverty and economic and political oppression and were to protect the weak, because all were created equally as children of God. And they were to love God and live in gratitude to him, for he was the high King of their land, the One who wanted to live among them and love his people. To love justice, to treat each other tenderly as equal children of God, to live gratefully before God—this the Israelites had to do to maintain God's kingdom in the cities of a pagan land.

Biblical Systems—and How They Fared

Deuteronomy describes the relationship God wanted for the people of his cities and nation as they developed their religious, political, and economic systems. For nearly two hundred years Israel was relatively successful in "singing the Lord's song" in the new land. Except for a few notable relapses, Israel faithfully practiced devotion to God, a corporate politics of justice for all the occupants of Canaan, and an economics of stewardship of all God had given them.

But as the years and generations and then centuries rolled by, Israel began to change. Slowly, inexorably, political power became concentrated in only two of the twelve tribes. Wealth began to accumulate in the hands of specific families. First winking at the law, then gradual injustice, and then outright disobedience of the law and covenant became prevalent. The uniqueness and power of Israel instilled by Moses in the desert gradually dissolved.

Then came a crisis—an external crisis. The dreaded Philistines from the Mediterranean invaded the land of Canaan. Weakened by their own spiritual and moral decay, Israel retreated frantically before the advancing Philistine army. In the face of this danger occurred one of the most poignant tragedies recorded in the Bible.

All the elders of Israel gathered together and came to Samuel at
Ramah. They said to him, "You are old, and your sons do not walk in
your ways; now appoint a king to lead us, such as all the other nations
have" (1 Sam. 8:4–5).

It seems a reasonable, even innocent, request. The very future of
Israel was being threatened by the Philistines, and a king would seem to
have the power to unite the twelve tribes, build a large army, and defeat
the invaders.

It was not an innocent request, however. God was Israel's king—the
God who had brought the people out of Egypt, the God who had
protected them in the wilderness, the God who had led them into the
Promised Land, the God who had graced them with "flourishing cities
you did not build." God was the high King of Israel, and no man! How
tragic are God's words to Samuel: "Listen to all that the people are saying
to you; it is not you they have rejected, but they have rejected me as their
king" (1 Sam. 8:7).

"They have rejected me. . . ." For Israel to choose to have a man as
their king was to say that they no longer trusted God. They could no
longer depend on him to protect them from an invading nation. They
would no longer depend on his laws to maintain justice in their cities,
because the justice they wanted—a justice favoring the rich instead of the
poor—was at sword's point with the justice demanded by God. Faced
with the decay of their nation's inward life and threatened by potential
defeat from the outside, Israel decided to depend on the empire's way
instead of God's ways. To decide to be like all the other nations of the
earth was to accept the conventional wisdom that a nation's destiny was
determined by its military power, political strength, and economic
production.

Thus, in the period of the kings Israel's theocracy ended, a theocracy
that had been carefully prescribed by Moses and functioning for more
than two hundred years. We can best see how a city's and country's
systems are corrupted by humanity and become demonic in their capacity
to generate evil if we study the economic, political, and religious dynamics
at work through the kings of Israel and Judah.

THE CORRUPTION OF THE SYSTEMS

We could cite a number of examples to trace the process by which
Israel's political, economic, and religious systems became corrupt. In the
story of Daniel we see a power-crazed Nebuchadnezzar, who on a whim
brought unbelievable oppression on Hebrew youth. Or we can observe
the political might of the Roman Empire joining forces with the economic
power of the Jewish religious institution in the time of Jesus to hold the
common people in thrall while justifying such exploitation by appealing to

Jewish religious nationalism. We could also turn to the time of Paul and view the urban churches he founded as they struggled against Roman power, the self-serving of Greek and Near Eastern religions, and a matrix of Jewish and gentile local and international economics.

We find the clearest biblical examples of urban corruption, however, during the time of the kings of Israel and Judah. Three kings in particular merit attention—Solomon, Ahab, and Josiah.

Solomon: The Economics of Privilege and Exploitation

Israel was warned about the dangers of monarchy when the people first pressed for a king while they were still in the period of the judges. In a profoundly prophetic passage, the charismatic leader Samuel told the complaining Israelites:

> "This is what the king who will reign over you will do: He will take your sons and make them serve with his chariots and horses, and they will run in front of his chariots. Some he will assign to be commanders of thousands and commanders of fifties, and others to plow his ground and reap his harvest, and still others to make weapons of war and equipment for his chariots. He will take your daughters to be perfumers and cooks and bakers. He will take the best of your fields and vineyards and olive groves, and give them to his attendants. He will take a tenth of your grain and of your vintage and give it to his officials and attendants. Your menservants and maidservants and the best of your cattle and donkeys he will take for his own use. He will take a tenth of your flocks, and you yourselves will become his slaves. When that day comes, you will cry out for relief from the king you have chosen, and the LORD will not answer you in that day" (1 Sam. 8:11–18).

Under King Solomon, what was once only a threat became stark reality. During his reign the Israelite empire reached both its greatest extent and its financial peak. Scripture graphically describes the growing power and wealth of the Israelite nation:

> And Solomon ruled over all the kingdoms from the [Euphrates] River to the land of the Philistines, as far as the border of Egypt. These countries brought tribute and were Solomon's subjects all his life. . . . For [Solomon] ruled over all the kingdoms west of the River, from Tiphsah to Gaza, and had peace on all sides. During Solomon's lifetime Judah and Israel, from Dan to Beersheba, lived in safety, each man under his own vine and fig tree (1 Kings 4:21, 24–25).

It sounds like the idyllic life for Israel—almost a second Garden of Eden. But the nation actually paid a terrible price for such development. The lifestyle of Israel's "rich and famous" became profligate. Consider, for example, the daily provision for the palace alone:

> Solomon's daily provisions were thirty cors [185 bushels] of fine flour
> and sixty cors [375 bushels] of meal, ten head of stall-fed cattle, twenty
> of pasture-fed cattle and a hundred sheep and goats, as well as deer,
> gazelles, roebucks and choice fowl (1 Kings 4:22–23).

The wealth and power accumulating in this one man's hands were
enormous by any standards:

> Solomon accumulated chariots and horses; he had fourteen hundred
> chariots and twelve thousand horses, which he kept in the chariot
> cities and also with him in Jerusalem. The king made silver as common
> in Jerusalem as stones, and cedar as plentiful as sycamore-fig trees in
> the foothills. Solomon's horses were imported from Egypt and from
> Kue—the royal merchants purchased them from Kue. They imported
> a chariot from Egypt for six hundred shekels of silver, and a horse for a
> hundred and fifty. They also exported them to all the kings of the
> Hittites and the Arameans (1 Kings 10:26–29).

Even Solomon's throne was an example of conspicuous consumption:

> Then the king made a great throne inlaid with ivory and overlaid with
> fine gold. The throne had six steps, and its back had a rounded top.
> On both sides of the seat were armrests, with a lion standing beside
> each of them. Twelve lions stood on the six steps, one at either end of
> each step. Nothing like it had ever been made for any other kingdom
> (1 Kings 10:18–20).

Far worse than such conspicuous wealth was the price being paid for
it. Israel was rapidly becoming a nation with radical class distinctions. The
king and the royal court along with landowners were accruing increasing
power and wealth, at least partly because they were exploiting the people
of the land, both foreigners and Israelites. Consider these terrible words of
condemnation:

> Here is the account of the forced labor King Solomon conscripted to
> build the LORD's temple, his own palace, the supporting terraces, the
> wall of Jerusalem, and [his treasure cities] Hazor, Megiddo and
> Gezer. . . . All the people left from the Amorites, Hittites, Perizzites,
> Hivites and Jebusites (these peoples were not Israelites), that is, their
> descendants remaining in the land, whom the Israelites could not
> exterminate—these Solomon conscripted for his slave labor force. . . .
> But Solomon did not make slaves of any of the Israelites (1 Kings 9:15,
> 20–22).

Solomon's resolve not to use Israelites as slaves did not last long. The
demands of this economic machine were such that, in his latter days, the
king resorted to the conscription of his fellow Israelites:

> King Solomon conscripted laborers from all Israel—thirty thousand
> men. He sent them off to Lebanon in shifts of ten thousand a month,

so that they spent one month in Lebanon and two months at home. Adoniram was in charge of the forced labor. Solomon had seventy thousand carriers and eighty thousand stonecutters in the hills, as well as thirty-three hundred foremen who supervised the project and directed the workmen. At the king's command they removed from the quarry large blocks of quality stone to provide a foundation of dressed stone for the temple. The craftsmen of Solomon and Hiram and the men of Gebal cut and prepared the timber and stone for the building of the temple (1 Kings 5:13–18).

Here, then, was the spectacle of an Israelite king, seated on the throne to maintain Israel as a nation of economic equality and political justice in a world of exploitation and oppression, but now so involved in "public works" that he had created virtual armies both of conquered peoples and of his fellow Israelites to undertake forced labor. For what cause were these people of God enslaved? The building of a temple for the worship of God! Somehow Israel could be taken out of Egypt, but Egypt had not been taken out of the king of Israel!

Solomon had become a painful contrast to Deuteronomy's instructions regarding the suitable king for Israel. Knowing the great dangers involved in a monarchy, God had warned:

When you enter the land the LORD your God is giving you and have taken possession of it and settled in it, and you say, "Let us set a king over us like all the nations around us," be sure to appoint over you the king the LORD your God chooses. He must be from among your own brothers. Do not place a foreigner over you, one who is not a brother Israelite. The king, moreover, must not acquire great numbers of horses for himself or make the people return to Egypt to get more of them, for the Lord has told you, "You are not to go back that way again." He must not take many wives, or his heart will be led astray. He must not accumulate large amounts of silver and gold.

When he takes the throne of his kingdom, he is to write for himself on a scroll a copy of this law, taken from that of the priests, who are Levites. It is to be with him, and he is to read it all the days of his life so that he may learn to revere the LORD his God and follow carefully all the words of this law and these decrees and not consider himself better than his brothers and turn from the law to the right or to the left (Deut. 17:14–20).

Solomon—the king who had asked for wisdom and had used that God-given intelligence to gather to himself wealth and power, women, and a potentate's court—had become everything the prophets of Israel had warned the people against for centuries. Solomon practiced unremittingly an economics of privilege and exploitation. And the result was an empire of such repression that it exploded in rebellion under the reign of his successor, Rehoboam (1 Kings 12). Because of Solomon's greed and lust, Israel's most powerful king sacrificed the heritage of his father.

Ahab: The Politics of Oppression

Economics that promote the exploitation of the poor and unfortunate as a means to accrue power and wealth for the privileged will inevitably lead to a politics of oppression. Wealth so gained must be protected, either by law or by violence, from those from whom it has been wrested. Thus politics is inevitably enlisted to secure that protection. It is that dynamic most clearly at work in the story of King Ahab of Israel.

Solomon's economics of privilege led, soon after his death, to revolution. The resulting explosion was the collapse of the Israelite empire and the creation of two rival Israelite states. In the north was "Israel," the larger of the two nations, ruled by the revolutionaries. In the south was "Judah," loyal to the descendants of Solomon and David. As is so often the case, those revolting against oppression eventually became the new oppressors. Formerly the revolutionaries, the kings of Israel's northern kingdom became far more cruel than the wealthy potentate they replaced. And the cruelest of the lot was Ahab.

King Ahab came to the throne forty-three years after Solomon's death. His rule, from its beginning in 879 B.C.E. to its end over twenty years later, was one of continuing religious and political oppression. His advocacy of the worship of Baal was a political move on Ahab's part, a strategy designed to weaken Israel's commitment to a constitutional and limited monarchy (because Yahweh was seen as Israel's ultimate monarch). Unlike Solomon, Ahab realized that the source of Israel's commitment to political justice lay in its basic commitment to Yahweh. If he were to become absolute dictator of Israel and rebuild Solomon's lost empire, Ahab would have to destroy Israel's faith in Yahweh.

Ahab was a strong leader and was feared by the Assyrians as a military genius. He led a coalition army that so badly defeated the Assyrian army that they were unable to invade Israel for sixteen years after his death.[2] Yet what would have been Ahab's greatest moment of glory as a king is not even mentioned in the Bible. Instead, the Bible gives an amazing amount of space to two events that would be considered historically small moments in the king's twenty-one-year reign. Those two events were the battle between Yahweh and Baal and the incident at Naboth's vineyard.

Elijah the prophet arose as the one man in opposition to King Ahab. To make Ahab's real intentions plain to Israel, Elijah's first task was to discredit Baal. He did so by challenging the priests of Baal to a battle between the two gods (1 Kings 18:16–46), the winner being recognized as the legitimate god.

The people of Israel gathered at Mount Carmel with Elijah and 450 priests of Baal. There both Elijah and the priests built altars and placed bulls upon them for sacrifice—one altar to Baal, the other to Yahweh. Elijah threw down the challenge: "You call on the name of your god, and I will call on the name of the LORD. The god who answers by fire—he is God" (1 Kings 18:24).

The priests of Baal began to cry to their god, begging him to send down fire. But nothing happened. Elijah mocked and ridiculed the harried priests; they prayed all the harder. For the half-day during which they cried to Baal, the god of fire did not answer with fire.

Elijah arose and commanded that twelve jars of water be thrown on the altar of Yahweh. He then offered one short prayer to God.

> Then the fire of the LORD fell and burned up the sacrifice, the wood, the stones and the soil, and also licked up the water in the trench. When all the people saw this, they fell prostrate and cried, "The LORD—he is God! The LORD—he is God!" (1 Kings 18:38–39).

"The LORD—he is God!" As this cry rose from the people, Ahab's hope for winning Israel to Baal was crushed. Although he had earlier succeeded in getting most of Israel to consider Baal, Yahweh's discrediting of the Canaanite god left no room for doubt in the Israelites' minds.

The issue here was not really religion; it was power. If Ahab could not undermine the Israelite commitment to law through discrediting their god, he could do so by direct force. In a show of strength Ahab broke the laws by seizing the vineyard of Naboth, a citizen of Israel (1 Kings 21:1–29), after Ahab's wife conspired to have Naboth killed. Elijah confronted Ahab with the fact that the king had sinned against Israel, against God, and against his own vows of kingship. But whereas Ahab did not succeed in turning the hearts of Israel from Yahweh to Baal, he did get away with his blatant exercise of power in Naboth's vineyard (despite his temporary penitence [1 Kings 21:28–29]). In spite of Elijah's public accusation, no charge was ever brought against Ahab and he defied the nation to keep him from illegally seizing property and committing murder.

In the incident at Naboth's vineyard the real issue was laid bare. Who ruled Israel, and who held the king to accountability? Before Ahab assumed the throne, Israel would have answered the question, "Yahweh rules Israel, and the king is God's servant; consequently, the king is accountable to the law of Moses and is responsible for its just and equitable adjudication." After Ahab's reign, many Israelites would have answered, "The king rules Israel and is accountable to no one."

Was the king above the law? The law of Moses called for the king of Israel to protect the law and thus protect the rights of the people. In the incident of the vineyard, Ahab proved that he could disregard the law and get away with it. He could exploit the law by disregarding it and thus oppress the people. It is noteworthy that Naboth was not one of the "ordinary people"; he was a part of the wealthy and ruling class. Yet because of Ahab's successful action, even the powerful had no guarantee under the law that their property—or even their lives—belonged to them.

Josiah: The Religion of Control

Have you ever started something with the very best of intentions and then found the action turning against you? I think that is what happened to Josiah, the boy king of Judah.

Solomon and Ahab both seemed quite clear about what they were doing. Solomon was committed to the creation of a privileged class, and if that meant economic exploitation of ordinary Israelites and foreigners alike, so be it! Ahab meant to possess full power and therefore relished the political oppression of Israel's powerful and powerless alike.

I do not think Josiah, however, meant to develop a religion that would seek to control the people. I believe he simply wanted to be a good and godly king; he responded with good intentions to the newfound law code. But "the best-laid schemes of mice and men" often go astray. They did for Josiah. He soon found himself trapped in a web of religious ritual and control from which he could not break free.

Josiah (640–609 B.C.E.) became king of the southern nation of Judah after it had had fifty-seven years of misrule. The northern kingdom of Israel had finally fallen to the Assyrian threat in 721 B.C.E. Although Judah initially sought safety in relationship with Yahweh under King Hezekiah, this commitment did not endure even to the end of his reign. With the Assyrian threat slowly crumbling, the two subsequent kings of Judah, Manasseh and Amon, led the nation into increasing economic and political exploitation, diverted by a Baal-centered religion of extreme sexual license and greed. When Amon's eight-year-old son, Josiah, ascended the throne, the country was ready for a change. Josiah began by cleaning up Solomon's temple. Eugene Peterson graphically describes what happened:

> As the temple was being renovated and repaired, Hilkiah the priest found an old book there. The book was brought to Josiah and read aloud to him. It was the book of Deuteronomy. Imagine the impact of that reading. Here is Josiah, disgusted with the evil of his father and grandfather and determined to do something about it, but not knowing quite how. He had no blueprint, no direction, no counsel. The only thing he had inherited from his father and grandfather was fifty-seven years of evil. Now he had this powerful document about the love of God and our worship of him, clear definitions of what is right and wrong, and explicit directions on how to make moral decisions and conduct intelligent worship.[3]

The message of the scroll was simply that God could not bless or protect Israel if she did not follow the Mosaic covenant. Obedience to the Sinai covenant was interpreted by Josiah and the priests of Israel in terms of liturgical reform, orthodox theology, a refusal to ally with heathen nations, and strict adherence to liturgical, dietetic, and health laws.

In compliance with the portions of Deuteronomy he and the priests chose to stress, Josiah launched a radical reform of Judah. He broke off all relations with Assyria and declared complete independence. He had all the altars and high places of Baal in the countryside destroyed, and all cult prostitutes were turned out. Worship was reformed; all shrines to Yahweh outside Jerusalem were demolished to compel centralization of worship at the temple. Everyone was expected strictly to obey the liturgical portions of the Deuteronomic law. The king himself became a chief participant in the worship at the temple and in liturgical reform. But such reforms were only skin-deep.

Jeremiah the prophet challenged Josiah's reform effort. He thought it shallow and boldly told Josiah so (Jer. 6:16–21). The prophet felt that the court's interpretation of Deuteronomy was dangerous because it held that Yahweh's demands were satisfied by liturgical reform and external compliance to ritual and regulations. True reform, Jeremiah pointed out, required social justice and personal repentance. His basic message was that Israel's commitment to Yahweh was superficial and that the supposed repentance of the people was no repentance at all, for they were not living by the economic, political, and social obligations of the Mosaic covenant.

Particularly disturbing to Jeremiah was the trap of logic into which the nation had fallen. Because the newfound scroll implied that God could not bless Israel unless the nation obeyed the ritualistic laws, the people and religious leaders believed that obedience to the law ensured God's protection. Remembering how God had earlier saved Jerusalem from the Assyrians (2 Kings 18:13–19:37), the people believed that God would preserve their country against all aggression.

In his famous "Temple Sermon" (Jer. 7:1–34), Jeremiah proclaimed that Israel was resorting to folly by believing that God would keep his city and temple from destruction simply because the people were practicing liturgical reform. The only basis for God's protection, the prophet declared, was that

> "If you really change your ways and your actions and deal with each other justly, if you do not oppress the alien, the fatherless or the widow and do not shed innocent blood in this place, and if you do not follow other gods to your own harm" (vv. 5–6).

The battle that Jeremiah faced had as its real issue the future of the national faith of Israel. Since the construction of the temple by Solomon three hundred years earlier, Israel had time and again proved unfaithful to the covenant. There was a continuing battle between prophet and priest, between covenant keeping and self-serving national religion. At the heart of the debate was the question of the nature of the Sinai covenant. The priests and the kings for more than three hundred years had insisted that both the Sinai and Davidic covenants were essentially liturgical and worship-oriented and had to do with the "religious" or "sacred" part of life. The prophets, by contrast, had maintained that the covenants were essentially life-oriented and thus were concerned with political justice, economic equality, and individual responsibility. This difference in understanding was the foundation for the struggles between Solomon and Israel, the battle between Elijah and Ahab, and now the conflict between Jeremiah and Josiah.

The self-interested interpretation that King Josiah and the priests of Judah gave to the rediscovered scroll of the law added a new dimension to this struggle, however. The Sinai and Davidic covenants were in danger of becoming the handmaid of official religion—a major step in turning the Hebrew faith from a servant-oriented religion to a religion of written law. A religion based on written law would increasingly tend to concentrate on obedience to that law rather than on a personal response to God. Jeremiah sensed this potential danger and battled to keep Judah faithful to the covenants.

Of course, the question must be asked, "Why would a king *want* a religion of liturgy, orthodox theology, and strict obedience in which he could participate?" Was Josiah drawn to a liturgical and legalistic interpretation because it would promote order and direction in his chaotic land? Was it that he saw religion as bringing stability to his nation, only to discover as time went on that such a formalized faith actually brought religious tyranny?

Religion can both be seduced by and seduce a nation's economic and political forces. It can be used to endorse or legitimize government and economic forces in any city or nation and thereby become a major means for controlling that society and its people. The history of Christianity is replete with examples of such mutual legitimization, where the official religion has blessed the political and economic orders and has been handsomely rewarded and protected by these forces. The recognition that this happens is expressed in the statement, "The church came to do good and ended up doing right well!"

A SCRIPTURAL SYNOPSIS OF SYSTEMIC SIN

The nature and extent of evil in a city are succinctly summarized by Ezekiel in his recital of Jerusalem's sins in Ezekiel 22. That chapter begins with God's challenge to Ezekiel:

> The word of the LORD came to me: "Son of man, will you judge her? Will you judge this city of bloodshed? Then confront her with all her detestable practices" (vv. 1–2).

Ezekiel's analysis of what has caused Jerusalem to become such a degraded city starts by citing the end of the process rather than its beginning. That city, created to be the city of God, has somehow become the city of Satan.

> "Say [to the city]: 'This is what the Sovereign LORD says: O city that brings on herself doom by shedding blood in her midst and defiles herself by making idols, you have become guilty because of the blood you have shed and have become defiled by the idols you have made. You have brought your days to a close, and the end of your years has come'" (vv. 3–4).

It is not simply that there is evil—great evil—being committed in Jerusalem, Ezekiel states. It is that the city itself has become infamous, detestable, murderous. Jerusalem had been intended by God to be an angelic presence in the world, but somehow she had become demonic. The city's very spirituality had profoundly changed from godly to satanic, making it "an object of scorn to the nations and a laughingstock to all the countries" (v. 4).

What had caused Jerusalem's profound spiritual shift? Ezekiel traces that shift quite clearly: Jerusalem's political (vv. 6–7, 25), religious (vv. 8–9, 26), and economic (vv. 12–13, 27) systems have become corrupt.

Jerusalem's princes have become "like a roaring lion tearing its prey" (v. 25). The political powers use their authority to treat Israelites with contempt, to enrich their own coffers, and to oppress the alien and mistreat the fatherless and the widow (v. 7). Thus the political authorities of Jerusalem have refused to fulfill their God-given, primary responsibility to seek justice for all the city's people. Rather, they have committed themselves to the oppression of the poor and powerless in order to increase their own power and wealth.

The economic leaders of Jerusalem are as guilty as the government officials, declares Ezekiel. They are like "wolves," voraciously tearing apart the people for the "unjust gain" they might receive (v. 27). For these leaders, everything is subject to its capacity to make money. Bribery, usury, excessive interest, and extortion are all acceptable activities for the rich (v. 12). The economic leaders, given the responsibility by God to be wise stewards of his people's resources, instead have become voracious exploiters of the people.

The religious establishment has also contributed to the spiritual death of Jerusalem, Ezekiel insists. They "do violence" to the law (v. 26), have "despised my holy things" (v. 8), and "shut their eyes to the keeping of my Sabbaths" (v. 26). These are the very people entrusted by

God to construct the city of God on each person's relationship with him; they are instead endorsing the political and economic leaders for the security and wealth they might receive.

Ezekiel goes on to say that the corruption of the political, economic, and religious leadership and systems of the city has not only eroded the godly foundations of the city, but has also seduced those who would normally hold such leadership accountable (v. 28). The prophets have always spoken God's word to Israel, demanding justice of rulers, equality and communality of business leaders, a commitment to personal relationship with God on the part of the priests. But the prophets have been seduced. The power and wealth and control of the systems have blinded those who are most likely to have eyes to see. They have been overwhelmed by the evil of the systems; "her prophets whitewash these deeds for them by [declaring] false visions and lying divinations" (v. 28). The prophets, formerly the symbol of Jerusalem's integrity, have allowed themselves to be captured by the systems rather than hold those systems accountable.

Finally, Ezekiel declares, such profoundly deep corruption of Jerusalem's systems has corrupted the people (vv. 8–11, 29). The ordinary citizens of Jerusalem—the victims of corruption—internalize the values of their leaders. Those oppressed by the systems turn on each other, oppressing "the poor and needy, . . . denying them justice" (v. 29) and following illegitimate sexual practices beyond belief (vv. 8–11). Thus the oppressed turn on each other rather than seeking to transform the system. Those exploited by business interests, instead of changing the system, seek to make as much money from each other as they can—legitimately or not. Those controlled by religion turn on each other, demanding an obedience to the minutiae of law and liturgy that not even the religious leaders require. So the people become the enemy, seduced by the power, prestige, and possessions of the city's rich, powerful, and pious.

Thus, Ezekiel teaches, Jerusalem's entire spirituality is corrupted. When the systems and the prophets and the people are all seduced, there is no one left who has eyes to see and ears to hear. All in the city have been seduced by Satan and have given themselves over to the sustenance and service of the demonic. Thus is the godly spirituality of a city destroyed, replaced by all that is dark, grasping, and evil in life.

CONCLUSION

The primary systems of a city are the economic, political, and religious institutions. These systems constantly interact and cooperate with one another, thereby forming either holy alliances or an unholy trinity. The systems have the potential to work for justice and economic equality for the people and wise stewardship of a city's resources if their functioning is based on both corporate and individual relationship with God. But systems can be demonic as well, enhancing the economic privilege of a few while exploiting the poor and powerless, using the political order to further such exploitation while maintaining a city's order, and turning faith commitment into formalized religion that legitimizes "the powers that be" while benefiting from the powers' largess.

What makes a city's systems evil? There are the natural sinful instincts of humanity—that part of all of us that seeks power, prestige, possessions, in the service of self-interest and the interests of those like us. What keeps God's kingdom out of us as individuals also keeps God's kingdom out of the city and its systems.

There is a far more powerful force, however, that presses a city's economic, political, and religious systems toward self-service and evil. That is the pervasive, overwhelming power of what the Bible calls the "principalities and powers." A biblical understanding of a city's principalities and powers—and particularly the demonic dimensions of such powers—is absolutely essential to effective ministry in that city. These demonic dimensions of a city's system are the subject of the next chapter.

Let us conclude this chapter by considering a stained-glass representation of King David and King Solomon in a church in Detroit, Michigan.

The window is divided into two panels. The second panel pictures Solomon dressed in sumptuous robes and holding a golden temple in his arms. His shoulders are hunched, and his arms cradle and protect that golden object. His body is weighed down with the problems of an empire. His face looks out at the observer with heaviness, anguish, and exhaustion.

The first panel shows King Solomon's father, David. David is wearing rather plain clothing and in his arms has not a golden temple, but a harp. As he plays the harp, David's body is straight, his head is thrown back, and he is singing energetically in praise to God!

Could it be that, as a man in love with God, David was a just and fair king, judging the cause of the poor and needy, weeping over the death of a son who had tried to kill him, and dancing in the worship of God? Is there in the city an alternative to the empire-building of a Solomon, an Ahab, or a Josiah? Can godly economics, politics, and religion actually be the way to run a city?

Chapter Three

OUR CITY AS THE ABODE OF SATANIC PRINCIPALITIES AND POWERS

My son and I stepped out of the airport and into the street. Immediately we were besieged by men grabbing at our suitcases, taxi drivers standing inches from our faces shouting, "Taxi, sir," scrawny women with exhaustion etched on their faces lifting begging hands, and deformed children calling for alms. We were part of a pilgrimage of first world Christians visiting and working with the church among the poor in Asia. We had just arrived in Calcutta, India, to work with the Missionaries of Charity, Mother Teresa's religious order.

The taxi ride to our modest hotel confirmed my impressions at the airport. Here was a city besieged. As we drove at breakneck speed through the streets, I could not help but be overwhelmed by the gaunt and desperate faces of the people, the endless squatter settlements of cheek-by-jowl, single-room shacks surrounded by ankle-deep mud, and the occasional glimpses of the rich apparently oblivious to the suffering around them. Walking the streets that night, I was stunned by the hoards of people bedding down on the sidewalks; I was later to discover that more than five hundred thousand people are forced to live on the streets of Calcutta, never to experience the luxury of a roof over their heads. As I distributed food to five thousand mothers the next day with the Missionaries of Charity, I found myself impressed by the stoic suffering of the poor as they waited quietly in line to receive the only sustenance that kept their families alive. Here was a city of suffering, disease, and impoverishment beyond any words to describe adequately.

The next day, however, we were treated to a profoundly different experience. We were walking to the Mother House of the Missionaries of Charity to begin our day's work. We picked our way past the ubiquitous street-dwellers as they tended small charcoal stoves, brushed their teeth in standing water, prepared appetizer-sized food for sale, squatted to urinate at the curbs. Suddenly we heard a great commotion down the street—the sound of beating drums, exploding firecrackers, and loud music. Then a large open-bed truck appeared, gaily decorated and filled with young men. They were singing, cheering, and waving to passersby. As the truck sped past us, I could see that many of the young men held large paper models of women, houses, cars, boats, and fine possessions. That was to be the first of many such parades that day and throughout the week.

We learned that these young men were worshipers of Kali, the Hindu goddess to whom the city of Calcutta is dedicated and after whom it is named. We had happened to arrive in the city at the close of the main annual festival in her honor. These young men had just left the temple of Kali, in which they had pledged their very souls to the goddess. In return, they had been promised that they might receive whatever they had displayed before Kali through the paper models they had built. They were now on their way to the sacred Ganges River, where they would place their models in the water. If the models did not sink as they floated out of sight, this would be an indication that Kali had heard the supplicant's request and it would be granted. For that object, which he might or might not receive, according to the whim of Kali, each young man had committed his soul to the goddess of Calcutta.

Who is Kali, who gathers the souls of young men? She is the goddess of darkness, evil, and destruction in the Hindu pantheon. This is the goddess to whom an entire city is dedicated.

Once I understood this, I understood Calcutta. I could finally identify the ominous, profoundly dark, and permeating impression I had felt since I had first entered the city. The spirit of Kali, like a malevolent power, possessed and hovered over her city. The urban world's worst poverty, the indignity in which street people were forced to live, and the way the rich and the city's systems and structures disregarded it all now made sense—for a profoundly evil presence brooded over this city and held it in her thrall.

We often talk about the "spirit" of a city. No matter how matronly a face someone tries to paint on her, Chicago is never far from the honky-tonk, bootleg gin, gangsters, and the smell of "naughty" excitement. One cannot walk the streets of Rome without hearing the tramping feet of the ancient legions and the whispered intrigue in emperors' courts and papal palaces. The spirit of Hong Kong is of commerce—whether legal or illegal, whether under capitalism or an adapted communism. Scratch the skin of Mexico City and you find the grandeur and gore of its Aztec past. Rio means festival; Moscow is firm, unyielding walls regardless of *perestroika;* and London keeps a proper face and a stiff upper lip in the midst of crumbled dreams of empire.

Every city has a "spirit" about it—an almost palpable essence distinct from every other city. It is a combination of that city's history, surroundings, and systems, the people who have moved through it, and the events that have occurred in it.

If we cannot name, understand, and cope with our city's spirit, we cannot hope to understand either the complexity of our city's spiritual warfare or the scope of ministry to which the church is called.

ST. PAUL'S URBAN ANALYSIS

The nine letters of St. Paul to select churches in the Roman Empire are actually urban letters. We do not tend to think of them that way, but eight of the nine were sent to churches in the principal cities of the eastern portion of the empire.[1] Corinth, Ephesus, Philippi, Colossae, and Thessalonica were the most important cities of their respective Roman provinces. Rome, of course, dominated the world.

The letters to these eight churches are like textbooks on urban ministry. Each book is filled with practical advice on doing ministry in that city and province. The considerable theological content is theology done in the midst of ministry; this is theologizing that comes out of Paul's attempt to instruct the church how to carry on effective ministry in the city.

One of Paul's primary concerns was to enable these urban churches to act rather than to react to their city, province, and empire. If they could not be assertive in undertaking ministry in their city and as part of the Roman Empire, they would eventually die. To be effective in ministry, it was necessary for Paul's churches to understand their urban and international context.

Thus Paul developed a theology that analyzed the systems of city and empire and presented principles and strategies for undertaking ministry in that light. In doing so, Paul was not simply speculating about the nature of urban and empire power, but was also basing his theology on Jewish and Old Testament social analysis that had been part of his earlier training as a Pharisee.

It is intriguing to see Paul's theology of evil in the city and empire mature over the years. The struggle to understand his urban environment honestly makes an initial appearance in early letters (1 Cor. 15; 1 Thess. 4). His theologizing on urban power underwent considerable maturation by the time he wrote his last letters to churches (Colossians, Ephesians), and increasingly came to dominate his letters. What was the mature analysis of St. Paul regarding the nature and extent of evil in the city and empire?

Principality and Power

To develop an adequate theology of evil in the city and empire, Paul suggested a level of evil beyond systems and structures that provided a connection between those systems and the Evil One. That typology can prove very helpful as we twentieth-century Christians attempt to understand the dynamics of evil and good in our cities.

What was Paul's understanding of evil? Its traditional formulation occurs in the King James Version of the Bible:

> In [Christ] we have redemption through his blood, even the forgiveness of sins: Who is the image of the invisible God, the firstborn of every creature; For by him were all things created, that are in heaven, and that are in earth, visible and invisible, whether they be *thrones, or dominions, or principalities, or powers* (Col. 1:14–16 KJV, emphasis mine).

"Thrones, or dominions, or principalities, or powers"—this is the formula Paul uses over and over again to describe the forces of evil throughout the universe. Evangelical Christianity has automatically placed an "other-worldly" interpretation on this formula, consigning what it describes to the supernatural world. But is that an adequate understanding of Paul's intentions? Consider what these words actually mean.

- *Throne*—The throne is simply the institution of power in a state, city, or economic body. Although today the "throne" of a country is found in its legislative, judicial, and executive systems, the "throne" of Paul's day was a literal chair of authority on a raised dais, symbolizing the "seat" of authority.

- *Dominion*—A dominion is the territory influenced or ruled by the throne; it is the sphere of formal influence of that structure of power. Thus the dominion of the United States is its fifty states and possessions and territories.

- *Principality*—The principality or prince is the specific person who currently occupies the throne. It can be the mayor of a city, president of a country, or chairman of an economic institution's board. The "prince," or specific person, can and will change, but the throne continues as long as that institution continues. This reality is captured in the British ritual at the death of the monarch, when the people cry: "The king [i.e., the specific person or 'principality'] is dead; long live the king [i.e., the throne or office of state, about to be filled by another person]."

- *Power*—The power of a throne comprises the rules, legalities, traditions, and sanctions that legitimize the throne's rule over that dominion and provides the authority by which the principality occupies that throne. Thus the "powers" that legitimize General Motors include its papers of incorporation, the bylaws according to which it structures its activities, its products, and maintaining a relationship of satisfaction with its customers. Removal of any of these powers would seriously curtail the capacity of General Motors to continue business.

The church has believed for centuries that the principalities and powers are solely spiritual forces that have their abode and authority in the "heavenlies." But such is a misuse of the words themselves. What we are about to discover is that such a traditional interpretation takes unwarranted liberty with Scripture.

We will try to show that the principalities and powers are the spiritual forces that work through the structures and systems of the city, nation, or universe. Such forces may be celestial (1 Peter 3:22). But the principalities and powers can also be godly or satanic forces that are solely terrestrial and earthly (Ps. 8), or both celestial and terrestrial at the same time (Ps. 103:13–22; Col. 1:15–20).

St. Paul's Doctrine of Corporate Evil

Paul did not systematically develop a doctrine of the principalities and powers. Precisely because his theology was developed "on the run," and in response to the needs and issues his churches faced, there is no single comprehensive presentation of his understanding of corporate evil. Consequently, from the insights he gives us we must construct a logical statement of his doctrine. When we do so, we discover that there are four basic assertions Paul makes about the principalities and powers.

1. The principalities and powers have been created by Christ, who is supreme over them. In Colossians 2:14–16, quoted earlier, Paul makes clear that the battle between God and Satan over the city is not a battle of equals. The very principalities and powers that can wreak such havoc in the city are under ultimate domination by God. This is so because God through Christ has created the principalities and powers. Just as the triune God has created humanity, has invested in it the capacity to create the city, and has created the systems and structures that bring order to each city, so God has created the principalities and powers that bring "spirit" to the systems and the city.

There are profound implications to this assertion. If God through Christ is the creator of the principalities and powers both on earth and in heaven, that means they have had to have been created good. If, like humans, they have been created good, it means that at present they are not beyond redemption. The principalities and powers that invade and possess the systems and structures of a city may be evil, but they are not irredeemably evil. Christ created them. Christ once ruled them. Christ will rule them again!

If the principalities and powers both on earth and in heaven were created good by God, why are they now seen as evil and what is the nature and extent of their evil authority?

2. Paul maintains that the principalities and powers have been captured by Satan and are now used by him for his nefarious work. The

apostle builds an argument on an Old Testament understanding of the person of Satan. Paul, who obviously had a healthy respect for the principalities and powers, warns the members of his churches against them. He writes in Ephesians,

> Finally, be strong in the Lord and in his mighty power. Put on the full armor of God so that you can take your stand against the devil's schemes. For our struggle is not against flesh and blood, but against the rulers, against the authorities, against the powers of this dark world and against the spiritual forces of evil in the heavenly realms (Eph. 6:10–12).

To the church in Colossae, Paul writes,

> See to it that no one takes you captive through hollow and deceptive philosophy, which depends on human tradition and the basic principles [or "elemental spirits"] of this world rather than on Christ (Col. 2:8).[2]

In passages such as these, we see Paul warning Christians of the powerful and deceptive strength of the principalities and powers. It is true that these spiritual authorities were created by Christ to be used by him in ordering human and heavenly society. But they have now become corrupt and evil with a seduction that can take Christians captive and a strength that requires of us "the full armor of God."

Paul examines the nature of the power of these demonic principalities to draw both people and a city's systems to serve their evil purposes. He states in Ephesians 2:1–3,

> As for you, you were dead in your transgressions and sins, in which you used to live when you followed the ways of this world and of the ruler of the kingdom of the air, the spirit who is now at work in those who are disobedient. All of us also lived among them at one time, gratifying the cravings of our sinful nature and following its desires and thoughts. Like the rest, we were by nature objects of wrath.

Both individuals and a city's systems are tempted to follow "the ways of this world and . . . the ruler of the kingdom of the air." We are so tempted because we desire to continue "gratifying the cravings of our sinful nature and following its desires and thoughts." What tempts the individual in personal life even more profoundly tempts those who operate the systems—the lust for power, the hunger for prestige, the mania for money and possessions, the need for a protective parochial spirit instead of a commitment to the larger good. But, Paul points out, such temptation is not an impersonal, inevitable part of our human nature. Such temptation comes from "the ruler of the kingdom of the air," who seeks to seduce both systems and people and bring them under his power.

What led the "prince of the air" astray? What caused the principalities and powers to deny their creation in God? Paul does not deal with this issue, probably because he does not think it necessary. In the Hebrew worldview, the answer was obvious. Paul would have depended on a passage such as Isaiah 14:12–15 to learn about the origins of evil and its captivating influence on the principalities and powers. This passage tells of how the angel Lucifer ("the morning star") had been cast out of heaven to earth because of his great sin.

> You said in your heart,
> "I will ascend to heaven;
> I will raise my throne
>   above the stars of God;
> I will sit enthroned on the mount of assembly,
>   on the utmost heights of the sacred mountain.
> I will ascend above the tops of the clouds;
>   I will make myself like the Most High."
> But you are brought down to the grave,
>   to the depths of the pit (vv. 13–15).

The great sin of which Lucifer was guilty is the sin of idolatry, of placing himself ahead of God and thus making the creature higher than its creator. This in turn is the sin of the principalities and powers: they have placed allegiance to Satan ahead of allegiance to God, their creator. Thus their spirituality is corrupted into a spirituality of idolatry so that it becomes a negative or evil spirituality. That idolatrous spirituality then seduces both the systems of a city and the people who cause those systems to function. Idolatry becomes the primary sin of the systems and people of any city—whether it is the worship of Kali or of Mammon (money), of Baal (power, sexuality) or of Caesar (nationalism).

3. Christ has come to conquer the sin of the powers and to set them free from their own bondage. Both the present activity of the principalities and powers and their intense commitment to the satanic control of the systems and people of the earth make it appear as if the powers are beyond redemption. In fact, our tendency is to consider them implacably evil. But that is not Paul's witness at all. Rather, he indicates that Christ has come as much to set them free as to set humanity free.

In Colossians 1:19–20, Paul writes of the principalities and powers,

> For God was pleased to have all his fullness dwell in him, and through
> him to reconcile to himself all things, whether things on earth or things
> in heaven, by making peace through his blood, shed on the cross.

The reference to "heaven" is a continuing reference to the "thrones or powers or rulers or authorities" of a previous sentence. Paul is here developing the idea that, through the cross, Christ will someday reconcile to himself not just the people and systems of the earth (see chapter 5 of this book), but also the principalities and powers. In themselves the powers are implacably evil. Through Christ, however, even they have the potential of transformation.

The process for such transformation, Paul insists, will not be easy for the principalities and powers. Their full commitment to idolatry and to leading humans and their systems into idolatry will have to be exorcised. That will mean humiliation of the powers. Paul writes,

> I pray also that the eyes of your heart may be enlightened in order that you may know . . . [God's] incomparably great power for us who believe. That power is like the working of his mighty strength, which he exerted in Christ when he raised him from the dead and seated him at his right hand in the heavenly realms, far above all rule and authority, power and dominion, and every title that can be given, not only in the present age but also in the one to come. And God placed all things under his feet and appointed him to be head over everything for the church, which is his body, the fullness of him who fills everything in every way (Eph. 1:18–22).

The intent of this passage—that all of life, including the principalities and powers, will be brought into subjection to Christ—is clear. Of particular interest, however, is the phrase "placed all things under his feet." This is a military term and literally means "to be brought under the heel." The image is one of a conqueror seated on his throne, his heel placed on the neck of his opponent prostrate in subjection before him.

Paul uses a similar image in Colossians 2:15: "And having disarmed the powers and authorities, he made a public spectacle of them, triumphing over them by the cross." Here the image is of the triumphal procession of a Roman emperor or general marching his opponents through the streets of Rome as the captives are jeered by the people (see further in chapter 6).

We see that the transformation of the principalities and powers will not come easily. The potential for redemption is given by Christ to the principalities, just as it is given to all people and systems. They will have to pay a significant price, however, both for their idolatry and for the way they lead people, cities, and nations into idolatrous worship.

4. The church is called to respond to the principalities and powers. In Ephesians 3:8–11, Paul makes this remarkable statement:

> Although I am less than the least of all God's people, this grace was given me: to preach to the Gentiles the unsearchable riches of Christ, and to make plain to everyone the administration of this mystery, which for ages past was kept hidden in God, who created all things. His intent was that now, through the church, the manifold wisdom of God should be made known to the rulers and authorities in the heavenly realms, according to his eternal purpose which he accomplished in Christ Jesus our Lord.

The task of the church, Paul declares, is to make known "the manifold wisdom of God" both to the principalities and powers and to the rulers and authorities of the systems they inhabit. It is the duty of the church to confront the powers and the systems with the biblical call to justice and redemption (again, see further in chapter 6). The church is to seek through Christ the transformation of the powers' inner spirituality, just as it is to seek the salvation of individuals and the liberation of the systems.

5. Paul presents the context in which all Christian ministry is to be maintained in the city:

> For I am convinced that neither death nor life, neither angels nor demons, neither the present nor the future, nor any powers, neither height nor depth, nor anything else in all creation, will be able to separate us from the love of God that is in Christ Jesus our Lord (Rom. 8:38–39).

We undertake our work and live in the city in the recognition that nothing is capable of separating us from the love of God found through Christ—not angels, not demons, not any powers, not the heights of heaven, nor the depths of hell. To live our lives and to undertake the ministry to which God calls us from this perspective gives us immense power and surety to be faithful "until that day."

Along with providing this brief synopsis of Paul's strategic insights on the principalities and powers, we will be looking at other passages he wrote on the topic. This survey has helped us to understand the nature and extent of evil in the city better, because we see now that it is not simply persons or systems that are evil. Their capacity for evil is directly related to their capacity to be possessed by the negative spirituality of principalities and powers. These dark forces invade the systems at the point of their greatest vulnerability—whether it is their lust for power that causes them to oppress both the powerless and those who would oppose them, their avarice for money and possessions that causes them to exploit the weak and poor, or their need to be in control that makes them seek to control the minds and spirits of all the city's residents.

Unless we understand those dark forces—their origins in God's light, their surrender to idolatry, their possession and seduction of the systems of a city, their inevitable defeat and spiritual liberation in Christ— we will not understand the nature and extent of evil in the city. If we do not understand, we will always be facing defeat because we understand neither the enemy nor the parameters of the warfare in which we are engaged.

Scripture analyzes the evil of a city a step further than we have done so far. The biblical writers assert not only that the individuals in the city are capable of great evil and that the city contains evil systems corrupted by the principalities and powers, but also that each city has its own spirituality, a spiritual force that invades and shapes every facet of that city's life.

THE SPIRITUALITY OF THE CITY

What do I mean by the "spirituality of the city"? How do we begin an exploration of such a spirituality? We begin it with an examination of the biblical concept of angels.

Today both liberal and evangelical Christians have a hard time with angels. Many of a more liberal theological persuasion simply dismiss the biblical emphasis on angels as being the attempt by a pre-scientific people to explain an apparently indescribable phenomenon of reality. Those of a more conservative theological bent may give recognition to the concept of angels, but relegate them to "heavenly" business and place wings and halos on them so that they do not need to be taken seriously. In either case the result is the same: the believer dismisses the biblical witness about the phenomenon of angels because it does not fit into a secular and scientific world perspective.

The reality, however, is that the Bible is full of references to angels. If we are to take the Bible seriously as our primary authority for faith and practice, then we must examine honestly what it has to say about angels. Precisely because their minds would not have been prejudiced by a scientific perspective of the world, it could be that the biblical writers had a profound understanding of reality that we miss today. Consider the relationship between cities and angels disclosed in Scripture.

The Brooding Angel

According to the biblical witness, every corporate unit of society is given its guiding, or "brooding," angel. This perspective of "brooding" is particularly important and is given voice as early as the creation story: "Now the earth was formless and empty, darkness was over the surface of the deep, and the Spirit of God was hovering over the waters" (Gen. 1:2). The sense of the Hebrew word *rachaph*, here translated "hover," is that of brooding, much as a barnyard hen or another bird broods over her nest and chicks. Thus, in this verse the image is one of God's protectively surrounding the earth he has just created, much as a hen guards and protects the egg she has just laid.

Each unit of society is protected and directed by its brooding angel. Because of this, in the book of Revelation the letters to the seven city churches in Asia Minor are not addressed to the churches, but to the protective angel of each church (Rev. 2–3). It is Jerusalem's angel who defeats the Assyrians and brings the miraculous deliverance of Jerusalem from her enemies! In what is considered a salvific event comparable to the parting of the Red Sea and Israel's return from Babylonian exile, the biblical writer records,

> That night the angel of the LORD went out [from the city] and put to death a hundred and eighty-five thousand men in the Assyrian camp. When the people got up the next morning—there were all the dead bodies! So Sennacherib king of Assyria broke camp and withdrew. He returned to Nineveh and stayed there (2 Kings 19:35–36).

But it is not only churches and cities that are protected by brooding angels. Nations are also. In a remarkable statement in Deuteronomy 32:8–9, Moses sings in his great canticle,

> The Most High assigned nations their lands; he determined where peoples should live. He assigned to each nation a god, but Jacob's descendants he chose for himself (TEV).

The phrase "a god" in this context is a Hebrew euphemism for "angel" (Job 1:6).[3] What Moses is declaring in this hymn is that every nation is watched over and protected by a guardian angel (Dan. 10:13; Pss. 29:1; 82:1–2; 89:6). Israel, moreover, is the only nation whose destiny is also directly supervised by God.

The angel of a city, Scripture tells us, exerts immense power and can radically influence the human institutions of the city. It even has the spiritual power to resist God! A vivid description of a brooding angel's power is presented in Daniel 10:1–11:2, which tells of a crisis in Daniel's life in Babylon. As in all the conflicts he faced, Daniel turned to God in prayer for direction and strength. This time his prayers seemed to be offered in vain. Finally, nearly a month after he began praying, Daniel fell into a deep sleep. Suddenly he was awakened. Next to his bed stood an angel, who said,

> "Daniel, don't be afraid. God has heard your prayers ever since the first day you decided to humble yourself in order to gain understanding. I have come in answer to your prayer. The angel prince of the kingdom of Persia opposed me for twenty-one days. Then Michael, one of the chief angels, came to help me, because I had been left there alone in Persia" (Dan. 10:12–13 TEV).

This is a most remarkable statement. Daniel had prayed to God. God prepared an answer to Daniel's prayer and gave it to an unnamed angel to deliver. On his way from the courts of God to Daniel in Babylon, however, the angel had to pass through the land of Persia. There he was confronted by the guardian angel of Persia, who was so powerful that he held God's messenger at bay for twenty-one days. The messenger angel would have never gotten through with God's answer to Daniel's prayer, except that Michael, the chief archangel, came to his aid. Even now, the angel told

Daniel, Michael continued to battle the angel of Persia. The messenger angel concluded, "Now I have to go back and fight the guardian angel of Persia. After that the guardian angel of Greece will appear. There is no one to help me except Michael, Israel's guardian angel" (Dan. 10:21 TEV).

What does this story tell us about angels? We should not allow our secular—supposedly sophisticated—scientific framework to get in the way of perceiving the truth revealed in this story. I believe that what the biblical writers are telling us in terms of the church, a city, and a nation is that everything in life has a spiritual dimension. The political system of a city consists of more than its people, electoral processes, structures, and institutions. That system is infused with a spiritual essence; it has unimagined and unexplored inner depths that are its "soul." The angel of a city is the inner spirituality that broods over the city. That spirituality has immense power, either for good or for ill.

The City's Inner Spirituality

What do we feel in Calcutta or Moscow or Bangkok or Mexico City or Washington or Nairobi? I suggest that what we sense is the soul of that city, its inner spiritual essence. Every city has an angel who broods over it. These angels infuse and dominate the principalities and powers, systems and structures, people groups and individuals of that city. There is that spiritual presence—either angelic or demonic (or displaying elements of both).

I always ask the participants in the urban workshops I lead to identify the angel of their city. They determine together who the angel of their city is, name and describe it, and then consider how it manifests itself in the city's structures, systems, and people and in their own churches. That exercise always proves to be the most stimulating event of the workshop. It comes as the last activity of a long and exhausting day. But rarely can I get people to go home once they have become involved in naming their city's angel. They intuitively sense that what they are involved in doing with their fellow Christians is crucial to their continuing ministry. Of course, they are right. To be able to name your city's angel and to understand how it is at work both exposes it and enables you to understand the dimensions the church's ministry must undertake if it is truly to confront the principalities and powers!

Every city has an interior spirituality. When the city's inner spirituality is under the authority of God (as was the messenger angel in the Daniel story), that spirituality is "angelic." When the city is under the authority of Satan (as was the angel of Persia), then it is demonic in its power and influence. All cities are caught in a spiritual warfare; the forces of God and the forces of Satan battle for that city's soul.

All of us have experienced moments of such battle. But we have not often recognized it as such and are consequently unable to confront the demonic elements in that battle effectively. Let me give one instance of how the lack of recognition of the dimensions of the battle cost one church its soul.

A presbytery is a regional ecclesiastical body of a Presbyterian denomination. It has jurisdiction over all that denomination's churches and mission units in a region. In one presbytery I was a member of a committee that was responsible, among other things, to work with troubled churches. One of the congregations was a downtown church that had once been large and prestigious but, like so many other city churches, had fallen on hard times. Its problems were far greater than declining membership rolls and income. For three generations this church had "run off" one pastor after another, some of whom were very talented and had previously had successful ministries. I began working with this church at a time when it seemed to be preparing to "destroy" yet another pastor.

I began meeting with the church's leaders and reviewed its history with them. The troubles had begun nearly fifty years earlier, before any of that church's current leadership were on the scene, but I discovered that most of them were unaware of that troubled history. From their perspective, the problems were always the fault of incompetent or unethical pastors.

As we probed that history, we encountered both significant insights and notable resistance. One leader said, "You know, we've always blamed our pastors for our problems. But it can't always be the pastor's fault. It is as if there is something almost alive in us that has to keep finding a victim to sacrifice!"

The committee of the presbytery finally came to the conclusion that this was a church hell-bent on self-destruction and that nothing we could do would cause them to seek salvation. We did not know exactly what had happened fifty years earlier. But something evil had occurred, and ever since then that evil had eaten away at the psyche of that church, gradually gaining power and becoming increasingly demonic. In a peculiar way, the transgressions of the fathers of that church seemed to be visited upon their spiritual children of the third and fourth generations. They were caught up in a destructive cycle they could not break. It was indeed as if there were "something almost alive in us." Unrecognized and unexorcised, it oppressed generation after generation of pastors and congregation until it was on the verge of destroying that church once and for all.

Whether it is a church, a city, an industry, a nation, every structure of human society has an inner spirituality. Every city has its brooding angel that hovers over its individuals, its families, its neighborhoods, its churches, its economic institutions, and its political order. Although that brooding angel might have dimensions of good in it, it is usually like that "something almost alive . . . that has to keep finding a victim to sacrifice."

Often we see a tragic picture of a city redeemed by grace and yet steadily succumbing to the spirit of lust, power, money and possessions, pride, or a stifling parochialism.

The city is a primary battleground between God and Satan for both the people and systems of human society. Behind the seduction of a city's systems and structures, behind the principalities and powers that form the spiritual essence of those systems, behind the often dark and destructive angel who broods over the city seeking to possess it—behind these stands the shadowy figure of the one known as Satan. It is the "father of lies" who is at both the heart and the head of a city's seduction.

We can discern Satan's urban strategy. He seeks to capture the soul of a city through the seduction of its systems and structures. In that seduction he uses the principalities and powers (the spiritual dimensions of the systems). By seducing the systems, Satan shapes the conditions of the city's formal and informal groups, families, and the lives of individuals so that he can seduce the people as well. Whenever he is successful in seducing systems or people by means of the principalities and powers, Satan is able to shape profoundly the interior spirituality (brooding angel) of that city and the rest of its institutions.

Why does Satan direct his offensive against the systems and structures of the city? There are two main reasons. First, those who provide the primary leadership to the systems are ripe for seduction. They tend to overestimate their own power because they are convinced they are in control. They tend to underestimate the potential of their system to operate independently of them (so that often the system dictates to these individuals rather than they to the system, whether in matters as minuscule as appropriate dress or in matters as important as steering the economy). They have little or almost no spiritual discernment so that it is almost impossible for them to conceive either of the demonic influence on their lives or of Satan's seduction of their system. The systems therefore provide an open arena for radical influence by the principalities and powers of the city.

Second, the church is woefully ignorant of this strategy. The city church places its primary effort into individuals and its secondary effort into church and family groupings. The church thus leaves the field open to Satan for exerting spiritual influence on both the city's systems and its interior spirituality.

God works primarily through people. Since his people insist on an individualistic approach to society (in spite of Scripture's clear emphasis on systems, principalities, and city-wide interior spirituality), they neither discern nor act upon the satanic strategy. As a result, God is prevented from using them to confront Satan in the halls of power of the city.

Sadly, when Christians do decide to enter into the political or economic arenas, they do so from a rather naive perspective. This perspective overestimates the influence of the individual and does not adequately account for the systems' resistance to change and their capacity to seduce or marginalize the individual. This naïveté is due to the difficulty Christians have in understanding the spiritual dynamism of a system. We essentially see systems as static, humanly conceived, and humanly driven machines. In reality they have a life of their own, a living spiritual dimension that, like a human, can resist, seduce, marginalize, or isolate those whom the system perceives as a threat to them and their power. That lively spiritual dimension of the system is its principality.

This is the discernible strategy of the Evil One, who would seek to control and dominate the city. Yet, off in the shadows of that city stands One who loves the city and weeps over it: "O Jerusalem, Jerusalem, you who kill the prophets and stone those sent to you, how often I have longed to gather your children together, as a hen gathers her [brood] under her wings, but you were not willing!" (Luke 13:34). It is the Christ who would brood over the systems and principalities of the city, who would gather its people like chicks and who would be both the city's brooding angel and more than angel. "But you were not willing!" This is the pain, the pathos, the dimension of the spiritual warfare in which your city is engaged.

A Word of Caution

There is one severe limitation in our reflections on the soul of a city: we could allow ourselves to be seduced by irresponsibility. Like Flip Wilson, the American comic of a generation ago, we can refuse to deal with the issues of a city by declaring, "The devil made me do it!" The danger of a theology that adopts this kind of attitude toward society is that it can be misused to justify apathy and evade personal responsibility. Like the church that was having problems in the presbytery, we can shift the blame and attribute the fault to someone else.

Scripture holds two truths in a delicate tension. It is true that the corporate structures of the city and all its people are under the influence of Satan and are therefore corrupt and evil (Eph. 2:1–3), even though all people are made in the image of God. It is also true that God holds accountable every individual and every structure of a city for the sin each entity commits. In the very book that presents Paul's doctrine of the principalities and powers most forcefully, the apostle directs,

> But among you there must not be even a hint of sexual immorality, or of any kind of impurity, or of greed, because these are improper for God's holy people. Nor should there be obscenity, foolish talk or coarse joking, which are out of place, but rather thanksgiving. For of this you can be sure: No immoral, impure or greedy person—such a man is an idolater—has any inheritance in the kingdom of Christ and

of God. . . . For you were once darkness, but now you are light in the Lord. Live as children of light (Eph. 5:3–5, 8).

Nothing we have explored either in this or the previous chapter should be construed to suggest that we are not accountable. Nothing about Satan's influence on our city, or its brooding angel, or the demonic possession of its systems and structures releases an individual from personal accountability toward God. Whether we are the mayor, a government bureaucrat, or an ordinary citizen, whether we are the president of a giant corporation, a worker in an office, or the pastor of a church that serves members of that corporation, whether we are the chairperson of the board of education, a teacher in the school system, or simply a parent wanting the best for our children—we are responsible. In a city that has the potential of being seduced by Satan and his angels, we are responsible before God and our fellow citizens for the ways our actions and our intentions either contribute to making our city the city of God or allow it to slide toward becoming the city of Satan.

In his epic work on the city, Lewis Mumford, the great Chicago urbanologist of a generation ago, considered why the church was unable to create "Christianopolis"—the Christian city. The church had the opportunity to do so during the Middle Ages, according to Mumford, but let the opportunity slip through its hands. The only truly formative forces at work in medieval towns were the monasteries, the Christian guilds (which centered employment in a sense of Christian calling), and the church. Why didn't the people build the city of God out of that focus of power and influence? Mumford answered his own question this way:

> If at the beginning the medieval city was truly shaped by Christian needs and interests, it was never completely transformed by the Christian challenge: the ancient powers and principalities were all too firmly lodged behind its walls. The jealous gods who had presided over the birth of the city in Mesopotamia and Egypt were more persistent and persuasive (in their seduction of the people) than the new teacher from Palestine. . . . The outline of that city was strong enough to give one hope for a new urban order, based on the religious and social premises of the most widespread of all the religions. But in the very growth of the town, . . . as life flowed back into this culture, as trade prospered and wealth accumulated, . . . that spiritual substance tended to disappear.[4]

Freedom or license, justice or exploitation, equality or oppression, love or lust, God or Satan—these have always been the issues in the struggles of the city. Will the jealous gods really prove more persistent and persuasive than the new Teacher from Palestine? The Bible declares, "No!"

Chapter Four

GOD'S INTENTIONS FOR THE CITY

One of the most urbanly oriented books of the Old Testament ends with these prophetic words:

"And the name of the city from that time on will be:

THE LORD IS THERE."

The prophet Ezekiel puts it very simply in that statement—God's intention for the city is that the Lord will be there. Like the Jerusalem in Ezekiel's vision, this can be our hope for our city. The Lord will so permeate the life and activities and even the spiritual essence of that city that its very name will proclaim that God is found inside that city's walls. Here, simply stated, is God's intention for the city!

As we have seen in the first three chapters, Scripture portrays the city as a primary battleground between God and Satan. For us to understand that battle, we have looked at the protagonists.

First, we looked at God's love for the city. We discovered that God is the creator of the city and is present in it. He loves and admires the city, seeing it as the jewel of his creation. God has invested the city in us and expects us to be responsible for its stewardship and development.

Scripture stresses that the city is central to God's plan of transformation and redemption of humanity and is therefore the locus of God's salvation of humanity. Consequently God feels compassion for the city; when he sees the city falling into sin and injustice, he is concerned for it and weeps over that sin.

Second, we examined the contest between God and Satan in terms of Satan's influence over the city. We stressed the importance of thoroughly understanding and not underestimating the nature and extent of evil in the city. We examined the systems and structures of a city and saw how these systems tend toward injustice and inhumanity toward the poor because those structures are captured by the evil focuses of self-interest, indulgence, and pride.

We looked behind the systems to their spiritual grounding in the principalities and powers that seduce and infuse the systems. These evil forces have their origin in the inner spirituality (the "corporate angel") of each city, which is greatly seduced by Satan to idolatry (making anything other than God god). This is the essential sin of the city and the locus of Satan's influence over the city.

On the basis of this biblical reflection we can confront the final issue concerning the nature of the city. The question we explore in this chapter is, "What are God's intentions for the city?" It is a pivotal question because the biblical answers will tell us what the city, under God, ought to be like. It will give us a clear sense of God's priorities for any city.

Furthermore, answering that question biblically will give us an increasingly clear perception of the salvific work God has done for the city through Christ. That will in turn lead us to explore the agenda the church needs to be pursuing in the city. Knowing God's priorities will give us clarity about the mission focus and objectives toward which we as God's people ought to be working in our city. Those objectives are the subject of Part II.

Let us turn now to the question, "What are God's intentions for the city?"

OLD TRUTHS IN NEW PACKAGING

It was 1962. We seminarians had just finished hearing a tape of a sermon preached by the late Peter Marshall, the exceptional pulpiteer of the New York Avenue Presbyterian Church in Washington, D.C. My seminary class in preaching had heard, over the previous hour, tapes of sermons by George Buttrick, E. Stanley Jones, and Ralph W. Sockman— all outstanding preachers of a previous generation. The tape recorder stopped whirring, and our professor began the discussion. "All right, class," he said, "tell me what was unique about these great preachers. What did they do that made them stand head and shoulders above their fellow preachers of twenty years ago?"

The class was silent as we sat and thought. Finally one intrepid soul hazarded a guess. "I would suggest, sir," he replied, "that the unique ability of each of these men was his ability to express the old truths of the gospel in new and fresh ways."

Expressing old truths in new ways is just what Jesus did. He took the ancient truths contained in the Old Testament, added to them the fresh insights of his personal relationship and greater knowledge about God, and consequently expressed in new, startling, and even controversial ways what God was seeking to do in the world.

Jesus found a new symbol for explaining what God was trying to do in the world. He introduced a new way of talking about God and God's intentions for human society. Yet the germ ideas for these new expressions were old ideas, because the symbol Jesus developed to present God's activity was a creative and unique adaptation of an essential Old Testament theme. It is crucial, for us to be effective as God's people in the city, that we clearly understand this symbol, for this symbol is the key that can empower us in our battle with principalities and powers.

The symbol Jesus used is "the kingdom of God." Jesus' essential message was summarized by St. Mark, who wrote at the beginning of his gospel,

> After John was put in prison, Jesus went into Galilee, proclaiming the good news of God. "The time has come," he said. "The kingdom of God is near. Repent and believe the good news!" (1:14–15).

What did Jesus mean by "the kingdom of God"? The word *kingdom* is defined as "a politically organized community or major territorial unit, having a monarchical form of government headed by a king or queen."[1] Rather than spiritualizing it, I suggest that Jesus meant for his symbol to be taken quite literally. I suggest that Jesus envisioned a given geographical area—the whole earth—operating under an economic, religious, and political system ruled by God.

Jesus' concept of the kingdom of God was actually a highly creative adaptation of Israel's existing self-understanding. As a result, our exploration of a kingdom theology begins with the Old Testament.

THE OLD TESTAMENT AND THE KINGDOM OF GOD

The phrase "kingdom of the LORD"—that is, the kingdom of God—occurs only once in the Old Testament, namely, in 1 Chronicles 28:5. But if the term is rare, the concept is not. The perspective that God ruled over Israel is the warp and woof of the Old Testament. We can describe the entire history of Israel in corporate terms that express the result of God's activity among that people: the Garden of Eden, the Abrahamic covenant (in which all peoples of the world would be blessed), the Promised Land, the Sinai covenant (made between the people and God), the People of the Covenant, the kingdoms of Israel and Judah, the "peaceable kingdom," and a new heaven and earth. These corporate terms were carried from the Old Testament into the New—not only in Jesus' expression "the kingdom of God," but also in "People of the Way" (the name Christians gave to each other; the term "Christian" was first used by pagans), the church, the Community of Promise, the New Jerusalem.

These are clearly not individualistic terms; they are corporate in focus and scope. They all deal with human society, testifying to Israel's and the early church's perception that God was working not only in individuals, but also in the world, seeking to bring about a new social order. God is always in the process of working creatively in the world to make us new again. His work is transformational; he is at work in our lives, in human society, in the total social order. Humanity is always becoming other than what it is right now as God works to re-create and redeem it.

A number of themes could be used to demonstrate the central theological and social commitment of Israel to the concept of the kingdom of God (as in the discussion of Deuteronomy in chapter 2 of this book). We will confine ourselves here, however, to three themes: oppression, peace, and poverty.

Oppression and Liberation

"I am the LORD your God, who brought you out of Egypt, out of the land of slavery" (Exod. 20:2). The story of God's effort to create a God-centered political, economic, and religious community began with the pain of oppression.

> During that long period [during which Moses was in exile], the king of Egypt died. The Israelites groaned in their slavery and cried out, and their cry for help because of their slavery went up to God. God heard their groaning and he remembered his covenant with Abraham, with Isaac and with Jacob. So God looked on the Israelites and was concerned about them (Exod. 2:23–25).

Why did the people groan? It was because of their burden under bondage to the empire. The Israelites were in slavery to Egypt; they were economically, politically, and spiritually beaten down by the power and might of the empire.

Such bondage is a recurring condition in Scripture. There are always the empires. There are always the principalities and powers, whether alive in Egypt or Assyria, in Babylonia or Greece, in Rome or in Israel itself. The "empire" is everywhere, oppressing individuals and families and tribes and nations in any way it can, politically or economically or spiritually. The empire is the very personification of evil, the abode of principalities and powers.

"The Israelites groaned in their slavery and cried out, and their cry . . . went up to God." The wording of this passage is crucial to the biblical understanding of the way God works in our lives and among the broken of the world. The people were so burdened, so oppressed, so crushed by their enslavement that they emitted what we can think of as an unearthly, almost animal-like groan.

Notice, however, that the text does not say the people cried to God! It says, "Their cry for help . . . went up to God." The enslaved Israelites did not initiate God's liberating work. God heard their pain and *he* decided to set them free! This dynamic is illustrated plainly in God's conversation with Moses, when the Lord said, "I have heard them crying out because of their slave drivers, and I am concerned about their suffering. So I have come down to rescue them from the hand of the Egyptians" (Exod. 3:7–8).

This important principle is critical and is stressed throughout Scripture. It is God who acts to save us. It is God who hears the groanings of his people and who then goes about to set them free. God acted to overthrow an empire. When God appeared to Moses at the burning bush in the desert, he said to that frightened shepherd,

> "And now the cry of the Israelites has reached me, and I have seen the way the Egyptians are oppressing them. So now, go. I am sending you to Pharaoh to bring my people the Israelites out of Egypt" (Exod. 3:9–10).

Through Moses, God offered liberation to Israel, and Israel accepted the offer. There were three factors at work that caused Israel to become free. We have seen that God heard the pain of his people and joined in that pain. In addition, the people took God at his word, believing that he could and would liberate them. They believed without witnessing the miracle-working power of God (for none of the miracles occurred until *after* the people had cast their lot with Moses and God). They simply believed the word of some apparently half-crazed shepherd who came stumbling in from the wilderness and was crying out that he had met God at a burning bush and that God had told him to set Israel free!

God was asking Israel to exercise the same kind of faith that their forefather, Abraham, had demonstrated. On the basis of little or no evidence, would they trust God? Would they believe that God, working through this strange shepherd, could set them free? It was not enough that Israel groaned. They also had to believe against all the apparent evidence that God could indeed set them free.

But Abraham's great example of faith, testified among the Israelites hundreds of years before Moses came stumbling out of the desert, entailed more than simply taking God at his word. Abraham had to act on that belief. Over time, he had to leave Mesopotamia, ignore the biological timeclock of fertility, and lay his son Isaac on the sacrificial altar. Hundreds of years later, Israel had to do the same thing. So the people had to obey as well as to trust, to act as well as to believe that God would set them free.

Moses had to tell Pharaoh the Nile River would be turned into blood before it actually was turned into blood. The Israelites had to celebrate that first Passover before the angel of death would come through Egypt, slaying the empire's firstborn. The children of Israel had to plunge into the parted waters of the Red Sea, believing that those waters, once parted, would not close in upon them. Joshua had to lead God's people into the Promised Land, uncertain whether they could defeat nations mightier than themselves.

The entire biblical pattern of liberation—whether of a nation from slavery or an individual from sin (2 Sam. 12:1–25)—is demonstrated in the story of the Exodus. First, God heard and joined in the pain of his oppressed people. Second, God asked those oppressed to believe that he could overthrow that empire. Third, God expected the oppressed to act on that belief.

But the biblical pattern doesn't end there. The dramatic account of Israel's miraculous salvation at the Red Sea illustrates another principle of liberation.

The people of Israel first stared in stunned amazement as they watched the waters of the sea close rapidly upon the trapped and panicking Egyptian army. Then a cheer arose from thousands as the Israelites realized that they were, indeed, free at last. The Scripture writer reports,

> Then Miriam the prophetess, Aaron's sister, took a tambourine in her hand, and all the women followed her, with tambourines and dancing. Miriam sang to them:
>
> > "Sing to the LORD,
> >   for he is highly exalted.
> > The horse and its rider
> >   he has hurled into the sea" (Exod. 15:20–21).

Israel held a party! The inevitable result when God liberates his people is that they will dance! If any Israelites stayed behind in Egypt, it was not they who danced; they remained enslaved. It was not the Egyptians who tried to prevent Israel's liberation who danced; they were destroyed. Only those who stepped out on faith, trusted God to set them free, and acted on that trust would dance the dance of freedom.

But what was that dance of freedom? It included Israel's celebrating its liberation, but it was more than that. That dance included meeting with God at Mount Sinai and receiving the Ten Commandments. It included Israel's painful correction following the idolatrous worship of the golden calf. It included being fed by God with manna in the wilderness. But most of all, Israel's dance of freedom included forty years in the wilderness as Moses took a collection of slaves and molded them into a nation, with a government, laws, and a faith that had the potential to keep the people perpetually free.

The Old Testament, through its stories of liberation, teaches us that liberation requires more than our belief that God can overthrow the empire that rules our lives. It requires more than our acting on that belief. It even requires more than celebrating God's victory in us. Our liberation—whether of ourselves, our family, our church, our business, our city, our nation, or the world—must include the difficult, painstaking task of building, under God, a new way of life for those liberated. We need to build a way of life that encourages us to act justly, to love mercy, and to walk humbly with our God (Mic. 6:8). That is the way to do God's dance of freedom.

The theme of "oppression and liberation" is exemplified in the story of the Exodus, but it moves throughout the Old Testament. This theme is the foundation on which the Old Testament perspective of the spiritual dimensions of nation-building is based. As such, it lays the groundwork for Jesus' understanding of the kingdom of God as the primary way to express God's work on earth.

Peace and Transformation

Peace is another theme that helps us appreciate the Old Testament origins of the concept of the kingdom of God. Jeremiah the prophet instructed the Israelites who were in exile in Babylon, "Seek the peace and prosperity of the city to which I have carried you into exile. Pray to the LORD for it, because if it prospers, you too will prosper" (Jer. 29:7). The English words "peace," "prosperity," and "prosper" are all translations of the same Hebrew word, *shalom.*

Shalom is a comprehensive word not easily translated into English, because our word *peace* is inadequate. The idea encompasses the manifold relationships of daily life, symbolizing Israel's ideal quality of life under the Law. Shalom is a state of wholeness and completeness possessed by a person or a group that includes good health, prosperity, security, justice, and deep spiritual contentment.

In the first place shalom is for each individual. It brings with it health and a good life (Ps. 38:3; Gen. 15:15). For an Israelite to wish people "shalom" was to wish them God's protection in battle or, if they were sick, God's restoration of their health (Dan. 10:19; Judg. 6:23). A person's shalom was synonymous with a good life, for it involved healthful sleep, a long life, prosperity, and a tranquil death after a full life (Gen. 15:1; Lam. 3:17; Ps. 37:11; Job 5:19–26; Lev. 26:6).

Shalom is also for the community. Peace is the normal and proper condition God intends for all people in relationship with each other. It is enjoyed most intimately in the family (Gen. 13:8), but it extends to the whole community as a "covenant of peace" (1 Sam. 20:42). Just as the peace of the individual is health and safety, the peace of the nation or of the family is prosperity and security (2 Sam. 17:3; Exod. 18:23; Ps. 125:5). Therefore, by wishing a family "shalom," you are wishing it economic prosperity. By wishing a nation "shalom," you are wishing it political security and freedom from strife and violence. There is an intimate relationship between a nation's peace and one's personal peace; thus Jeremiah states that a person is to work for the good of a city because personal shalom depends on whether that city experiences shalom through individual efforts and the efforts of the community of faith.

The most important perspective about the Jewish concept of shalom is the relationship of peace to God. There is no shalom apart from God (1 Kings 22; Mic. 3:5-11; Jer. 6:13-15). Because God is the supreme ruler of the universe, all true peace originates with him (Isa. 52:7; 55:12; 57:19). True peace exists where people are acting in loving and just ways toward each other, and that occurs only when people are living in covenant together under God (Ezek. 34:25-30; 37:26; Isa. 54:10). It is the blessing of God coming to us that makes our relationships whole. In this way biblical peace is closely allied to salvation and right relationship with God (Isa. 49:22-26; 60:12-14). It is only God's salvation and transformation of us that can give us a sense of fulfillment, satisfaction, or security. Therefore to offer people "shalom" is to offer them the peace that comes from God, a peace that we can receive only as we submit to God and that our city can receive only as it submits to his kingly lordship.

The connection between personal peace, a society's justice, and relationship with God is presented in Psalm 85. This psalm mourns over the evil that has fallen on Israel, and the psalmist asks, "What needs to happen in order to enable Israel to live in peace again?" The psalmist answers,

> I will hear what the LORD God has to say,
>   a voice that speaks of peace,
> peace for his people and his friends
>   and those who turn to him in their hearts.
> His help is near for those who fear him
>   and his glory will dwell in our land.
>
> Mercy and faithfulness must meet;
>   justice and peace embrace.
> Faithfulness shall spring from the earth
>   and justice look down from heaven.
>
> The LORD will make us prosper
>   and our earth shall yield its fruit.
> Justice shall march before him
>   and peace shall follow his steps (vv. 8-13).
>   (The Grail, The Psalms)[2]

What had to happen if Israel was to live in peace? The people must "turn to [God] in their hearts." Both mercy and faithfulness must spring forth from the people. Only as they choose to embrace "justice and peace" in their corporate life will they know both national transformation and true peace.

A profound statement about biblical peace is contained in Isaiah 11:1–11. In 720 B.C.E. the Israelites had just survived the worst beating they had ever received as a nation. The massive Assyrian war machine had come down on the two little kingdoms of Judah and Israel, had conquered and destroyed the northern nation, and had made the other a vassal of the Assyrian empire. After taking all the gold and silver, slaves, and women that they wanted, the Assyrians had withdrawn, leaving behind a battered Judah licking its wounds.

It was inevitable, then, that the Israelites began to ask, "Does God really have any power at all? Is he really at work in the world, creating shalom? Does he really intend to use a beaten, poor, weak nation like us to be a sign of his kingdom in the world?"

In the midst of this confusion and despair, Isaiah the prophet spoke to the people. He held up God's vision for humanity. Isaiah charged Israel not to lose sight of that vision, because God's kingdom surely would come, led by God's Man.

What was that divine vision for humanity that Isaiah proclaimed?

> The wolf will live with the lamb,
>   the leopard will lie down with the goat,
> the calf and the lion and the yearling together;
>   and a little child will lead them.
> The cow will feed with the bear,
>   their young will lie down together,
>   and the lion will eat straw like the ox.
> The infant will play near the hole of the cobra,
>   and the young child put his hand into the viper's nest.
> They will neither harm nor destroy
>   on all my holy mountain (vv. 6–9).

God's peaceable kingdom, as envisioned by Isaiah, is the re-creation of the Garden of Eden—the creation of a new human order ruled by God. It is a level of human existence that we find hard to envision, because it is foreign to our experience of a war-filled, conflict-ridden, voracious world. This social order passes all bounds of probability, symbolized by wolves and leopards living peaceably with lambs and goats, with lions and bears taking on the demeanor of cattle, and children playing fearlessly with benevolent snakes. Isaiah's description is, indeed, of a peaceable kingdom, which, in his words, "will be peace, . . . quietness and confidence forever" (32:17).

If there is to be a peaceable kingdom, how is leadership to be practiced by the Man of God who will govern this kingdom? First, this person and those who administer the kingdom with him must exercise responsible political leadership. They must evidence "the Spirit of wisdom and of understanding" (Isa. 11:2). They must be able to apply their wisdom to the rule of their people, being decisive in their judgments and wise in their counsel. They must be motivated by "knowledge and . . . the fear of the LORD" (v. 2). Those who rule others must themselves be ruled by God, responsible to him for what they do.

Second, if God's society is to occur on this earth, humanity must seek to create a just and equitable government. Observe Isaiah's description of the governance of this peaceable kingdom:

> [God's ruler] will not judge by appearance,
>   nor decide by hearsay,
> but [must] act with justice to the helpless,
>   and decide fairly for the humble.
> He will strike down the ruthless with his verdicts,
>   and slay the unjust with his sentences.
> Justice shall gird him up for action,
>   he shall be belted with trustworthiness (vv. 3–5 MOFFATT).

Third, if God's kingdom is to be built, humanity must be reconciled to all of life. Each person in the kingdom must be reconciled with every other person, and humanity must be at one with nature. There is, explains Isaiah, no hope for the human race unless there is a permanent end to all forms of conflict—between nation and nation, ruler and ruler, person and person, humanity and nature. We must seek to come together again, seeking to "neither harm nor destroy on all my holy mountain" (Isa. 11:9).

How is all this possible? How can we achieve such a vision for a peaceable humanity? In a world so deeply torn with strife, distrust, and manipulation, how can God's dream for society ever come true? This great statement on shalom made by Isaiah concludes with the condition necessary for the creation of this peaceable kingdom: "For the earth will be full of the knowledge of the LORD as the waters cover the sea" (v. 9).

What does Isaiah mean by "the knowledge of the LORD"? The Israelite meaning for the word "to know" was much richer than our word. When we use the infinitive *to know*, we usually mean "to comprehend" or "to understand." To the Hebrew people, however, *to know* meant "to perceive and experience to the very depths." Unlike our concept of knowledge, it was not used in conjunction with ideas, but with people. Thus, for a Hebrew man to "know" a woman meant that they had developed a deep and all-pervading relationship, symbolized by sexual union.

For Isaiah to state, therefore, that God's kingdom would come on the earth when humanity was filled with the knowledge of the Lord was, in reality, to say that it would come when all humanity and each individual had developed a deep and all-pervading relationship with God. The foundation for the kingdom of God was the creation of a whole new way of life on earth. This would be a way of life in which each person and all humanity would know and love and be committed and obedient to the Lord.

Such a new style of life would have to include the transformation of the individual because it would have to be personal and experiential. That style of life would also have to include the restructuring of all human society—economically, politically, and religiously—based on a selfless, God-obeying humanity rather than a self-serving humanity.

This radical transformation can occur only by the intervention of "a shoot" that will come "from the stump of Jesse" (Isa. 11:1)—a new Man upon whom "the Spirit of the LORD" will rest (v. 2). This Man will provide the power for the conversion of the individual and the reform of society's structures. He will become transforming good news to people and to society alike, because "he will delight in the fear of the LORD" (v. 3). The full realization of shalom will depend on this Man, for out of his own shalom he will introduce humanity to true shalom, and thus God's kingdom of justice and peace will be created.

The Old Testament concept of shalom, therefore, provides another basis for Jesus' proclaiming a theology of the kingdom of God. As liberation in the Old Testament is centered on the rescuing of nations and cities from oppression, so the Old Testament perspective on peace concentrates on the transformation of individuals and the corporate structures of society by a right relationship with God.

Commitment to the Poor

The Old Testament is rooted in a concern for the poor. The overwhelming power of that concern is somewhat obscured by our English translations, which consistently render the word *justice* as "righteousness" and *oppression* as "suffering" or "tribulation," thus spiritualizing and compromising the real and obvious intent of the author.[3] Let it be said that much of the focus of the Old Testament is on justice for the poor.[4]

Part of the difficulty in understanding this focus lies in the differences between Hebrew expression in the Old Testament and our ways of thinking and communicating. Whereas we speak abstractly about "exploitation," the Old Testament authors wrote of "widows, orphans, prisoners, and slaves." Whereas we speak of "social justice," they would deal with a workman's wages being withheld or an immigrant defrauded. Whereas we might address a "community concern," the Hebrews would be concerned about what happened to a widow and her children deprived of the protection and earning power of her murdered spouse. Thus, for us to appreciate fully the Jewish community's deep concern for the poor and marginalized, we must abstract a biblical social analysis from their concrete actions and statements. Or perhaps we would have more impact on our world if we Christians, instead of speculating about social analysis from the Scripture, would instead seek to find practical means "to act justly and to love mercy and to walk humbly" with our God (Mic. 6:8).

The Old Testament analysis of poverty is stated succinctly in Amos 2:6–7: "For three sins of Israel, even for four, I will not turn back my wrath. They sell . . . the needy [ebyon] for a pair of sandals. They trample on the heads of the poor [dallim] . . . and deny justice to the oppressed [anawim]."

In this passage, three different types of poverty are identified by the prophet. The ebyon are people totally dependent on others, those who are utterly destitute and must beg in order to survive. Those who are dallim are the physically weak and materially poor—they simply have neither the capital nor the strength to make it financially in life. Finally, there are the anawim—those who know themselves to be of no account, the people broken under their weight of poverty so that they are entirely dependent on others for their survival. Today we would call the ebyon the exploited, the dallim the impoverished, and the anawim the oppressed.

What is significant in this passage is not the analysis it contains about the Israelites' understanding of the nature of poverty, however. The significance is that God condemns Israel for allowing some of its people to be exploited, impoverished, or oppressed. "For three sins of Israel, even for four, I will not turn back my wrath. . . ."

What did God want Israel to do regarding poverty? What did he expect from his chosen people? God's expectations are laid out quite clearly in Deuteronomy 15.

> At the end of every seven years you must cancel debts. This is how it is to be done: Every creditor shall cancel the loan he has made to his fellow Israelite. He shall not require payment from his fellow Israelite or brother, because the LORD's time for canceling debts has been proclaimed. You may require payment from a foreigner, but you must cancel any debt your brother owes you. However, there should be no poor among you, for in the land the LORD your God is giving you to possess as your inheritance, he will richly bless you, if only you fully obey the LORD your God and are careful to follow all these commands I am giving you today (vv. 1–5).

This is one of a number of Old Testament statutes (the most far-reaching being the Day of Jubilee) that sought to regulate the economic and political life of Israel through its religion. This particular law was obviously aimed at minimizing the wealth-accumulating capacity of some Israelites at the expense of the less fortunate and weaker. By requiring all creditors to forgive the indebtedness of all Israelites every seven years, this law would prevent any group of people from amassing unreasonable wealth and power.

It is noteworthy that this regulatory legislation existed specifically and avowedly on behalf of the poor. The motivation behind the seven-year debt forgiveness was that "there should be no poor among you," and if Israel was faithful to protect the rights of the poor and provide means by which they could be liberated from their poverty, then "in the land the LORD your God is giving you to possess as your inheritance, he will richly bless you."

In other words, this law was one attempt among many to control the systems of Israel. Apparently Israel accomplished this goal until the time of Solomon, as we saw in chapter 2. Under the Jewish law fully applied, unjust structures creating increasing inequality between rich and poor were not to be tolerated, and solidarity with the poor and oppressed was to be fostered along with respect for the poor. Why? "Remember that you were slaves in Egypt and the LORD your God redeemed you [from slavery]" (15:15).

But this is not all that Israel was called to regarding the poor.

> If there is a poor man among your brothers in any of the towns of the land that the LORD your God is giving you, do not be hardhearted or tightfisted toward your poor brother. Rather be openhanded and freely lend him whatever he needs. . . . Give generously to him and do so without a grudging heart; then because of this the LORD your God will bless you in all your work and in everything you put your hand to (vv. 7–8, 10).

Having just systems and making sure those systems operate justly are not enough. God wanted the Israelites to *care sincerely* about their poor. Old Testament concern for the oppressed, exploited, and marginalized was not merely a matter of cold calculation of obligation and duty; it was to be acted on out of a heart of genuine compassion and sensitivity. It was not enough to create just systems; the nation had to long for justice and love those who were victims of injustice.

Earlier I mentioned a life-transforming trip my son and I took to Calcutta in 1982. There we were privileged to meet with Mother Teresa, but we were even more privileged to work with her Missionaries of Charity among Calcutta's hungry, sick, and orphaned.

One thing Mother Teresa said to us was, "When you minister with us to the poor and needy, I want you to look at them with eyes of love and touch them with hands of love and speak to them with words of love. Because it is not simply to the poor to whom you are ministering. It is to Christ. And each poor person, for the moment he is before you, is Christ to you and you are Christ to him. I urge you to look at them and see Jesus!"

I did that as I ministered to the hungry, the destitute, and the orphaned. In doing so, I discovered a strange thing happening to me. The holy rage I felt for the systemic economic injustices of India and the part the northern hemisphere has played in creating those injustices still burned within me. But I also found the beauty of the poorest of the poor. And I found a dimension of Christ I had never known before.

On my return to the United States, I shared my experience with the congregation of my church.

> When I left India, I was relieved to be going for I had been shocked, hating its dirt, its filth, its seeming disregard of life. But now, I realize that I am, in some mystical way, tied up in the lives of Calcutta's poor and they in mine—for we are all part of every man.
>
> It was those little kids in the orphanage who did this to me—those beautiful little kids, swarming all over me, wanting to be cuddled, crying when I left—the little girl who was afraid, the two sisters who held each other's hands while crying, the two little boys who loved being swung through the air and who would sock each other to get up first in my lap.
>
> It was those hungry men, women, and children in line for their daily bulgur who did this to me—the patriarch with long white beard who bowed solemnly to me, the young woman with long, silky black hair who flashed me the most grateful smile, the little boy who tricked me into giving him more than his allotment of food.
>
> It was the kids swarming around me in the streets to have their pictures taken. It was the leprous man so proudly showing me his one-day-old baby. It was the blind watchman so conscientiously guarding the gate of the Missionaries of Charity. It was all these people who did it—so beautifully and hopefully responding to life, when they have so little future before them. How is it possible to respond to them but with the deepest of compassion?[5]

The passage in Deuteronomy 15 calling Israel to both systemic and compassionate commitment to its poor ends in a rather unexpected way:

> There will always be poor people in the land. Therefore I command you to be openhanded toward your brothers and toward the poor and needy in your land (v. 11).

"There should be no poor among you" (v. 4), and here are regulations to make that commitment a reality. Yet, "there will always be poor people in the land" (v. 11). This statement is not an expression of doubt in the writer nor a lament on a grim reality. The statement is a tragic prophecy! The Israelite system had been constructed to minimize the aggregation of the poor among them. The Hebrews had been called as well to compassion toward their underprivileged, for all had been slaves in Egypt. But the statement "there will always be poor people in the land" was a recognition that such legislation and compassion would probably not work.

Israel was first and foremost a community. As we have seen, it was intended to be the political, economic, and religious kingdom of God. The absence from that kingdom of the death-dealing elements of every other kingdom—oppression, conflict, poverty—would be the continuing sign that this was indeed the community of faith. The continuing existence of the poor in the land would be an ongoing witness to the world of the absence of justice, shalom, and equality in that nation. *That* would be a sign that the kingdom of God had not fully come in Israel!

I suggest that such a theological interpretation of Israel's history as I have attempted to reconstruct here provided the context for Jesus when he came preaching, "Repent, for the kingdom of heaven is near" (Matt. 4:17). Seeing these themes of oppression/liberation, conflict/peace, and poverty/equality in the context of Israel's self-understanding as God's holy nation helps us understand some of the roots of Jesus' thinking that would have contributed to his formulation of a theology of the kingdom of God. Let us now examine Jesus' teachings regarding the kingdom of God.

JESUS AND THE KINGDOM OF GOD

> After John was put in prison, Jesus went into Galilee, proclaiming the good news of God. "The time has come," he said. "The kingdom of God is near. Repent and believe the good news!" (Mark 1:14–15).

Jesus came preaching, "The kingdom of God is near." The Jewish people quickly responded to that message because it rekindled dreams long lying dormant of the Old Testament's "peaceable kingdom." People soon began to realize, however, that Jesus had something more in mind than people sitting in peace under fig trees in an all-Jewish kingdom especially blessed and protected by God. They recognized that Jesus' vision of the kingdom was far more comprehensive than theirs, for the kingdom of which he spoke was an international order of justice, love, and freedom from want.

When Jesus spoke of his vision of the kingdom, "the large crowd listened to him with delight" (Mark 12:37). But the powerful and the rich heard him with increasing anxiety and foreboding. What was the message of Jesus that brought joy to the poor but filled the strong with dread?

Kingdom Parables

Nowhere in the Gospels does Jesus present a systematic scheme of the kingdom of God, because by the very nature of his life and ministry, Jesus taught "on the run." Rather, in his parables we uncover the fullest expression of Jesus' theology of the kingdom. The thirty-six parables recorded in the Synoptic Gospels fall easily into six primary divisions that expose to us what Jesus believed about the kingdom.

1. *The first set of parables explains what God is like and what he wants from humanity.* Each of these parables portrays God as a patriarchal Jewish father who both loves his family but also bears the rule over his children and wants them to live under the shelter of his love. Such parables as the lost son (also known as the prodigal son, Luke 15:11–32), the lost sheep (Luke 15:3–7), the lost coin (Luke 15:8–10), and the workers in the vineyard (Matt. 20:1–16) all proclaim the story of the loving father-king.

In the parable of the lost son, for example, the son wants his share of the inheritance so that he can live as he pleases. His father gives it to him and the son hurries into a far country, where he squanders his inheritance in riotous living. Eventually he is reduced to caring for pigs and eating their slop—the most demeaning task any Jew could possibly have. While he is in this squalor, he comes to his senses and decides to return in humility to his father, asking that he be made one of the servants. The father sees his son coming from far off, runs to him, and instead of making the son a servant, orders a feast—"for this son of mine was dead and is alive again; he was lost and is found" (Luke 15:24).

Here Jesus shows that God is a loving father who cares deeply about us, his children, but will not prevent us from acting in self-centered ways. Our "Jewish Father God," however, will stand at the door and wait for his children to return, ready to receive them with acceptance and joy. God is like a parent. He is loving, forgiving, concerned, willing to allow the children the freedom they demand—even if it leads to self-destructive behavior—yet full of the knowledge that freedom is found only when they live under their parent's roof and rule. This first grouping of Jesus' parables, therefore, tells us that God wants us to live under his loving rulership.

2. *The second group of parables deals with the struggle between God and Satan.* God wants the world to be in God's kingdom, but the powers of evil are always at work undermining him and working to thwart his intentions. Some of these parables—the hidden treasure (Matt. 13:44), the pearl (Matt. 13:45–46)—stress that the kingdom of God is in our midst. It is spreading throughout the world and into the hearts of people; it is there for us to claim. Other parables in this group, while acknowledging the steady infiltration of God's kingdom, also point out how the powers of evil are arrayed against the kingdom to stop its advance. These parables are the weeds (Matt. 13:24–30), the net (Matt. 13:47–50), and the growing seed (Mark 4:26–29).

In the parable of the weeds, as an example, a farmer sows good seed on his land. At night, however, an enemy creeps into his fields and sows tares in an effort to destroy the farmer's crop. Jesus teaches here that the powers of Satan are arrayed against God's kingdom, doing everything possible to thwart and stop its advance. We see that the battle for God's kingdom is not simply a matter of accepting or rejecting people or just and oppressive systems. It is a cosmic battle between God and Satan, and we as God's people are caught up in it.

3. *The third group of parables proclaims the message that God's kingdom is here on earth right now—but only in a partial way.* There will be an unspecified period of time before God's kingdom has fully come on the earth. But it will come, and God wants us to be a part of that kingdom. Parables in this group are the servants on watch (Mark 13:32–37), the talents (Matt. 25:14–30), the mustard seed (Mark 4:30–32), the yeast in the dough (Matt. 13:33), the wicked servant (Matt. 24:45–51), the ten virgins (Matt. 25:1–13), the wedding banquet (Luke 12:35-40), the ten minas (the second parable of the talents, Luke 19:11–27), and the persistent widow (Luke 18:1–8).

The story of the ten virgins is a good example from this group. Ten virgins are waiting to light the way of the bridegroom as he comes to his marriage feast. Five of the virgins have adequate supplies of oil to keep their lamps lit; five do not. The bridegroom is late, and the lamps of the five foolish virgins have gone out. Needing additional oil, these five set out for the market to buy the oil. While they are gone, the bridegroom arrives, the five wise virgins light his way into the banquet hall, the doors are shut, and the five returning virgins find that they are excluded from the feast.

In this parable the bridegroom represents Jesus, who is coming to claim his kingdom. The kingdom's present reality is symbolized in his being the bridegroom, not the fiancé. The wedding ceremony has already taken place, but the wedding feast has not yet been held; this will consummate the marriage. In other words, the kingdom has not yet come in its totality. The bridegroom *will* come (the kingdom will someday be accomplished on the earth) and we (like the virgins) are invited to be a part of that kingdom. We are instructed to watch for the coming of the bridegroom. Whether we watch wisely or foolishly will decide whether we enter the kingdom.

4. *The fourth set of parables deals with the attitude of God toward our entrance into the kingdom.* God will exclude no one from the kingdom; we choose to exclude ourselves. The parables in this group are the great banquet (Luke 14:15–24), the friend at midnight (Luke 11:5–13), the tasks of the servants (Luke 17:7–10), the lost sheep (Luke 15:3–7), the sower (Matt. 13:3–23), the two sons (Matt. 21:28–32), and the wedding banquet (Matt. 22:1–14).

Let's look at the parable of the great banquet as an example. A man gives a great feast and invites the leading citizens to attend. One by one they make excuses for not attending. The host angrily instructs his servants to go into the highways and byways of the city to invite the ordinary people to come. The clear meaning of the parable is that God excludes no one from the banquet table of the kingdom—people exclude themselves. The invitation is for all people. It will be the common people, however—the poor, the ordinary folk—who will be most likely to respond. Each person must respond personally to the invitation to attend the banquet, and one's wealth or power will have much to do with one's predilection toward accepting or rejecting that invitation.

5. *The fifth series of parables exposes the radical difference between the kingdom of God and our daily experience.* God's kingdom is a different way of life; we relate differently toward God, others, our inner selves, and the world. The parables in this group are the good Samaritan (Luke 10:25–37), the rich fool (Luke 12:13–21), the Pharisee and the tax collector (Luke 18:9–14), salt and light (Matt. 5:13–16), the evil spirits in a man (Matt. 12:43–45), the seat of honor (Luke 14:7–14), the rich man and Lazarus (Luke 16:19–31), the sheep and the goats (Matt. 25:31–46), and the unmerciful servant (Matt. 18:23–35).

These parables illustrate a number of characteristics of the kingdom of God, and we will look briefly at three of them. In the parable of the good Samaritan, Jesus teaches that all people are our neighbors. Those living in the new kingdom are called to minister to the neighbor in trouble. Orientation toward the needs of others is the essence of the new life we are called to practice as people who have agreed to be in God's kingdom.

The story of the rich fool is not a polemic against wealth, but rather deals with the rich person's self-centeredness and pride. The word "I" is used more often in the rich fool's speech to himself than in any other passage in the Bible. He is therefore the antithesis of kingdom life, which is to be a "we" life instead of an "I" life. Life in the kingdom is to be lived for and with others in a community of love.

Finally, in the parable of the Pharisee and the tax collector, Jesus presents humility as a characteristic of kingdom life. In all these parables, however, the essence of what Jesus is illustrating is that life in the kingdom is entirely different from our everyday living. Yet it is a way of life we can practice—both individually and corporately—right now.

6. *The final group of parables deals with how one enters into the kingdom.* These parables teach that entrance into the kingdom comes in only one way: by believing in Jesus Christ. Two parables that make this point are the story of the tenants (Mark 12:1–9) and the wise and foolish builders (Matt. 7:24–27).

In the latter parable, Jesus points out that those who obey his teachings will discover the only true foundation on which God would have them build their lives. Those who ignore his words will come to ruin. Only those who accept him and his teaching will experience the kingdom of God in their hearts.[6]

The kingdom of God, as taught by Jesus in his parables, is to be a new order upon the earth. It was envisioned by Jesus as a corporate order. Entrance into that kingdom can come only as a personal decision. One would have to respond intentionally to God's redeeming love in order to enter the kingdom. The end of personal conversion in Jesus' teaching, however, was not to be conversion itself, but active commitment to fulfilling God's kingdom.

God's chief aim, Jesus proclaimed, is to create a new world order, entered into through personal repentance. The kingdom is the ultimate focus of God's intentions. Like any other empire, the kingdom of God would have its political, economic, social, and religious dimensions. It would be a corporate reality.

This is made particularly obvious in the parable in which Jesus likens the kingdom of God to "a mustard seed, which is the smallest seed you plant in the ground. Yet when planted, it grows and becomes the largest of all garden plants, with such big branches that the birds of the air can perch in its shade" (Mark 4:31–32). The symbolism that Jesus chose would have been crystal clear to any good Jew. In the Old Testament a tree was the symbol most used to describe a great empire, and the smaller nations encompassed by that empire were represented as birds finding shelter under its branches.[7] So in this parable Jesus is teaching that the kingdom of God will start very small—with only himself and a little band of disciples—but it will grow and grow until it becomes a mighty empire, spreading through the whole world and gathering all the nations under it as a tree attracts birds.

Thus the kingdom of God is worldwide. Jesus sees it as an empire of God's rule over all the earth. Like any other kingdom, it has its political, economic, and religious dimensions; it is not just "spiritual."

It is intriguing, however, that although Jesus describes what the kingdom will be like, he does not present any particular form of government, any economic theory, or any social or educational platform for that kingdom. He does not give the slightest hint whether the government would be democratic or dictatorial, whether the economy would be capitalist or socialist, whether its society would be voluntaristic or communal in nature.

Jesus does describe the kingdom of God as a society where war is absent, where there is neither proverty nor hunger nor injustice. He describes the kingdom as a world in which all class hatred, racial prejudice, and national differences have been swept away. The new society Jesus proclaimed will be one in which the hungry are fed, the thirsty given drink, the stranger welcomed, the naked clothed, and the prisoner freed.

It is a mark of Jesus' great wisdom that he did not identify the systems of the kingdom. As a result, the church has never had to identify with any particular political system and call it "kingdom politics." It has never had to endorse one economic structure and label it "godly economics." It has never had to single out a religious and social system and say, "This is the only way God wants us to live." Instead, the church has been able to proclaim God's kingdom in every political system from the Roman Empire to modern-day democracy. It has been able to call humanity to practice caring economics in all nations, whether their economies have been feudalistic, socialistic, or capitalistic. The church has been able to press for social justice in every nation through two thousand years, regardless of the social system or religion that nation might embrace. Rather, throughout the whole world, wherever God's people may be found, the kingdom of God is growing and advancing in all governments and in spite of those governments.

Further, Jesus' refusal to indicate one political, economic, or social-religious system for the kingdom presses the church both to proclaim the Good News in every society and to work for immediate, short-term social changes that improve the conditions of people. The church does not have to try to get its society to conform to predetermined political, economic, or social theories. Instead, Christians can work pragmatically on behalf of the kingdom of God right where they are, proclaiming the Good News with their lips, by their actions, and in their lives as they seek to be responsive to the particular needs and problems of the people and their neighborhoods, cities, and nations.

The Kingdom and the Poor

If anything can be said of Jesus, it is that he was a person committed to the poor. He proclaimed this solidarity with the broken of life in his very call to ministry, when he quoted the prophet Isaiah.

> The Spirit of the Sovereign LORD is on me,
>   because the Lord has anointed me
>   to preach good news to the poor.
> He has sent me to bind up the brokenhearted,
>   to proclaim freedom for the captives
>   and release from darkness for the prisoners,
>   to proclaim the year of the LORD's favor (Isa. 61:1–2).

The "year of the LORD's favor" is a Jewish euphemism for the Year of Jubilee, which was an Old Testament tradition (Lev. 25:8–54) whereby every fifty years all the rich Israelites had to surrender all their property and all the poor Israelites were forgiven their debts. Thus everyone started all over again. It was, in other words, a periodic effort to redistribute the wealth of Israel.

In quoting this passage, Jesus was symbolically saying to his hearers, "The task to which I have been called by God is to preach good news to the poor. I will work to release captives. I will recover the sight of the blind. I will set free those who are oppressed. I will seek the redistribution of the wealth of this country."

Jesus was a partisan of the poor. He ate with tax collectors, he numbered prostitutes among his friends, he healed the lepers and the blind (who were the rejects of Jewish society), he reached out to the Gentiles, women, and children who were all relegated to second-class citizenship, and he fed the hungry. When asked by disciples of John the Baptist for evidence that he was indeed the Messiah, Jesus answered,

> "Go back and report to John what you have seen and heard: The blind receive sight, the lame walk, those who have leprosy are cured, the deaf hear, the dead are raised, and the good news is preached to the poor. Blessed is the man who does not fall away on account of me" (Luke 7:22–23).

To the rich young man, Jesus said, "One thing you lack. . . . Go, sell everything you have and give to the poor, and then you will have treasure in heaven. Then come, follow me" (Mark 10:21). To the rich, Jesus said, "Woe to you who are rich. . . . Woe to you who are well fed now. . . . Woe to you who laugh [make merry] now" (Luke 6:24–25). Like all the major prophets of the Old Testament, Jesus was an advocate for the poor, the oppressed, and those not receiving justice. Athol Gill writes in a monograph, "From Down Under":

> Jesus grew up on the margins of Galilean society far removed from the centre of economic and religious power. In his ministry he was open to a wide range of people, but he was particularly drawn to the outcasts, the marginalized and oppressed people of Galilee. The religious and political authorities were offended at the way he overturned contemporary economic and religious customs. But he saw his teaching and lifestyle as a reflection of the nature of God and his kingdom which he believed was breaking into history through his ministry. In the light of the kingdom he called people to follow him in his ministry.[8]

The gospel accounts contain a surprisingly large amount of evidence about Jesus' commitment to the poor and his perception that "theirs is the kingdom of heaven." His incarnation involved not only becoming flesh, but also living among the poor and weak. A strong argument can be made for Jesus' being born, not into a poor, but into a middle-class family. His work and religious and academic training would indicate that he was middle class. Yet, in his ministry he chose to move among the outcasts and the needy, he had nowhere to lay his head, and he was intentionally poor (indicated by his borrowing a boat or a coin on occasion).

But Jesus' commitment to the poor went beyond identification with these people. He challenged those who would oppress the poor. His confrontations with the Jewish rulers, with the temple priests during his ejection of the temple money-changers (which many biblical scholars think was the incident that actually led to the decision to execute him), and continually with the Pharisees and Sadducees were all indications of Jesus' rage at the refusal of the leaders of Israel to be responsive to the plight of the poor. Even more intriguing was Jesus' indifference to Roman claims to power.

Jesus' identification with the poor was also an act of solidarity with them. By living among them, by taking time to listen to them, by teaching in their terms, by choosing many of his disciples from among them, by worshiping and eating and having fellowship with them, Jesus made it clear that he stood in solidarity with the poor.

Jesus' concern for the poor went beyond restoring to them a rightful share of society's power and wealth. He was concerned about their humiliation and rejection by society. So he went out of his way to affirm them and to seek their restoration and healing. Most of his healings fall into this category, because they were healings of "ordinary" people who were also rejected by their society. Their healings were, in many instances, healings not simply of their bodies but of their souls as well.

It is perhaps in dealing with money that Jesus made his clearest statement about the relationship between rich and poor. In the Gospels Jesus talked more about money than any other subject except relationship with God, simply because he saw one's perspective on money as pivotal in life. What people do with their money and the attitudes they have toward it will determine a great deal about whether they open their hearts to the poor and needy. Consider passages like these:

"Watch out! Be on your guard against all kinds of greed; a man's life does not consist in the abundance of his possessions" (Luke 12:15).

" 'Bring in the poor, the crippled, the blind and the lame . . . [for] not one of those men who were invited will get a taste of my banquet' " (Luke 14:21, 24).

"If you want to be perfect, go, sell your possessions and give to the poor, and you will have treasure in heaven. Then come, follow me" (Matt. 19:21)

"It is hard for a rich man to enter the kingdom of heaven" (Matt. 19:23).

Perhaps the statement of Jesus that most clearly illustrates his solidarity with the poor and his chastisement of the rich is the Lukan Beatitudes. It is intriguing that one often hears sermons on the Beatitudes as they are presented in the gospel of Matthew, but rarely as they appear in Luke. The Luke passage has as much scriptural authority as the more familiar blessings of Matthew 5.

"Blessed are you who are poor,
    for yours is the kingdom of God.
Blessed are you who hunger now,
    for you will be satisfied.
Blessed are you who weep now,

for you will laugh.
Blessed are you when men hate you,
    when they exclude you and insult you
    and reject your name as evil, because of the Son of Man. . . .

"But woe to you who are rich,
    for you have already received your comfort.
Woe to you who are well fed now,
    for you will go hungry.
Woe to you who laugh now,
    for you will mourn and weep.
Woe to you when all men speak well of you,
    for that is how their fathers treated the false prophets."
                                    (Luke 6:20–22, 24–26)

In reality, Jesus' understanding of and commitment to the poor went far beyond that of the Old Testament prophets. Jesus was the first person in Scripture to perceive that the poor are not only those who have little money, but also those (wealthy or not) with impoverished human spirits. He understood that the oppressed are not simply the weak who were taken advantage of by the rich and powerful, but also the oppressors themselves. He not only railed against the Pharisees for creating a religious system that enabled them to control the populace, but also warned them that they were becoming slaves to their own religion, which was controlling their lives and keeping them from God.

For example, Jesus saw that Nicodemus could never experience the liberating new birth as long as he allowed his obedience to the religion of the Pharisees to dictate his priorities. Jesus perceived Pilate would be kept from knowing the truth as long as he kept the spears of the Roman army against the chests of the Israelites. Jesus knew that the rich young man in Mark 10 was as spiritually impoverished by his money as were the poor materially impoverished by his refusal to give. It is intriguing that, whereas Luke has it, "Blessed are you who are poor, . . . you who hunger now, . . . you who weep now" (as we pointed out above), Matthew puts it, "Blessed are the poor in spirit, . . . the meek [of heart], . . . those who hunger and thirst for righteousness" (Luke 6:20–21; Matt. 5:3–6). Luke concentrated on the physical and social realities of Jesus' ministry, while Matthew understood its psychological and spiritual implications.

Who, truly, are the poor? According to Jesus, all of us are! For the hungry are not only those people who lack bread, but those who lack love. The thirsty are not simply those who need water; you and I may thirst for righteousness. The naked are not simply those who seek to be clothed; you and I may long to be clothed in dignity, with a sense of being worthwhile or really wanted by someone. Jesus was the very first to know and to teach that every human being is poor—poor in heart if not in body. All of us, from the greatest to the smallest, from the richest to the most oppressed, are people who have been deprived of some of those critical elements that contribute to making us whole, fulfilled, joyous, compassionate, God-filled people. And that brings us to a very intriguing, but often obscured fact about Jesus—namely, that there were people in Israel whom Jesus did not like.

A friend of mine once said, "You know, Bob, you don't have to like someone in order to love him!" That makes sense. There have been times when as a parent I have not liked my children or what they were doing, particularly in their rebellious teen years. That dislike of them and their actions never took away from my continuing, deep-seated love for them. The same can be said of Jesus. Jesus never met a man he did not love, but he dealt with many men and women he did not like!

A Jewish rabbi once wrote of Jesus,

> I sometimes think that if Jesus had given a little of the gentleness and love which he displayed for the tax-collectors and the outcast to his Rabbinic antagonists, some of them might have been won over to his cause. After all, they too were human beings and although Jesus seemed to forget it, they, too . . . were sinners with souls to save.[9]

Actually, Jesus did not forget that. He knew that those rabbis were sinners, destitute and impoverished and oppressed by their religious system. The problem was that *they* did not see that they were sinners. Instead, they would stand in the temple and pray, "God, I thank you that I am not like other men—robbers, evildoers, adulterers—or even like this tax collector" (Luke 18:11).

What caused Jesus to dislike someone was that person's refusal to see himself or herself as a destitute and impoverished sinner in need of God's transforming love. Jesus did not like those people who used their wealth or power or religion to separate themselves from the needy, saying, "I am not like other men."

When people fail to perceive that their wealth may be depriving a poor person of the necessities of life, when they fail to see that their yearning for security may be causing political oppression to peasants in another country, when they fail to sense that their religion may be geared to make them feel good about themselves and the way they choose to live rather than helping them to perceive their need of God's forgiveness and love, then, Jesus tells us, such people have eyes that do not see and ears that do not hear. Consequently these people are enemies of God and of his Son.

But if, having much money or little, you are poor in heart; if, holding great political power or little, you hunger after a right relationship with God and justice for your nation's weak; if, being actively involved in a church or on its fringes, you seek to love those in need and are "meek" or "little" before God—then you are a friend of Jesus. You are one of those who can hear and receive the Good News he has for you.

What was the Good News, the Gospel, that Jesus proclaimed? "The kingdom of God is near!" (Mark 1:15). Jesus described this kingdom, with its Old Testament roots in liberation, peace, and justice, as a new order of right relationships with God and humanity, acted out in commitment to the materially poor and the poor in heart. This kingdom was the center of Jesus' preaching, healing, and ministering.

In Luke 17:20–21 Jesus summarizes his doctrine of the kingdom of God in one pithy statement: "The kingdom of God does not come with your careful observation, nor will people say, 'Here it is,' or 'There it is,' because the kingdom of God is within you."

Although it is not obvious in the English translation, the Greek in this passage has an intentional play on words. Jesus uses the word *entros*, which can be equally translated "within" or "among." Consider the implications of these choices.

"The kingdom of God is within you." Jesus' intention for humanity is that all might experience the transformation of their own inner poverty. Entering into God's kingdom means to come into contact with the inner self, to respond to God's saving action in our lives, and under that protective love to begin discovering our full personality—our strengths, our weaknesses, our potentials, and the evil and good powers at work within us.

"The kingdom of God is among you." Jesus' intention for humanity is that we might experience the kingdom life in our midst. God is at work among us to create in our midst a new community—a community of people who love each other the way God loves them. The creation of this new community, Jesus taught, was his means for bringing to earth God's social order. That new social order would be *practiced* by the church in its corporate life. It would be *witnessed to* by the church as it calls the world to accountability. And it would be *lived out* by the church as its people invest their lives in a commitment to the pain of the world by confronting poverty, oppression, injustice, or coercive religion in the world.

"The kingdom of God is within you . . . among you." This was Jesus' dream for humanity. This is what the prophets in the Old Testament proclaimed as they envisioned their new Jerusalem. This is God's intention for the city!

THE KINGDOM OF GOD AND THE CITY

It may be obvious that there has really been little mention of the city in this chapter. That is intentional. What I have wanted to do is present rather thoroughly my understanding of the biblical doctrine of the kingdom of God. Its implications for the city will be explored thoroughly later on in this book. But it seemed important to take the time to explore the theology of the kingdom. Why? Because *the kingdom of God is the primary paradigm for understanding God's call to the church in the city.*

Colin Marchant, reflecting on his years of ministry in East Ham, a borough of London, writes:

> Underneath our human concern [for the city's poor] and analysis, behind our experiments and projects lay the pattern of human life as intended by God, set out in the Scriptures and focused in Jesus Christ—and so often ignored, even by Christians. The covering-up and the accretions, however skilful and impressive, could not obscure the deeper realities which must eventually break through: God's purpose and human sin; God's grace and His people; God's justice and His world plan.
>
> Were Christians really different in their attitudes and life-style from non-Christians? How far had the church faced, and grasped, the wholeness of Scripture? *In short, how far had the Kingdom, or rule, of God become embodied and made real in the people of Christ?*[10]

This is the underlying question facing the church in the city. How far has the kingdom of God become embodied and made real in the city's people of God? God's primary intention for the city is to bring God's kingdom into that city—to permeate its political, economic, and religious structures, to transform the lives of its inhabitants, to exorcise evil and unrepentant principalities and powers, and to place over that city, not a brooding angel but a Christ who would gather the city to himself. It is God's intention to transform every city into the city of God by making of that city the embodiment of God's rule.

God would seek to do this in every city by creating in that city a new community: the church. That community would be the very embodiment of God's kingdom in the city. In its life together, the church would practice that new social order. Through its witness, the church would call the city to participate in God's kingdom. By its solidarity with the economically, politically, and spiritually poor of the city, and by its confrontation of the powers that would seek to control and oppress rather than recognize their own poverty, the church would work for God's kingdom. That is why Marchant insists that the underlying question to every church in every city is this: How far has the kingdom of God become embodied and made real in the life, witness, and social action of your church in this city?

The church as the embodiment of the kingdom of God is the dream. We have been very far from the dream, both when we were people who had not received the Gospel and even now as people who believe but who struggle to live and practice it. What, or who, can empower us to be the kingdom community we have been created and called to be?

The task of the rest of this book will be to explore how the church can, indeed, be the kingdom community, witness to Christ and his kingdom, and seek to practice the kingdom in a way that comforts the city's afflicted and afflicts the city's comfortable. We will investigate how God has worked to empower the kingdom community and to redeem the city through Jesus Christ. We will examine that vocation to which God calls the church in the city and the instructions God has provided to enable God's people to act out that vocation. We will explore the sources of power God has given to sustain the kingdom community as it seeks to embody and make real the kingdom of God in even the darkest and most demanding ministries in the city.

A POSTSCRIPT

Sam Kamaleson, a noted Methodist preacher from Madras, India, and a vice-president of World Vision International, was speaking to the three hundred pastors assembled at a conference on urban ministry held near Ahmadabad, India. His address focused on the story of Sodom and Gomorrah in Genesis 18 and 19.

Dr. Kamaleson developed a theme that brought an entirely new insight to me and to all the pastors gathered there. I could hardly wait to get back to my library in the United States. Was Kamaleson right in his interpretation of that controversial passage? If he was, it would reveal an entirely new dimension to God's love for the city, one that would remove much ambiguity from that intriguing passage about Abraham's bargaining with God for the deliverance of Sodom.

When I returned home to California three weeks later, I made a beeline for my reference books. There I discovered that Dr. Kamaleson's insights were clearly supported by such noted Old Testament scholars as E. A. Speiser and Gerhard von Rad.[11] Sam was right!

What was this interpretation that so electrified three hundred Indian pastors and one American pastor?

In Genesis 18, Abraham is visited by three men who predict the birth of Isaac and announce, "The outcry against Sodom and Gomorrah is so great and their sin so grievous that I will go down and see if [they should be destroyed]" (vv. 20–21). It became quickly apparent to Abraham that the three visitors were not men, but manifestations of the Lord God. According to verse 22, "The men turned away and went toward Sodom, but Abraham remained standing before the LORD." In audience before God, Abraham began his famed negotiations for the rescue of Sodom and Gomorrah from divine destruction.

Dr. Kamaleson told his audience that the earliest manuscripts do not support the reading, "Abraham remained standing before the LORD." He contended, instead, that there is significant textual evidence to indicate that the passage originally read, "The LORD remained standing before

Abraham"! Who was begging whom for the city? Could it be that a scribe, thinking this reading could not possibly be right, reversed the text?[12]

Even if this suggested original reading is not true, Genesis 18 remains a profound statement of God's love for the city, the role of intercession, and the presence God's people have in a pagan society. But if it *is* true, it has profound implications for our understanding of the church's responsibility in its city.

If the passage truly reads, "The LORD remained standing before Abraham," it means God was the supplicant before Abraham. It was *God* who was advocating Sodom's deliverance before *Abraham!* It is as if God were saying to the patriarch, "I listen to the entreaties of my people. Go on, Abraham, ask me! Ask me to spare Sodom for fifty people—and I'll do it." Abraham asks in faith, and God grants.

"Go on, man, ask me for forty!"

"Lord, spare the city for forty people."

"Done! Go on, ask me for thirty!"

"Lord, thirty."

"Done. Ask for twenty!"

If Abraham had asked for it, would God have spared the city for one family—the family of Lot? Would he have spared it for Lot alone? If the wording of Genesis 18:22 has indeed been reversed, then the answer clearly is yes! God so loved Abraham and so loved Sodom and Gomorrah, he would have given to Abraham the city for anything the old man had asked. God *wanted* the city saved. God's sense of justice, however, demanded judgment.

"Go on, man, ask me! I want to forgive; I want to stave off judgment." Beyond his request for ten people Abraham could not go. So it was that the bargaining stopped—*not because God lacked mercy, but because Abraham lacked sufficient nerve.*

Considered this way, Abraham's response to God standing before him for Sodom is another trial of faith. Could he believe God for the birth of the promised son? Abraham turned to Hagar instead of Sarah, and Ishmael was born. Could he believe God for the pregnancy of Sarah? Sarah laughed and Abraham wavered. Could he sufficiently believe God for the city? He could not; he could not barter with God far enough. This makes Abraham's later trust in God—when he faced God's demand for Isaac's sacrifice—even more remarkable. It is an indication of how Abraham had grown over the years in his trust in God.

That is God's cry as he stands before us and pleads for the city. We are called by God to be his community, both the foretaste of the kingdom and its present embodiment. All that the city will know of God's kingdom, it will know from our life together, our witness, and our commitment to the city's broken, hurting, and poor.

"Go on, man, ask me! Go on, woman, ask me for the city!" Do we have sufficient nerve to ask God for our city—the nerve to *be* in the city, to *proclaim*, and to *work for justice*, for what God calls the church to be? Are we willing to be the embodiment of the kingdom of God in our city?

"Go on, church, ask me!"

PART II

THE CHURCH: GOD'S URBAN ADVANCE

Chapter Five

WHAT DID JESUS DO FOR THE CITY?

Lord Jesus Christ:

When you entered the city, the people spread a carpet of palm branches before you, and shouted, "Blessings on him who comes in the name of the Lord."

Lord Jesus, we want to join them in their welcome and their praise.

When you were handed over to the authorities, flogged and put to death, you still seemed more like a king than a criminal.

Lord Jesus, even your cross looks like a throne: always and everywhere you are in control.

When the people's praises turned to jeering and they shouted, "Crucify!" you prayed for their forgiveness.

Lord Jesus, we know that we are the same sort of people as those who jeered at you in the city: we too need your forgiveness.

When you were raised from the tomb, people were brought to see in your living and your dying the surpassing love of God.

Lord Jesus, nothing in all creation can separate us from the love of God which we meet in you.

Praise and honour, glory and might, be to him who sits on the throne and to the Lamb, for ever and ever. Amen.

Caryl Micklem[1]

In the first section of this book, we explored the city biblically. We have examined the essential biblical theme about the city as battleground between God and Satan. We have examined God's creative and compassionate love for the city and God's intentions to re-create the city, its systems, and inhabitants, into the kingdom of God.

We have also taken considerable time to try to understand biblically the nature and extent of evil in the city—so that we have explored this evil, not only as individual, but as corporate, systemic, and demonic. Our reason for taking such a careful look at a biblical theology of evil becomes apparent in this chapter. We will now explore a biblical understanding of the work of God through Christ which is as big as the evil of any city!

Jerusalem the Bride: Part 3

A foretaste of Christ's transforming work for the city is expressed throughout the Old Testament. Perhaps no passage is as graphic as that described in the third portion of Ezekiel 16—Jerusalem as the bride of the Lord God.

In chapter 1, we examined the first portion of this passage, in which the city is described as an innocent young woman with whom God falls in love. Marrying her, God rescues her from her poverty and raises her to the status of queen. "Your fame spread among the nations on account of your beauty," God says to his beloved queen, "because the splendor I had given you made your beauty perfect" (Ezek. 16:14).

But Jerusalem succumbed to wealth, beauty, and power. In chapter 2, we examined the second portion of this Scripture, Ezekiel 16:15–34, which describes the city's intentional fall from grace. Jerusalem trusted in her beauty (v. 15); she was impressed by herself and her status in the world. Then increasingly she prostituted herself: "you lavished your favors on anyone who passed by." She began offering her sons and daughters in human sacrifice to the gods of Canaan and of the nations around Israel (vv. 23–24). In "Jerusalem the Bride: Part 2," we saw the decline and destruction of a soul—not an individual's soul, but the soul of a nation and a city. For Ezekiel has described for us in chapter 16 a city's intentional, willful, long-term abandonment of God.

The allegory of the city as bride does not end with Jerusalem's fall. In Ezekiel 16:35–63, the prophet shares what God will do to win his city back to himself, her husband. Ezekiel hears God say,

> I will hand you over to your lovers, and they will tear down your mounds and destroy your lofty shrines. They will strip you of your clothes and take your fine jewelry and leave you naked and bare. They will bring a mob against you, who will stone you and hack you to pieces with their swords. They will burn down your houses and inflict punishment on you in the sight of many women (Ezek. 16:39–41).

First, God as lover will punish Jerusalem for her whoring (idolatry and rejection of him). Israel had followed a course of political expediency and practical politics and abandoned God and followed the gods of the more powerful nations around them: Egypt, Assyria, and Babylonia.

Such disloyalty to God will not benefit Israel at the end. Her "lovers"—the other nations with whom Jerusalem consorted—will eventually conquer Israel, destroy Jerusalem and its temple, raze the city, take as booty all of Israel's wealth, and carry the people off into bondage.

As we pointed out in chapter 2, the seriousness of such rejection and blatant disregard of God is given poignant voice in Ezekiel's comparison of Jerusalem's crime to the sins of her sister cities Sodom and Samaria.

> Now this was the sin of your sister Sodom: She and her daughters were arrogant, overfed and unconcerned; they did not help the poor and needy. They were haughty and did detestable things before me. Therefore I did away with them as you have seen. Samaria did not commit half the sins you did. You have done more detestable things than they, and have made your sisters seem righteous by all these things you have done (Ezek. 16:49–51).

Social injustice (especially toward its own poor), exploitation, sexual perversity, pride, gluttony, arrogance, and complacency are all terrible sins, and together are capable of destroying the soul of a city. Nothing, however, is as evil as idolatry—making something other than God god and rejecting the One who can actually bring salvation. This was Jerusalem's sin; the city placed national security ahead of God.

God does not stop with Jerusalem's punishment. Ezekiel's allegory does not end with the city in Babylonian captivity. There is to be a restoration! God will redeem!

Although the focus of Ezekiel 16 is on Jerusalem, in reality the chapter ought to be called "A Tale of Three Cities," for it is also about Sodom and Samaria as well. These cities, of course, stand symbolically for their respective nations: Judah (Jerusalem), pre-Israelite or gentile Canaan (Sodom), and Israel (Samaria, the northern kingdom's capital city). The chapter deals with the nature of the sinfulness of all three cities and God's condemnation and redemption of them. This is even though God has covenanted with only one of them—Jerusalem.

Verses 53–63 conclude the chapter. These verses deal with the forgiveness and restoration of the three cities. Ezekiel writes,

> However, I will restore the fortunes of Sodom and her daughters and of Samaria and her daughters, and your fortunes along with them, so that you may bear your disgrace and be ashamed of all you have done in giving them comfort. And your sisters, Sodom with her daughters and Samaria with her daughters, will return to what they were before; and you and your daughters will return to what you were before (vv. 53–55).

Here is the grace of God! The Lord promises redemption to each city, even though none deserves it. In verses 53–55, God promises to restore the cities that stand as symbols of the Israelite and gentile worlds. The condition for such restoration, however, is "that you may bear your disgrace and be ashamed of all you have done" (v. 54). Repentance and a turning to God is a precondition of God's redemption and transformation of a city (see also Jonah 3–4).

The redemption of Samaria, Sodom, and Jerusalem is pure grace! None of these cities deserves redemption, nor is there anything they can do which will require God to forgive them and thus earn their redemption (v. 59). They are made new and whole again simply because God chooses to forgive them. Because he is a God of love and of commitment, God saves cities because he chooses to save. It is simply part of God's character to want to save!

This is magnificently put by Ezekiel in terms of the covenant. God says in this chapter,

> I will remember the covenant I made with you in the days of your youth, and I will establish an everlasting covenant with you. . . . So I will establish my covenant with you, and you will know that I am the LORD. Then, *when I make atonement for you* for all you have done, you will remember and be ashamed and never again open your mouth because of your humiliation, declares the Sovereign LORD (Ezek. 16:60, 62–63, emphasis mine).

God will atone for Jerusalem's crimes! He will accomplish that atonement through a new covenant. Because of God's commitment to Jerusalem through the old covenant, Ezekiel emphasizes, God will create a new and more extensive covenant with Jerusalem that will bring about the city's atonement. That new covenant, though made only with God's people, will reach out into the rest of the world and include within it Samaria (Israel) and Sodom (the gentile world).

Thus it is that God chooses to forgive and accept Jerusalem the fallen, idolatrous bride. Thus it is that God chooses to save three cities. All that any of the three cities can do in response is to repent of their sin in the light of such unmerited grace and to accept that they are forgiven.

What a powerful descriptive allegory! God let the people know that he intended to redeem three cities, cities that were symbolic of the Jewish and gentile nations. It is such an Old Testament understanding of the salvation of the city that provides us with an introduction to understanding what it is that Christ has done for the city.

ON TO JERUSALEM TO DIE

> From that time Jesus began to make it clear to his disciples that he was destined to go to Jerusalem and suffer grievously at the hands of the elders and chief priests and scribes, to be put to death and to be raised up on the third day (Matt. 16:21 JB).

The very words Matthew chooses to introduce the theme of Christ's impending doom indicate how important Jerusalem—*the* city—figured into Jesus' understanding of God's plan of salvation.

- "Jesus began to make it clear"—Jesus did not make this statement once; rather he stated over and over again to his disciples what would happen to him.

- ". . . that he was destined"—It was not optional for Jesus to go to Jerusalem. It was not preferable. It was obligatory that it be Jerusalem to which Jesus was to go to do that work which meant the world's salvation. It was part of God's design.

- ". . . to go to Jerusalem and suffer grievously at the hands of the elders and chief priests and scribes, to be put to death and to be raised up on the third day." It was to Jerusalem that Jesus had to go to die. Why? I suggest that the primary reason was that Jerusalem was the archetypal battleground between God and Satan for the souls and life of all humanity.

In the Bible, Jerusalem is not simply *a* city. It is *the* city. It was not just the capital city of the nation of Israel, the site of the temple (and thus the repository of the Hebrew cultic practices), or the center of Jewish faith. Jerusalem was the gathering place of all the systems—the religious, political, and economic systems of Israel, the spiritual center of the Roman world, and the physical abode of the Law. Jerusalem was the city most brooded over both by God and Satan, the city which, in its very name, symbolized the battle between God and Satan for spiritual control.

As the archetypal city, Jerusalem symbolized and stood in the place of all other cities. Every first-century Jew believed Jerusalem was the vortex and focus of humanity's spirituality. Therefore, to die in Jerusalem was to die at the spiritual center of the universe. That was why Jesus had to go to Jerusalem to die.

Salvation for a City

Where else can one possibly begin to deal with Jesus' relationship with the city of Jerusalem than with Luke 13:34–35?[2]

O Jerusalem, Jerusalem, you who kill the prophets and stone those sent to you, how often I have longed to gather your children together, as a hen gathers her chicks under her wings, but you were not willing! Look, your house is left to you desolate. I tell you, you will not see me again until you say, "Blessed is he who comes in the name of the Lord."

This pivotal passage, its parallel in Matthew 23:37–39, and its companion passage of Luke 19:41–44 provide us with four insights which underlie the biblical theology of salvation for the city!

God's love for the city is exceedingly patient. Jerusalem, Jesus stated, had killed its prophets and stoned those who had brought unacceptable news from God. The one-thousand-year history of Jerusalem from David to Herod could best be depicted as a continuing and lengthy rejection of any new way God might be at work in the midst of his people. God's people continually rejected any godly activity that demanded the least bit of sacrifice on their part.

Jerusalem's history included a wide spectrum of sin. The sin over which Jesus mourns is not simply the accumulation of the wrongdoing of Jerusalem's individuals. It is also corporate, systemic, and demonic sin, permeating every structure and aspect of city life. Yet God goes right on loving the city, forgiving her, and patiently starting all over again. God's love for the city seems unending, so that we see Jesus weeping at the city's obdurateness rather than threatening its obliteration.

Christ longs to see the city become the city of God. "How often I have longed to gather your children together, . . . but you were not willing!" Jesus says. One can almost hear the pain in his voice. The city—as the abode of Satan as well as of God—always has killed its prophets and stoned its messengers. Yet Christ longs to see the city come to him, to become what it had been created to be: the city of God. In order for it to be what it can be, Christ has already done all that is necessary for the city to be redeemed and renewed. But it will not!

The city's refusal breaks Jesus' heart, for he knows the spiritual, social, and physical desolation toward which the city is propelling itself inevitably. He longs for it to choose him instead. As a result, his heart is broken over the city's blindness and its unwillingness to accept the outstretched hands of love and appeal.

Humanity refuses the city of God. Luke 19:41 describes Jesus as weeping over the city, and Jesus' words in Luke 13:34–35 are filled with such pain that they can come from nothing other than a breaking heart. Jesus weeps over Jerusalem precisely because the potential for the inhabitants' salvation came to them, and they refused it.

This is why the city does not benefit from salvation. It is not that God does not provide it—he has provided it through Jesus Christ. Humanity refuses it. The city will not accept its salvation; it refuses the vision of itself as the city of God.

It is particularly important to note that the city's rejection of Christ is a corporate rejection. Jesus does not address people here. He addresses the city: "How often I have longed to gather your children together, . . . but *you* were not willing" (Luke 13:34). It is the city which Jesus longs to gather to him as a hen gathers her chicks. It is the city's systems Jesus longs to fill with God's redeeming love. It is Jesus who wants to be the brooding hen over that city and its principalities and powers, rather than for the city to allow Satan's angel to shape its interior spirituality. But it is the city that refuses to receive Christ as Lord of its corporate life. It is the city—and not simply its inhabitants—which therefore must be rejected.

Inevitable consequences come upon the city that rejects Christ. "Look," Jesus sobs in Luke 13:35, "your house is left to you desolate." In the companion Lukan passage, Jesus is even more specific:

> "The days will come upon you when your enemies will build an embankment against you and encircle you and hem you in on every side. They will dash you to the ground, you and the children within your walls. They will not leave one stone on another, because you did not recognize the time of God's coming to you" (Luke 19:43–44).

Both the Luke 13 and Luke 19 passages are statements that simply cannot be individualized or "spiritualized" away. These are corporate statements, made to a city. A city will be destroyed because a city refused to recognize the redemptive events occurring in it. Because the city rejected its moment of salvation, its opportunity was gone—and salvation would have to await a Second Coming.

Thus Jerusalem is doomed to a continuing cycle of destruction and restoration—even today! It still cannot see its salvation drawing nigh, nor, apparently, does it even seek it. Instead, nearly two thousand years after Jesus spoke these words, Jerusalem—and its present jingoistic state arrayed against Palestinian refugees—gives itself more fully than ever to accumulating power, prestige, possessions, and a parochial solidarity!

God's love for the city is exceedingly patient. Christ longs to see the city become the city of God. Humanity refuses the city of God. Inevitable consequences come upon the city which rejects Christ. These four emphases in the story of Jesus weeping over Jerusalem provide for us the framework for thinking about what it is that Jesus has done for the city.

Christ's Saving Work for the City

In this section, we will look at six pivotal Scriptures written by St. Paul and St. John (the New Testament's most visionary thinkers) that help us to discern the salvific work Christ has done for the city.

Romans 8:18–23, a truly mind-expanding passage, reads:

> I think that what we suffer in this life can never be compared to the glory, as yet unrevealed, which is waiting for us. The whole creation is eagerly waiting for God to reveal his sons. It was not for any fault on the part of creation that it was made unable to attain its purpose, it was made so by God; but creation still retains the hope of being freed, like us, from its slavery to decadence, to enjoy the same freedom and glory as the children of God. From the beginning till now the entire creation, as we know, has been groaning in one great act of giving birth; and not only creation, but all of us who possess the first-fruits of the Spirit, we too groan inwardly as we wait for our bodies to be set free (JB).

Consider what Paul is saying here. He is contending that creation—the world, the cosmos, the universe—is enslaved to decadence and sin as much as are human beings. But it "still retains the hope of being freed, like us, from its slavery to decadence" (vv. 20–21). Creation is as capable of being saved by Christ as are we! As that which will be saved, creation will enjoy the same benefits of salvation as will humans, and to the same degree, for creation will "enjoy the same freedom and glory as the children of God" (v. 21). Finally, creation is presented as being alive and as actively involved in the salvation process as is a human being ("creation still *retains the hope* of being freed" [vv. 20–21, emphasis mine]).

We see then that in Romans, Paul is teaching that there is no dichotomy between the individual and his corporate environment (whether social or physical). It is all of one cloth. It is all corrupted by sin. And God has provided for the redemption of it all. That, by inference, would include the city.

Why should Christ die for the world as well as for the individual? What is the purpose for which the universe faces decadence today and hope of eventual salvation? Paul states it in the pivotal sentence of this section: "The whole creation is eagerly waiting for God to reveal his sons" (v. 19; literally, "waiting for the revelation of the sons of God").

The salvation of the cosmos is not planned by God simply because the cosmos is evil. Its redemption is intended by God because it is the environment in which humanity lives and which has been sinned against by humankind. The material world shares humanity's destiny. "It was cursed for man's sin . . . and is therefore now deformed: impotent and decadent" (Gen. 3:17, 19–22 JB). It longs for its own salvation, as much as humanity yearns for wholeness. Only Christ can set the cosmos free!

Colossians 1:15–20 is one of Paul's most illuminating statements about Christ. He writes,

> [Christ] is the image of the invisible God, the firstborn over all creation. For by him all things were created: things in heaven and on earth, visible and invisible, whether thrones or powers or rulers or authorities; all things were created by him and for him. He is before all things, and in him all things hold together. And he is the head of the body, the church; he is the beginning and the firstborn from among the dead, so that in everything he might have the supremacy. For God was pleased to have all his fullness dwell in him, and through him to reconcile to himself all things, whether things on earth or things in heaven, by making peace through his blood, shed on the cross.

This is a remarkable statement of Jesus as co-Creator. It stresses that Jesus is the physical manifestation of God. He is co-eternal with God ("He is before all things") and, as the second person of the Trinity, shared with the first person in creation ("firstborn over all creation"). He created everything that is in the universe as well as on the earth, everything material, and everything spiritual. He is therefore the creator of thrones, powers, rulers, and authorities—that is, he is the creator of both the demonic/angelic possessors of power and the political, economic, religious, and social systems, structures, and personalities of power.

The assertion that Christ is the creator of the principalities and powers does not mean that he created the Roman state or a Marxist or capitalist state today. To contend this would be to suggest that he is responsible for the state's inequities, injustices, or suppressions. Rather, Christ is the creator of the powers themselves (the demonic/angelic forces behind the systems) and of the underlying need in humanity to structure, systematize, and order its life together. That this capacity to order life can be captured by the needs of people and systems to serve their own purposes and for self-aggrandizement does not invalidate Christ's creation of both the need and ability to order. It only reveals how that innately positive need can be led astray.

All that is created, but especially the demonic/angelic forces behind the systems and the powers of life, has been created in, through, and for Christ. They are created, Paul contends, as an integral part of the universe God has planned. They are empowered by the power of God, from whom the angelic/demonic/systemic/human need to structure and order comes. They are created for only one purpose: "to glorify God and to enjoy him forever"—in other words, to be centered on God and the service of God's creation. Therefore, for the powers to become diverted into lusting after possessions, power, prestige, and parochialism is particularly grievous, for it is a total reversal of that purpose for which they have been created.

Jesus is not only co-creator with God of all the structures and powers of the cosmos. He is also their redeemer. The final portion of this passage from Colossians (1:18–20) deals with Jesus' redemption of the cosmos. Paul points out that Christ, the creator of the created order, was also the first to conquer death in that system, "so that in everything he might have the supremacy"(v. 18). Then Paul makes this unusual statement: "For God was pleased to have all his fullness dwell in him" (v. 19).

This verse is extremely difficult to translate. What it literally says is "because [God] wanted the *plēroma* to dwell in him." *Plēroma* is the substance that fills up a gap or hole, like a patch. It is likely that Paul is trying to express the concept that, through Christ, the entire cosmos is being filled with the creative presence and redemptive power of God.

Paul finishes this remarkable passage with the words, "through him [Christ], to reconcile to himself [God] all things, whether things on earth or things in heaven, by making peace through his blood, shed on the cross" (v. 20).

Through his redemptive work on the cross, Jesus Christ has reconciled the entire cosmos ("whether things on earth or things in heaven") to God. All things are reconciled through him, and they are reconciled for or to him.

Who is reconciled? Everyone. Everything. Not just people, but "thrones . . . powers . . . rulers . . . authorities" ("thrones . . . dominions . . . principalities . . . powers," KJV): the heavenly order (the angelic and demonic forces) and the earthly order (the systems and structures, the material world, all human beings). Everything and everyone.

John 3:16–17 is perhaps too well known for us to be analytical toward it. We recite it without much thought, our minds shaped by its primary use—as the Scripture passage used to introduce an individual to Christ.

In the light of such popularity, it is important to assert that the Greek word John uses which is frequently interpreted individualistically ("God so loved Bob Linthicum that he gave . . .") is not an individualistic word. It is the word *cosmos*—the entire created order. It does not mean the physical earth; the word *oikoumenē* was used for the inhabited world. Nor does it mean people; the word *laos* would be used if referring only to humans.

The word *cosmos* was used in Scripture to refer to the universe, the heavens, and the earth and all its inhabitants (both human and non-human), the scene and systems of human activity. It is an all-encompassing word and means "the totality of existence."

To capture the power and implications of what John was writing in this passage, let me translate it this way:

> For God so loved the cosmos that he gave his one and only Son, that whoever believes in him should not perish but have eternal life. For God did not send his Son into the cosmos to condemn the cosmos, but to save the cosmos through him.

It seems terribly important to me that John chose to use the word *cosmos* in this passage. Perhaps the most precise of all biblical writers in his use of Greek, John would not have used the word if he had not meant cosmos. If he had meant *people,* he would have said so. This passage is not written to deal simply with the redemption of human beings (although it includes them). It is referring to the redemption of the universe, the geophysical world, the social systems and structures of humanity, and the entire human enterprise—in other words, the entire created order. It is the cosmos that God does not want to condemn, but which he wants to save and for which he has provided a way of salvation through his one and only Son.

Second Corinthians 5:17–20 is Paul's great declaration of the reconciling work of God.

> If anyone is in Christ, he is a new creation; the old has gone, the new has come! All this is from God, who reconciled us to himself through Christ and gave us the ministry of reconciliation: that God was

reconciling the world to himself in Christ, not counting men's sins against them. And he has committed to us the message of reconciliation. We are therefore Christ's ambassadors, as though God were making his appeal through us. We implore you on Christ's behalf: Be reconciled to God.

The phrase that leaps out at me from this passage is, "All this is from God." This is where the focus must lie. Both the work of reconciliation and the use of his people as agents of reconciliation are motivated, instituted, and implemented by God. The Lord does the work—sometimes through us, sometimes in spite of us—but it is he who does the salvific work. That is how the world is to be transformed from a world at enmity with God to a world at one with God: through the work of God in Christ.

In verse 19, most translations state, "God was in Christ reconciling the world." The New International Version translates it correctly: "God was reconciling the world to himself in Christ." This wording emphasizes reconciliation (i.e., the work of Christ) rather than the person of Christ; this is more appropriate to the context. The work God did and is doing through Christ is the work of reconciliation. And it is not just individuals or humanity he is reconciling; it is the whole world.

Our task, in this ministry of reconciliation, is not the reconciliation itself; only God can do that, particularly at the systemic and cosmic levels. Our task is to proclaim what God has already done. We are to be Christ's ambassadors in a godless world, the envoys of heaven sharing with the world the Good News that they are already reconciled, that the war is over, and they no longer need to keep "kicking against the goads," but can receive God's salvation through Christ for their own lives.

Revelation 11:15–18 deals with both judgment and grace.

The seventh angel sounded his trumpet, and there were loud voices in heaven, which said:

> "The kingdom of the world has become
> the kingdom of our Lord and of his Christ,
> and he will reign for ever and ever."

And the twenty-four elders, who were seated on their thrones before God, fell on their faces and worshiped God, saying:

> "We give thanks to you, Lord God Almighty,
> the One who is and who was,
> because you have taken your great power
> and have begun to reign.
> The nations were angry;
> and your wrath has come.
> The time has come for judging the dead,
> and for rewarding your servants the prophets

and your saints and those who reverence your name,
     both small and great—
and for destroying those who destroy the earth."

"The kingdom of the world has become the kingdom of our Lord." Note that the Scripture does not say "the kingdoms of the world" (as Handel does in his "Hallelujah Chorus"). There is a profound difference between *kingdoms* and *kingdom.*

To say "kingdoms of this world" is to say that the political entities, various nations, and their rulers, will be transformed or converted into the kingdom of God. But to say "the kingdom of this world" means the current world order. The cosmos—the created order, the earth and its inhabitants, the whole of human activity, the world alienated and at enmity with God, the world in the grip of Satan and his demonic powers—that world will be converted into the kingdom of God! Every knee will bow and every tongue confess Christ as Lord. And those people, systems, and powers that steadfastly refuse to bow the knee will decree their own inevitable fate. Thus, in reality, all knees will bow and tongues confess, whether in praise or in despair. Because the kingdom of this world will, indeed, become the kingdom of our Christ.

"The time has come . . . for destroying those who destroy the earth." The earth (the systems, the cosmos) is not inherently, *ipso facto,* evil. It has the marks of alienation from God because of the alienation of the people on it. The people are destroying the earth, and that is what causes it to be corrupt and decaying. If there is evil on the earth, it is because of the evil of its inhabitants. (The phrase "destroying the earth" takes on a very literal and expanded meaning today, as industrialized humanity pollutes the environment, devours natural resources, levels mountains, destroys rain forests, and allows the ultimate desecration of the earth with the potential of nuclear holocaust). So the time will come "for destroying those who destroy the earth"!

But the kingdom of this world will become the kingdom of his Christ. The transformation will happen. There will be judgment. There will be mourning for a depleted and corrupt world. One corporate entity ("the kingdom of the world") will be transformed into another corporate entity ("the kingdom of the Lord"). And Christ's redemptive work will be finished with the transformation of the entire cosmos!

What insights do these Scripture passages give us about Christ's redemptive work in the city? We can see some common themes moving throughout all of them. All stress that Christ saves more than people. His work of salvation is one of redemption of the individual, of humanity's systems, of the corporate dimensions of human activity, and even of the spiritual powers which infuse and radically influence the systems and the corporate existence (and the individual existence) of humanity. Every structure—the family, the church, the community, the nation, the universe, yes, and the city—falls from grace, sins grievously against its Maker, and yet is so loved by him that he has provided a way to its salvation and transformation through Christ.

John writes, "The reason the Son of God appeared was to destroy the devil's work" (1 John 3:8). The purpose of Christ's coming is to enervate the devil, to eliminate his power, to destroy his effectiveness. If the city is the battleground between God and Satan, this passage reminds us that Christ came to the city to die in order to undo all that Satan has done in the city among its people, systems, and principalities.

THE SALVATION OF THE CITY

Perhaps the most comprehensive statement in Scripture regarding the breadth of salvation—including the salvation of the city—is Romans 7:7–8:4. That passage perhaps throws the most light on what Christ has done for the city.

Why Humans Cannot Make a Good City

What keeps humanity from God? Paul, in this Romans passage, names these alienating powers as sin, death, and the law. Of the three, it is the law that is most critical, because the law exposes sin as sin (Rom. 7:7) and thus reveals our physical death as spiritual death (v. 9). But what is the law?

When Christians hear the word *law* used in Scripture, we automatically assume this is a reference to the Jewish Torah. But I suggest that, for Paul, with his sophisticated theology of the principalities and powers, the law meant far more than the Pentateuch and its accompanying traditions. The law, to Paul, was the religious, cultural, political, and economic array of rules and regulations which ordered all life throughout worldwide Judaism. In other words, to Paul the law is a "system," inevitably infused by the principalities and powers. To read the book of Romans from this understanding is to make this book intensely relevant to the struggles of living as God's people in today's city.

Paul first presents in this passage why human beings cannot make a good city. People simply cannot build a utopia—whether it is an ideal church, a city that works, or a Marxist or capitalist state. Here is Paul's rationale for such apparent lack of faith in humanity:

> Once I was alive apart from law; but when the commandment came, sin sprang to life and I died. I found that the very commandment that was intended to bring life actually brought death. For sin, seizing the opportunity afforded by the commandment, deceived me, and through the commandment put me to death. So then, the law is holy,

and the commandment is holy, righteous and good. Did that which is good, then, become death to me? By no means! But in order that sin might be recognized as sin, it produced death in me through what was good, so that through the commandment sin might become utterly sinful (Rom. 7:9–13).

When there were no laws or systems ordering life, Paul declares, humanity was "alive" in God. When the systems of a city and a nation came into existence, however, sin sprang to life and we died spiritually. He is not saying that before there were systems there was no sin and no spiritual death. He is saying simply that without systems, which by their very presence decree right and wrong, humans had no awareness that what they might be doing would destroy or enhance the ordering of life.

Was the creation of these systems by God the creation of evil, Paul asks? Not at all. It was not that the systems were themselves evil, for humanity was inspired by God to create them for humanity's own good. The systems of a city bring structure and order and direction to life. By their very existence, however, the systems of a city or nation spiritually kill humanity. Here is the reason: the very nature of our sinfulness—our very proclivity toward sinfulness and lawlessness—seizes the opportunity to take advantage of the systems.

There is something in every human that wants to "beat the system." We create systems to bring life and direction to our communities, but our uncontrollable need to turn everything to our advantage corrupts these same systems. We not only observe this phenomenon at work in our city or state. Each of us can readily recall numerous examples of pastors or church leaders who drag down the very institution they once worked tirelessly to build up—simply because they cannot cope with community changes going on near the church or with opposition to their policies. Often such leaders work to protect the "purity" of the church even when such protection destroys its unity and peace.

Thus it is that we end up corrupting the systems we create. These systems, intended to bring life, often bring death instead. That is why humans cannot make a good city—no matter what their ideological persuasion.

Why We Are Our Own Worst Enemy

Paul recognizes that there is something demonic in him—and in everyone—that always wants to beat the system and use it for personal ends. This is true even when one does everything possible to control this all-consuming drive. Paul puts it in the most graphic words.

My own behavior baffles me. For I find myself not doing what I really want to do but doing what I really loathe. Yet surely if I do things that I really don't want to do, I am admitting that I really agree with the Law.

> But it cannot be said that "I" am doing them at all—it must be sin that has made its home in my nature (Rom. 7:15–17 PHILLIPS).

We do not always consciously intend to beat the system, Paul contends. In fact, it is the exact opposite. We create and maintain and obey our city's political, economic, and religious systems—and do so with every good intention. But it is at an unconscious level that we seek, not "the peace and prosperity of the city" (Jer. 29:7), but our own good. We are often not even aware of this drive within us. And, if we are "good" people, the awareness of such drive is the cause of much despair and turmoil within us. It is as if something demonic is at work in us (as indeed it is) as well as at work in our city. Paul writes,

> My conscious mind wholeheartedly endorses the Law, yet I observe an entirely different principle at work in my nature. This is in continual conflict with my conscious attitude, and makes me an unwilling prisoner to the law of sin and death. In my mind I am God's willing servant, but in my own nature I am bound fast to the law of sin and death! (Rom. 7:22–23 PHILLIPS).

It has been put best by the comic strip character Pogo the Possum. He said, "We have met the enemy—and he is us!" The enemy is not simply the system. The enemy is not simply "them"—the maintainers and creators of the systems: the "political oppressors," the "economic privileged," the "controllers of the religious systems." The enemy is "us"—for within each person in the city seeking to be financially secure is the longing to be privileged. Within each person feeling oppressed hides the urge to become the oppressor—despite all the rhetoric to the contrary. Within each person liberated by the saving work of Christ lies the "fundamentalistic" need to turn one's experience into the primary measurement of everyone else's relationship with God—this is the desire to control that which God has given as free gift to the city. We are the enemy. If we do not recognize that reality (but instead divide the city into "good guys" and "bad guys"), we are either avoiding reality or are being dishonest about ourselves.

"We have met the enemy—and he is us!" It is our own deeply ingrained and perfidious nature that will keep on corrupting every system which we create and in which we participate. What hope is there then—for me, for my church, for my city—if even I am the enemy?

Thanks Be to God for Jesus Christ!

Paul answers his own question, "Who will rescue me from this body of death?" with the response, "Thanks be to God—through Jesus Christ our Lord!" (Rom. 7:24–25). Only Jesus can save the city! Only Jesus can release individuals, the systems we create, and all of the created order from the power of sin, death, and the law. How does Christ accomplish this miracle? Paul writes:

> Through Christ Jesus the law of the Spirit of life set me free from the law of sin and death. For what the law was powerless to do in that it was weakened by the sinful nature, God did by sending his own Son in the likeness of sinful man to be a sin offering. And so he condemned sin in sinful man, in order that the righteous requirements of the law might be fully met in us, who do not live according to the sinful nature but according to the Spirit (Rom. 8:2–4).

"The law of the Spirit of life set me free from the law of sin and death." It is beyond our ability to redeem the systems we create, because of our unconscious, uncontrollable need to exploit our systems and the people "serviced" by them. Only God can free us from this "body of death." This he does, not by giving us the ability to overcome our systems, but by providing for us a new system, the "system" of the Spirit of life in Christ Jesus.

The systems of God are able to liberate us from the control of the systems ordering the world. God has done what the systems could not do, because we have thoroughly and pervasively corrupted and demonized all systems. God has already done for us what we cannot do for ourselves, for we cannot reform our systems because we have been "weakened by the sinful nature." God has done this by "sending his own Son in the likeness of sinful man to be a sin offering" (Rom. 8:3).

It is through Jesus Christ, Paul declares, that God has fulfilled the obligations of all the systems. All the demands that our systems make upon us, all the demands that the specter of death and corruptibleness of our own personalities make upon us, have been met and satisfied in Christ. In his death, Christ has met all the conditions of the law, all the conditions of the systems. He faced the worst of death for us; he plumbed the depths of human depravity—both individual and collective depravity. In that condescending act Christ took upon himself all that personal, corporate, and systemic evil could ever do. By taking such evil upon himself, Christ has liberated us—and the city—from evil's complex grasp.

And that is what Jesus has done for the city!

TO JERUSALEM TO SUFFER AND DIE

We began our exploration of the New Testament's understanding of Jesus' saving work for the city by examining together Matthew 16:21. In this passage, Jesus told his disciples that he had to go to Jerusalem where he would suffer, be killed by the systems, "and on the third day be raised to life." That passage acted as the paradigm for our development of a theology of both individual and corporate salvation.

We did not, however, explore the rest of that passage. The

remainder of that Scripture passage is as important as Jesus' announcement that he intended to follow God's call into Jerusalem. Here is how that story ends:

> Peter took [Jesus] aside and began to rebuke him. "Never, Lord!" he said. "This shall never happen to you!"

> Jesus turned and said to Peter, "Get behind me, Satan! You are a stumbling block to me; you do not have in mind the things of God, but the things of men."

> Then Jesus said to his disciples, "If anyone would come after me, he must deny himself and take up his cross and follow me. For whoever wants to save his life will lose it, but whoever loses his life for me will find it. What good will it be for a man if he gains the whole world, yet forfeits his soul? Or what can a man give in exchange for his soul?" (Matt. 16:22–26).

Jesus came to the city to die for the city, its systems, and its people. And Christ asks us to participate in what he has done. We are to take up our cross and follow him into the city—there to be willing to minister, to suffer and, if need be, to lose our lives. His death was not an esoteric exercise occurring at the limits of human understanding. It was a death coming out of great love and intense commitment to the city, its systems, and its people. So it is that the Christ demands of those who would follow him into the city that they have his same level of commitment to the city's afflicted and comfortable and the exploiters and exploited of its systems, its principalities, and powers. He even wants us to look seriously at the pernicious corruption in us all.

For our Lord was not crucified in a gothic cathedral on a golden cross placed upon a marble altar between two silver candlesticks. He was crucified on a rugged cross between two thieves, on the city's garbage heap, at the kind of place where cynics talk smut and thieves curse and soldiers gamble. That is where Christ died. And that is what Christ died about. That is where Christ calls his church to be. And that is what Christ calls his church to be about!

Chapter Six

THE VOCATION
OF THE URBAN CHURCH

As a visiting professor at Eastern College, I was leading a workshop for graduate students in the M.B.A. program that prepares students to commit their lives to small-scale community-based economic development both in the third world and in impoverished urban areas of the United States. After I concluded my presentation, I was surrounded by students who wanted to talk further. Among them was a black student, obviously older than most of the others, waiting quietly on the sidelines.

After the other students had finished visiting, that student introduced himself to me. "I am an African," he told me. "I come from Nigeria, and I have been a pastor in Lagos [a major city in Nigeria] for many years. I came to Eastern two years ago to work on my M.B.A., because I felt if I were truly to minister to the people of Nigeria, I had to do more than preach the Gospel. I had to practice it as well. For me that meant getting into the workplace. So I'm here to get my degree in economic development, and then I plan to go back to Nigeria to help generate small Christian businesses."

This Nigerian pastor continued, "My big question as a pastor always was, 'Is what I am doing really making a difference in the life of my people? Are the activities of our church at all relevant to the struggles of their everyday lives as Christians in a pagan city?' I often wondered if it was. And what you said tonight made a great deal of sense to me. You were showing me for the first time that the church can really make a difference in the city—if it understands what its job is!"

To understand what its job is—this is the essence of each city church's struggle. What is the church's mission and what are its tasks in the city? There is no more important question for Christians to ask and to answer than that, because its answer will shape all that churches will be and do and say in the city.

In chapter 5 we explored the scriptural truth that individual and corporate evil, the evil in the city's political, economic, and religious systems and structures, and even the systems' demonic possession by principalities and powers—the full breadth of evil in the city—are covered by the blood of Jesus Christ. There is no dimension of sin, death, or the law for which God has not provided redemption through Christ.

What this means for the church is simple and profound: it is not the responsibility of the church to save the city! Only Christ can! Each church in the city needs to testify to this truth in all of its pronouncements, programs, activities, and actions. The church is not called to be the victorious, triumphant Savior, for One already is that Savior.

We do not save the city. As Christ's ambassadors and servants, however, we are to undertake a unique ministry and assume a strategic responsibility in the city. In the next four chapters, we will explore that biblical responsibility, as we deal with the mission (vocation) and ministry (roles) of the church in the city. In this chapter, we will examine the mission or vocation of Christ's church in the city.

MIRACLE IN A CITY

Our exploration of the vocation of the church in the city begins with one of the most pivotal miracle stories in the Gospels: the healing of a man born blind (John 9:1–39). It is pivotal because it is the only miracle in the Gospels in which a person is healed of an affliction that had warped his life from birth. A birth-related affliction was, of course, of particular importance to the Jews of Jesus' day. The conventional thinking was that an infirmity from birth was a justly deserved result of inherited sin. As a just punishment, therefore, such an affliction could never be healed. This is why both the people and the religious leaders kept asking the healed man and his parents, "Is this your son . . . the one you say was born blind? How is it that now he can see?" (v. 19). Their incredulity at such a miracle occupies the bulk of the story, simply because such healing was patently preposterous! That the miracle occurs in a city, Jerusalem, is not incidental to the story, as our study will show.

> As he went along, [Jesus] saw a man blind from birth. . . . [Jesus] spit on the ground, made some mud with the saliva, and put it on the man's eyes. "Go," he told him, "wash in the pool of Siloam" (this word means Sent). So the man went and washed, and came home seeing (vv. 1, 6–7).

The healing did not end simply with that poor man's restored sight. This man had been victimized by a lifetime of ostracism, and all around him perceived this as the result of great sin. Even Jesus' disciples were not above asking, "Rabbi, who sinned, this man or his parents, that he was born blind?" (v. 2). Jesus' response was anticipatory of the complete work of salvation God would do in this man. "Neither this man nor his parents sinned," said Jesus, "but this happened so that the work of God might be displayed in his life" (v. 3).

Once Jesus had physically healed the man born blind, Jesus began spiritually healing him, for this man had been marginalized and ostracized by his society. Jesus spiritually healed the man in four stages.

It is worth noting here that Jesus never conditioned his acts of mercy on a person's acceptance of him as Savior and Lord. Jesus did not minister to people only on the basis of spiritual need; he ministered to injured, hurting human beings irrespective of their responses to him. When Jesus did heal a person with a receptive heart, he used his acts of mercy as an opportunity to introduce the person to his saving work. In the man born blind Jesus had found a receptive heart.

Jesus first healed the man's physical blindness (vv. 1–7). We have already examined that healing.

In the second level of healing, the man responded to One whom he perceived as simply a man (vv. 8–12). The man born blind had encountered a man who treated him with compassion rather than shunning him. This man had to change his perception of human beings, because at least one of them had cared enough about him to free him from lifelong enslavement. Questioned by the people,

> He replied, "The man they call Jesus made some mud and put it on my eyes. He told me to go to Siloam and wash. So I went and washed, and then I could see" (v. 11).

The third level of spiritual insight and healing came to the man when he realized that, because his miracle was very astounding, this Jesus had to be more than a mere man. When asked by the Pharisees his opinion of Jesus in view of the fact that Jesus had given him sight, the man replied, "He is a prophet" (v. 17). That was a risky statement for the man to make, given the Pharisees' hatred of Jesus. But what we see here is a man, freed of his physical blindness, becoming increasingly bold as the blindness of spiritual oppression is removed from him as well.

This man's final level of the spiritual liberation occurred when he realized Jesus' true identity. After his intense questioning at the hands of the Pharisees (whom the increasingly bold man directly insulted and even humiliated, vv. 27–34), the man met Jesus a second time. "Do you believe in the Son of Man?" Jesus asked him (v. 35). I can imagine that the man's heart began to beat faster because he knew instinctively the answer to that question. He responded:

> "Who is he, sir?" the man asked. "Tell me so that I may believe in him."

Jesus said, "You have now seen him; in fact, he is the one speaking with you" (vv. 36–37).

Remember that the man had never seen Jesus with his newly healed eyes, because Jesus had sent him alone to the pool of Siloam. Consequently the first time the man ever laid eyes on Jesus was in this, their second encounter!

Then the man said, "Lord, I believe," and he worshiped him (v. 38).

The healing of the man born blind was now complete!

The central motif of this story, however, is not the four-stage healing of the man born blind. The entire meaning and thrust of the story is caught up in the man's response to his accusers: "One thing I do know. I was blind but now I see!' (v. 25).

"I was blind but now I see!" That this is the central point of the entire story is made clear in the story's conclusion, spoken by Jesus:

Jesus said, "For judgment I have come into this world, so that the blind will see and those who see will become blind" (v. 39).

"I was blind but now I see!" was not only the testimony of the man in John 9. This healing is considered one of the most pivotal miracle stories in the Bible precisely because the apostolic church recognized that, in a very profound way, this man's words somehow encapsulated the entire testimony of what God had done for the whole church. Christians preserved this story, not only because it displayed Christ's power and compassion, but because it also testified to what Christ had done for them all. They had all been blind. And, with the touch of the Master's hand, they all could now see!

I suggest that this miracle, occurring in a city, is recounted to enable us to understand the essential vocation of the church in the city. The John 9 story brings order and direction to the work and mission of the church in metropolis. It tells us that we are not only the people of the city who were once blind but now can see, but we are also the people whose task it is to expose to those in the entire city how they are blind, yet how they—if they so choose—can see!

I WAS BLIND

How do we understand the blindness of the city? Perhaps a Scripture of particular instruction to us is not one that uses the imagery of blindness, but rather one that gives us further insight into the church's interaction with the principalities and powers of city or empire. St. Paul wrote in Colossians:

When you were dead in your sins and in the uncircumcision of your sinful nature, God made you alive with Christ. He forgave us all our sins, having canceled the written code, with its regulations, that was against us and that stood opposed to us; he took it away, nailing it to the cross. And having disarmed the powers and authorities, he made a public spectacle of them, triumphing over them by the cross (Col. 2:13–15).

In this passage Paul gives us insight into the unique work of the church in the city (and in the empire) by showing us the unique work of Christ. The work Christ did for us was to free us from the power and influence of the "powers and authorities." He "disarmed" and "made a public spectacle" of them.

The extremely vivid image Paul is using here, of course, is the triumphal procession. When a Roman general conquered an enemy, he would make a triumphal procession into Rome, marching through the city streets not only his conquering army, but his foe's defeated troops, the hostages and booty taken and, finally, the vanquished general or king. It was, for any Roman general, the supreme moment of his career when he was granted the right to a triumphal procession.

Thus Paul is describing Jesus as the conquering general who parades the defeated and vanquished principalities and powers through the city they once sought to rule. They are thus made into a public spectacle, where the citizens of that city heap abuse and scorn upon them.

How did Christ defeat the principalities and powers of city and empire? Paul tells us that Christ "canceled the written code" (i.e., the system or mosaic of religious, cultural, political, and economic rules and regulations which ordered all life throughout both Judaism and the Roman Empire).[1] He forgave us our sins, freed us from the authority of the city's and empire's systems over our lives, and granted us freedom in Christ. By such redemptive action, the power of the systems and their principalities (both earthly and demonic) has been broken, both over the church and over all society.

It is particularly intriguing to note the variety of words used by translators to indicate what Paul believed Christ did to "the written code." In his death, Christ "overrode" the systems; he "did away" and "set aside" the systems; he "canceled" and "took it out of the way."[2] The Greek word means "rubbing out" the record of a debt; it signifies the actual act of canceling the debtor's note. Paul suggests that Christ took that note of indebtedness held against us, nailed it up on the cross for all to see that it had been forgiven, and then erased any record that there had been any indebtedness in the first place.

In other words, Paul is telling the Colossian Christians that the debt which Roman society and the Jewish religion had always told them they owed actually did not exist. It had been erased by Christ! All along, the Christians had been obeying a lie! They went on believing that they were under the authority of Roman law and the Jewish religious system, and they never were because ever since Christ died for them, they were freed from the power of the law. All these commands and teachings were man-made rules and regulations, but everyone, including the Christians, had accepted them as absolute truth.

In the light of the awareness that we have been victims of the lie, Paul asks, what should be our response? Well, "since you died with Christ to the basic principles of this world, why, as though you still belonged to it, do you submit to its rules?" (Col. 2:20). Why do you Christians go on believing the lies and submitting to the authority of those lies? Why don't you start living your lives as those freed from the world's regulations, responsible only to Christ? Why don't you start practicing the truth in your relationships with each other, in the social order, and with all humanity? And why don't you start exposing the lies by which the principalities and powers hold humanity in bondage? We see that Paul wrote the remainder of Colossians 2 and then 3:1–9 to illustrate how Christians, redeemed from the power of the principalities, continue to live under that power because they do not live out freedom in Christ. Chapter 3 shows what life would be like if Christians lived under the authority of heaven rather than under the domination of the Roman and Jewish systems and their principalities.

By exposing the systems and the principalities for what they actually are—the means to control humans and drag them down to hell—Christ has created the means for the liberation of the city and all its people.

This Scripture thus gives us clear insight into a portion of the primary vocation of the church in the city. The mission of the church, first, is to proclaim, "I was blind." It is to confess that both it and all who now call themselves Christians were once seduced by the tempting and intimidating lies of the city and the world. And it is to challenge those outside the church to perceive how both they and the structures they have created to order life have also been seduced by those same controlling lies.

Let's look briefly at how the church faithfully sought to expose the lie of the systems, the principalities, and powers during the church's first three centuries of life.

The lie of first-century Judaism was that by obedience to the Law, people would find life. Those obedient to the Law could not see that their very obedience to it was killing them, because they could not accept how their sinful nature would corrupt the system upon which they would depend for life. So those in the first-century cities of the Roman Empire who depended upon the Jewish Law to bring them life were actually being led into spiritual death by the principalities and powers.

There were significant benefits in following the Law. If there were not, no one would have practiced it. The Law of Jesus' and Paul's times presented to people a fair, understandable, and predictable universe.

Everything about life had been neatly set down in the Law, and thus in a chaotic, damaging world, life for obedient Jews became quite predictable and comfortable. The Law may have been terribly limiting, but limits give people the sense of familiarity and security.

How did the church expose the controlling, dominating lie of the Law? It did it through the theology of the Cross and Resurrection. It is asserted that the Law creates a fair, understandable, and predictable universe, administered by good and fair men. Then how is Christ's death explained? A man deeply loved by the people, considered a prophet by many of them, a man who had done nothing but good, healing the sick, raising the dead, feeding the hungry, bringing hope to the poor—this man was put to death by the very "good and fair" men who administered the Law, doing so through the very dictates of the Law. That which had been created to maintain a fair, understandable, and predictable existence for all had, in the hands of threatened men, become unjust, insane, and manipulative—a tool for doing evil rather than accomplishing good. And the resurrection of Jesus from the dead exposed to all that the Law, created to be just and reasonable, had instead become irredeemably evil, for the Resurrection witnessed to the fact that it was the Law that had put to death him who was indeed the Christ, the way of salvation for the world.

The lie of Rome was that it held ultimate power and authority over all people. Rome convinced the then-known world that it held the power of life and death over all people and all nations. The *Pax Romana* was a peace enforced at the point of a spear. No state could conquer Rome (Hannibal discovered that), and Rome could sweep through any nation that might offer resistance to its marching legions (innumerable triumphal processions witnessed to that). Rebellion, whether of slaves, subjects, or states, was futile. The presence of executing crosses throughout the empire was constant, mute testimony to what awaited anyone who would dare challenge or try to escape from the authority of Rome. Rome was the author of life and death!

There were distinct benefits to living under such tyranny, for Rome acted as a benevolent despot. The world did know peace under the *Pax Romana* for more centuries than it had experienced before or since. The nations and peoples of the Mediterranean world knew more prosperity, a higher standard of living, and a level of urbanization that it would take nearly another two thousand years to equal. Life was enhanced by the ease of transportation over Roman roads and over seas free of pirates, communications which could travel with amazing speed from one end of the empire to the other, and a predictable legal system. Yes, there were many apparent rewards for cooperating with such a "beneficent" system. But cooperation came at the price of freedom, justice, and integrity.

The church exposed the lie of Rome's invincible power. This is the only explanation that truly makes sense out of Rome's episodic persecution of the church for two centuries. Those emperors who scorned and attacked the church rightly perceived that the greatest enemy Rome faced was not the Huns or Visigoths, but the Christians. This was so because the Christians witnessed constantly, in word and deed and life, that it was their God and not Rome who truly possessed the power of life and death.

In the hands of the Christians, the interpretation of the death of Jesus Christ at the hands of Rome constantly proclaimed the limits of Roman power. Christ could face the most brutal death and punishment that any system—human or demonic—could devise yet he could liberate millions through that death. Rome could kill him, but it could not stop him from saving the broken and hurting of the empire.

The Resurrection was perhaps more of an offense to the Romans than to the Jews. The empty cross in every worship site was a constant testimony both to the faithful and to any discerning Roman that Rome's supposed power over life and death was a fiction. The Christians had a far greater power than Rome's capacity to put them to death. Christ had risen from the dead; Christ lives! And because he lives, all those who follow him in death will also live, the Christians believed. Rome does not control life and death. Christ does! In this way it would be the martyrs of Christ, and not the soldiers of Attila, who would break the power of Rome.

And today? What are the lies that the city's systems and their principalities and powers tell us today? What is the task of the church—the people of God who have experienced Christ's crucified and resurrected power—in dealing with these lies at the core of our society?

The city and country will remain nameless. I was visiting some urban ministries partially funded by World Vision and came to one place that was in a particularly destitute part of that city. Nonetheless, this Christian ministry had become a beacon of hope in that slum of thieves, prostitutes, and beggars. It provided schooling for children, job training for adults, health care for all, and the gospel of Christ's saving love.

We had visited the community center, had talked with some of those who participated in this ministry, had walked the streets of that slum, and had gone into some of the shacks in which people lived. The two leaders of this ministry—a man and a woman—escorted me out of a shack and down the street. We turned the corner. There we came upon a scene that chilled my blood. On the street lay a man, writhing in pain. Above him towered five police officers, mercilessly beating him.

Quickly the woman escorting me leaped into action. She stepped between the man and the police, who were momentarily startled into inaction by our sudden appearance. Shielding the man with her body, the woman confronted the police, who in their surprise backed off. Producing a pad and pencil, she began writing down their badge numbers, firmly saying she was going to report them to their commandant. Like whipped schoolchildren, the police quickly got into a squad car and, with tires squealing, drove rapidly away.

As the woman was bending over the man and offering him first aid, the other Christian leader explained to me why they had intervened. The police regularly "shook down" the residents of this neighborhood, illegally demanding of them a monthly payment for police protection. This man had refused to cooperate; he was being beaten in retaliation.

Once the woman was convinced that the man was not seriously hurt, we continued on our way, visiting people in their homes. As we were talking to one community resident, another policeman suddenly appeared at the door and asked us to step out onto the street. We did—and we could not believe what met our eyes!

A troop carrier, a paddy wagon, and a squad car were in the middle of the street. Climbing out of the vehicles were about thirty police officers, all armed with riot gear and assault weapons. They quickly formed a perimeter around the street, isolating us from everyone else. Several of the police went after the man they had been beating. With shoves from butts of rifles, they ushered the leaders of this ministry and the beaten man into the paddy wagon and took them off to jail. The poor people of that neighborhood gathered in little groups, whispering in horror at the fate of those who would protect them.

Two hours later, a young boy came running down the street, excitement and joy on his face. "They are coming back!" he cried. "The Christians are coming back!" Suddenly, there they were—the leaders of that Christian ministry, the man who had been beaten by the police, the woman who had defended him with her own body. They were walking toward us with dignity and confidence.

We soon heard from them their story. When they arrived at the police station, that young woman insisted on going directly to the commandant. There she pressed charges against her accusers and ended up winning his support against those who had beaten that man.

Now that slum community came alive with celebration. For both he who had been a victim and they who had been his Christian defenders had been arrested and were now freed again; they had met the enemy and they had won!

As I reflected on this event later, I realized I had witnessed an extraordinary display of the vocation of the church. The church is at work not just in the Jerusalem of Jesus' ministry or the Rome of Paul's time, but in a city and country of the third world today.

In that city, the church was truly being the church. For by its actions, it was exposing the lie of a system's naked use of power. It was revealing that such power trembles even before one determined Christian woman!

Is exposing the lie a legitimate mission of the church in today's city? Three biblical images help us to answer that question.

The first image is found in John 11:43–44. Jesus' close friend, Lazarus, has just died. Jesus comes to Lazarus' home in the town of Bethany, where his sisters, Mary and Martha, both assail Jesus with the same accusation: "Lord, . . . if you had been here, my brother would not have died" (vv. 21, 32). Jesus went weeping to the tomb of his friend. There at the tomb, Jesus stood surrounded by the friends of Lazarus.

> Jesus called in a loud voice, "Lazarus, come out!" The dead man came out, his hands and feet wrapped with strips of linen, and a cloth around his face. Jesus said to them, "Take off the grave clothes and let him go" (vv. 43–44).

The second image is found in 2 Kings 6:15–17. The Arameans are at war with the Israelites. The king of Aram, realizing that it is Elisha the prophet and not the king of Israel who is his real enemy, surrounds the prophet's home city of Dothan. But the king of Israel has provided no troops to defend the city. It seems as if it is only Elisha, his servant, and the townspeople against the mighty army of Aram. When Elisha's servant sees the armed host of Aram, he trembles with fear.

> "What shall we do?" the servant asked.
>
> "Don't be afraid," the prophet answered. "Those who are with us are more than those who are with them."
>
> And Elisha prayed, "O LORD, open his eyes so he may see." Then the LORD opened the servant's eyes, and he looked and saw the hills full of horses and chariots of fire all around Elisha.

The third image is found in Revelation 21. The Christians in the Roman Empire are under siege. The persecution they are suffering is the worst the church has ever had to face. They do not know if they can continue to withstand the might of Rome. Then John writes a book about a world at warfare with itself. And from the rubble and fire and death of a destroyed capital city as powerful as Rome, he writes:

> I saw the Holy City, the new Jerusalem, coming down out of heaven from God, prepared as a bride beautifully dressed for her husband. And I heard a loud voice from the throne saying, "Now the dwelling of God is with men, and he will live with them. They will be his people, and God himself will be with them and be their God. He will wipe every tear from their eyes. There will be no more death or mourning or crying or pain, for the old order of things has passed away" (vv. 2–4).

What do these three images tell us about the present vocation of the church in the city? In the story of Lazarus' resurrection, the people of God must share in the miracle, for they must "take off the grave clothes and let him go [free]." In Elisha's prayer, God reveals to the prophet's servant that what seems real is only apparent, for in reality the ostensibly vulnerable people of the city of Dothan are being well protected by God.

In the face of Roman persecution, the Christians are reminded that it is God and not Satan who will have the last word, as God creates a city in which all people will live face to face with the Lord.

In other words, each of these stories is designed to change the reader's perspective of reality! Each one reminds us that things are seldom what they seem, even in the city! Each story tells us that God is a miracle producer and that we play a primary role in each miracle.

The basic premise of this urban biblical theology is that the city is a primary battleground between God and Satan, between the Lord of Light and the Prince of Darkness. Now, if you were the Prince of Darkness and had gained control of the systems and structures of your city through the principalities, how would you exert your primary influence in that city?

You would do it by getting the people to believe in a lie. You know God can raise people from the dead and that he will raise all of us at the last day. You would convince the people, however, that life ends at a tomb, with a helpless Christ assailed by despairing mourners crying, "Lord, if you had been here, my brother would not have died." You would convince people that they could not participate in a resurrection and that they can do nothing to unbind and set free the poor, the imprisoned, and the defeated.

If you were Satan, you would know that the city is surrounded by angelic hosts and chariots of fire, protecting its people from you and your principalities and powers. But you would convince them that they are helpless, that you and the city's systems have all the power, and that all the people can do is tremble with fear and cry out, "What shall we do?"

If you were Satan, you would know that city life will not end with suffering and persecution and an economy and politics dominated by the Romans of this world. But you would keep from the people's eyes the vision of a city "coming down out of heaven from God, prepared as a bride beautifully dressed for her husband." Instead, you would deceive the people into thinking that their only alternative is to cooperate with a harlot Babylon—or be beaten and arrested and killed!

Satan is the master of the lie. The systems and structures of the city he seeks to possess have also mastered the lie. The primary vocation of the church in the city is both to expose such lies and to proclaim the truth of God's great intentions for the city and all its inhabitants. By exposing the lie we become people who can say of ourselves, "Once we were blind (and bought into the 'world's' perception of reality). And because we can now see how we were seduced by the master of the lie and his principalities which dominate the city's political, economic, and religious systems, we can become the people who can enable both others and our society to perceive how they have been blinded as well." "I was blind. . . ."

BUT NOW I SEE

Ephesians 3:8–12 helps us to formulate the second portion of the vocation of the church—our response, in the light of our confession of former blindness and seduction. This passage focuses on perceiving what it is we offer to the city to replace the lies with which people lived their former lives. What is it that they see, now that they can see? It is written:

> Although I [Paul] am less than the least of all God's people, this grace was given me: to preach to the Gentiles the unsearchable riches of Christ, and to make plain to everyone the administration of this mystery, which for ages past was kept hidden in God, who created all things (vv. 8–9).

Paul's unique call was "to preach to the Gentiles." But what is he to share with them? He is to proclaim "the unsearchable riches of Christ," the "mystery which for ages past was kept hidden in God." It is not a simple Christianity which Paul feels called to share with Gentiles—a faith reduced to "the four things God wants you to know." He is to share "the unsearchable riches," the full dimensions of the gospel of the Cross and the Resurrection. But these riches are not apparent. The riches are a "treasure hidden in a field" (Matt. 13:44), a "pearl of great price" (Matt. 13:45–46), a "lost coin" so precious that the one who has lost it sweeps the entire house searching for it (Luke 15:8–10). What is the mystery of God's saving work, hidden from humanity for millennia and only now revealed through Jesus Christ? Paul writes:

> [God's] intent was that now, through the church, the manifold wisdom of God should be made known to the rulers and authorities in the heavenly realms, according to his eternal purpose which he accomplished in Christ Jesus our Lord. In him and through faith in him we may approach God with freedom and confidence (Eph. 3:10–12).

The "mystery" is God's "eternal purpose which he accomplished in Christ Jesus our Lord." It is, consequently, the full work of salvation Christ has done for all of human society, in all its breadth and complexity. It is not just conversion, and it is not simply for individuals—for even "rulers and authorities in the heavenly realms" need to know this "manifold wisdom."

This Scripture passage is not simply a statement on salvation, however. It is also a statement of mission. "His intent," Paul wrote, "was that now, *through the church*, the manifold wisdom of God should be made known." It is the calling of the church in the city to witness to the manifold work God has done for the city, its people, systems, and powers, through Christ. That witness is a call to the city to recognize its spiritual depth and to allow those depths to be transformed by Christ.

Perhaps we can see more clearly what Paul is proposing as the primary mission of the church by considering a story about two city prophets and their kings.

Jeremiah and Zedekiah. It is the last days of Judah. The nation, under the hegemony of the Babylonian Empire, has revolted against the king of Babylon. The Babylonian army has left its homeland and is on a forced march to Judah to deal with the rebellious nobility. King Zedekiah, trembling at what his actions have produced, seeks counsel from the prophet Jeremiah. The news he hears from Jeremiah is not what he was hoping to hear:

> Then Jeremiah said to Zedekiah, "This is what the LORD God Almighty, the God of Israel, says: 'If you surrender to the officers of the king of Babylon, your life will be spared and this city will not be burned down; you and your family will live. But if you will not surrender to the officers of the king of Babylon, this city will be handed over to the Babylonians and they will burn it down; you yourself will not escape from their hands.' "
>
> King Zedekiah said to Jeremiah, "I am afraid of the Jews who have gone over to the Babylonians, for the Babylonians may hand me over to them and they will mistreat me."
>
> "They will not hand you over," Jeremiah replied. "Obey the LORD by doing what I tell you. Then it will go well with you, and your life will be spared. But if you refuse to surrender, this is what the LORD has revealed to me: . . . All your wives and children will be brought out to the Babylonians. You yourself will not escape from their hands but will be captured by the king of Babylon; and this city will be burned down" (Jer. 38:17–21, 23).

Zedekiah, in this account, is both the principality (symbol of the state) and the personification of Judah's systems. He is also a very frightened king. Jeremiah the prophet is making what appears to be a treasonable recommendation—that Zedekiah surrender to the king of Babylon. The only authority that Jeremiah has for making this demand is that he insists he speaks for the Lord (and the fact that his prophecies in the past have come true give credence to this claim).

Of course, the demand Jeremiah is laying on Zedekiah is extreme. For the king to concur with this prophecy would be for him also to commit treason. His expressed fear of his advisers (see vv. 19, 24–27) is an indication how opposed the court is to any consideration of surrender. To obey this word from the Lord, the king would have to give up all his prerogatives and powers as king and throw himself on the mercy of God for deliverance.

Will Zedekiah follow Jeremiah's advice? His fear of his court and his sense of fatalistic commitment to the path he and his advisers have determined tell us that he will not. He refuses to look at the crisis facing him from any other perspective than that of his own and his advisers' perspectives. He will not follow the command of God, even if it means his salvation. Therefore Zedekiah's doom—and Jerusalem's—is assured.

Isaiah and Hezekiah. Over one hundred years earlier, another king of Judah faced a similar problem. Sennacherib, king of the Assyrians, had invaded the land of the Israelites and was approaching the gates of Jerusalem. All that was left under King Hezekiah's control was the city itself. And the massive Assyrian army had laid siege to that city.

Like Zedekiah after him, Hezekiah sought the advice of a prophet of God. Isaiah said to Hezekiah,

> "This is what the LORD says: Do not be afraid of what you have heard— those words with which the underlings of the king of Assyria have blasphemed me. Listen! I am going to put a spirit in him so that when he hears a certain report, he will return to his own country, and then I will have him cut down with the sword" (Isa. 37:6–7).

Immediately after Hezekiah received this word from God, he received another word: the demand from Assyria for Judah's unconditional surrender. The Scripture then reports:

> Hezekiah received the letter from the messengers and read it. Then he went up to the temple of the LORD and spread it out before the LORD. And Hezekiah prayed to the LORD: "O LORD Almighty, God of Israel, enthroned between the cherubim, you alone are God over all the kingdoms of the earth. You have made heaven and earth. Give ear, O LORD, and hear; open your eyes, O LORD, and see; listen to all the words Sennacherib has sent to insult the living God. . . . Now, O LORD our God, deliver us from his hand, so that all kingdoms on earth may know that you alone, O LORD, are God" (Isa. 37:14–17, 20).

This was a profoundly different response to a very comparable situation. Although the predicted results for Hezekiah would suggest that he did not have as much at stake as did Zedekiah (deliverance for Hezekiah; domination for Zedekiah), I would contend that was not the case. God actually promised deliverance for both men, because if Zedekiah obeyed God's command he, his family, and his nation would be delivered safely into Babylonian exile with no loss of life.

Both men had the same issue at stake: who would rule the nation— the king or God? Hezekiah was willing to trust God, and place both his fate and the fate of Jerusalem in God's hand, even if all the evidence was that Sennacherib's mighty army would crush the little nation. Zedekiah was unwilling to trust God, and even until the final moment of Jerusalem's destruction, continued to grasp onto what little power he had left.

In reality, both prophets were looking for the same thing from the principality of their city. Both of them were seeking to transform the inner spirituality of their king, the court, and, consequently, the city and nation.

They wanted both kings to see life from a perspective other than their previous commitment to practical politics and self-service. Hezekiah, once "blind," had eyes that could see, and his kingdom was given back to him. Zedekiah would not allow himself to see, and his kingdom was torn from him. He simply could not depend on God for his deliverance.

"I was blind, but now I see." The vocation of the church in the city is to seek that city's spiritual transformation. That transformation must include (for it to be transformation) the corporate systems and structures and their principalities and powers. That can occur only as the church exposes the lies on which the city is built. It will occur only as the church so "lives and moves and has its being" in the city that it exhibits to all people and systems of the city a new creation: the kingdom of God.

If the vocation of the church in the city is to be the people who proclaim, "I was blind, but now I see," how does that influence the way the church deals with each segment of the public with which it comes in contact? For example, what becomes the responsibility of the church toward the leaders of the city's structures and systems? The church bears responsibility to uncover the truth about the ways those structures and their leaders operate and serve their own interests—and to call them to both accountability and repentance. It is to hold up to this leadership a new heaven and a new earth so that this leadership may see a different vision of the city: the city as it could be under the lordship of Christ (see chapters 4 and 12).

What becomes the responsibility of the church toward the people who are seduced and deceived, but who benefit from the city's self-serving structures and systems? The church bears the uncomfortable responsibility of afflicting the comfortable, but to afflict with great compassion and love. It must expose to these people the lie of their service to the city's systems; these people must see that they benefit only at the poor's expense. In addition, as the church tells the truth in love, it must also present the hope of the Gospel: that we can all be new in Christ. That newness must include ways these people can act responsibly so as to address the full spectrum of human pain and poverty in that city that the city begins to become a new creation.

What becomes the responsibility of the church toward the city's exploited, powerless, and hurting, as well as the innocent who have been taken advantage of by all who have benefited from their city's systems? The church may both rejoice in comforting those who are being afflicted and bear the uncomfortable task of exposing the truth that the victims also victimize. The church is both to present to the poor God's great love and acceptance of them and to call them to become all that God has given them the potential to be. God wants poor people to discover their unique call in Christ as they seek to minister to the city; ministering to the city includes ministering to those who have taken advantage of the poor.

What becomes the church's responsibility toward the city's principalities and powers? The task is to expose the principalities and powers and their infiltration of the warp and woof of the city's political, economic, and religious life. And it is to claim dominion over them by naming the Name throughout the whole life of the city.

What becomes the responsibility of the church to itself? The advice of Paul to the Christians in Galatia is also appropriate advice to the whole church as it considers its soul within the context of its ministry to its city's systems, to the principalities, and to the seduced and exploited:

> Brothers, if someone is caught in a sin, you who are spiritual should restore him gently. But watch yourself, or you also may be tempted. Carry each other's burdens, and in this way you will fulfill the law of Christ. . . . Let us not become weary in doing good, for at the proper time we will reap a harvest if we do not give up. Therefore, as we have opportunity, let us do good to all people, especially to those who belong to the family of believers (Gal. 6:1–2, 9–10).

We began this section by examining Paul's formulation of the vocation of the church as he presented it in Ephesians 3:8–12. He saw his responsibility (and therefore, by extension, the responsibility of the church) as "to make plain to everyone the administration of this mystery [of the unsearchable riches of Jesus Christ], which for ages past was kept hidden in God" (v. 9). "But what is this mystery?" we asked. "And how is that mystery to be shared with the world?"

The mystery is that "God so loved [the city] that he gave his one and only Son." Christ's death and resurrection—and all that was accomplished through it—is sufficient to redeem the city. Redeeming the city means not only redeeming the people, but also its systems, principalities, and powers. God's intent, Paul wrote, "was that now, through the church, the manifold wisdom of God should be made known to the rulers and authorities in the heavenly realms, according to his eternal purpose which he accomplished in Christ Jesus our Lord" (vv. 10–11). God sends his church to the city, in all its complexity, as the vehicle to make known the mystery of what he has done for it.

What, then, is the vocation of Christ's church in the city? I would suggest that in its life, work, and witness, the church's vocation is to be *the people who were blind but now see*, and who thus invite the blind city to see. The primary responsibility of the church is to enable the systems and structures and the people to see their city from an entirely new perspective, and then help them to act according to that new perspective. People and systems, no longer blinded, can see through the lies Satan tells them about the city. They are then able to see themselves as children of God and their city as the city of God; they are then able to act consistently on what they see.

In a word, the vocation of the church in the city is to be the dreamer and the advocate for a city given over to God. The church is to be the people of the vision—those who can see through Satan's lies to a city as God would have it. The church is to be the people of action—those who call the city's structures and systems to accountability, who defend those oppressed and exploited by those systems, and who minister to those who are deceived but who benefit from that city's principalities.

We Christians cannot bring into being such a city, but we can work, pray, proclaim, and be on the side of the angels! To do so means that we must commit ourselves to work toward the transformation of our city's inner spirituality. That transformation happens only through the Gospel. This is the vocation or mission of the church of Jesus Christ in each city of the world.

Earlier in this chapter I spoke of the way Christians in a third world urban slum came to the defense of a poor man being beaten by the police. When that poor man arrived at the jail, he pled with the Christians arrested with him, "Do not leave me here. They will beat me until I am almost dead. You are my only hope!"

For the poor and oppressed of the city, for the city's rich and middle class, for the systems and structures which are lusted over by Satan, Christ—and Christ's church—is the only hope. Do not leave them there in their sins until they are almost dead. Touch their eyes with Christ's love so that the once-blind can now see. Let them see a vision of their city where God will make his home, where they shall be his people and he will be their God, and all tears shall be wiped away. Call them to join in Christ's triumphal procession which claims victory over their city's principalities and powers. Let Christ raise them from their deadly tomb and let the church unbind them and let them go free. Hold out for them the assurance that when they spread out before the throne of grace that which is overwhelming and which they cannot face, God will hear their prayer and will rescue them from almost certain conquest. And remind them that they need have no fear, for protecting them from the Evil One are the angelic hosts and their chariots of fire.

Church of Jesus Christ, be for your city the church you have been called by God to be!

Chapter Seven

THE PRESENCE AND PRAYER
OF THE CHURCH IN THE CITY

In this and the next two chapters we will explore biblical insights into the work in the city to which God calls the church. We will discover that the Scriptures are startlingly specific concerning the tasks God expects his people to undertake as the primary means for living out the vocation to which he has called us. The paradigm for this study will be one of the most profound ecclesiastical statements in Scripture: Jeremiah 29:1–13.

THE URBAN CHRISTIAN: EXILED OR CALLED?

My daughter and her family live near the U.S. city of Detroit. Recently when I was there to visit, I noticed a rather intriguing plaque hanging on the wall of their home. It was a photograph with golden lettering on it. The photograph was any camera buff's dream—pine trees near the foreground framing the picture, a crystal-clear lake mid-scene, and in the background a majestic snow-capped mountain against a cloudless sky. Across that plaque was inscribed the promise from Scripture:

"I know the plans I have for you," declares the Lord, "plans to prosper you and not to harm you, plans to give you hope and a future."

It is a magnificent biblical promise that is engraved on the photograph of that plaque—in fact, one of my favorite promises of Scripture. But that promise was not made among pine trees and crystal-clear lakes and snow-capped mountains. Instead, this was a promise made in a city and given, conditionally, to an urban people of God.

This great promise was contained originally in a letter written by Jeremiah the prophet to the Israelites who had been taken as captives to the city of Babylon at the start of the Exile. All that remained of once-proud Israel—the little country of Judah—had been invaded twice by

Nebuchadnezzar, the king of the Babylonian Empire. As we saw earlier, Jeremiah had warned the king of Judah, Zedekiah, that the little nation would be destroyed and the king greatly punished if he did not surrender. The king before Zedekiah, Jehoiachin, had also been warned he would taste the fury of the Babylonians.

Zedekiah refused to heed Jeremiah's advice—and he paid dearly for this decision. Babylonia viciously conquered the nation, razed the city of Jerusalem, burned the temple to the ground, and even spread salt on the remains so that nothing would ever grow there again. True to Jeremiah's prophecy, the Babylonians killed Zedekiah's sons before his eyes, then gouged out his eyes, bound him with bronze shackles, and dragged him as a slave to their capital city of Babylon.

But it was not only the king whom the Babylonians took captive to their city. It was the policy of Babylonia to export to their country all the people of a conquered nation who could possibly provide leadership to that nation. Only peasants would be left behind to tend the fields and raise the livestock for Babylonia's benefit. In both invasions of Judah by the Babylonians, the best of Israel's leadership was taken into captivity. Thus Jeremiah tells us that the surviving elders, the priests, the prophets, the court officials, and even the craftsmen and artisans were all taken as slaves to the city of Babylon. Although Jeremiah's letter was written initially to the captives of the first deportation—the one under Jehoiachin—it applied equally to the captives who were ordered on a forced march to the Babylonians' capital city in the second deportation.

There in that heathen city the Israelite captives began to despair. They grieved for their land, began to lose all hope, and became depressed. It was to those despairing, grieving captives that Jeremiah's letter came. The contents of that letter to those enslaved Israelites is a message that every urban Christian needs to hear.

> This is what the LORD Almighty, the God of Israel, says to all those I carried into exile from Jerusalem to Babylon: "Build houses and settle down; plant gardens and eat what they produce. Marry and have sons and daughters; find wives for your sons and give your daughters in marriage, so that they too may have sons and daughters. Increase in number there; do not decrease. Also, seek the peace and prosperity of the city to which I have carried you into exile. Pray to the LORD for it, because if it prospers, you too will prosper."

> This is what the LORD says: "When seventy years are completed for Babylon, I will come to you and fulfill my gracious promise to bring you back to this place. For I know the plans I have for you," declares the LORD, "plans to prosper you and not to harm you, plans to give you hope and a future. Then you will call upon me and come and pray to me, and I will listen to you. You will seek me and find me when you seek me with all your heart. I will be found by you," declares the LORD,

"and will bring you back from captivity. I will gather you from all the nations and places where I have banished you," declares the LORD, "and will bring you back to the place from which I carried you into exile" (Jer. 29:4–7, 10–14).[1]

The promise is an urban promise. And it is a conditional promise. It is a promise made to residents of one city—Jerusalem—who have been taken as political hostages and captives to another city—Babylon. It is a promise of their sons' and daughters' eventual return, but not theirs (for in seventy years, all the original adult hostages would be dead). But it is a promise based on their faithful fulfillment of its condition.

God promises to work for the good of the exiled Israelites if "you will call upon me and come and pray to me. . . . You will seek me and find me when you seek me with all your heart" (Jer. 29:12–13). His blessings on them in captivity and their consequent return to the Promised Land are conditional, for these are based on their receptive response to God. But how are they to seek after God? Where will they find the Lord?

They will find God in the city—not in the city of Jerusalem, but in the enemy city, the evil city, the heathen city—Babylon! God will bless the Israelite exiles if they seek after the peace and prosperity of Babylon!

The pivotal passage in Jeremiah's letter is that famed Scripture we discussed earlier in this book. It is the "John 3:16" of urban Christians:

Seek the peace and prosperity of the city to which I have carried you into exile. Pray to the LORD for it, because if it prospers, you too will prosper (Jer. 29:7).

The passage is translated slightly differently in other English versions of the Bible. For example:

Seek the welfare of the city where I have sent you into exile, and pray to the LORD on its behalf, for in its welfare you will find your welfare (RSV).

Work for the peace and prosperity of Babylon. Pray for her, for if Babylon has peace, so will you (LB).

Were the Hebrews "exiled" or "sent" to Babylon? The Hebrew word actually contains both meanings. It would be translated most accurately with the awkward phrase, "I have caused you to be carried away captive." The word means "exile"—that is, "forced removal from one's country." But it also suggests that what happened to the Israelites was not simply circumstance; they were "sent" into exile by God.

"You have been *exiled* to this city," God is in essence saying to the Israelites in Jeremiah's letter. You people of the covenant are in the city of Babylon because you were brought there by force. Your nation was conquered, and you were dragged to that wicked city by your Babylonian captors. That is the *circumstance* which brought you to this city.

"You have been *sent* by God to this city," Jeremiah is also suggesting in his letter. You are not in Babylon simply because of the exigencies of war or the particularly repressive policies of the Babylonian Empire aimed at emasculating a conquered nation. It is that God, in the Lord's infinite wisdom, needs you in this city. God needs the presence of his people in this city—and the reason for the same will become clear later on. You Israelites are in Babylon because God wants you there. The repressive policies of the Babylonians were the tool God used to get you there! You are sent by God into the city—that is his *design!*

I suggest that this is a message, not only to Jews exiled to Babylon, but to all urban people of God. Why are you in the city in which you live? You may have been born there. You may have decided to move there. You may be in that city because you took a job there or have built a career there. You may be in that city because your spouse or a loved one is there. You may have come to that city to be educated or to retire there. But none of those reasons are why you actually live in that city. Those are simply the *circumstances* God has used to bring you there.

Why are you in the city in which you find yourself? You are there, Jeremiah suggests, for one reason and one reason alone. You are in your city because God has *called* you there. You are in your city by God's design, by God's will. Whether God's plans for you in that city turn out to be plans for your peace and not for your disaster depend upon whether you can see yourself as being called by God into your city, and then whether you can seek to live faithfully according to that call.

One of the greatest urban preachers of all time was the late D. L. Moody, the creator of the modern evangelistic crusade. Over one hundred years ago, Moody centered his twenty-year evangelistic ministry in Chicago and London. His impact on both cities has been greatly underrated. Untold numbers of the citizens of those two great cities professed Jesus Christ as Savior and Lord for the first time. In addition, under Moody's moral leadership, the problems of poverty, of unemployment, of inadequate education of the lower classes, of the social sins of prostitution and alcoholism, and of distress of those people whose lives had been broken by such sin were profoundly addressed.

A few years ago some letters of Moody's were discovered among the effects of a close friend. Among them were found these words that Moody had written to this friend:

> The city is no place for me. If it was not for the work I am called to do, I would never show my head in this city or any other again.[2]

I regret that Moody never learned to enjoy the city, because the city —any city—is a rich and stimulating community to experience and to know and love. God loves the city—and so can we!

What is remarkable to me, however, is what this statement reveals about Moody's motivation. He said, "The city is no place for me," yet he was in the city. Why? Because he felt called to it. He was in Chicago by God's will. He was in London by God's design. It was God's purpose that Moody do his great work in the city. And Moody was not disobedient to that heavenly vision!

"Seek the peace and prosperity of the city to which I have carried you into exile," says the Lord. Christians in the city have a destiny and purpose to be there, because they are there by God's design and will.

Where, then, do we seek God? In the city—where God has called us. That is where we will find God. But how do we live into God's urban call to us? How does God expect God's people to work for the peace and prosperity of their city?

PRAYING FOR THE CITY

Pray to the LORD for [the city], because if it prospers, you too will prosper (Jer. 29:7).

When the psalmist joins Jeremiah in urging God's people to pray for the city, his instructions are to "pray for the peace of Jerusalem" (Ps. 122:6). This is the biblical writers' essential call to God's people for urban prayer—to pray for the peace or shalom of the city. The Hebrew *shalom* means contentment, fulfillment, unity with one another, accord, prosperity, and a genuine commitment to each other's good (see chapter 4 for a discussion of the Hebrew concept of *shalom*). But what does it mean to pray for a city's peace?

When we Christians pray for a city, we tend to pray for it in one of two ways. Either we pray that the city will be reached by the Gospel and that many people will be redeemed, or we pray for the well-being of the Christian enterprise in that city (that is, praying for ourselves, our families, our own church, and the body of Christ in that city). Scripture calls us, however, to much more comprehensive prayer than for the success of the Christian enterprise in that city. Let's look at some biblical insights on praying for the city.

Psalm 122 provides the essential model for urban prayer.

> Pray for peace in Jerusalem:
>   "Prosperity to your houses!
>   Peace inside your city walls!
>   Prosperity to your palaces!"
> Since all are my brothers and friends,
>   I say, "Peace be with you!"
> Since Yahweh our God lives here,
>   I pray for your happiness (vv. 6–9 JB)

Pray for the City's Economic Health

First, the psalmist calls us to pray for the economic health of the city: "Prosperity to your houses!" Here is a cry for the city to be a city of economic well-being, not simply for the wealthy but for all the city's inhabitants. No one in the prosperous city is to be poor, rejected, marginalized, or cast off by society. God wants our prayers to be prayers for the economic well-being of the city and for all its citizens.

Such concern is given voice by Jeremiah:

"This is what the LORD says: 'You [people] say about this place, "It is a desolate waste, without men or animals." Yet in the towns of Judah and the streets of Jerusalem that are deserted, inhabited by neither man nor animals, there will be heard once more the sounds of joy and gladness, the voices of bride and bridegroom, and the voices of those who bring thank offerings to the house of the LORD, saying,

"Give thanks to the LORD Almighty,
for the LORD is good;
his love endures forever."

For I will restore the fortunes of the land as they were before,' says the LORD." . . .

"Then this city will bring me renown, joy, praise and honor before all nations on earth that hear of all the good things I do for it; and they will be in awe and will tremble at the abundant prosperity and peace I provide for it" (Jer. 33:10–11, 9).

God will restore the fortunes of the desolate city, for he is concerned about the economics of the city. God is concerned about urban economics precisely because it is wealth that either liberates or oppresses the city. A city can be a wise steward of its wealth, equitably distributing its resources, eliminating its poverty and building for the "common wealth" of that city. Or its wealth can be used to build great monetary empires for a few of the most acquisitive, grasping individuals and organizations, while exploiting the poor for every last farthing. Jesus taught that money has both a destructive dark side to it (Luke 18:18–30) and also a bright side which can lead to profound liberation for individuals and their society (Luke 19:1–10).

It is precisely because money is so important to the building of a godly city that God commands us to pray for the way our city uses its wealth. God is concerned about the economic health for all the citizens of the city, and so should we be concerned!

Pray for the Safety of the City

Pray for "peace inside your city walls!" (Ps. 122:7 JB). The psalmist further instructs us to pray for the safety of the whole city, for both its internal fabric of common life and its external life. If one is to pray comprehensively for the safety of a city, that means praying in two distinct ways. One way is how conservatives would most advise us to pray; the other is the way liberals would want us to pray. Perhaps both of them are right!

We should pray for the safety of a city's citizens: safety from conflict, from violence, and from crime against individuals and property. The very nature of shalom is one of "every man [sitting] under his own vine and under his own fig tree, and no one will make them afraid" (Mic. 4:4). If the crime of a city is not being reduced and is not kept under strict control, then no citizen feels safe. When the citizenry of a city lives in fear, then that city is in the midst of psychological collapse.

There is another dimension of prayer for a city's safety: prayer for those who commit its crimes. Scripture repeatedly calls upon God's people to pray for those in prison and to become their advocates. "Remember those in prison as if you were their fellow prisoners," the author of Hebrews advises the church, "and those who are mistreated as if you yourselves were suffering" (Heb. 13:3).

It is easy for humans, particularly the frightened and intimidated, to become vindictive. There is no place for that in the Christian community! Therefore we are to pray for those in prison, both for their salvation and for their rehabilitation. We are to pray for the police, that they will flee both corruption and unjust practices. We are to pray for the judicial system, that it will be uncompromisingly just and fair to all its citizens rather than showing favoritism toward those accused of "white-collar" crime or those who hold significant political or economic power.

We are to pray for our city's safety.

Pray for the Political Order

Pray for "prosperity to your palaces" (Ps. 122:7 JB). If there is any focus for prayer stressed in Scripture, it is prayer for the government. Thus Paul advises Timothy, "I urge, then, first of all, that requests, prayers, intercession and thanksgiving be made for everyone—for kings and all those in authority, that we may live peaceful and quiet lives in all godliness and holiness" (1 Tim. 2:1–2).

The prayer for "prosperity to your palaces" is not simply a prayer for the financial and political well-being of those who lead government. It is, in reality, prayer that the king might act worthy of kingship.

The model for our political prayers is given to us in Psalm 72:

> Endow the king with your justice, O God,
>   the royal son with your righteousness.
> He will judge your people in righteousness,
>   your afflicted ones with justice.
> The mountains will bring prosperity to the people,
>   the hills the fruit of righteousness.
> [The king] will defend the afflicted among the people
>   and save the children of the needy;
>   he will crush the oppressor. . . .
> For he will deliver the needy who cry out,
>   the afflicted who have no one to help.
> He will take pity on the weak and the needy
>   and save the needy from death.
> He will rescue them from oppression and violence,
>   for precious is their blood in his sight (vv. 1–4, 12–14).

God's people are to pray for a reformation of the political process. We are to pray for our political leaders: not that they be successful, but that they be just; not that they build power for themselves, but that they empower the commonwealth. We are to pray that our city's politicians "defend the afflicted among the people and save the children of the needy . . . [and] crush the oppressor" (that could include the economic as well as the military oppressor).

The mark of an authentic political leader, the psalmist tells us, is that his or her primary concern will be to "deliver the needy who cry out, the afflicted who have no one to help . . . take pity on the weak . . . and save the needy from death." Rather than accruing power and prestige personally or for the political party, or consorting with the economic powers of the city, the governmental leader is to be compassionately concerned for the city's hurting, marginalized, poor, and powerless. "Precious is their blood in his sight."

God's people are to pray so that they may gain political leaders like this. It is for the transformation (conversion) of politicians into such statesmen that we are to pray. It is for the reformation of the political process of the city, so that it creates peace instead of strife, justice instead of a party spirit, and prosperity for all its people, including economic redistribution for the poor.

One may be surprised at Scripture's strong emphasis on God's people praying for the economic system, the judiciary, and the political powers of a city. But is this not an indication of the biblical writers' profound understanding of the dimensions of the potential evil and potential good of a city? In chapters 1 through 4 we developed the idea that the city is a battleground between God and Satan with the political, economic, and religious systems as the primary arena where that battle is waged. If this is true, then it makes a great deal of sense that this is where the prayers of the church need to be focused. God's people should be praying for justice in the way their city treats money, the way its judiciary adjudicates, and the manner in which its political leadership governs. There is more to pray about in the city, however.

Pray for the People

> Since all are my brothers and friends,
> I say, "Peace be with you!"
> Since Yahweh our God lives here,
> I pray for your happiness (Ps. 122:8–9 JB).

The psalmist reminds us to pray for the people of the city—the ordinary folk, the "little people" who make up the great populations of each city. We are to pray shalom upon them all, no matter who they are, what they believe or do not believe, whether or not they work for the good of the city, whether or not they recognize that we are working for the good of the city. We are to pray God's peace upon them all: economic peace, the peace of safety, the peace of justice.

Isaiah develops this theme in a passage written in the face of the Israelite jingoism of his day.

> Let no foreigner who has bound himself to the LORD say,
> "The LORD will surely exclude me from his people."
> And let not any eunuch complain,
> "I am only a dry tree." . . .
> "To the eunuchs . . . I will give within my temples and its walls
> a memorial and a name
> better than sons and daughters. . . .
> And foreigners who bind themselves to the LORD
> to serve him, . . .
> these I will bring to my holy mountain
> and give them joy in my house of prayer.
> Their burnt offerings and sacrifices
> will be accepted on my altar;
> for my house will be called
> a house of prayer for all nations" (Isa. 56:3–7).

We are to pray for the happiness of all the people of the city—foreigner as well as Israelite, eunuch as well as parent—for God welcomes all to God's holy mountain (i.e., Jerusalem). God's temple is to be a house of prayer for all nations; the common factor of the people of God is not a bloodline, but a relationship to God.

Why should we pray for all the people of our city, even those who are not like us? For one simple reason: "Since Yahweh our God lives here, I pray for your happiness" (Ps. 122:9 JB). Because God lives in our city, this makes all the city's residents my urban brothers and sisters, whether or not *they* recognize that reality. I am to pray for their happiness and joy. I am to pray that they will discover God's shalom. And I am to pray for them for no other reason than that they happen to live there with me!

Pray with Importunity

Scripture not only shows us how we are to pray for our city; it shows us with what seriousness we are to take on this responsibility. In Isaiah 62, the prophet instructs the people of God:

> I have posted watchmen on your walls, O Jerusalem;
>   they will never be silent day or night.
> You who call on the LORD,
>   give yourselves no rest,
> and give him no rest till he establishes Jerusalem
>   and makes her the praise of the earth (Isa. 62:6–7).

The image is rather comedic. The prophet is suggesting that the believers should pray so insistently that they should not take any rest—but they are not the only ones not to rest. They have to be sure that God does not get any rest, either. They must so keep besieging him with their concern for Jerusalem that he finally accedes to their importunity in order to get a good night's sleep!

What Isaiah dreams about and what the psalmist encourages, we see actually carried out through one city's praying community of believers. The earliest Christians in Jerusalem gathered in desperate prayer upon the arrest of Peter and John, the church's most pivotal leaders. These apostles were being confronted by the Jewish Sanhedrin who were looking for a way to put them away permanently.

Because the leaders of the Sanhedrin could not decide what to do with Peter and John, however, they warned the men not to preach any longer in the name of Christ. Then the Sanhedrin let the men go free. Peter and John gathered with that praying community of believers and shared with them how the chief priests and elders had to release them. "When [the people of the church] heard this," Scripture tells us, "they raised their voices together in prayer to God" (Acts 4:24).

Praising God for his miraculous deliverance of Peter and John, that little band of believers prayed, "Now, Lord, consider their threats and enable your servants to speak your word with great boldness. Stretch out your hand to heal and perform miraculous signs and wonders through the name of your holy servant Jesus" (Acts 4:29–30). Then, just as they had prayed, God immediately worked in and through that little community of faith in amazing and very specific ways. Luke tells us:

> After they prayed, the place where they were meeting was shaken.
> And they were all filled with the Holy Spirit and spoke the word of

God boldly. All the believers were one in heart and mind. No one claimed that any of his possessions was his own, but they shared everything they had. With great power the apostles continued to testify to the resurrection of the Lord Jesus, and much grace was upon them all. There were no needy persons among them. For from time to time those who owned lands or houses sold them, brought the money from the sales and put it at the apostles' feet, and it was distributed to anyone as he had need (Acts 4:31–35).

It is intriguing to note what came out of that little prayer meeting. As a result of the prayers of God's people for the city of Jerusalem and its leadership:

- The Christians were filled with the Holy Spirit.
- They preached the Word of God boldly.
- They became united as a church.
- They cared for each other's physical, economic, and social needs.
- They built a life together that was a sign to the inhabitants of the city of the corporate and individual way of life that they coveted for the entire city.
- They testified openly to the resurrection of Jesus Christ.
- "Much grace was upon them all."

In other words, the interior life of the church was transformed by their prayers; yet those prayers were not for themselves, but for their city and its leaders. Those earliest Christians committed themselves to prayer for their city's chief priests and elders, and in doing so the lives of the *Christians* were transformed! Their intention was to pray for their city and a result was that the church changed to become sign, word, and deed to the city of that which they were seeking for the city! They became their own best advertisement!

Whether displaying humor (as in Isaiah 62) or solemnity, the biblical writers' injunctions are for steady, insistent prayer for the city. God's people are not to take lightly the privilege given to the church to pray for the city. This is prayer which is not to be focused upon the Christian nor upon the church, but upon the totality of that city, in all its economic, political, judicial, social, and spiritual dimensions. Only such intentional praying will reach the city and change the church. It is only upon the bedrock of the intentional praying of God's people that a city can be built "whose architect and builder is God" (Heb. 11:10).

Prayer is both absolutely necessary and strategic. But it is not sufficient. The church has not fulfilled its call to city ministry by praying. How else does God expect his people to work for the peace and prosperity of their city?

BEING GOD'S PRESENCE IN THE CITY

"Build houses and settle down; plant gardens and eat what they produce. Marry and have sons and daughters; find wives for your sons and give your daughters in marriage, so that they too may have sons and daughters. Increase in number there; do not decrease" (Jer. 29:5–6).

We see that the Israelites taken as captives to Babylon have chosen to become fixated in the past or to dream of the future. They concentrate upon recalling what life was like back in Jerusalem, or dream only of what they hope will be an imminent return to Israel. Their attitude is beautifully captured by the psalmist who wrote,

> By the rivers of Babylon we sat and wept
> when we remembered Zion.
> There on the poplars
> we hung our harps,
> for there our captors asked us for songs,
> our tormentors demanded songs of joy;
> they said, "Sing us one of the songs of Zion!"
> How can we sing the songs of the LORD
> while in a foreign land?
> If I forget you, O Jerusalem,
> may my right hand forget its skill.
> May my tongue cling to the roof of my mouth
> if I do not remember you,
> if I do not consider Jerusalem
> my highest joy (Ps. 137:1–6).

Jeremiah would not stand for such avoidance of reality. His instructions to the Jewish exiles in this letter found in Jeremiah 29 were direct and even harsh. Your task in Babylon, the prophet said, is not to dream of the "good old days" nor yearn for your return to the Promised Land. Your task is to get on with your life in that place in which God has placed you right here and now.

"Build houses and settle down; plant gardens and eat what they produce" (v. 5). Enter your city's economy and contribute to it; purchase a home in the city and settle into your neighborhood. Marry, have children, raise them to adulthoood, see them married, and enjoy being a grandparent. Make an investment of yourself and your family in Babylon, Jeremiah insists.

"Increase in number there; do not decrease" (v. 6). The prophet seeks to teach the discouraged people: become God's presence in the city which has been given to you and the city will be blessed by your presence. Live and move and have your being, as God's people, in the city where he places you. Be what you are—God's living presence in the city.

What is that presence in a city? Recalling the story about the search for a sufficient number of godly people to save Sodom and Gomorrah, Jeremiah writes,

> Go up and down the streets of Jerusalem,
>   look around and consider,
>   search through her squares.
> If you can find but one person
>   who deals honestly and seeks the truth,
>   I will forgive this city (Jer. 5:1).

In Sodom, it was a search for ten godly people—the lowest number for which Abraham had the nerve to bargain (see chapter 4). For Jerusalem, it is a search for one. Whether ten or one, the implication is the same. The presence of godly people in a city will save it from destruction. As long as there are godly people in a city, it will never be captured by Satan. The influence of the demonic and unjust may seem overwhelming in that city, but the presence of God's people will keep that city from succumbing to evil.

The presence of godly people is absolutely essential to the survival of a city. Scripture teaches that, not by being overtly "Christian," but just by the consistent, quiet, committed living-out of their faith, the godly people provide for their city both an example and a moderating presence.

The Pentateuch offers an image to illustrate the importance of godly people in a city. In Leviticus 1, the writer describes the offerings that are to take place in the temple:

> The LORD called to Moses and . . . said, "Speak to the Israelites and say to them: 'When any of you brings an offering to the LORD, bring as your offering an animal from either the herd or the flock. . . . [The priest] is to wash the inner parts and the legs with water, and the priest is to burn all of it on the altar. It is a burnt offering, an offering made by fire, an aroma pleasing to the LORD" (Lev. 1:1–2, 9; see also vv. 13, 17).

The burnt offering, of course, had no salvific quality in and of itself. What made it of redemptive value was the commitment of the person who brought that offering. If it was a sin offering, it was that person's sense of his own sinfulness and his need for salvation from God, symbolized in that offering, which brought about expiation. If it was a thanksgiving offering, it was that person's sense of gratitude and of praise to God which made that offering of worth. If it was a tributary offering, its value lay in that person's desire to give of his crops, his flocks, and his bounty as a response for all that God had given him.

The burnt offering which the Israelites were here instructed to perform, therefore, was not meant simply as a ritualistic act. It was meant to be symbolic of the offering of their lives. The lives of God's people were to be "an aroma pleasing to the LORD," a sweet-smelling fragrance rising to

God. God's people were to be an intentionally godly presence in the city; they were to be a sanctifying force which would bless the city with their living personification of God. This act of worship was to symbolize the reality which they were to live out.

A second and straightforward statement of the Christian's role is presented by the ever-practical James. He writes,

> My dear brothers, take note of this: Everyone should be quick to listen, slow to speak and slow to become angry, for man's anger does not bring about the righteous life that God desires. Therefore, get rid of all moral filth and the evil that is so prevalent and humbly accept the word planted in you, which can save you.
>
> Do not merely listen to the word, and so deceive yourselves. Do what it says. Anyone who listens to the word but does not do what it says is like a man who looks at his face in a mirror and, after looking at himself, goes away and immediately forgets what he looks like. But the man who looks intently into the perfect law that gives freedom, and continues to do this, not forgetting what he has heard, but doing it— he will be blessed in what he does.
>
> If anyone considers himself religious and yet does not keep a tight rein on his tongue, he deceives himself and his religion is worthless. Religion that God our Father accepts as pure and faultless is this: to look after orphans and widows in their distress and to keep oneself from being polluted by the world (James 1:19–27).

These are not easy words. By the way a Christian lives, James teaches, he or she testifies for or against Christ. If she listens carefully to those around her, if he holds his tongue and does not try to dominate conversations, if she controls her anger, if he seeks to live out the expectations of the Word of God consistently, if she shows compassion for the hurting, marginalized, and vulnerable of the city, if he avoids both corporate and individual sin—he or she will be a quiet and continuing testimony to Christ. On the other hand, if a person allows himself to conform to the low ethical and moral expectations of the majority of people in the city, or if she speaks of faith but is not obedient to the Word, then by their very lifestyles all that such Christians witness to by word or deed is exposed as hypocrisy.

If Christians are living out the Christian life before the world, they become a transforming presence, James insists. Their lives become an almost painful reminder to the city of the quality of life that can be lived if one chooses to live in communion with God and the neighbor.

Perhaps the most profound treatment of the importance of being God's presence in the city is given by our Lord. Jesus uses two metaphors to describe the impact his followers should have on the city:

"You are the salt of the earth. But if the salt loses its saltiness, how can it be made salty again? It is no longer good for anything, except to be thrown out and trampled by men.

"You are the light of the world. A city on a hill cannot be hidden. Neither do people light a lamp and put it under a bowl. Instead they put it on its stand, and it gives light to everyone in the house. In the same way, let your light shine before men, that they may see your good deeds and praise your Father in heaven" (Matt. 5:13–16).

Christians, Jesus suggests, are like salt. Their unobtrusive presence in a city both flavors that city and preserves that city from decay. Christians are also like light. They illuminate all that is going on in the city. By their lifestyle they expose the lies of the city's systems and principalities which would seek to dominate that city for their own selfish ends. By the priorities practiced in their lives, the Christians exhibit to the city the beautiful and joyful example of what that city, given over to Christ, could truly become.

Jesus uses the idea of Christians as salt and light as his paradigm in the Sermon on the Mount (Matt. 5–7). What are those people like whose presence flavors and preserves a city? What is the personality and what are the priorities of those people who, by their lifestyle, expose to the city the evil of that city's ways and are an example of a much better way of living? Jesus gives us the attributes of such believers in that portion of the Sermon on the Mount which has become known as the Beatitudes. "Salty" and "light-filled" Christians, Jesus tells us in Matthew 5, are people of humility (vv. 3–4) and meekness (v. 5), those who hunger and thirst after personal righteousness and corporate justice (vv. 6–7), and who exhibit purity of heart (v.8), a commitment to peacemaking (v. 9), and a willingness to suffer for Christ and his kingdom (v. 10).

In their treatment of the people, groups, and systems of the city, such people of God go far beyond the expectations and limitations of the Law. The Law says, "Do no murder." Christians recognize that to treat people contemptuously is to destroy them (Matt. 5:21–25). The Law says, "Do not commit adultery." God's people live by the recognition that to look at any human being with lust is an act of rape (vv. 27–30). The Law says, "Anyone who divorces his wife must give her a certificate of divorce." Followers of the Christ recognize divorce as the destruction of human relationships and therefore as inappropriate for Christians (vv. 31–32). The Law says, "Do not break your oath." Salty Christians will not operate by promised intentions, but by direct and transparent actions (vv. 33–37). The Law says, "Eye for eye and tooth for tooth." Christians, however, live with a spirit of forgiveness, not of retribution (vv. 38–42). The Law says, "Love your neighbor and hate your enemy." Godly people recognize that a city or society cannot function unless it is built on compassionate concern for all its people, irrespective of how one might feel about any of them (vv. 43–48).

The characteristics of Christ's people include advocacy for and compassionate involvement with that city's poor and needy (Matt. 6:1–4), a life of intercessory prayer for that city (vv. 5–15), and a quiet commitment to personal spiritual formation (vv. 16–18). What will be an overriding characteristic of such people, whether at any given moment they are working with the poor, praying for the city or spending time with Christ, is that all such activity will be unobtrusive and hidden (vv. 1–18). The reason this is so is that such people are interested not in human attention, but in being faithful to God (vv. 19–24).

Those who can be God's presence in the city can be so because of their focus.

> "No one can serve two masters. Either he will hate the one and love the other, or he will be devoted to the one and despise the other. You cannot serve both God and Money" (Matt. 6:24).

God's people have decided not to pursue power (Matt. 7:15–23), prestige (Matt. 6:16–18), possessions (Matt. 6:24–34), or the advocacy of their own little group (Matt. 7:1–6, 13–14). Rather, they are people simply committed to the love of God and the service of the people of their city. Because they are so constituted, God's people will be free of the constraints of worry (Matt. 6:25–34) and the need to judge others (Matt. 7:1–6) but will instead live open and receptive lives (Matt. 7:7–12). It will be such people who, by the very way they "live and move and have their being," will be God's gracious Good News lived out in their city.

Jeremiah advises the Israelite exiles in Babylon to live into God's urban call to them by becoming a godly presence in their adopted city (see Jer. 29:5–6, quoted earlier). God says the same to God's people today. Whatever the circumstances might be that have brought you to your city, what God most wants out of you as a Christian in that city is to live fully into your circumstances.

Buy a house or rent an apartment, God instructs you and me. Find your vocation and enter into your city's economics. Buy and sell. Give and take. Love your neighborhood; commit yourself to its people. Laugh and cry with them. Celebrate and mourn with them. Make an investment of yourself and your family in your city.

Be God's moderating presence wherever you might be in the city— flavoring all of life with the beauty of your life, preserving your city from spiritual decay, shedding God's light on the lies of your city's powerful, exhibiting to all around you the quality of life God means for all to live in the city. Become God's transforming presence at your work, your school, and your community as your life becomes an aroma pleasing to the Lord. Live and move and have your being, as God's person, in your city. And in this gentle and unassuming way, become God's profound blessing to your city, your neighborhood, your working place, your family, and yourself.

In the Chicago church I served from 1969 to 1975, there was a man in his early forties who was mentally retarded. Jack was certainly not bright, but he was sincere and caring. Jack impressed me with his Christian commitment. He could not *understand* much about the Gospel, but what he missed in comprehension he made up for in caring.

Every Sunday, when Jack left the worship service, he and I would go through the same ritual. As the pastor of the church, I would be greeting people at the door. Jack, when he came by, would always tell me that he could not stay for our coffee hour. I would urge him to stay, but his answer was always the same. "Can't, dear," he would reply (he called everyone "dear"). "I have to get to my deliveries."

Now, these "deliveries" were Jack's livelihood. Seven days a week, fifty-two weeks a year, Jack delivered medicine and other goods for a local pharmacy. In good weather and in bad, in heavy traffic and in light, in the morning and at night, Jack would be seen pedaling slowly along on his bicycle, faithfully making his deliveries. In a community with a soaring crime rate, Jack alone had access to most of the apartment buildings. In a neighborhood in which people desperately feared one another, Jack alone would be welcomed past the front doors of private homes.

In 1983, eight years after I had left that Chicago church to pastor a church in the Detroit area, I opened a letter from my mother, who still lived in Chicago. Out tumbled a newspaper clipping. I opened it and began to read. To my amazement, it was an article about Jack. I was not prepared for what I read. Let me share a part of that article with you.

> "You know, whenever I was sick and feeling despondent," said Mrs. Vera Wombwell, "it was when Jack came to bring the medicine that I would get cheered up. He was a wonderful little man. He could come here on cold and windy, rainy nights and pick up my prescription and ride over to the store on his bike, get it refilled, and bring it back to me.
>
> "He'd say, 'Now dear, how do you feel? You look a little better already, dear.' Then he'd do a little dance and say he had to be off. He had his work to do."
>
> "Jack, he was a good boy," says his mother, sitting tearfully in her apartment. "And he loved that job. It meant so much to him. He loved to ride the bike and to be outside.
>
> "He never got sick. He never complained about the cold. He was out on icy streets, in busy traffic, in thunderstorms and he was never hurt. Why did it have to happen now? This way? On a sunny day on a side street where there was no traffic?"
>
> Perhaps the driver of the car that sped out of the alley did not see Jack, pedaling slowly along on his delivery bike. Perhaps the driver did not

care, for when the car hit Jack and he fell on the street, breaking his collarbone and cracking his head, the car did not stop.

The car sped away instead, leaving Jack lying next to his bicycle, hurt and confused. When he was taken to the hospital, he said only that his head hurt.

Before the day was over, Jack had fallen into a coma. He stayed in the coma for five days. On Monday, Jack died.

"And everybody, everywhere along the street is talking about Jack," Vera Wombwell said. "You see, in his own way, Jack did more for the people around here than any big city official or any preacher or any social worker.

"You don't have to be rich or famous or handsome or smart or have people remember you," said Mrs. Wombwell. "You can be quiet and honest and good. You can be just a simple little man. Just like Jack!"[3]

As the church in the city, God has not called us to be above our city, fellowshiping only with God's people while singing, "This world is not my home; I'm just a-passing through." Nor are we simply in the city, committed to our own welfare without contributing to the city's good. As children of God, we are called to be for our city and with our city, casting our lot with this city. We are to pray for our city. As we will discover in the next chapter, in addition we are to work for justice for our city's powerless and proclaim the Gospel in our city.

Underneath it all, however, we are to be the people who live our lives joyfully and hopefully and profoundly in the city, being the very presence of God to the loneliness and fear and deep hunger of our city's people and systems and principalities—just like Jack! For only as we so live into God's call to us in our city will God fulfill his promise to us:

"I know the plans I have for you," declares the LORD, "plans to prosper you and not to harm you, plans to give you hope and a future" (Jer. 29:11).

Chapter Eight

THE PRACTICE AND PROCLAMATION OF THE CHURCH IN THE CITY

> Work for the good of the [city] to which I have exiled you; pray to Yahweh on its behalf, since on its welfare yours depends (Jer. 29:7 JB).

Sometimes what is not said is as important as what is said. This is the case in this strategic sentence in Jeremiah's letter to the Israelite exiles in the city of Babylon. The letter reaches its apex in this sentence, as Jeremiah tells the people what their essential focus should be while in exile.

In telling them what their focus should be, he also tells them—by not telling them—what their focus should not be. He does not say to the exiles, "Work for your own good or your family's good in Babylon." He does not even say, "Work for the development and maintenance of religious centers which can preserve your faithfulness to Yahweh in this strange land." Jeremiah simply says, "Work for the good of the city to which I have exiled you." The focus of the people of God is to be on the shalom of that pagan city, because "on its welfare yours depends."

How do God's people work for the good of their city? What activities constitute the appropriate ministries in which the church should be involved in the city?

In the previous chapter, we explored how God calls each of us as Christians and all of us as the church to pray for the city. We discovered that the prayers of God's people are to cover all aspects of a city. This includes praying for the city's economic health, for safety from conflict, for an end to violent crime, for a reformation of the political process, for the well-being and happiness of all who live in that city, and for justice for all, but especially justice for the poor.

We further explored the absolutely pivotal presence of God's people in the city. We are not to take our presence lightly. To be a godly presence is to be both example and moderator, flavoring and preserving the city, sanctifying and transforming it by being the people God created us to be.

While prayer and presence are certainly strategic ministries of the church in the city, they do not comprise the total activity of the urban people of God. For the church is also called to *work* for the welfare of the city. The church works for the kingdom of God in the city in two ways: through its proclamation and through its practice.

PRACTICE OF THE CHURCH IN THE CITY

I was leading a workshop of pastors from Brasilia, the capital city of Brazil. In the course of the workshop, I asked these urban pastors the question, "What is the work of the church in the city?" They began to make a list, including in it such items as "pastoral care," "evangelism," "the Christian education of the children," "youth work," "preaching," "teaching," "counseling," "fund-raising and stewardship," "maintenance of the temple" (the church building), and "care of the congregation." I then suggested to them that very few of these activities could be supported from Scripture as the work of the church. Some could be supported as the nurturance of a Christian community, but others are not even mentioned in Scripture. Yet they play a prominent role in the work our churches do today.

That evening, as I reflected on that day's events, I found myself wondering, "Were the responses by these pastors peculiar to this group? Or do pastors throughout the world perceive the work of the church as the maintenance of the church?" I decided to raise this question in each workshop I would lead that year to see what I would discover.

By the end of the year, I had decided that I had discovered a primary reason why the church throughout the world seems to have a hard time coping with city ministry. In workshop after workshop in Africa, Southeast Asia, the Indian subcontinent, the United States, and Latin America, pastors had consistently identified the maintenance of the life and institution of the church with the work of the church. To be faithful in doing God's work in the city, pastors uniformly believed, the church was called to build up its interior life and maintain its institution.

As I first suggested to those Brazilian pastors, this perception of ministry cannot be supported from Scripture. Rather, the biblical writers provide a consistently different answer to the question: "What is the church called to do in the city?"

One Scripture passage that helps direct our thinking regarding the work of the people of God in the city is Isaiah 65:18–25.[1] This Scripture deals with the prophet's dream of a new heaven and a new earth built around a rejuvenated and transformed Jerusalem. Here is revealed God's agenda for the city, and consequently, with the added insights of related Scripture, what the agenda of God's people ought to be, as well.

Discovering the City's Joy

> I will create Jerusalem to be a delight
>   and its people a joy.
> I will rejoice over Jerusalem
>   and take delight in my people;
> the sound of weeping and of crying
>   will be heard in it no more (vv. 18–19).

We do not often think of our city as the City of Joy—but this name is to be more than simply the title of a book. God wants to delight over the city and wants God's people to find joy in the city, as well. In chapter 1, we discussed the importance of allowing ourselves to celebrate our city, and to discover in it all that is of good report. God loves our city. So should we.

The church is called to be a cheerleader to the city. It is also called to name all that is evil and dark about the city, and particularly to confront the city's systems and structures when they act in exploitive and oppressive ways. In order truly to be effective in the city, however, the church cannot allow itself to be overwhelmed by its city's evil. It must take delight in its city, in the people surrounding the church, and in each other in the community of faith. There is much to love in every city!

Health Care and Longevity

> "Never again will there be in [the city]
>   an infant that lives but a few days,
>   or an old man who does not live out his years;
> He who dies at a hundred
>   will be thought a mere youth;
> he who fails to reach a hundred
>   will be considered accursed. . . .
> For as the days of a tree,
>   so will be the days of my people" (Isa. 65:20, 22).

The city is to be a place of health, and the church has the responsibility to work for the longevity and health care of its inhabitants. "Sons are a heritage from the LORD, children a reward from him," declares the psalmist (Ps. 127:3). To live in the kind of health conditions that deprive people from raising their children to adulthood or take adult life prematurely is unacceptable. The work of the church must include advocacy for adequate health care for all the city's inhabitants.

To advocate adequate medical care without also dealing with the very conditions of the city that produce ill health is to be short-sighted. The church must be concerned about the stress of city life, which is a major contributor to both psychological and physical breakdown.

There were a number of emotionally scarred and mentally ill people in our Chicago neighborhood, folks who had been released from the state-run mental hospital to local residential-care facilities. Because these people spent most of their days wandering the community, our church opened a day-care center, primarily funded by the State of Illinois. About one hundred mentally ill people from these nearby residential-care homes regularly came to our center.

I once had a conversation with the resident psychiatrist of the day-care center about the causes of mental illness. He said to me something I will never forget.

"Bob," he said, "there is only one difference between you and the people who attend our day-care center. They have faced one overwhelming stress or a series of stresses with which they could not cope. You have not faced that stress or stresses in your life yet. But there is a limit to the amount of stress with which you are capable of living—there is just so much you can tolerate in this city, and no more. If events happen to you that push you past that level of stress, you will be here in this day-care center, just like them."

To deal with health care in the city is to deal with the issue of stress. The congestion of traffic, the competitiveness of work in a technologically sophisticated society, the expectations upon us to deal with constantly changing and rapidly accumulating information caused by computerization, the stress of living in such close proximity to each other (twenty thousand people lived within a four-block radius of our church in Chicago), and the intense and frantic pace of life all contribute to the breakdown and ill health of twentieth-century urban people. An essential part of the work of the church in the city is to question today's urban life-style and to offer a viable alternative within the Christian community.

Health care must also include environmental concern. Here in Los Angeles we have the saying, "We Los Angelos don't believe in any air we can't see!" You really can see it—see it on your clothes and on every surface of your home, smell its acrid odor with every breath you take, and feel it burning in your lungs. To be concerned with the health of humans in the city means that one must be concerned with the health of the environment. That means all aspects of the environment, not just air pollution and smog, but the contamination of water (the main cause of sickness and death in most cities of the third world), the disposal of sewage, trash, and the debris of city life, the increasing consumption of fossil fuel, and the mining and harvesting of non-replaceable natural resources (such as the strip-mining of Africa and Latin America and the harvesting of the rain forests of Brazil and Southeast Asia).

Health care in the city, therefore, means more than adequate medical care for all; it also means dealing with the variegated stress of the city and with the city's environmental issues. The Bible indicates that such concern needs to be part of the work of the church in the city.

Housing

They will build houses and dwell in them; . . .
No longer will they build houses and others live in them.
(Isa. 65:21, 22)

Isaiah instructs God's people to be concerned about how people live in the city. Housing, he says, must be for all the people, irrespective of their wealth or poverty. The psalmist also reminds us that God wants his people involved in providing for those in need (Ps. 127:1–2), and surely housing is one aspect of that.

When one deals with urban housing in the modern world, he or she must face three housing issues: adequacy, distribution, and safety.

The church is to work for adequate housing for all, so that everyone has a home and no one is forced to live on the street. Today, at this very moment, more than forty million children have been abandoned by their parents and are living on city streets. In São Paulo, Brazil, alone, seven hundred and fifty thousand of them live by their wits and cunning. Between half a million and a million people live on the streets of Calcutta, India; they are born there, grow to adulthood there, marry there, bear and raise their children there and die there—never once in their entire lives experiencing a night under a roof![2] Even in a country as wealthy as the United States, homelessness has become an epidemic as urban dwellers become accustomed to the bag-ladies and grate-dwellers and the people sleeping in the doorways, the parks, and on the sidewalks throughout our U.S. cities. God is displeased with such inequality and expects his people to work for adequate housing for all the people.

The church is to work for just housing, housing fairly distributed to everyone, whether one is powerful or a "nobody" in the city, whether one is rich or is poor. Isaiah states it magnificently: "No longer will they [the common people] build houses and others live in them." In other words, the prophet is saying, "God wants people to be able to live in the houses they build, to receive housing—not because they are capable of purchasing housing, but because they are human beings!" There is something radically sick with society when people are forced to live without any housing (never mind adequate housing), while others live in sumptuous surroundings.

Finally, the church is to be committed to safe housing. It is a shock to enter into a squatter settlement of a third world city; these settlements, erected overnight by the people migrating to the city, cling tenuously to the side of steep hills or over precipices, their unpaved streets deep in mud churned up by countless passing feet, their houses built of cardboard, packing crates, metal sheets, and mud-bricks. Unsafe? One torrential rainstorm, one mud- or landslide will cause that urban settlement to go tumbling into the depths below.

Such conditions are not found in the third world alone. One needs only to enter any inner-city slum of the United States or Europe to find people living in shocking and deplorable conditions behind the facade of buildings that look substantial from the outside. The church is to work for safe and well-built housing so that there are no tenements, no slums, no cardboard and tin shacks, no barrios, no bustees or favellas. To work for safe and decent affordable housing for all city dwellers is a part of the work of the urban church.

Economic Development

> They will plant vineyards and eat their fruit.
> No longer will they . . . plant and others eat. . . .
> My chosen ones will long enjoy
>   the works of their hands.
> They will not toil in vain (Isa. 65:21–23).

Isaiah calls the church to work for economic development in the city. Jobs are a priority for God in the city he desires to have for humanity. Jobs should, consequently, be a priority to the church as well.

Scripture stresses the importance of building an adequate economic base under an entire people. Jeremiah instructs the king of Judah, for example,

> "This is what the LORD says: Do what is just and right. Rescue from the hand of his oppressor the one who has been robbed. Do no wrong or violence to the alien, the fatherless or the widow, and do not shed innocent blood in this place. For if you are careful to carry out these commands, then kings who sit on David's throne will come through the gates of this palace, riding in chariots and on horses, accompanied by their officials and their people. But if you do not obey these commands, declares the LORD, I swear by myself that this palace will become a ruin" (Jer. 22:3–5).

The king is expected to maintain a just economy; he is particularly responsible for making sure that the oppressed, the foreigner, the widow, and the orphan—society's most vulnerable people—are equitably and favorably treated. The Year of Jubilee and Israel's other economic cycles were all designed for orderly regulation and adjustment of the economy, so that wealth would not become increasingly centralized in the hands of a powerful few, while the poor only became poorer.

St. Paul, in his advice to slaves and masters, asks of the slaves nothing more than Roman law required—that they obey their masters, but to do so out of love for Christ rather than out of fear of the master. For Christian masters, however, Paul requires treatment of slaves far beyond the requirements of the law—for they are to treat the slaves with respect, commitment to their needs, and in ways that are expressive of their love for Christ. Further, Paul instructs the masters not to threaten their slaves "since you know that he who is both their Master and yours is in heaven, and there is no favoritism with him" (Eph. 6:9).

Scripture passages like these indicate how both Old Testament Jews and New Testament Christians were seeking to deal with economics justly and equitably. Although their economic specifics are irrelevant for our own day, their operating premises can be instructive for us as we seek to build an urban economics for the twentieth and twenty-first centuries. Promotion of economic justice, control of the distribution of an economy, particular attention to the hurting of any urban society, and using the law of love as the highest code by which a city structures itself all become principles upon which economic development must be based.

In the worldwide capitalist, socialist, and socialist/capitalist economies that exist in today's urban society, of particular importance is employment. In the first world, as technology becomes increasingly complex, an ever-expanding number of people become technologically obsolete—and so do their jobs. This results in a steady expansion of the unemployed and unemployable. This, in turn, leads to a steady expansion in illegal means of making money along the seamy underside of the city: prostitution, drug-dealing, and criminal activity. Thus, a permanent underclass of the poor and disenfranchised emerges in the cities of the first world, most often along ethnic and racial lines.

In the third world, economies are weak, dominated by balance-of-payments and debt-reduction that hold those economies in thralldom to the first world. Consequently, those economies are often oriented toward the production of raw materials and processed goods for first world markets rather than the production of goods for their own people. The result, in the cities, is a large unemployed sector—normally between thirty-five percent and seventy percent of a city's population. Without a welfare or social security system which can economically sustain these people, they are doomed to become the forgotten "wretched of the earth." Most respond to their dilemma by entering the "informal sector" of their economy (although some choose the criminal or subsistence routes). Rather than seeking to be employed, those entering into the "informal sector" create their own jobs and businesses; they thus form an informal economy next to the formal and primary economy of their city and thus build an economic base for themselves.

How does the church biblically respond to the economic imbalance of its city? In one way or another, the church must become involved in economic development—the creation of jobs, the organizing of people to create community industries and trades, job re-training, economic self-determination, advocacy of the poor. Though the strategies and action plans should differ from city to city, the essential principles are the same.

The church is called to strive for a city where there is a job for everyone and in which no one is forced to work below his level of skill. Isaiah calls us to bend our godly efforts to the development of a secure, balanced economy, a theocratic economy which enables each person to work and to make a valuable contribution to the furtherance of the well-being of that city.

Relationship with God

> They will be a people blessed by the LORD,
>   they and their descendants with them.
> Before they call I [the LORD] will answer;
>   while they are still speaking I will hear (Isa. 65:23–24).

Perhaps that which most separates a biblical vision for the city from the utopias of dreamers such as John Stuart Mill, Adam Smith, and Karl Marx occurs at this point. Each such visionary builds his utopia on the premise that such an ideal world is achievable. Each utopia is built on the premise that humanity is essentially good and if the formula devised by the visionary is followed, then society will reach that utopia.

Scripture, on the other hand, operates on the premise that although humanity is made in the image of God, that image is implacably scarred by the existence of sin (thus humanity is redeemable only by the action of God). Human beings will therefore corrupt every good plan humanity devises. Only God can make society work, as he redeems us and then creates in us a new community (Jesus' "kingdom of God"). The difference, therefore, between the utopias of visionaries and the kingdom of God is that the first is centered on the perfectibility of humanity and the latter is centered on God. Relationship with God is the center of the transformed biblical city. Human utopias avoid that relationship.

Isaiah brings out that insight most clearly in this passage on the idealized Jerusalem. In the city as God intends city to be, God will be in such close relationship with his people that "before they call I will answer; while they are still speaking I will hear." Relationship between God and God's people will be so intimate that he will respond to their longing for him even before they have placed words on that longing. The description is almost one of a lover responding to his beloved at the moment before she reaches for his reassurance, or of a mother anticipating the needs of her baby even before the baby begins to cry. This is the intimacy God covets between Yahweh and the people of the city.

The Bible is full of insights regarding relationship with God as the base upon which the city should be built or reformulated. Consider the following:

> When the LORD your God brings you into the land he swore to your fathers, to Abraham, Isaac and Jacob, to give you—a land with large, flourishing cities you did not build, houses filled with all kinds of good

things you did not provide, wells you did not dig, and vineyards and olive groves you did not plant—then when you eat and are satisfied, be careful that you do not forget the LORD, who brought you out of Egypt, out of the land of slavery.

Hear, O Israel: the LORD our God, the LORD is one. Love the LORD your God with all your heart and with all your soul and with all your strength (Deut. 6:10–12, 4–5).

> Unless the LORD builds the house,
>   its builders labor in vain.
> Unless the LORD watches over the city,
>   the watchmen stand guard in vain (Ps. 127:1).

[And Jesus wept,] "O Jerusalem, Jerusalem, you who kill the prophets and stone those sent to you, how often I have longed to gather your children together, as a hen gathers her chicks under her wings, but you were not willing!" (Luke 13:34).

But you have come to Mount Zion, to the heavenly Jerusalem, the city of the living God. You have come to thousands upon thousands of angels in joyful assembly, to the church of the firstborn, whose names are written in heaven. You have come to God, the judge of all men, to the spirits of righteous men made perfect, to Jesus the mediator of a new covenant, and to the sprinkled blood that speaks a better word than the blood of Abel.

See to it that you do not refuse him who speaks. If they did not escape when they refused him who warned them on earth, how much less will we, if we turn away from him who warns us from heaven? . . . Therefore, since we are receiving a kingdom that cannot be shaken, let us be thankful, and so worship God acceptably with reverence and awe, for our God is a consuming fire (Heb. 12:22–25, 28–29).

"And the name of the city from that time on will be:

THE LORD IS THERE."

(Ezek. 48:35)

It is the task of the church in the city to introduce its citizenry to God in Christ. This is its primary calling and its exclusive calling. It is not the church's only calling, but it is primary and exclusive. If the church does all the rest, but leaves this task undone, then it has been irresponsible and derelict to its unique call.

Shalom with the Neighbor

> "The wolf and the lamb will feed together,
>   and the lion will eat straw like the ox,
>   but dust will be the serpent's food.
> They will neither harm nor destroy

on all my holy mountain,"
says the LORD (Isa. 65:25).

The end, the goal, of the city in Isaiah 65—just as it is in Jeremiah 29—is "shalom." And that, as we have explored in chapter 4, is an Old Testament way of referring to the concept of the "kingdom of God." God's agenda for the city ends with that which proves whether this city is indeed the city of God—whether or not its populace lives in shalom. St. Paul witnesses to the same intention when he writes, "But now in Christ Jesus you who once were far away have been brought near through the blood of Christ. For he himself is our peace, who has made the two [previously alienated Jew and Gentile] one and has destroyed the barrier, the dividing wall of hostility [between them]" (Eph. 2:13–14).

It is the responsibility of the church in the city to work for this shalom. This is expressed by Jeremiah in the passage which provides the focus for both this and the previous chapter: Jeremiah 29:7. It actually reads, "Work for the shalom of the city to which I have exiled you; pray to Yahweh on its behalf, since on its shalom your shalom depends." It cannot be said any plainer than that!

Perhaps the most eloquent statement regarding the responsibility of the people of God to seek the shalom of their city is found in another passage: Isaiah 58:6–9:

"Is not this the kind of [worship] I have chosen:
to loose the chains of injustice
    and untie the cords of the yoke,
to set the oppressed free
    and break every yoke?
Is it not to share your food with the hungry
    and to provide the poor wanderer with shelter—
when you see the naked, to clothe him,
    and not to turn away from your own flesh and blood?
Then your light will break forth like the dawn,
    and your healing will quickly appear;
then your righteousness will go before you,
    and the glory of the LORD will be your rear guard.
Then you will call, and the LORD will answer;
    you will cry for help, and he will say: 'Here am I.' "[3]

The most appropriate worship of God is sometimes the service of humanity. A primary responsibility of the church in the city is to seek the reconciliation and shalom of its people.

Isaiah 65 is extremely helpful as we begin to perceive and name the work to which God calls the urban church. But it does not include an exhaustive list. There is much more. Let's look briefly at some of the other work of the church.

Advocacy for the Poor

God's disposition toward the poor is perhaps one of the most important themes in Scripture. We have traced that theme throughout this book, for there is no way to talk about the city and ignore its poor.

Integral to God's commitment to the poor is Yahweh's assumption that the chief defenders of the poor must be God's prophets, apostles, and people. It is a primary task of the church in the city to be the advocate and champion for those who are poor. We are often their only voice—a voice to which the principalities and powers of a city must listen.

This strategic role of the church was given magnificent voice by Dom Helder Camara, the saintly bishop of the Roman Catholic Church in Brazil who, over two generations, transformed the Brazilian church from a church of the powerful to a church of the people. He stated,

> The first great discovery we made . . . was that even illiterate people . . . still know how to think. It's impossible to work with the people, even in those situations where you're a teacher, without learning from them. You teach and you learn, teach and learn.

> When we saw that people who didn't know how to read or write still knew how to think, we felt an urgency to prove this to the government. So we worked with the poor and simple people in base Christian communities, helping them to come to the conviction that no one was born to be a slave or a beggar. No one![4]

There are many instances in Scripture of godly people's advocacy of the poor. But perhaps one of the most dramatic was Jeremiah's confrontation with King Jehoahaz. One can hardly imagine more stern words than these which Jeremiah delivered to Jehoahaz, as he sat in the throne room of his palace in Jerusalem:

> "Hear the word of the LORD, O king of Judah, you who sit on David's throne—you, your officials and your people who come through these gates. This is what the LORD says: Do what is just and right. Rescue from the hand of his oppressor the one who has been robbed. Do no wrong or violence to the alien, the fatherless or the widow, and do not shed innocent blood in this place. For if you are careful to carry out these commands, then kings who sit on David's throne will come through the gates of this palace, riding in chariots and on horses, accompanied by their officials and their people. But if you do not obey these commands, declares the LORD, I swear by myself that this palace will become a ruin" (Jer. 22:2–5).

Then Jeremiah refers to the expensive palace the king has just constructed, a palace which was built with the slave labor and upon the broken backs of Jerusalem's poor. In his prophecy, Jeremiah refers to

Jehoahaz' father, King Josiah, a king who was both godly and deeply committed to the poor.

> "Woe to him who builds his palace by unrighteousness,
>   his upper rooms by injustice,
>   making his countrymen work for nothing,
>   not paying them for their labor.
> He says, 'I will build myself a great palace
>   with spacious upper rooms.'
> So he makes large windows in it,
>   panels it with cedar
>   and decorates it in red.
>
> "Does it make you a king
>   to have more and more cedar?
> Did not your father have food and drink?
>   He did what was right and just,
>   so all went well with him.
> He defended the cause of the poor and needy,
>   so all went well.
> Is that not what it means to know me?"
>   declares the LORD.
> "But your eyes and your heart
>   are set only on dishonest gain,
> on shedding innocent blood
>   and on oppression and extortion" (Jer. 22:13–17).

Now that is advocacy!

Preaching like that did not make Jeremiah a popular prophet. His efforts were not rewarded with a large sanctuary and people's praise. Jeremiah did maintain his integrity, however, spoke the truth, and "defended the cause of the poor and needy." That is why he is considered today one of the most outstanding preachers in the Bible.

The church is called to be a strong voice for those in the city who are poor and a defender of their causes. The church is also called to put its body where its mouth is.

Empowerment Through Self-Determination

Along with advocacy of the poor, the church is expected by the biblical witness to work for the empowerment of the city's powerless. The church must stand up for the urban poor. The church must work in its city so that economic development can occur, adequate housing be built, and safety and health care be guaranteed for the poor. The church must take seriously its task to "preach good news to the poor" (Luke 4:18). In the final analysis, however, if the church does not find ways to come alongside the poor to support them as they seek to take charge of their own situations, it has not really done its job in the city. After all, the people who are best able to assume responsibility for solving a problem are the people who have the problem. That applies as much to the city's poor and powerless as it does to anyone else. The church therefore must be involved in working with the people for their self-determination.

The Bible places quite a bit of emphasis on the importance of empowerment and self-determination, especially with the poor and powerless. We will spend the entire next chapter exploring that emphasis in detail through the life and ministry of Nehemiah. It is important that now we take the time to look at several other passages of Scripture that enable us to catch a glimpse of this most godly way for undertaking ministry in a community and city.

Isaiah 61 provides us our first insight into this principle:

> The Spirit of the Sovereign LORD is on me,
>> because the LORD has anointed me
>> to preach good news to the poor.
> He has sent me to bind up the brokenhearted,
>> to proclaim freedom for the captives
>> and release from darkness for the prisoners,
> to proclaim the year of the LORD's favor
>> and the day of vengeance of our God. . . .
>
> They will rebuild the ancient ruins
>> and restore the places long devastated;
> they will renew the ruined cities
>> that have been devastated for generations (vv. 1–2, 4).

Who are "they"? It is clear, as one reads this entire prophecy, that those who will rebuild the devastated city will be the poor, the brokenhearted, the captives, and the prisoners referred to in the first two verses. The city will not be rebuilt by the Anointed One upon whom the Spirit of the Sovereign Lord came. His task, instead, is to deal with the issues that are immobilizing them and keeping them from rebuilding their city. The poor of the city are the hopeless, the brokenhearted bound up in their grief, the captives and prisoners jailed by their own sense of limitations. It is the job of the Anointed One to say to them, "You are free. You are free in God. And he sets you free to take charge of this city." And they do!

A second example is found in Acts 15. This event had little to do directly with the poor, brokenhearted, captives, and prisoners of the city, but rather concerned the leadership of the early Christian church. At issue was whether Gentiles could become Christians without first becoming Jews. The issue had been building a long while, during which time Paul and Barnabas continued their missionary activities among Gentiles throughout Asia Minor. These people were becoming Christians without making a prior commitment to Judaism. Therefore in Jerusalem the church held its first council and to it came the leaders to deal with this issue. In other words, the people having the problem decided to solve the problem. Rather than turning to James (the administrative head of the church) or to Peter (the spiritual head of the church) to adjudicate the issue, all those concerned with the issue met together and discussed and debated until they came to resolution. Happily, Paul and Barnabas succeeded and the church became a gentile movement. The church solved the problem, not by fiat or adjudication, but by corporately assuming responsibility for the problem and solving it among its members.

A third example is found in Paul's letter to Titus, when he writes, "The reason I left you in Crete was that you might straighten out what was left unfinished and appoint elders in every town, as I directed you" (Titus 1:5). Here is another example of self-determination. The leadership of the church in Crete is selecting and appointing elders who will then rule their respective churches. Paul was not seeking to administer those churches from afar. He organized those churches, trained leadership through Titus, and then set the people in charge to run their own churches, for good or for ill. Paul believed that the people had to be empowered to assume responsibility for their own situations.

This is a critical insight for the work of the church in the city. If people are not empowered to take charge of their own situations, they remain either victims or objects to be pitied. It is irrelevant whether they are poor or middle class or wealthy; if people believe they are helpless to do anything about the forces that constrain them, then they are indeed helpless. And the church is the most liberated body ever created by God, because Christ has freed us from that which once oppressed, minimized, and nearly destroyed us. That is the essence of the Gospel. Therefore, our strategic and unique role in the city is to work with all those people, groups, and structures that feel powerless and out of control so that we may enable them to discover freedom and liberation themselves.

Stewards of the City

A crucial way for the church to look at the city is to recognize that the church is not foreign to the city. It has been placed by God in the city to be its primary steward. The city is a massive investment made both by God and by humanity. Humanity provides for the stewardship of that city's political, economic, social, and material investment through the systems and structures of that city. As we have seen from Scripture, however, the city is also a considerable spiritual investment; in fact, it is to be understood primarily as a spiritual entity. How is the spirituality of the city protected and nurtured and allowed to grow? It will either be done through the church or through the demonic forces of that city. Consequently, the church has as a major responsibility the stewardship of the spirituality (and therefore the materiality) of its city.

This is given eloquent voice by the author of Deuteronomy, who reminds Israel that the land and the cities in which the people live have been given to them, not built by them: "cities you did not build, houses filled with good things you did not provide, wells you did not dig, vineyards and olive groves you did not plant" (Deut. 6:10–11). God has made an investment in Israel. How is Israel to be a good steward of that investment?

> Be careful that you do not forget the LORD, who brought you out of Egypt, out of the land of slavery. Fear the LORD your God, serve him only and take your oaths in his name. Do not follow other gods, the gods of the peoples around you. . . . Be sure to keep the commands of the LORD your God and the stipulations and decrees he has given you. Do what is right and good in the LORD's sight, so that it may go well with you and you may go in and take over the good land that the LORD promised on oath to your forefathers, thrusting out all your enemies before you, as the LORD said (Deut. 6:12–14, 17–19).

Jesus stressed the church's stewardship responsibility for the city when he told the parable of a fig tree that would not bear fruit and that the owner (God) wanted to cut down. "Sir, [the servant who took care of the vineyard replied], leave it alone for one more year, and I'll dig around it and fertilize it. If it bears fruit next year, fine! If not, then cut it down" (Luke 13:8–9).

Just as a city depends upon the prayers of the church for its welfare, so, too, the city depends upon the church's faithful stewardship. Most often, the city is unaware that its spirituality is being cared after by the church; perhaps it is not even aware of its spirituality. But just as the church's prayers for the city are done in a closet and not for the city to see, so the church works behind the scenes to make the city pure and holy before God. That is why the church involves itself in health care, housing, economic development, and advocacy of the poor—for, whether addressed or ignored, all those profoundly affect the depth of spirituality of the city, for good or for ill.

PROCLAMATION TO THE CITY

D. L. Moody was once asked how he would define a great urban preacher. His definition is a classic statement. He responded, "A truly great urban preacher is the pastor who climbs into the pulpit each Sunday with the Bible in one hand and the newspaper in the other."[5]

What Moody was stressing, of course, is that it takes an awareness of both the Bible and one's urban reality to make proclamation effective. The Bible may be good news, but if it is not applied to our world, it is news that is irrelevant to us. The newspaper, by contrast, is always relevant news, but without biblical interpretation, it is only bad news.

Proclamation requires both a conceptual framework (i.e., the Bible) and one's context (the newspaper). This book seeks to build a biblically founded conceptual framework for doing urban ministry. Without allowing it to interact continually with your own context, however, it is simply a theoretical exercise. This is particularly true both of preaching and of evangelism. What, then, does the Bible have to tell us about proclaiming the Good News in the city?

Old Testament Proclamation

Evangelistic proclamation is not strongly developed in the Old Testament, primarily because the Israelites sought to maintain the purity and integrity of their nation. They perceived themselves as a "peculiar" people, unlike the other nations around them, both because of their worship of Yahweh (rather than the Canaanite, Mesopotamian, and Egyptian deities) and because of their committal to a law code which stressed covenantal responsibility, not individual license. It was not that Gentiles could not become a part of Israel; they certainly could and often did (e.g., Ruth the Moabitess who became the forebear of Israel's greatest king). It was simply that they were not sought.

Nonetheless, one cannot begin an exploration of the nature of the church's proclamation in the city without beginning with the church's Old Testament roots. Two Old Testament passages particularly point the way in understanding the church's responsibility for urban proclamation. The first passage is Isaiah 61:1–4, which we examined briefly earlier in this chapter, but want to explore more thoroughly now.

> The Spirit of the Sovereign Lord is on me,
>   because the Lord has anointed me
>   to preach good news to the poor.
> He has sent me to bind up the brokenhearted,
>   to proclaim freedom for the captives
>   and release from darkness for the prisoners,
> to proclaim the year of the Lord's favor
>   and the day of vengeance of our God,
> to comfort all who mourn,
>   and provide for those who grieve in Zion—
> to bestow on them a crown of beauty
>   instead of ashes,
> the oil of gladness
>   instead of mourning,
> and a garment of praise
>   instead of a spirit of despair.
> They will be called oaks of righteousness,

a planting of the LORD
for the display of his splendor.
They will rebuild the ancient ruins
and restore the places long devastated;
they will renew the ruined cities
that have been devastated for generations.

The opening lines of this prophecy, of course, were the words Jesus used to inaugurate his ministry. This indicates the importance he attached to this passage.

As indicated earlier in this chapter, this Scripture passage deals primarily with the liberation of the marginalized and oppressed of the city so that they could assume for themselves the rebuilding of their city. The passage also deals with their spiritual liberation.

First, note what it is that the person or people who are the subject of the prophecy are to do. As God's anointed ones, they are "to preach," "to bind up," "to proclaim," "to comfort," to "provide,"and "to bestow." The Anointed One is to play primarily a pastor-preacher role. As preacher, the Anointed One proclaims and preaches. As pastor, he binds up, comforts, provides, and bestows. Therefore, this passage has to do primarily with the proclamation of the Good News. And, as pointed out earlier, it is in the cities that this Good News is to be proclaimed.

Second, note to whom the Anointed One is to preach and to pastor. It is to "the poor," "the brokenhearted," "the captives," "the prisoners," "all who mourn," and "those who grieve." Proclamation is essentially seen as a task of the Anointed One to the afflicted of society. In this passage, those who are powerful, self-possessed, and wealthy are conspicuously absented from hearing and receiving the Good News proclaimed by God's Anointed One! Could that be so because they do not see their need for such good news? And could this passage have shaped Jesus' antipathy for those seduced by their own power, prestige, property, and parochialism?

Third, note the results of the work of the Anointed One. The poor have good news preached to them, the brokenhearted are bound up, the captives are freed, the prisoners are released, the mourning and grieving are comforted and "the year of the LORD's favor" is proclaimed (see chapter 4 on the Year of Jubilee).

The work of the Anointed One is to result in good news preached to the poor. The task is not completed simply with preaching, however. "The blind receive sight, the lame walk, those who have leprosy are cured, the deaf hear, the dead are raised" (Matt. 11:5). Unless the brokenhearted are bound up, people in captivity freed, prisoners released, the grieving ones comforted, and the city's economy regularly redistributed ("the year of the LORD's favor"), then the proclamation is inadequate.

Word and work are all of one cloth in the city; to do one without the other is to be guilty of heresy.

Perhaps the most poignant Old Testament statement about proclamation is that of the book of Jonah. Jonah is all about proclamation—about proclamation in a city.

"Go to the great city of Nineveh and preach against it," the Lord commanded Jonah, "because its wickedness has come up before me" (Jonah 1:2). This was not a task Jonah particularly relished. When he realized he was not going to change God's mind, Jonah ran away rather than assume his responsibility. God followed Jonah, causing a great storm to occur around the ship on which Jonah was fleeing. Jonah was thrown overboard. "But the LORD provided a great fish to swallow Jonah, and Jonah was inside the fish three days and three nights" (1:17). Reconsidering his situation, Jonah repented of his refusal to follow God's will and submitted to God's call. Consequently, Jonah was unceremoniously vomited up on shore by the fish.

Much chastened, "Jonah obeyed the word of the LORD and went to Nineveh" (3:3), there to proclaim its destruction. To Jonah's consternation, the people of Nineveh—from the king to the lowest commoner—accepted Jonah's message of doom and repented of their sin. Never was there a preacher more disappointed when people actually believed and acted on his message!

> When God saw what [the Ninevites] did and how they turned from their evil ways, he had compassion and did not bring upon them the destruction he had threatened. But Jonah was greatly displeased and became angry (3:10–4:1).

Jonah could not accept the forgiveness which God exercised toward the people of Nineveh. "I knew that you are a gracious and compassionate God, slow to anger and abounding in love, a God who relents from sending calamity" (4:2). The only compensation Jonah felt he might receive from preaching doom to the Ninevites was that he would see them destroyed by God. And now, because Yahweh is "a gracious and compassionate God," Jonah was not even going to get the satisfaction of seeing that happen.

God provided an object lesson for Jonah (history's first Sunday school lesson?) in the rapid growth and death of a vine which temporarily provided shade to Jonah who was still waiting outside Nineveh, hoping against hope it would be destroyed. Now Jonah was really angry! God replied to Jonah's anger:

> "You have been concerned about this vine, though you did not tend it or make it grow. It sprang up overnight and died overnight. But Nineveh has more than a hundred and twenty thousand people who

cannot tell their right hand from their left, and many cattle as well. Should I not be concerned about that great city?" (4:10–11).

With that admonition, the book of Jonah ends, never to answer for us how Jonah reacted or whether he repented of his fierce nationalism and hubris.

The book of Jonah was written in a period of Israel's history when it had become significantly nationalistic (even jingoistic) and introspective. That period could either be during the reign of Jeroboam II (786–746 B.C.E.), when the prophet Jonah lived (2 Kings 14:25), or around 350 B.C.E., when Israel was withdrawing from all contact with the gentile world under the reforms of Ezra and Nehemiah. In either situation, the intent of the prophecy would be the same. Convinced that God hated the foreign nations even more than they did, the Israelites were eagerly waiting for the day of judgment (Amos 5:18–20) when all the nations would be condemned and only Israel and Judah would be saved.

Jonah's story came as a reminder to Israel that God was as concerned for all the "Ninevehs" of the world as he was for Israel. The Israelites' refusal to share God's Good News with the rest of the world was really an attempt to run from the task God had given them, but he would pursue them and work supernaturally in order to have them do his bidding. For God is "a gracious and compassionate God, slow to anger and abounding in love," who is "concerned about that great city" of Nineveh where there were "more than a hundred and twenty thousand people who cannot tell their right hand from their left" (the possible reference to the children in Nineveh) and concerned about all the other cities of the world as well.

In the book of Jonah, proclamation plays a highly strategic role. It is what Jonah was called to do and is what brought about the repentance of the Ninevites. It was proclamation to a foreign, heathen city—a concern for even the Gentiles' response to God. In this the book of Jonah goes even beyond Jeremiah's call to the Israelites to "seek the peace and prosperity of the city" of Babylon, for in Jeremiah we see no sign of a commitment to the conversion of Babylon to Yahweh. Here, therefore, is Old Testament evangelistic proclamation at its very best, for it comes from the heart of God, who states, "Should I not be concerned about that great city?"

Jesus on Proclamation

What did Jesus understand as his mission? His quotation of Isaiah 61:1–2 at the inauguration of his ministry is one indication of his self-understanding. That he would select a passage on which to begin his ministry that stressed preaching Good News to the poor, freedom for the prisoner, recovery of sight for the blind, freedom for the captive, as well as proclaiming the Year of Jubilee (Luke 4:18–19) shows his priorities. Perhaps an even more direct statement occurs later in Luke 4:

> At daybreak Jesus went out to a solitary place. The people were looking for him and when they came to where he was, they tried to keep him from leaving them. But he said, "I must preach the good news of the kingdom of God to the other towns also, because that is why I was sent." And he kept on preaching in the synagogues of Judea (vv. 42–44).

In Matthew 9:35–38, Jesus suggested not only what his mission should be about, but what his followers' mission should focus on as well. This passage tells us that Jesus traveled throughout Judea teaching, preaching, and healing. It further reported that "when he saw the crowds, he had compassion on them, because they were harassed and helpless, like sheep without a shepherd" (v. 36). Finally, he said to his disciples, "The harvest is plentiful but the workers are few. Ask the Lord of the harvest, therefore, to send out workers into his harvest field" (vv. 37–38). Jesus thereby indicated that he expected his followers to imitate him in like ministry.

Jesus perhaps gives his clearest statement of purpose in response to the thinly disguised question of John's disciples, indicating John's increasing fear that he might have been mistaken in naming Jesus as the Messiah. John's followers ask Jesus, "Are you the one who was to come, or should we expect someone else?" Jesus replied,

> "Go back and report to John what you have seen and heard: The blind receive sight, the lame walk, those who have leprosy are cured, the deaf hear, the dead are raised, and the good news is preached to the poor. Blessed is the man who does not fall away on account of me" (Luke 7:22–23).

All these passages indicate Jesus' understanding of his mission as that of proclamation: proclamation by preaching, by teaching, by healing, and by compassion for the poor and marginalized of Jewish society.

What Jesus expected out of his followers is given particular voice in Matthew 10:1–10, when he sent the disciples out on a preaching mission. As he sent them forth, Jesus said:

> "Go . . . to the lost sheep of Israel. As you go, preach this message: 'The kingdom of heaven is near.' Heal the sick, raise the dead, cleanse those who have leprosy, drive out demons. Freely you have received, freely give" (vv. 6–8).

In the companion passage in Luke 10, Jesus instructs his disciples:

> "When you enter a town and are not welcomed, go into its streets and say, 'Even the dust of your town that sticks to our feet we wipe off

against you. Yet be sure of this: the kingdom of God is near.' I tell you, it will be more bearable on the day for Sodom than for that town.

"Woe to you, Korazin! Woe to you, Bethsaida! For if the miracles that were performed in you had been performed in Tyre and Sidon, they would have repented long ago, sitting in sackcloth and ashes" (vv. 10–13).

In the Great Commission, Jesus instructs his followers to "go and make disciples of all nations, baptizing them . . . and teaching them to obey everything I have commanded you" (Matt. 28:19–20).

In all these statements, it is clear that Jesus saw the mission of his followers to be comparable to his: to preach, to teach, to heal, to present the Good News, to warn, to act in compassion toward the broken in body and soul.

Proclamation in the Book of Acts

Examining the passages in the book of Acts regarding proclamation gives us insight into the early church's assumptions concerning the place of proclamation in the urban ministry of the church.

The beginning chapters of Acts are filled with Christians in Jerusalem sharing their faith: in the temple, among the beggars and the broken, even before the Jewish Sanhedrin. The book presents excerpts from sermons preached by Peter, John, and Stephen. When Philip met the treasurer of the queen of the Ethiopians, he asked the man (who was reading Isaiah 53), "Do you understand what you are reading?" The Ethiopian eunuch responded, "How can I unless someone explains it to me?" (Acts 8:30–31). Philip shared the story of Jesus with the man and he received Christ and was baptized.

Simon Peter's sharing of the Gospel with the family and household of Cornelius, a Roman centurion, was a significant breakthrough for the church, for it was the first time the Gospel was received by a Gentile with no Jewish commitment. The text states:

While Peter was still speaking these words, the Holy Spirit came on all who heard the message. . . . Then Peter said, "Can anyone keep these people from being baptized with water? They have received the Holy Spirit just as we have." So he ordered that they be baptized in the name of Jesus Christ (Acts 10:44, 46–48).

With the entrance of Paul into the leadership of the church, the focus of the book of Acts shifts to missionary journeys to Greek and Gentile cities. In the city of Pisidian Antioch, after his message was rejected by the city's Jews, Paul shared with gentile listeners Isaiah 49:6: "I have made you a light for the Gentiles, that you may bring salvation to the ends of the earth." It is then recorded in the book of Acts, "When the Gentiles heard this, they were glad and honored the word of the Lord; and all who were appointed for eternal life believed" (13:48).

After considerable ministry in a large number of cities in Asia Minor, Paul was in the city of Troas. There Paul received a vision "of a man of Macedonia standing and begging him, 'Come over to Macedonia and help us'" (Acts 16:9). Not disobedient to that heavenly vision, Paul and his companions crossed from Asia into Macedonia and Greece. Thus the Gospel was introduced into Europe.

Perhaps the greatest instance of proclamation in Acts was Paul's daring speech in the city of Athens—a classical application of Moody's principle that great urban preaching combines Bible and newspaper, Christian theology and the particularities (and even peculiarities) of that context. Paul began his evangelistic thrust in Athens with the words,

> "Men of Athens! I see that in every way you are very religious. For as I walked around and looked carefully at your objects of worship, I even found an altar with this inscription: TO AN UNKNOWN GOD. Now what you worship as something unknown I am going to proclaim to you" (17:22–23).

Although most of Paul's hearers that day (being sophists) rejected him, some responded. Some said, "We want to hear you again on this subject" (v. 32). But the author of Acts also reports, "A few men became followers of Paul and believed" (v. 34).

Actually, from Acts one can discern quite clearly Paul's missionary methods.[6] Paul went only to cities to evangelize and to plant churches— he did not visit villages or towns for this purpose. He did not seem to choose a city haphazardly, either. It is quite obvious, in studying the book of Acts, that the cities in which Paul invested considerable time and built strong churches were all the politically, economically, and religiously paramount cities of their Roman regions. Paul was an urban pastor and church planter!

When he entered into a city, Paul did not enter alone but brought with him his lieutenants trained both to evangelize and to build a community of believers. His first visit in each city would be to the local synagogue (e.g., Acts 13) where he would proclaim the Gospel. Normally he was met with scorn and rejection, but there were always a few Jews who listened and responded to his message (Acts 14:1–7).

Paul would then go to a gathering place of the Gentiles in that city (see Acts 17). There he would proclaim the Gospel to the Gentiles and, most often, would again be met with scorn and rejection. But, again, there would be the few who would listen and respond (vv. 30–35).

Gathering those responsive Jews and Gentiles, Paul and his lieuten-ants would withdraw from public ministry in that city. They would then begin the intensive discipling of these new Christians (Acts 18), not only teaching them about the Christian faith but also preparing them to develop and maintain a church (which was actually modeled upon a Jewish synagogue). As Paul and his team worked with these new converts, he would particularly encourage the Christian community to call forth each other's gifts, that each might contribute to the building of that local body of Christ (1 Cor. 12:1–14:40; Eph. 4:7, 11–13, etc.). Out of that process, the leadership of the church would be discerned and chosen, and leaders would receive the intense attention of Paul and his team.

Finally, it would be time for Paul and his team to leave the fledgling church (Acts 19:1–22), but by this time the foundation had been built for the church to develop and grow strong. And even though the church had to make its own way in its pagan city, it was not alone, for it continued in contact with the church in Jerusalem and sister churches throughout the region. Paul and his disciples maintained a written dialogue with each of these churches and often returned for visits.

Who Is to Proclaim?

"Everyone who calls on the name of the Lord will be saved." How, then, can they call on the one they have not believed in? And how can they believe in the one of whom they have not heard? And how can they hear without someone preaching to them? And how can they preach unless they are sent? (Rom. 10:13–15).

Who are those who are called to proclaim the Gospel to those who have not heard it? Who has been sent by God to the cities throughout the world to share the Good News? The author of Acts presents the answer to that question in a most winsome way:

Now those who had been scattered by the persecution in connection with Stephen [his execution] traveled as far as Phoenicia, Cyprus and Antioch, telling the message only to Jews. Some of them, however, men from Cyprus and Cyrene, went to Antioch and began to speak to Greeks also, telling them the good news about the Lord Jesus. The Lord's hand was with them, and a great number of people believed and turned to the Lord (11:19–21).

Who was sent? The entire church—those people fleeing from Jerusalem, fleeing for their lives!

Throughout his epistles, Paul stresses which Christians he believed were called by God to proclaim the Gospel in their cities. In writing to the Philippian Christians, he states:

I thank my God every time I remember you. In all my prayers for all of you, I always pray with joy because of your partnership in the gospel from the first day until now, being confident of this, that he who began a good work in you will carry it on to completion until the day of Christ Jesus (Phil. 1:3–6).

Further on in his letter to the Philippian church, Paul reflects on his imprisonment in Rome. He writes,

> Now I want you to know, brothers, that what has happened to me has really served to advance the gospel. As a result, it has become clear throughout the whole palace guard and to everyone else that I am in chains for Christ. Because of my chains, most of the brothers in the Lord have been encouraged to speak the word of God more coura-geously and fearlessly. It is true that some preach Christ out of envy and rivalry, but others out of good will. . . . The important thing is that in every way, whether from false motives or true, Christ is preached. And because of this I rejoice (1:12–15, 18).

It does not take much digging into Paul's writings to realize that his answer to the question, "Which Christians are to proclaim the Gospel in the city?" would be a very brief answer. It would be: "Everyone!" It is the task of the whole body of Christ in a city—all of its members—to share the Gospel in word, in deed, and in life together. All urban Christians are called to be evangelists—proclaimers of the Gospel to those in the city whose lives they touch.

Why is proclamation absolutely essential to the work of the church in the city? As we have explored over these past two chapters, the work of the church in the city is that of presence, prayer, practice, and proclama-tion. Without prayer, ministry in the city will lack the spiritual foundation and strength upon which it must be based; by its very nature, however, prayer is a hidden ministry. Presence is the final authentication of urban ministry, for if the corporate life of the church and individual lives of Christians are not consistent with their practice and proclamation, their unfaithful lifestyle will invalidate all that their work and witness seeks to accomplish. Practice is necessary because the essence of the Gospel is to be on the side of the hurting, the poor, the marginalized, the oppressed, the broken of this world; the world knows this, perhaps even better than we do. If our proclamation and our practice are not consistent with each other, it will be our proclamation which invariably will be discounted.

Proclamation therefore must be consistent with our practice, pres-ence, and prayer. But proclamation also plays its own unique role in the city. If those in the church seek to live Christlike lives but provide no verbal witness as to why this is so, people will simply conclude that we are "nice people." If we defend the cause of the widow and orphan but provide no interpretation of why we are committed to the broken and hurting in the world, people will conclude that the church is simply made up of social reformers. It is proclamation—and only proclamation—that gives explanation for "the hope that is within us." It is only as the church shares its faith that people are aware that the church has any faith at all. Without proclamation, the work of the church in the city is incomplete.

The Gospel exists to be shared. We are responsible for sharing the faith that is within us with those who have not heard it. Paul said it for us all: "Woe to me if I do not preach the gospel!" (1 Cor. 9:16). Whether we are a pastor preaching from an urban pulpit, an evangelist sharing the gospel on a street corner, or a faithful layperson witnessing to the people with whom we work, it is the great privilege of the people of God to proclaim the Gospel. It is a privilege we should never take for granted or assume lightly.

Let me suggest that, rather than being the first thing and the constant thing that we do, proclamation should be a later thing we do. In the city, our proclamation must be built upon the foundation of our presence, our prayer, and our practice—our involvement in ministering to the social, economic, and political needs of the poor and oppressed.

I once had a person say to me, "Words . . . words . . . words. That's all I hear from you Christians—a constant volley of words. Words from your pulpits, words over the radio, words in every conceivable magazine, book, or newspaper. Words . . . words . . . words. If your actions began to compare in volume to the sheer number of your words, this world would be a far better place in which to live. Why don't you Christians talk less and act more?"

That's harsh criticism, but criticism we should listen to. We Christians do talk too much! We also talk too early! In the city, you have to earn the respect of those you wish to evangelize. You can win their respect only by showing that you care as much about them and the problems with which they have to deal as you care about their souls. Proclamation is a critical part of the work of the church in the city. It is primary. But it is not first. We Christians should be slow to speak but quick to act, proclaiming the Gospel only in relation to our acts of compassion and of our commitment to the poor of body or of soul.

ST. PAUL'S SECRET FOR EFFECTIVE URBAN MINISTRY[7]

What is the ministry that the church is called to practice in the city? The Bible calls us to proclaim the fullness of the Gospel in and to the city, to evangelize, to discover and celebrate our city's joy, and to address issues of health care, infant mortality, stress in city life, environmental pollution, the need for housing which is adequate, fairly distributed and safe, and economic development (especially for the jobless). We are to advocate for the poor, seek empowerment of the powerless, urge upon the city a personal relationship with God, seek the peace and reconciliation of all peoples in the city, and become stewards of the city's inner spirituality.

That is a pretty tall order! How can the church handle such a large and complex responsibility? It is St. Paul, Christianity's greatest urban missionary, to whom we turn for direction.

We do not often think of Paul as an urban pastor, but we have seen that he was one. The churches he organized and then served were all in cities. Every letter he wrote to a church, with the exception of the epistle to the Galatians, was written to a city church. And his focus in each letter was to provide the theological framework (the Bible) and instructions in ministry (the newspaper) to enable each church to be more effective in ministering to its city.

In the book of Ephesians, Paul presents the primary principles upon which he operated as an urban pastor. Those principles help us to understand how the church realistically can practice a holistic faith in the city and undertake the work and responsibility God has laid upon it.

"As a prisoner for the Lord, then, I urge you to live a life worthy of the calling you have received" (Eph. 4:1). With this verse Paul begins his reflection on how the church can undertake the full-orbed ministry to which it has been called by God. Each member of the church, Paul states, has been called by God to serve God and humanity in a particular way. That is each believer's vocation. Paul then instructs us to live our lives in conformity to our vocation. It is our vocation that shapes how we are free and how we are constrained to live—not the other way around! Our lives are to be a consistent display of our vocation, so that our lives do not defame but rather support the work to which God calls us.

Our vocation can be practiced only within the community of faith. Each member of the church is to work actively to maintain the peace and unity of the church, Paul teaches. Each of us is, at the same time, to recognize and call forth the vocations to which each individual in the church has been called by God. Consequently, it is critical to recognize that each of us is "graced" or gifted by God to practice that vocation to which we have been called (Eph. 4:17).

With the stage thus set, Paul is now able to move to the heart of his teaching on undertaking biblical and yet achievable ministry in the city. This teaching is found in Ephesians 4:11–16. We will look initially at verses 11–13.

> [Christ] gave some to be apostles, some to be prophets, some to be evangelists, and some to be pastors and teachers, to prepare God's people for works of service, so that the body of Christ may be built up until we all reach unity in the faith and in the knowledge of the Son of God and become mature, attaining to the whole measure of the fullness of Christ.

Here Paul presents the single most important principle of successful city ministry. It is the principle upon which Paul built his entire ministry.

It is a principle I discovered early as a city pastor, and it transformed my ministry. It is a principle which, when consistently used, has always had a transforming impact upon a church's city ministry.

Paul points out that, in every church, there are apostles, prophets, evangelists, pastors, and teachers. I would suggest that the people to whom Paul is referring are not people occupying offices, but church members performing specific functions. There are those in any church, Paul is saying, who perform the function of apostle, of prophet, of evangelist, of pastor, and of teacher. In the New Testament, all references to these positions, whether in a local church or in the universal church, are functional references—that is, people performing particular tasks. Over the centuries, however, the church has turned these functions into offices that a person often occupies for life.

What are these functions? The apostle exercises authority for ruling the life of the church. The prophet calls the church to social responsibility. The evangelist proclaims the Gospel to those who have not heard it. The pastor shepherds, or nurtures, the people who have received the Gospel. The teacher instructs Christians in their faith.

According to Paul, a primary task of the urban pastor is to discover and call forth those in the congregation to whom God has given these gifts of leadership. Every church has in it those who have been placed there by God who can exercise authority, call the church to accountability, proclaim the gospel, nurture the people, and instruct in the faith. The pastor's job is to discover those people, call them forth, and train them to do that work even more effectively. A sign that a congregation is, indeed, the legitimate church of Jesus Christ is the presence in it of people functioning as apostles, prophets, evangelists, pastors, and teachers.

In the first urban church I pastored, one of the members struck me as a particularly nurturing individual. I spent time with Ward and discovered he had a profound ability to care for people. The more I got to know Ward, the more convinced I became that he was called to be a pastor—a nurturer of souls. The governing body of our church and I called Ward forth to be a "pastor" of our congregation—not an ordained clergyperson—but a member of the congregation placed there by God to care for its members. That became his "job," his vocation at the church, under the authority of our governing board and of me. Ward became a far more effective pastor than I ever was, but he became such because I gave him the room to exercise that calling.

Now the crucial question we must ask is this: "Why has Christ appointed some people in every church to function in these capacities?" Paul responds, "[Christ did this] to prepare God's people for works of service" (Eph. 4:12). This is the single most important principle for effective urban ministry! What that passage tells us is that *the urban church is not meant to be a shelter; it is meant to be a seminary!*

A shelter is a place where people come to escape the cold, the pain, and the discomfort of city life. We must keep in mind, however, that the people of the church are not those to be ministered unto. The church is not a shelter.

As a seminary, according to Paul, the church is meant to be a training ground, a school in Christian living, a center in which the people of God are educated to be God's ambassadors out in the world. All God's people are called to ministry in the world—to be salt, to be light, to be God's presence in the city. All God's people are to be praying for the city, to be practicing their faith in the economic, political, and social issues and concerns in which they get involved, and to be proclaiming the Good News of salvation in Christ.

It is not the job of the ordained pastor to be priest, prophet, and evangelist to the city. It is the job of every Christian. And the primary purpose of the urban church is to be the training ground or "seminary" preparing each Christian to undertake his or her ministry in the city.

That is why God does not give to one man or woman the job of being the pastor of the church. That is why God, in his infinite wisdom, places in every congregation some people who can bear rule, others who can call the church to social responsibility, others who can proclaim the Gospel, others who can nurture and pastor people, and still others who can instruct. Your church will be successful in reaching out to your city to the degree that you can discover those people, call them forth, train them, and imbue them with God's vision for the city—and then use them to prepare all the members of your congregation to become Christ's ministers to all of your city.

What Paul actually presents as the operating strategy for the urban church is the strategy of self-development. The primary task of the urban pastor, Paul teaches in Ephesians 4, is to enable his church to become self-sufficient. The worst possible pastor in the world, to Paul's mind, is the pastor who makes her people dependent upon herself—upon her preaching, her teaching, her administration, and her pastoral care. The truly effective pastor, Paul teaches, is the one who enables her congregation to become self-determined, to become a congregation that perceives its call from God to minister to the city and carries out that ministry through its life, witness, and community involvement. The essential characteristic of an urban ministerial style must be a commitment to self-development.

What is true for the local urban church can also become true for the neighborhood, the larger community, and the city itself, Paul teaches. First, self-development begins with the pastor as God liberates him or her from needing to be in control of the congregation or from making people dependent upon "the pastor." The pastor is freed to take the risk of calling forth and developing the God-given gifts of congregation members to do their ministry within that congregation and to the world (Eph. 4:11–15).

Second, Paul teaches that congregation members are then liberated to assume their rightful responsibilities in the church and in witness to the world. Their minds and spirits are freed and they are liberated internally (vv. 17–24). Their actions and ethics in the world are transformed (vv. 25–32). Their lives take on new focus, as their priorities are straightened out and each person finds that ministry in the city for which he or she has been created, called, and gifted by God (Eph. 5:1–20).

Third, the transformed, newly vitalized and focused congregation can then have a profound impact upon its immediate neighborhood, its larger urban community, and even upon the city itself. Paul tells us that a church so liberated will become a liberator of the city. The self-determination and development of people will spread from the church to the city. It will transform marriages (Eph. 5:21–33) and lead to the liberation of women (v. 33), the protection of children (Eph. 6:1–4), the defense of the poor and the oppressed (v. 9), and the restructuring of the economic and political systems of the city (vv. 5–9). As a result, all people will be freed from that which oppresses them and will become all that God created them to be.

Finally, Paul teaches that such a liberated church and its people will become those who can effectively confront the systems and structures of their city and the forces which lie behind those structures. "Put on the full armor of God so that you can take your stand against the devil's schemes," the apostle warns us. "For our struggle is not against flesh and blood, but against the rulers, against the authorities, against the powers of this dark world and against the spiritual forces of evil in the heavenly realms" (Eph. 6:11–12).

Only the people of the church can become both the liberated ones and the true liberators of the city. Only the people of the church can be spiritually equipped and protected to confront and to withstand the evil power of the principalities of their city (Eph. 6:10–20). Only the people of the church can then see through Satan's lies. Only the people of the church can battle against Satan for the interior spirituality of that city and of the people who live there.

Following the strategy presented in Ephesians, the church becomes God's effective instrument for urban ministry. It becomes capable of communicating the Gospel effectively to the lost, able to minister in transforming ways to the poor and exploited and to the rich and powerful, and able to practice an authentic life together in the Spirit. By so practicing both the preparatory (apostle, prophet, evangelist, pastor-teacher) and sustaining ("work in the world") vocations, the church will create the preconditions in which the practice of its unity and peace will become inevitable. The church will then grow and build itself up in love, not by concentrating on growing or by making itself a loving fellowship, but by each person's discovering his vocation, doing her unique work of ministry both in the church and to the city, and supporting fellow Christians as each undertakes his or her specific vocation.

This is how the church practices its faith holistically and comprehensively in the city. This is how it effectively addresses issues of the city's joy, health care, longevity, stress, pollution, adequate and fair and safe housing, economic development and jobs, relationship with God and individuals' reconciliations with neighbors, advocacy for the poor, empowerment and self-determination, and stewardship of its interior spirituality. This is how the urban church carries out both the Great Commission and the Great Commandment effectively. This is Paul's secret for the practice of the faith in the heart of the city!

To what has God called the church in the city? The body of Christ— your church, my church—has been called by God to place before the city God's vision for that city. That vision is one of a city wholly given over to God, freed from Satan's influence, a city whose principalities and powers, systems and structures have been as transformed by the shed blood and saving work of Christ as have been its people. In the light of Jesus Christ's sacrifice for the city, the church issues a continuing call to the city which exposes the lies which limit its people's lives, which calls its systems and structures to accountability, which defends the cause of the poor and oppressed, and which both comforts and afflicts those who have been seduced and yet benefit from its systems.

The means by which the church issues this clarion call to each city is through its presence, prayer, practice, and proclamation. God's vision of the city as he would have it is presented in and through the church's life together. That vision is empowered by the church's practical, continuing prayer for its city. That vision is carried out in the practice of the church, as it carries out ministries of compassion, self-determination, and advocacy for the poor, and ministries calling that city's systems—and the demonic powers lying behind those systems—to accountability. That vision is given voice by the church, as it proclaims to the city the good news that it can experience the transforming love of Christ.

This, all of this, is the work of Christ's body, the church, to which God calls all of us and each of us in our city. Nothing less will suffice! And yet there is one thing more. There is a particularly godly way for undertaking such ministry to our neighborhood, larger community, and city. That more godly way we will explore in the next chapter.

Chapter Nine

GODLY WAYS
FOR COMMUNITY MINISTRIES

I was meeting with an executive of a large parachurch mission organization which is becoming involved in third world urban ministry. He explained to me that he had been studying the urban work of other mission organizations so as to inform his own group in the formation of its urban strategy. He thought that perhaps the directions World Vision was taking in its Urban Advance would be helpful to his organization.

I asked him how his survey was going. His response disturbed me greatly. "What I've discovered, Bob," he replied, "is that most parachurch organizations and denominations have formulated mission strategies, but almost all of them are having trouble in implementing those strategies. Great strategies, but little successful implementation!"

Now, if that does not intimidate you before you begin sharing about the urban strategy and implementation of your organization, I do not know what will. I trust that what I shared with him that day about World Vision's urban work in the third world provided a more optimistic perspective for him.

We have examined thus far in the second section of this book the insights Scripture gives to us for the formulation of our own urban mission strategy. But is it "great strategies, but little successful implementation"? Where in Scripture do we see evidence that the body of Christ really can be effective in holistic ministry in the city?

To answer that question, we must first ask: "What are the marks of truly effective urban ministry?" I suggest there are four:

- Are the systems of a city being confronted and offered real potential for change?

- Are the poor and exploited of the city provided the vehicles by which they can bring about change in their situation?

- Are the middle class and the powerful given the opportunity to join in common cause with the poor to confront the systems of the city and seek their transformation?

- Is there a spiritual transformation that is going on in that city, or are the changes only social? Are the lives both of that city's poor and of its powerful being changed by God?

Therefore we must ask ourselves: "Is there in Scripture any example of an urban ministry which exhibits these four marks of truly effective ministry?" There are examples in Scripture of ministries that significantly addressed their cities, but one example of a city ministry stands head and shoulders above all the others.

This ministry confronted the city's systems and saw significant transformation occur. This ministry organized the people of that city— both its poor and its powerful—to reverse the destructive directions of that city. A result of this ministry was a profound spiritual transformation, not only of the city itself, but of an overwhelming majority of its people. This ministry of presence, prayer, practice, and proclamation exposed the lies of the powers that would have exploited that city, and it engaged the people in creating for themselves a new vision of what it meant for them to be "the city of God." This vision was so profound that it altered for all time the self-understanding and mission directions of the Jewish people.

The ministry was that of Nehemiah. The time was 445–433 B.C.E. The city was Jerusalem. The memoirs of Nehemiah's ministry, which became the Old Testament book of Nehemiah, provide us with the best textbook I believe has ever been written on how to undertake urban ministry successfully that transforms more than people. Let's examine that textbook to discover how to do ministry God's way!

BEGIN WITH YOURSELF[1]

In the month of Kislev in the twentieth year, while I was in the citadel of Susa, Hanani, one of my brothers, came from Judah with some other men, and I questioned them about the Jewish remnant that survived the exile, and also about Jerusalem.

They said to me, "Those who survived the exile and are back in the province are in great trouble and disgrace. The wall of Jerusalem is broken down, and its gates have been burned with fire."

When I heard these things, I sat down and wept (Neh. 1:1–4).

Thus begins the book of Nehemiah. It begins with relatives of a man named Nehemiah coming to the capital of the Persian Empire, Susa, to visit him and to share with him the sad news that the once glorious Jerusalem had, since the Babylonian exile, eroded into a destitute and forsaken city. Who Nehemiah was and why he was in the Persian capital city is not revealed until later in the story.

Nehemiah, upon hearing the sad news, dissolves into tears. His grief is not a short grief. He tells us, "For some days I mourned and fasted and prayed before the God of heaven." First, Nehemiah wept! He allowed his heart to be broken with the things that break the heart of God. He did not try to avoid the pain nor dismiss his grief as he went about his daily tasks in Susa. Instead, he gave himself permission to live into that pain and to feel it to the very core of his being. Nehemiah understood grief and saw that its exploration is often the way people discover their vocations—for God always calls us to address a particular pain of the world.

Then Nehemiah prays (Neh. 1:5–11). His prayer is a model of how to be honest about one's grief but then to move beyond it in order to discover what calling God has for us through that grief. The prayers of Nehemiah that lasted "for some days" included the celebration and praise of God, even in the midst of the man's grief (vv. 5–6). Nehemiah confesses the sins of his people which have contributed to the present disaster, as well as his family's and his own contribution to that disaster (vv. 6–7)! "I confess the sins we Israelites, including myself and my father's house, have committed against you," he prayed.

In his praying, Nehemiah is not beneath reminding God of the commitments the Lord has made to Israel, and especially the promise, "I will gather [the Israelites] from [exile] and bring them to the place I have chosen as a dwelling for my Name" (v. 9). Claiming that promise, Nehemiah asks God to show him—through his grief—what God wants him and God's other servants to do about the city (vv. 10–11).

Nehemiah does not yet have a clear-cut plan of action for dealing with Jerusalem's dilemma. He does know, however, the next risky step of faith God is asking him to take. So he prays God's favor upon that step: "Give your servant success today by granting him favor in the presence of [the king]" (v. 11).

Now comes one of the most striking statements in the book of Nehemiah —striking for its simplicity and directness: "I was cupbearer to the king" (v. 11). What was a cupbearer, and why does Nehemiah mention it at this point in the story?

This is not a statement of fact. This is a statement of strategy. The cupbearer played quite an important role in the Persian court.[2] His status was ahead of courtiers, eunuchs, gatekeepers of the palace, singers, and bakers—the people who made the court function. The role of the cupbearer was to select and present the wines and other drinks to the Persian king and queen during their meals, at state banquets, and on any other requested occasion. Because he was often alone in the presence of the king, the monarch would have complete trust in him and often strong attachments would develop. Because the cupbearer was also alone in the presence of the queen, he was a eunuch; it is reasonable to assume that Nehemiah was also a eunuch.

When Nehemiah states, therefore, "I was cupbearer to the king," he is making more than an occupational observation. He is honestly appraising his situation and looking for possibilities in that situation.

Nehemiah's heart is broken over the fate of his city and as he has brought his pain to God in prayer, he feels increasingly that he is called by God to do something about that city. He does not have great amounts of money. He holds no political office. He is not a recognized leader of Persia or of Israel. But he is cupbearer to the king. Several times a day he is alone in the Persian emperor's presence. He is respected by that king, and his advice is appreciated.

This is who Nehemiah is. What, now, could he do with his position to address his concern for Jerusalem? Although highly irregular, he could take the risk of sharing his concern with the king. The risk was real, because if the king took offense, Nehemiah could lose not only his job but also his head (Esth. 4:9–11). But Jerusalem was worth the risk!

Chapter 1 of Nehemiah gives the essential grounds for undertaking God-empowered urban ministry. Nehemiah began with himself. So should we. The starting place for us is with the question, "What makes me weep over my city?" If you answer that question, "Nothing makes me weep over this city," you had better get out of urban ministry because you do not belong there. Only a man or woman who allows his or her heart to be broken with the pain and the plight of the hurting poor and/or the hurting powerful of the city belongs in ministry there. To be effective in urban ministry, you must have a heart that is as big as the city itself. Such a heart develops only as one gives one's self the permission to live into and feel the pain of the city's people.

Then, like Nehemiah, bathe your tears in prayer. Prayer needs to come out of pain. When we cry to God over what breaks our hearts, he will make clear what he is calling us to do in the city. Only out of our own brokenness and vulnerability can God show us how he wants to use us to empower people to—

> Rebuild the ancient ruins
>   and restore the places long devastated; . . .
> renew the ruined cities
>   that have been devastated for generations (Isa. 61:4).

Out of such willingness to open your life to the pain you feel about the city and out of your willingness to bathe your tears in prayer, God will lead you to appraise honestly your situation and to look for possibilities! You will discover, in God's timing, how God is calling you to contribute to the effort to empower and liberate the city's broken. Also, you will be enabled to take that next risky step of faith that takes you from reflection and quiet nurturing of the pain to action to deal with the issue.

It is terribly important, however, that you not rush the incubation of the pain. It is important that you take your time in perceiving and understanding God's call to you to do ministry in a new way in the city. Rushing the incubation will only bring forth a premature effort, a ministry not sufficiently grounded in God's struggle with you to have the depth necessary to have a sustaining work of empowerment and liberation.

Martin Buber, the great Jewish mystic, said it best when he wrote,

> When a man grows aware of a new way in which to serve God, he should carry it around with him secretly, and without uttering it, for nine months, as though he were pregnant with it, and let others know of it only at the end of that time, as though it were a birth.[3]

The day finally comes to keep it a secret no longer. The call is brought forth as if it were a birth. And you go to the king with your pain.

BUILD YOUR NETWORKS

Nehemiah went to the king; he looked sufficiently downcast that the king asked, "Why does your face look so sad when you are not ill? This can be nothing but sadness of heart" (Neh. 2:2). So it was that Nehemiah shared with the king his burden and the king responded to Nehemiah's pain. The response was to approve Nehemiah's request.

> Then I prayed to the God of heaven, and I answered the king, "If it pleases the king and if your servant has found favor in his sight, let him send me to the city in Judah where my fathers are buried so that I can rebuild it" (Neh. 2:4–5).

Permission granted, Nehemiah also gained the support of the queen (v. 6), the governors of Trans-Euphrates (v. 7), the keeper of the king's forest (v. 8), and strategic army and cavalry officers (v. 9). When he arrived in Jerusalem, Nehemiah moved in among the people, lived among them without telling them what he wanted to do (vv. 11–12), spent considerable time studying the situation, and sensitively visited with the people (vv. 13–16).

What was Nehemiah doing? He was building the foundation upon which all the rest of his ministry in Jerusalem would be based. He was building his network. The success of everything else that he would do was built on the strength of the foundation he laid in those networks.

Networking is the first task any urban pastor needs to do in his or her community. It is also perhaps the most important task. For on the strength of his or her networks will stand or fall the ministry.

What is networking? It is the building and maintaining of those contacts which will enable all of those in that network to carry out ministry more effectively to and with the exploited, the pagans, and the church in that city.[4] Networking is the intentional and systematic visiting of the people in a community by pastor and church people to lead to that community's organizing of itself to cope with its most substantive problems. That is what Nehemiah did—and what we are called to do also.

If networking is built upon biblical foundations—such as we observe here in Nehemiah's story—it will enable the urban church to reorder and prioritize its life and mission so that it will be able to join effectively with the poor and exploited of its city in their (and perhaps in the church's) liberation. By so joining in common cause, the church will gain the credibility to proclaim the Gospel to those who have formerly despised it.

Underlying the biblical concept of networking is the essential assumption that all human beings, however uneducated, exploited, and beaten down by life, have a greater capacity to understand and act upon their situation than the most highly informed or sympathetic outsider. Every human being, no matter how deprived, is created in the image of God and as such is no less innately capable of determining his future than the most highly educated and self-determined individual. As Dom Helder Camara put it, "The first great discovery we made was that . . . people who didn't know how to read or write still knew how to think."[5]

Nehemiah was not the only biblical networker: among the finest were Moses and Paul.[6]

Moses, as he met with God at the burning bush (Exod. 3:1–4:17), had been carefully prepared by God for the task awaiting him. "Who am I, that I should go to Pharaoh and bring the Israelites out of Egypt?" Moses asked God incredulously (3:11). But God knew why he had chosen this apparently forgotten shepherd on the backside of the desert. As the son of a Hebrew slave, Moses had been miraculously delivered from Egyptian infanticide (Exod. 1:8–2:7) and had been subsequently well educated (Exod. 2:8–10). His commitment to the Jews and to their liberation was so great that he would later risk his own life and career in order to rescue an Israelite in distress (Exod. 2:11–15). It could truly be said of Moses that he was a Hebrew of the Hebrews.

Moses was also an Egyptian of the Egyptians, however. "When the child grew older," Exodus 2:10 tells us, "[his Hebrew mother] took him to Pharaoh's daughter and he became her son. She named him Moses, saying, 'I drew him out of the water.' " Moses was, according to Josephus, considered a prince of Egypt, a member of the royal family. The treasures of Egypt and its political influence as the world's most powerful nation were all available to him (Heb. 11:24–26). Tradition has it that Moses was one of Egypt's most competent generals who successfully led a campaign against the Ethiopians. This was a man who understood the Egyptians— how they thought, what they prioritized, how they organized themselves. Even as a shepherd on the backside of the desert, Moses had access to the pharaoh, whom he could later confront to demand, "Let my people go!" And once the Israelites had been let go, Moses had the Egyptian knowledge to organize this great host for a march across the desert.

Finally, Moses was a man of the desert. For forty years he had lived in the desert, made his livelihood at herding sheep, married and raised a family there. As well, he had entered into the family of Jethro, the priest of Midian who taught him how to survive in the desert and later helped him to organize and administer the vast company of freed slaves from Egypt (Exod. 18:13–27). From his desert associates, Moses was spiritually taught and strengthened so that he was prepared to lead his people through the forty years of wilderness wanderings.

Once Moses met God at the burning bush and received his vocation for the remainder of his life, it is intriguing to note how Moses used the network he had built over the years. Aaron, his brother and a Levite leader, provided him credibility and entree to the Hebrew people. He used his contacts in Egypt to do what no other Israelite could do—enter Pharaoh's presence at will. Moses used Joshua and Caleb as lieutenants to organize the people; he used his father-in-law to train Israel's leaders in desert survival. Without the network Moses had built over the years, or without his continuing ability to network during his confrontation with Pharaoh and his ability to lead the people during their forty years in the desert, Israel's exodus from Egypt could never have happened.

St. Paul is a New Testament example of remarkable networking. Like Moses, Paul was a man magnificently prepared by God for the vocation to which God had called him. He was a man who thoroughly understood and was totally devoted to the Jewish faith and nation. In his own words, he testified, "[I was] circumcised on the eighth day, of the people of Israel, of the tribe of Benjamin, a Hebrew of the Hebrews; in regard to the law, a Pharisee; as for zeal, persecuting the church; as for legalistic righteousness, faultless" (Phil. 3:5–6).

At the same time, Paul was a man who understood and appreciated the Gentiles. Born and raised in the gentile city of Tarsus, Paul was a Roman citizen—a political lever he would use often for the sake of the church and his vocation. He understood the Greek culture, Roman law, gentile society, pagan religions, even Roman sports. He therefore knew profoundly the people to whom he had been called to minister. No wonder Paul could write,

> To the Jews I became like a Jew, to win the Jews. . . . To those not having the law I became like one not having the law . . . so as to win those not having the law. To the weak I became weak, to win the weak. I have become all things to all men so that by all possible means I might save some" (1 Cor. 9:20–22).

When Paul was converted to Christ, God sent Ananias to him with these words: "Go [to Paul]! This man is my chosen instrument to carry my name before the Gentiles and their kings and before the people of Israel" (Acts 9:15). This was exactly what Paul did. For the remainder of his life, Paul became a tireless evangelist, spreading the Gospel throughout Judah, but primarily into the gentile world. Paul's three successful missionary journeys into the pagan Roman Empire transformed Christianity from a Jewish sect into a worldwide faith for Jew and Gentile alike.

The effectiveness of those journeys was significantly enhanced by Paul's networking skills. The leaders he would gather from across the Roman Empire for evangelistic thrusts, his capacity to adapt his message to the people with whom he was dealing (evidencing his great appreciation and knowledge of their respective cultures), his building of an empire-wide network of skilled urban pastors and leaders who could be sent to troubled churches, his strategy for planting and growing churches in great urban centers (which was examined in the previous chapter), and his ability to deal with his protagonists testified to his skill. Paul was a supreme networker.

How can networking be done effectively in the city? Networking is based upon the living out of the Incarnation in the neighborhood in which your church has been placed by God to do ministry. That means living among the people, even if it is an urban slum or squatter settlement. An incarnational ministry is one which casts its lot with the neighborhood's people, working among them, spending time visiting with them, walking the streets, coming to know and care about and love them. Networking is built upon this incarnational foundation.

Even though I always lived in the community in which my church was situated, my primary responsibility was, of course, to my church. With the demands of a pastorate, I discovered that if I did not schedule specific time for neighborhood ministry and networking, it would not happen. Consequently, I followed the discipline of committing one day a week to neighborhood or community ministry. For the first year, I spent this time networking. I spent that neighborhood ministry day visiting people in my community: other pastors, business leaders, local politicians and party leaders, educators and service providers, but primarily I visited ordinary folk. In one of the churches I served, I challenged the church's leadership to join me, and we eventually had fifty-two church members visiting in our community each week.

What was it that we were trying to accomplish from our networking? Essentially, we were seeking to learn about that community from its residents and those who worked in it. From them we could discover the issues they were concerned about. We could identify who were the community's real leaders—the gatekeepers, caretakers, flak catchers, and brokers who make a community live (rarely are the real leaders of an urban community its formal leadership; those people only think they are the real leaders). We sought to uncover the people in the community who had a real burden for it and/or for one of its primary issues.

Why would a pastor and church want to learn such things from the community's people? If the church is going to minister effectively in its community, it must be addressing the issues the people perceive as the issues; no other issues really exist. If the church is going to join with the people in dealing with their issues, it is necessary to have the real leaders of the community involved; otherwise any such effort lacks acceptance and credibility in the neighborhood's eyes. If the church and community are to deal with those issues, the people who have a real burden for those issues need to be involved in planning and undertaking the actions to address those issues. They are the people who care the most about an issue and thus are the ones most motivated to do something about it.

How do you discover the people's issues, the community's leadership, the people who care? You ask the people! They will tell you. But you will not get this kind of information from them until you have first invested yourself in them by living among them and identifying with them. Such information-sharing comes as the end-product of trust.

There are some proven methodologies and techniques for effective networking. One's skill at networking can be enhanced by such training, but it is not the intention of this book to teach such techniques. Increasingly, people are writing materials[7] and offering seminars and urban workshops throughout both the first and third worlds which develop the skills of pastors and church leaders both in networking techniques and in the practice of other related urban strategies.[8]

What does networking do for the urban church?

- It builds and nurtures a wide and steadily expanding system of relationships with the true leaders, concerned people and groups, and the ordinary folk of your community.
- It identifies those people in the community with whom your pastor or your church may want to build relationships.
- It influences the preaching and teaching of the church (as the church seeks to be responsive to the issues and needs uncovered in the community).
- It influences the church's plans and programs in and for the community.
- It affects the interior life of the church, sometimes in profound ways.
- It creates a community awareness of and respect for your church, and adds significantly to your church's credibility by creating a community consciousness of your church.
- It identifies possible future evangelistic contacts.

- It either confirms or requires the church to adjust the research it may have gathered on the community.

Most of all, however, what networking can do for your church is to prepare you to take that next risky step of faith that can transform your ministry and your relationship with your community and city. That is the next step that Nehemiah takes.

ORGANIZE THE COMMUNITY

Having completed both his networking and his original research, Nehemiah gathered together "the priests . . . nobles . . . officials [and] any others who would be doing the work" (Neh. 2:16)—that is, the powerful and the people. Then a remarkable thing happened.

> Then I said to them, "You see the trouble we are in: Jerusalem lies in ruins, and its gates have been burned with fire. Come, let us rebuild the wall of Jerusalem, and we will no longer be in disgrace." I also told them about the gracious hand of my God upon me and what the king had said to me. They replied, "Let us start rebuilding." So they began this good work (Neh. 2:17–18).

Based on his networking with the people and the officials, and based upon his own personal research, Nehemiah identifies that issue which the people feel is most pressing: their sense of vulnerability due to their broken and ruined walls. As we will discover later on in this study, the broken-down walls of Jerusalem were not the real issue, but it was the issue the people felt the most; it was their *most urgent* issue. Therefore, it was the issue around which to organize that community.

Nehemiah organizes the people around that issue. He says to them, "You see the trouble we are in: Jerusalem lies in ruins and its gates have been burned with fire." You can imagine the heads nodding in agreement as he speaks; someone finally has had the courage to say openly what all of them had been feeling covertly.

Then Nehemiah, in essence, says to the people, "What are *we* going to do about it?" Notice that he did not say, "This is what the king of Persia is going to do about it," nor did he say, "This is what the priests or the local officials are going to do about it." He says, "Let *us* rebuild the wall of Jerusalem." "Let us assume responsibility for our own situation, and do something about it."

Nehemiah also testifies to "the gracious hand of my God upon me and what the king had said to me." In other words, Nehemiah assured them that they did not stand alone in the task of rebuilding the walls. The emperor of the entire Persian Empire was standing behind the project, not just with his personal endorsement, but by his funding and provision of much of the materials to the project (Neh. 2:7–9). Moreover, God had so blessed this endeavor that it was obvious that the Lord was behind the effort, too.

Neither king nor God would rebuild the walls, however. God and king would provide all the support necessary for the project to be completed. But it would be up to the Israelites living in Jerusalem to assume responsibility for their own situation and actually rebuild their own walls.

Nehemiah was obeying the supreme law of community empowerment, a law consistently disobeyed or ignored by the church. The primary principles of undertaking truly effective and godly community ministry are these:

- The people who are best able to deal with a problem are the people most affected by that problem.

- People who are excluded from full participation in the social, economic, or political life of their city or community can be empowered to participate only when they act collectively.

When most churches decide to minister to the people of their community, the members take it upon themselves to study that community and determine its primary issues and needs. Then, based on their findings, the church selects and determines the project or program needed to solve that problem or address that need. Once the church has decided what the solution needs to be, it goes ahead and implements, operates, and maintains that program.

Such an approach to community ministry is destined to fail! In this scheme, the ownership of the problem, the solution, and the program to implement that solution lies in the church—not in the people. It is the church's program. The people of the community have no ownership in it. They may attend it and participate in it, but they will always be spectators and clients, never participants and goal-owners.

The church may want the community's people to become that program's goal-owners and may urge the people to provide leadership to the program. In fact, that may be an integral part of the programmatic plan, but the people will not assume that role in that program. The church will probably never be able to determine why the people of the community use but will not run the church's program because it will always perceive its own intentions as having been honorable and God-inspired. Instead, the church will blame the people (especially if they are poor and/or of another ethnic or racial group) for being lazy and not assuming responsibility. But they are not lazy or irresponsible, just disenfranchised. Disenfranchised people always resist programmatic leadership by remaining spectators and clients.

The fate of the program is inevitable. It will function successfully as long as the church is willing to commit its people, money, materials, and building to make it successful. But it will eventually "burn out." Once programmatic exhaustion has occurred and the well-intentioned pastor can no longer get sufficient volunteers or money or resources to maintain the program, that program will die.

As I look back on twenty-five years of ministry in the cities of Milwaukee, Rockford, Chicago, and Detroit, I realize that my churches and I probably created hundreds of programs for the communities surrounding our churches. Not one of those programs continues today! But in Rockford, Chicago, and Detroit, I was involved in the development of community organizations. Every one of those organizations—developed between 1967 and 1982—thrives today and remains an outstanding voice for the poor and marginalized in its community.

It is the destructive tendency of the church to do ministry *for* a neighborhood's people, particularly the poor. But who then is in control? When we do ministry for the poor, the church is in control. The church decides what the people's problem is, what the solution should be, and what the project should be to implement that solution. The church is deciding everything. Therefore, even though that program might minister effectively to the physical or economic needs of the poor, it has actually pushed them down and enervated them further because it has deprived the poor of self-empowerment.

What, then, should the church do in the city? How should it address issues of health care, longevity and infant mortality, stress, environmental pollution, housing, economic development, advocacy, empowerment, stewardship of the city, relationship with God, and shalom with the neighbor? Let it follow the example of Nehemiah. Let it follow the example of Paul (see previous chapter). Do not do things for people! Do not come into Jerusalem with all the king's workers, money, materials, and supplies and rebuild the walls for them. Instead say to them, "Let *us* rebuild the walls together," and join with the people as they collectively take charge of their own situation and rebuild the walls themselves. Only the people who are most affected by a problem can best deal with that problem. And they can best deal with that problem only when they work on it collectively.

True urban ministry will not occur when churches develop projects *for* the poor. True and effective urban ministry exists only when the city's churches work together *with* the poor to identify their needs and determine the actions the poor and the churches need to take together. Only out of such an atmosphere will ministry *by* the poor occur for their own development. That is the approach that empowers people—that enables them to deal effectively with their own problems. That is the role of *servant* leadership to which the church is called in the city. And that is the process which enables the urban communities of the poor and of the church to minister to each other and, consequently, to set each other free!

Because the church does not often appreciate this way of looking at ministry, most city ministries make the same fateful error of taking a programmatic approach, over and over again. Thank God Nehemiah did not make that mistake—or Jerusalem would never have been rebuilt, Israel would not have been saved from disintegration, and Jesus would never have come to save the city!

How does Nehemiah empower the people of Jerusalem so that they can solve their own deteriorating situation? Already, he has—

- Allowed their plight to burn into his own soul to such a degree that he is obsessed with bringing about their empowerment.

- Networked with the powerful in order to gain their personal support, money, and resources.

- Networked with the people in order to ascertain what they perceive as their city's most urgent and immediate issues.

- Personally researched the situation to determine the accuracy of both his perception and the people's perception of their most urgent issue.

- Challenged and inspired the people to take charge of their own situation.

Now what? Where does Nehemiah go from here? How does he actually organize them to rebuild their own walls? Chapter 3 of the book of Nehemiah gives us Nehemiah's action-plan.

> Eliashib the high priest and his fellow priests went to work and rebuilt the Sheep Gate. They dedicated it and set its doors in place, building as far as the Tower of the Hundred, which they dedicated, and as far as the Tower of Hananel. The men of Jericho built the adjoining section, and Zaccur son of Imri built next to them. . . .
>
> Next to [Shemaiah], Hananiah son of Shelemiah, and Hanun, the sixth son of Zalaph, repaired another section. Next to them, Meshullam son of Berekiah made repairs opposite his living quarters. Next to him, Malkijah, one of the goldsmiths, made repairs as far as the house of the temple servants and the merchants, opposite the Inspection Gate, and as far as the room above the corner; and between the room above the corner and the Sheep Gate the goldsmiths and merchants made repairs (vv. 1–2, 30–32).

What initially appears to be a list of the people and families who worked on the wall is actually the people's action plan. If you trace on a map of Jerusalem each group's repair work, you will discover that the wall around the entire city has been repaired, beginning and ending with the Sheep Gate. After his initiating challenge to the citizens of Jerusalem, Nehemiah organized the people to accomplish the initial action. They were, together, going to rebuild the entire perimeter wall of that city.

Once the people began to rebuild their wall, they began to take charge of their own situation.

There is no indication from the text that the plan of action was Nehemiah's. All it tells us is that Nehemiah challenged them to rebuild those walls and defended the people against their critics. Most likely, it was the people who developed the plan of action—not by sitting around at endless meetings, but just by getting to work!

They did not simply work on the walls. They spent time, as well, reflecting on their activity together—particularly when they met opposition from within or from outside (Neh. 4:6–14; 5:1–7). Early in the empowering process, Nehemiah built in the factor of community reflection and action. That process continued long after the completion of the walls and became the base by which Nehemiah led the people of Jerusalem into profound community reformulation.

I have discovered in my own community organizing that the quickest way to move from theory into practice is around the process of reflection and action. At this point in the process, my networking of that community has provided me with three crucial pieces of information: the issues the people identified as most urgent and crucial; the real leaders of the people; and those people, both Christian and non-Christian, who are deeply concerned about those issues.

As I have examined the results of my networking, I have noted those issues most raised by the people. Then I go to the real leaders and the concerned people who have most voiced those issues (obviously, such networking requires carefully keeping accurate records). I ask them to come together to discuss the issues, and I share the names of pivotal people from the community also committed to those issues.

We get together in issue-based coalitions around each issue. There we begin to reflect together about that issue. We seek to understand the issue, to examine that community need. Soon into the process, I ask the question, "What are *we* going to do about it?" From that question, the group determines the first action or project they will undertake.[9]

We then tackle and successfully complete the project or action. It is very critical in this early stage of empowerment that the fledgling coalition get accustomed to winning. An integral problem for the poor and marginalized of a city is that they have lost at the hands of the system all their lives. Therefore, victory is imperative in order to communicate to that neighborhood, the community groups, and churches that together they can win! Consequently, as the coalition selects its initial actions, it needs to choose activities that cannot fail. And these projects should be ones for which the coalition assumes full responsibility.

During that initial action and particularly after it, the coalition gathers to reflect upon it. What did they learn from it? What went well? Why? What went poorly? Why? What should we pat ourselves on the

Reflection		Action	
Examining community needs	▶	Initiating project or other action to address needs	▶
▶ Examining impersonal forces	▶	Developing more substantive projects	▶
▶ Examining systems and structures	▶	Serving as advocate for equitable treatment	▶
▶ Examining one's own complicity	▶	Developing substantive, community-transforming projects	

back about? What can we learn from this experience that we could do better next time? What have we learned about ourselves, our community, our community groups and churches, the government, business community, etc.? Such reflection should then lead to the determination of the next, and slightly more challenging, action. That action should lead to deeper reflection. This should lead to an even deeper action. Then more profound reflection and so on and on and on.

Three things will inevitably come out of this kind of community empowerment (see diagram).

First, the coalition will move through an ever-deepening process of reflection and action. Second, natural leadership will rise like cream to the top of the coalitions. This leadership can be called forth, encouraged, and strengthened through various leadership-training activities, and used to support the community empowerment process. Incidentally, this was the one substantive mistake Nehemiah made in his organizing of the Jerusalem community; he did not identify, call forth, encourage, and use other leaders. The result was a near-disastrous power vacuum which, upon Nehemiah's return to the court of the Persian king, almost destroyed that noble experiment (Neh. 13:4–31).

Third, such action and reflection will quickly reveal to coalitions organized around different community issues that they will more effectively reach their respective objectives by working together and enabling each other. On this basis coalitions can come together, along with the churches and other community-based groups in that neighborhood, to create the community's organization. Such an organization represents the interests of the entire community rather than a single constituency (e.g., rose-growers, a fraternal organization, the Presbyterians, etc.). Such an organization gives a sense of identity, direction, and purpose (particularly as it engages the community in setting community goals) and deepens the sense of community relationship.

Earlier I suggested that if the church is to be truly effective in doing urban ministry, it must move away from developing projects *for* the poor and marginalized and toward a perspective which seeks to come alongside the people to work *with* them in the reformulation of the community's life. The process I have just presented to you is one which enables ministry like the latter to happen.

Using this process, the church acts as partner-servant with the people and groups of its community. Through its networking, it identifies the real and felt issues of the people of that community, and the pivotal leaders and motivated community people who can address these issues. The church acts to pull these people together into coalitions formed around the issues the people have identified as most important. Then the church joins with the coalition (and, later, the community's organization) to analyze the issues and reflect on the more substantive forces lying behind those issues. It joins with the coalition to share in the development and implementation of projects and actions the coalition and community see as necessary. Such projects will be owned by the community and the people will invest significant effort to make those projects work. The church can be a part of that entire process, participating with the community in the implementation of those projects and providing those resources the church is best equipped to provide and for which the community asks. Thus, the church will be an integral part of the reformulation of that community, will be respected and trusted in that enabling role, and will have the permission of the community to share that faith which makes such selfless ministry possible.

As an illustration of this empowering process at work, let me share one example of organizing, involving a church I pastored. This coalition was built by the churches and people in the poorest urban census tract in the United States: a deteriorated community in Detroit, Michigan.

In 1981, a group of clergy and community leaders in this Detroit slum began to gather together to reflect on its future. Over the previous fifteen years, this neighborhood had been (in the words of one community resident) "messed over and messed over and messed over." It had been the recipient of various city, state, and federal "rehabilitation" projects. All that had come out of these efforts, however, was a discouraged and powerless people, over seventy percent unemployment, a neighborhood devastated with decaying, rat-infested homes, a deteriorating business section, several untenable apartment buildings, and entire blocks of the community so torn up it looked as if they had been bombed.

A coalition of concern was born out of those meetings in 1981 and 1982. They decided to call themselves "People In Faith United" or PIFU (our motto was: "How can you get mad at an organization that calls itself PIFU?"). These community and church people decided, initially, to tackle an issue which could be addressed with some certainty of success: the isolation of the community's senior citizens. The coalition began its first program—a senior citizens' luncheon program. It was created, staffed, and funded entirely by the people and churches of that neighborhood.

It was in 1982 that I was invited to be a part of the PIFU coalition. I introduced to PIFU the ideas of organizing as a "community organization" and of mobilizing as a support network several suburban churches that were in close geographic proximity to the PIFU neighborhood. People In Faith United became a legal community organization and the suburban churches began to join.

We were ready now to tackle more intensive problems—the need for emergency help and for youth programming. The Episcopal diocese helped us develop an emergency food pantry and a counseling and advocacy service (especially for community residents receiving government support). The people and churches of the community also began a youth ministry, funded primarily by the Presbyterian denomination. Both projects provided the first opportunities for members of the suburban churches to join with community people and churches in volunteer ministry in this neighborhood. Recognizing the great amount of hunger in the community, residents and PIFU church members volunteered their time to enable the local Lutheran church to begin a soup kitchen; soon it was serving more than two thousand meals each week.

Finally, by 1983, the people were ready to tackle the community's major issues: housing and unemployment. The PIFU neighborhood's future, community residents and church members alike began to realize, lay in enabling its people to find permanent employment and become homeowners (ninety-four percent rented their homes and apartments). Only a community with employed homeowners would have a future.

The community organization opened a job placement service which, in its first year of service, placed more than 120 community residents in jobs. This was soon followed by a program that trained people for newly emerging work in Detroit. By its second year of operation, our jobs program was placing three hundred people a year.

The group formed a housing corporation. My congregation, recognizing the importance that the development of affordable, decent housing meant to the future of that community, granted me a four-month leave of absence so that I might become PIFU's first full-time housing director.

We created an initial housing and community reformulation plan and purchased our first houses. People In Faith United devised with the people of the community a scheme by which residents could make the down-payment on their homes by working on the renovation of all the houses being remodeled at the time. Thus, poor community residents could begin the purchase of a home with only enough money to make the monthly mortgage payments. In order to provide adequate funding under this community reformulation plan, PIFU used its suburban churches to build a fiscal network outside PIFU. This informal network consisted of pivotal people and organizations in Detroit—large businesses, major Detroit fiduciary institutions, a national housing network, and all strategic governmental agencies. People In Faith United eventually employed permanent housing staff, I returned to my pastorate (although I continued to work in the community organization as a volunteer), and actual housing development began.

As I look back on the development of PIFU, I realize what was most important was not the programs it generated but the opportunity it afforded to the beaten people of that community to stop being victims and to begin taking charge of their situation. Perhaps this was most symbolized in the community's decision to give itself a name. It had always been known only by a numerical designation assigned to it by the City of Detroit. The people decided to give it an identity, because it had become truly a community to them; they named it "Fox Creek."

The process of empowerment that Nehemiah and PIFU and countless community groups have used (and which I have summarized above) is now given a technical name: "community organization." Nehemiah would not have called it that, nor would have Moses or Paul (two other great community organizers). But that is what they were doing—mobilizing a powerless or marginalized community to identify and deal collectively with the problems that were destroying them. Obviously, it is not the purpose of this book to make a full presentation of community organizing principles or methodology. Rather, my purpose is to demonstrate how it relates both biblically and practically to a church's empowerment of a city's poor and marginalized—the best, most responsible, and most biblical ministry that church can provide to its city. (Regarding community organization, the notes section for this chapter presents both a reading list and leads for training opportunities.)[10]

DEAL CREATIVELY WITH CONFLICT

Empowerment of the poor and marginalized will inevitably create conflict. Those who hold power will not like the poor or the marginalized taking charge of their situation (and thus taking power away from the power-brokers). Those who have always been beaten down by life will often be tempted to abuse their newly discovered power, for the poor and the marginalized are as capable of doing evil as are people of power!

Conflict is the sign that effective empowerment of the ordinary people of a community or city truly is occurring. If those who hold the power and who benefit from the maintenance of the status quo begin to resist the work of the community's organization, and if those in the organization seek to misuse their power, then empowerment is working! This was as true for Nehemiah as it is for the church working among the disadvantaged today.

Conflict around the people's efforts to rebuild Jerusalem's walls surfaced in two ways. First, resistance came from without.

> But when Sanballat, Tobiah, the Arabs, the Ammonites and the men of Ashdod heard that the repairs to Jerusalem's walls had gone ahead and that the gaps were being closed, they were very angry. They all plotted together to come and fight against Jerusalem and stir up trouble against it. . . . Our enemies said, "Before they know it or see us, we will be right there among them and will kill them and put an end to the work" (Neh. 4:7–8, 11).

Who were Sanballat, Tobiah, and the Arabs of whom Nehemiah speaks? Sanballat was the governor of Samaria, Tobiah was the governor of the Persian province of Trans-Jordan (immediately east of Palestine), and one of the Arabs referred to was Geshem, the highly influential father of an Arabian king (Kain of Kedar) who had united the Arabian tribes into a desert confederation (Neh. 2:10, 19). These men were the people responsible for maintaining order throughout Canaan and were nominally accountable to the Persian emperor. In addition, "the Arabs, the Ammonites and the men of Ashdod" were the peoples maintaining and benefiting from the trade and industry of the region by exploiting the Jews' cheap labor.[11]

In other words, those resisting the actions of the people of Jerusalem as they sought to improve their conditions were the political and economic establishments of Palestine—the primary systems shaping the life of all the peoples around Jerusalem.

Trouble, however, was not just from "without the camp." It was also inside.

> Now the men and their wives raised a great outcry against their Jewish brothers. Some were saying, "We and our sons and daughters are numerous; in order for us to eat and stay alive, we must get grain." Others were saying, "We are mortgaging our fields, our vineyards and our homes to get grain during the famine. . . . Although we are of the same flesh and blood as our countrymen and though our sons are as good as theirs, yet we have to subject our sons and daughters to [their] slavery . . . because our fields and our vineyards belong to [them]."
>
> When I heard their outcry and these charges, I was very angry. I pondered them in my mind and then accused the [Jewish] nobles and officials. I told them, "You are exacting usury from your own countrymen!" (Neh. 5:1–3, 5–7).

Just like all the Palestinian Jews, the Jewish nobles and officials had been living under the oppressive policies of Sanballat, Tobiah, Geshem, and "the Arabs, the Ammonites and the men of Ashdod." But given the chance, these middle-level Jewish leaders were taking advantage of their people's newly won self-determination to oppress their fellow Jews. Having gained some measure of independence, the oppressed had turned into the oppressors! They were practicing business in such a way that they were putting poorer Jews into economic subjection to them.

What was Nehemiah to do? How was he to deal with the opposition of Palestine's political and economic systems to the rebuilding of the wall? How would he deal with the economic betrayal of God's people by God's people?

Dealing with External Resistance

Nehemiah's first attempt was to seek to build relationships with Sanballat, Tobiah, and Geshem (Neh. 2:10–20). Only when such negotiations failed did Nehemiah move to more firm action.

A basic rule of working for the empowerment of people is that there are no permanent enemies! The redemptive side of the strong advocacy of the weak or marginalized is that no person or system need remain an enemy. There are inevitably times in the organizing of people for self-determination when the political, economic, and even religious systems of a city will oppose such activity. At such moments the church has no alternative but to confront those systems and their leaders. But there is no reason why such conflict must continue. The intentional effort of any good community organizer is always to try to turn an enemy into a friend.

This principle was clearly seen in PIFU's work, described earlier. When we were in the initial stage of building community empowerment (the senior citizens' program, the soup kitchen), we ignored the systems of Detroit, and they ignored us. In fact, they were probably not even aware of our activity in that slum. We were irrelevant to each other.

When we moved to the second stage of organizing, our relationships with the city's systems and gate-keepers changed profoundly. The very nature of the work of our emergency food pantry and our counseling and advocacy center moved beyond dealing with immediate needs to more substantive issues. The people's pantry/center and the systems of the city began confronting each other consistently when the neighborhood's people were being ignored or manipulated by those systems. This occurred particularly when city agencies would give our people the runaround on providing welfare benefits to the people; these were benefits the agency was required by law to provide (and when you had a community with over seventy percent unemployment, those welfare payments made the difference literally between life and death). As well, the youth ministry got us into conflict both with the Detroit police (particularly regarding harassment) and a crime syndicate (in the marketing of drugs throughout the community). The city's systems, both legal and illegal, were acting as blocks to the self-development of our community's people. And PIFU had to assume the role of advocating the poor's cause and confronting those systems.

The third stage of community empowerment, however, required an entirely different stance toward Detroit's systems. Though we continued confrontation and advocacy where it was necessary, our primary stance had to be that of being partners with our former enemies. We could not rebuild our community's houses nor provide and train for jobs without the cooperation of Detroit's people and systems of power.

When people of our community and I went to a particular city official whom previously we had confronted rather sharply, he said to us, "Why should I cooperate with you people? After all, you've given me nothing but headaches!"

The response of one of our people was brilliant. He said, "We will continue to give out headaches if our people are being denied what is rightfully ours by law. But our problem has never been with you; it has simply been with the city's bureaucracy. What you want is what we want. You want a city that works—where people are working at jobs, living in their own homes, caring for their neighborhood, and paying taxes as both workers and homeowners. That's what we want for our neighborhood, too. But we can't get what we want for our neighborhood without your support. And, frankly, you can't get what you want for our neighborhood without our support—particularly when it comes to votes. So why don't we stop quarrelling and start working together?" And we did.

There are no permanent enemies. As a young community organizer, I made and maintained enemies. I soon began to realize how fruitless and faith-denying that attitude was. Consequently, in my latter years of community organizing, I began to seek ways to turn into friends those I had to confront. Like lawyers who fight in the courtroom and then go to a companionable lunch together, I would try never to alienate anyone whom I had to oppose. The way I found most helpful was to separate the person from the issue. I would keep reminding myself that it was the issue over which the other person and I were in conflict, not each other as human beings. Therefore, I would try to find ways to build our personal relationship even in the midst of our conflict: asking after the person's family, talking about items of mutual interest (even if it had to be the Detroit Tigers or the Chicago Cubs), writing a complimentary note after a confrontation, etc. It is a glorious thing to see that kind of personal attention pay off when you build a friendship rather than contribute to an estranged relationship.

When Nehemiah had to deal with external resistance, therefore, he first tried to heal the breach—to turn potential enemies into friends. He failed—not because he made no effort to negotiate, but because Sanballat, Tobiah, and Geshem rejected his overtures. What did Nehemiah do then?

> I stationed some of the people behind the lowest points of the wall at
> the exposed places, posting them by families, with their swords,

spears and bows. . . . When our enemies heard that we were aware of their plot [cf. Neh. 4:7–9] and that God had frustrated it, we all returned to the wall, each to his own work.

From that day on, half of my men did the work, while the other half were equipped with spears, shields, bows and armor. . . . So we continued the work with half the men holding spears, from the first light of dawn till the stars came out. . . . Neither I nor my brothers nor my men nor the guards with me took off our clothes; each had his weapon, even when he went for water (Neh. 4:13, 15–16, 21, 23).

When reconciliation or negotiations with oppressive systems and their people fail, a community must respond through confrontation. To confront the principalities and powers, one must first understand them (after all, the first rule of warfare is "Know your enemy"). One gains understanding of his enemy through a power analysis.

A power analysis is a study one makes of a system or subsystem in order to understand how it is functional and dysfunctional, who are its pivotal players and how they influence each other, and what are its strengths and where it is vulnerable. When completed, a power analysis is of immense help to a community organization as it works to empower people. Through it, one can determine a system's or subsystem's points of vulnerability and thus take action against that system at such points. The analysis enables a community organization to identify a system's key players and to determine a strategy to deal with those players.

This sounds terribly theoretical and somewhat boring. But it is actually of immense practical advantage to the people as they seek to deal with those who would seek to use the community for their own advantage. For example, the community organization with which I worked in Chicago (the "Organization of the North East," or ONE) became aware that banks, insurance companies, and other fiduciary institutions had "red-lined" our two communities. Red-lining is when corporations determine together to approve no loans, only offer insurance with extremely exorbitant premium payments, and otherwise make it difficult for people to maintain their homes and for firms to do business in the community. The practice is illegal in the United States. Red-lining eventually leads to the deterioration of a community and its abandonment by its current occupants.

With the neighborhoods vacant or deteriorated, the fiduciary institutions are able to buy up the neighborhood's land and buildings at speculative rates. Once they have gained control of the land, these speculators can follow a number of strategies (renovation, razing, rebuilding, industrial development, etc.) which eventually result in immense profits for the speculators.

When we first realized that red-lining might be going on in our community, we began seeking incontrovertible evidence that this was occurring. We began a power analysis of the institutions involved. The evidence soon mounted in convincing volume and our power analysis of each participating institution soon made it clear that the most vulnerable of those institutions to public pressure were the banks. Their vulnerability lay, our analysis revealed, both in their dependence on the good will of their investors (therefore, they could not afford bad publicity) and in the maintenance of those investments (therefore, they could not sustain a widespread sudden withdrawal of funds). We also discovered that the churches in the community had major investments in those banks. Through those churches, we could reach about sixty percent of all the people living in the community. Our power analysis, therefore, gave us our strategy.

You can fairly easily guess what our strategy was. We contacted the churches and pivotal people. We got signed affidavits from them that each institution and individual would withdraw funds at our command, thus risking a "run" upon the bank. We met with the bank president and, backed with these affidavits, got the bank to reverse its lending policies. Although there was never any admission of collusion with other fiduciary institutions (we were not seeking a confession; we were seeking a change), people could once again obtain home-improvement and business loans. With the withdrawal of that bank from the scheme, the attempted red-lining of that community quickly collapsed.

There is every evidence that Nehemiah did a power analysis of the situation there in Jerusalem (although he would probably not have called it that). As he considered how to deal with the political and economic powers of Palestine, he would have realized that he could not convince them to be receptive to the way the people of Jerusalem were organizing. But he also recognized that, even though they accused him of treason (Neh. 6:6–7), they would not appeal to the emperor because of Nehemiah's own influence with the emperor. In fact, they might harass the people unmercifully, but they would not desire any news of their harassment to get to the emperor's ears.

Those who opposed Nehemiah were, however, capable of attacking the Jews building the wall (probably claiming it was desert bedouins who mounted the attack.) Therefore, Nehemiah mobilized the Israelites for battle, with half standing guard while the other half built the wall.

This was not Sanballat, Tobiah, and Geshem's only attempt to undermine Nehemiah's work. After the wall was completed, they sought to lure Nehemiah into a clandestine meeting where they hoped to kill him (Neh. 6:1–14). Nehemiah would not be fooled.

Nehemiah's strategic dealing with the political and economic establishment of Palestine provides us with considerable clues for dealing with external resistance. The people make a power analysis in order to discover their foe's vulnerability and then plan their strategy around that vulnerability. Once that strategy is formulated, the community's organization then prepares for and gets ready to take action. When that action occurs, it takes the form of confrontation, rather than violence. This is a particularly important point. It is significant that Nehemiah's strategy presented Sanballat and the others with the threat of violence. But no violence ever occurred. Nehemiah used confrontation, rather than violence.

Violence is the sign that confrontation has failed. Violence is an admission of failure. As long as the community organization is using confrontation, it is in control of the process. If, however, it allows violence to occur, it has lost control and the systems have gained the upper hand, for they operate primarily through violence. It is the aim of the community organization to press the confrontation, but to avoid violence.

It is hard for us Christians to talk about power, power analysis, planning strategies against an enemy (we want to be the friends of everyone), and confrontation. But the issue is: how do we deal with the systems and structures of the city in order to enable the people to be empowered? How do we enable the poor, the marginalized, and the victims of a city's principalities and powers to be spiritually and physically freed from their demonic power? St. Paul named the action for what it truly is: spiritual warfare (Eph. 6:10–18). After all, one does not fight a war with sweet words!

Dealing with Internal Injustice

The most debilitating threat to a people who are taking control of their own lives is not the activity of the system without, but the betrayal of people from within. Nothing is as devastating as the person or group who seeks to use a community's organization for personal aggrandizement. This is what happened to Nehemiah, as we learn in chapter 5 of his book.

The people of Jerusalem came to Nehemiah with a serious threat. In order to get food, the "ordinary folk" of Israel were borrowing money from wealthier Jews who, in turn, were charging exorbitant interest, foreclosing on property, and even forcing indebted Israelites to turn over their children (who, because of the laws of the time, could be claimed to pay a debt as much as could property) to be sold as slaves (vv. 1–6). Nehemiah was furious when he uncovered such internal injustice in Israel. He gathered the wealthy, the nobles, and the officials together and confronted them.

> So I [said to them], "What you are doing is not right. Shouldn't you walk in the fear of our God to avoid the reproach of our Gentile enemies? I and my brothers and my men are also lending the people money and grain. But let the exacting of usury stop! Give back to them immediately their fields, vineyards, olive groves and houses, and also the usury you are charging them" (vv. 9–11).

When Nehemiah became aware of legal but unjust profiteering of Jews by Jews, he confronted them. From this confrontation we can learn a great deal about how to confront our friends. Nehemiah dealt with them honestly and directly, exposing their sin. But he never attacked the profiteers personally. He separated the sin from the sinner, the people from the problem (vv. 6–13). He never accused the wealthy Jews of being exploiters of the people, like the Gentiles before them; he accused the wealthy Jews of engaging in exploitation. There is a profound difference! One can stop an *action*—and the wealthy Israelites did stop their usury when their sin was exposed to them.

But Nehemiah did more than confront. Although he was not guilty of such action, Nehemiah identified himself with those who were guilty by indicating that he could fall to the same temptation as did they (vv. 14–19). He shared with them how he had hemmed himself about to keep himself from taking advantage of the people. And he went even further than that. He worked as hard in the rebuilding of the wall as any Jew, and he openly and intentionally avoided any semblance of profiting personally from his leadership of the Jews.

> I devoted myself to the work on this wall. All my men were assembled there for the work; we did not acquire any land. Furthermore, a hundred and fifty Jews ate at my table, as well as those who came to us from the surrounding nations. . . . I never demanded the food allotted to the governor, because the demands were heavy on these people (vv. 16–18).

Nehemiah followed principles I found absolutely essential to maintain my integrity as a community organizer and pastor. I discovered that I, as a leader of the people, could not ask them to do anything I was not willing to do myself. Whether you are a pastor of a church or a leader in your community's organization, you must work alongside the people and must observably undertake the most difficult and risky aspects of that work. Nehemiah did not just organize and supervise; he picked up mallet and chisel and went to work on that wall. So should we (especially those of us who are pastors).

Second, I discovered that it was imperative that I not even appear to profit in any way from my leadership in the community organization. Even the slightest hint of profiteering compromises the integrity of your work and allows others to question your motives. Nehemiah did not financially profit by his effort to rebuild the wall of Jerusalem; in fact, he spent more of his personal resources than he was paid as governor of Palestine. When he returned to the Persian court, he went back a poorer man than when he left. That is how ministry must be done among the poor in the city if it is to have integrity.

A community organization has great potential. As this section has reminded us, however, it also has a great capacity for evil. Whenever people gain power, they can use that power for self-aggrandizement. The poor are no less likely to do this than are the rich, for the poor are subject to the same temptations as are the powerful. But if God's people—the church—have really entered into the life of that slum or squatter settlement, if they have identified with the people and worked side by side with them in the cause of justice and are willing to undertake the most difficult and risky aspects of that work, if the church and its people give themselves away rather than profit from their involvement, then that church gains a profound credibility in that community. Because of its integrity, its willingness to risk, its freedom to ask the hard questions, and its lack of self-interest, the church can become the conscience both of that organization and of the community. It can become the body that most shapes the spiritual grounding of that empowering effort.

It goes even further than that, however. The church that has undertaken that kind of incarnational ministry and has placed itself on the line with the poor is a church that gains a profound respect in that community. In being willing to lose its life, it saves it. The people of that community will listen to that church, will listen to what it has to say and the Gospel it has to proclaim. That slum or squatter settlement knows that church did not have to risk its existence by joining in common cause with them. But it did so risk and did so join and did so work. In return, the people will want to know what motivated the church to commit itself thus to the people. They will want to hear about a Christ who also incarnated himself in our world, and they will often respond to that Christ. That is why, today throughout the world, the city churches which most uniformly experience growth are churches which are involved intensely in community organization. That was my experience as an inner-city pastor. It is now the experience of hundreds of city pastors.

Confront the people responsible, condemn their actions but not them as persons, expect them to mend their ways, participate yourself in the recognition that all face the same temptation, work alongside the people, and do not intentionally profit by your own participation—these are the lessons Nehemiah teaches us on dealing with internal injustice among the poor and marginalized, the people with whom we are working for their empowerment.

SEEK THE COMMUNITY'S TRANSFORMATION

The real problem was not the walls. The walls were simply Jerusalem's most immediate and urgent problem. The walls were now built. But if the Jerusalem community was truly to have a future, it would have to move from dealing with the lesser problem to the greater. The people had now proven to themselves that they were capable of such a mighty work as rebuilding a city's walls. Could they be equal to an even greater task—rebuilding the life of Jerusalem?

> Now the city was large and spacious, but there were few people in it, and the houses had not yet been rebuilt (Neh. 7:4).

How was Nehemiah going to rebuild the life of a nation? The essential problem of defeated, poor, or marginalized people is that they believe they are incapable of coping with the world. They accept and believe internally all the lies the systems and the people served by the systems tell them. They believe they are inferior.

Sociologists are fond of talking about a "culture of poverty." What they mean by that phrase is that poverty is not simply an absence of money or the lack of daily sustenance. Nor for marginalized people is the problem simply that society has, in some way, set them aside. The problem is that the poor perceive themselves as adequate only to be poor and the marginalized believe they somehow deserve their marginalization. They are resigned to their poverty, their powerlessness, their rejection by the people and systems that matter in life.

This is why the Gospel is such "good news to the poor." The Gospel says to the poor, "You do matter! You are important! You are important enough for God to have provided for your salvation. You are important enough for Christ to have died for you. *You are somebody!"*

When a community is beaten by life, it too adopts a "culture of poverty." It may have adequate monies to function, but it is dysfunctional because it believes it deserves no better. Each of us can remember countless city neighborhoods into which we have entered where that sense of depression and resignation is so palpable that we can almost reach out and touch it. The issue is this: how can a community convinced it is unacceptable learn both to accept itself and to reformulate its own existence into a corporate life that is meaningful and full of hope? And what is the role of God's people, the church, in the transformation of such a depressed community? This was the issue Nehemiah faced upon the completion of Jerusalem's walls.

Reflection

Reflection is an integral part of the process needed to transform a community. Such reflection must include several strategic ingredients which lead toward the reformulation of the community's life. The first ingredient is a new and more liberated evaluation of the people's worth and capability, based upon their capacity to identify and deal with their corporate problems and to confront the systems and win. That is why community transformation cannot be addressed until the people are empowered as presented earlier. The people must have evidence that they are capable.

A second ingredient is a rediscovery and reinterpretation of the community's cultural heritage. As a part of community rebuilding, the people need to celebrate their corporate past and to revise and integrate that heritage into the rebuilding process. A third ingredient is the people's social analysis of their culture. Through this process, the people are enabled to perceive how that society's systems have contributed to their malaise; this helps the people stop self-destructively minimizing or blaming themselves. A final ingredient is the people's recognition of their own complicity in their situation and, consequently, their own sinfulness, which is forgiven. As a result, their lives are transformed by God.

We see all these ingredients present as Nehemiah helps the people deal with the substantive problem of rebuilding the life of Jerusalem.

> When the seventh month came and the Israelites had settled in their towns, all the people assembled as one man in the square before the Water Gate. They told Ezra the scribe to bring out the Book of the Law of Moses, which the LORD had commanded for Israel. . . .
>
> Ezra opened the book. All the people could see him because he was standing above them [on a platform]; and as he opened [the Book of the Law], the people all stood up. Ezra praised the LORD, the great God; and all the people lifted their hands and responded, "Amen! Amen!" Then they bowed down and worshiped the LORD with their faces to the ground. . . .
>
> Nehemiah said, "Go and enjoy choice food and sweet drinks, and send some to those who have nothing prepared. This day is sacred to our LORD. Do not grieve, for the joy of the LORD is your strength.". . .
>
> Then all the people went away to eat and drink, to send portions of food and to celebrate with great joy, because they now understood the words that had been made known to them. . . .
>
> Day after day, from the first day to the last, Ezra read from the Book of the Law of God. They celebrated the feast for seven days, and on the eighth day, in accordance with the regulation, there was an assembly (Neh. 8:1, 5–6, 10, 12, 18).

After the people of Jerusalem rebuilt the wall, they had a party! What a party it was; it lasted for seven days! At that party, they read from the Book of the Law of Moses and praised God. They feasted, rejoiced, and played together.

The task facing Israel was a profound one, for the people had to shift from a commitment to rebuild the walls of Jerusalem to the realization that their real task was to rebuild the life of their community. Nehemiah began that shift through community celebration. He provided the opportunity for the people to celebrate the great work of their hands and the even greater work in their spirits—which occurred because of the work of their hands. Nehemiah orchestrated the victory celebration within the context of reminding the people of their great heritage in being Israelites. They worshiped; they partied; they celebrated with great joy.

Community celebration is the best vehicle I have discovered for enabling a people to reflect substantively on their previous empowering actions and to discern the next risky—but necessary—steps for building community. Celebration gives permission to rejoice at what the people have accomplished, to congratulate and honor each other, to stand in solemn assembly together and reflect on what has happened, and to discern the next precarious steps the community needs to take in its interior transformation. When the community allows for overt worship (and I have yet to work in a secular community organization where worship of God was not a natural response to substantive victory), celebration is the natural locus for recognizing the source of the community's strength and its potential in the God who calls it to enter the future with him.

The church has celebration built into its life every week. A community does not. Yet celebration is the single most effective activity for enabling a community to reflect on its just-completed actions and to move out into the future. A primary responsibility of the community's organization, therefore, is to provide regular opportunity for the community to celebrate together. For it is its celebration which both demonstrates the depths of the community's potential and provides the incentive for next actions which lead toward the transformation of that community.

Celebration on what the community has accomplished (and on God's blessings on that endeavor) is not sufficient to bring about that community's transformation. The second ingredient is the rediscovery of that community's cultural heritage. Note how that happened in Nehemiah's effort to reformulate the life of Israel.

> On the twenty-fourth day of the same month, the Israelites gathered together, fasting and wearing sackcloth and having dust on their heads. . . . And the Levites . . . said: "Stand up and praise the LORD your God, who is from everlasting to everlasting.". . .
>
> "You are the LORD God, who chose Abram and brought him out of Ur of the Chaldeans and named him Abraham. . . . You saw the suffering of our forefathers in Egypt; you heard their cry at the Red Sea. You sent miraculous signs and wonders against Pharaoh, against all his officials and all the people of his land, for you knew how arrogantly the Egyptians treated them. . . . You came down on Mount Sinai; you spoke to them from heaven. You gave them regulations and laws that are just and right, and decrees and commands that are good. . . . You gave them kingdoms and nations, allotting to them even the remotest frontiers. . . . You made their sons as numerous as the stars in the sky,

and you brought them into the land that you told their fathers to enter and possess. . . . They captured fortified cities and fertile land; they took possession of houses filled with all kinds of good things, wells already dug, vineyards, olive groves and fruit trees in abundance. They ate to the full and were well-nourished; they reveled in your great goodness" (Neh. 9:1, 5, 7, 9–10, 13, 22–23, 25).

The people of Israel not only celebrated the work of their hands—the rebuilding of the wall of Jerusalem. They not only celebrated their newfound communal strength and self-determination and the love and favor of God so obviously showered upon them. Israel also recounted its history. The people remembered from whom they had come. They recited the events that shaped them into a great and glorious nation.

Why was it important for the Jews gathered in their rebuilt Jerusalem to recite their history? First, it reminded them of their great origins, their illustrious past. It said to them, "You have not always been a defeated, weak, and persecuted people. You were at one time a nation with which God made covenant, you were miraculously delivered from Egyptian slavery as God humbled the mightiest ruler of that time, you were chosen by God out of all the nations on the face of the earth and given a land— this land—which was then flowing with milk and honey. You were given a city—this city of Jerusalem—as the city in praise of God. All this you were. And all this you are, because the blood of your ancestors still courses through you. The commitment of God to your ancestors is a commitment that still is made to you. And as you are faithful, God will honor that covenant and will bless you, just as the Lord blessed your ancestors when they were obedient to him."

Every community has a history; every people has moments of glory and honor. Reclaiming the history of a community and/or its people is essential for its transformation from a defeated to a self-determined people. That is why the black history movement is vitally important to Afro-Americans. It reminds such people of color of their great heritage— of the great nations they built in Africa, the kings from which they are descended, the creativity and dignity with which they resisted the abasement of slavery, and the great contributions Afro-Americans of the past made in politics, government, economics, music, art, science, and religion in the United States. All of this is a way of saying, "We *are* somebody; look what great blood courses through *our* veins!"

The second reason for recounting the past is to demonstrate to the people that their ancestors overcame even greater obstacles than they now face. And "since we did it before, we can do it again!" Such a recognition breeds a self-confidence in a previously defeated people, convincing them that they can handle a task that, on the surface, seems overwhelming— even rebuilding the wall of Jerusalem!

In addition to celebrating the people's capacity for self-determination (demonstrated by successfully organizing and taking action) and the community's cultural heritage, a third ingredient in community transformation is the social analysis of their culture. Nehemiah leads the Israelites in making such a social analysis, in order that they might understand why a people greatly loved by God could become powerless.

> "We are slaves today, slaves in the land you gave our forefathers so they could eat its fruit and the other good things it produces. Because of our sins, its abundant harvest goes to the kings you have placed over us. They rule over our bodies and our cattle as they please. We are in great distress" (Neh. 9:36–37).

The people of Israel are discontent. Their worship of God, their celebration of the great "work of their hands," and the recital of their illustrious history have all worked to increase their discontent over their present pitiable state. Why do they live in such powerlessness, such deprivation? The reflection over their history shows them that it is not God's doing. Neither are they an incapable people, for both their history and their own recent action of rebuilding the wall demonstrates to them that they are capable of great things.

Why do they live in poverty and powerlessness? "We are slaves today . . . in the land you gave our forefathers. . . . [Our] abundant harvest goes to the kings . . . [who] rule over our bodies and our cattle as they please." On reflection, the Jews of Jerusalem realize that they are weak and poor because the nation's political and economic systems are intentionally and purposefully arrayed against them to the benefit of those who run those systems. That is biblical social analysis!

The problem does not lie solely with the unjust operation of the nation's and city's systems. The problem also lies within themselves.

> "[Our foreparents] turned their backs on you, became stiff-necked and refused to listen. For many years you were patient with them. By your Spirit you admonished them through your prophets. Yet they paid no attention, so you handed them over to the neighboring peoples. But in your great mercy you did not put an end to them or abandon them, for you are a gracious and merciful God.

> "Now therefore, O our God, the great, mighty and awesome God, who keeps his covenant of love, do not let all this hardship [we are experiencing] seem trifling in your eyes—the hardship that has come upon us, upon our kings and leaders, upon our priests and prophets, upon our fathers and all your people, from the days of the kings of Assyria until today. In all that has happened to us, you have been just; you have acted faithfully, while we did wrong. Our kings, our leaders, our priests and our fathers did not follow your law; they did not pay attention to your commands or the warnings you gave them. . . . They did not serve you or turn from their evil ways" (Neh. 9:29–35).

"You have acted faithfully, while we did wrong." The fourth ingredient of reflection which leads to community transformation is a recognition of the community's and one's own culpability. As we reflected earlier, Pogo the Possum so profoundly put it, "We have met the enemy, and he is us."

Israel is not under Persian authority simply because the systems are arrayed against it. That is a significant part of the problem, but not the whole problem. Israel is under oppressive political and economic authority because of the irresponsible way God's chosen people chose to live and still choose to live. They have been their own worst enemy, and they have consequently contributed to their own malaise.

The discontent that needs to be fostered in a neighborhood or city to motivate the people enough to seek their community's transformation must not only center on the problem "out there." It must also center on the enemy within the community's midst and within each of us. We are a part of the problem. True community reformulation cannot occur until we admit to the evil within us, confess our own complicity and our ancestors' complicity in contributing to our bondage or marginalization, and throw ourselves upon the mercy and forgiveness of God.

Secular community organization rarely reaches this community-transforming place because it has difficulty turning to God for forgiveness for the people's sinful contribution to their own disenfranchisement. To turn to God would be to cease being a secular organization; it would mean admitting to the spiritual dimensions of a community's and a city's bondage. Thus the empowering work of the church in the city is strategic, because only the church can deal with sin and salvation in relation to both the deterioration and the transformation of a community. This is the particularly godly contribution the church can make to the empowerment of the marginalized and defeated people of the city.

It should be noted how late in the empowerment process one's own complicity is introduced. An essential problem of powerless people is their quickness to blame themselves for all that happens to them. To raise the issue too quickly is to defeat the entire empowerment process. This is so because, recognizing one's own culpability, a powerless person will only retreat into self-blame and the blaming of the poor around him. However, once a community has moved into participation in a coalition around the issues, has tasted a series of victories when dealing with the issues, has participated in considerable social analysis, and has dealt successfully with conflict, that community is ready to look at its own contribution to its bondage or marginalization. It has gained enough self-respect and dignity of character that its people can tolerate reflection upon their corporate and individual culpability. Because the people now have more self-confidence, they can look frankly and openly at their own sin and not be devastated or immobilized by it.

Action

Community transformation actually occurs when the people move beyond reflection to an intentional and ever more difficult action. The stepping-stones mentioned previously will lead toward community transformation, but only the intentional corporate action of the individuals of that community will lead to community reformulation. Chapter 10 of Nehemiah tells what the people of Israel decide together to do in order to rebuild the life of Jerusalem and of the nation.

> All who separated themselves from the neighboring peoples for the sake of the Law of God, together with their wives and all their sons and daughters who are able to understand—all these now join their brothers the nobles, and bind themselves with a curse and an oath to follow the Law of God given through Moses the servant of God and to obey carefully all the commands, regulations and decrees of the LORD our God (Neh. 10:28-29).

In order to rebuild the life of Jerusalem—to transform that community—the people determined together to obey a discipline that included not marrying Gentiles, not trading with Gentiles on the Sabbath, cancelling all debts every seven years, supporting the temple through an annual tithe of their income and goods, contributing time each year to work in or for the temple, and even contributing their firstborn sons for temple service (Neh. 10:30-39).

Such a plan of action would be repressive except for one factor. This discipline was set by the people on the people. There is no evidence in the text of Nehemiah's participation in or leadership of the process at all. This plan of action was an act of participatory democracy.

An essential ingredient of a community's action must be participatory decision-making. The people of the community have been powerless precisely because they have been effectively excluded from the decision-making process of the city's political and economic (and perhaps even religious) systems. From the very origins of the community organization—when coalitions are pulled together around issues identified by the people—it must be the people (and not the organizer nor the church) who must determine the actions the coalitions will take to address these issues. As the organization moves from issue-identification to reflection and action and the confrontation of the city's systems and structures, each decision on community objectives, strategies, and tactics must be made in a participatory manner. As the community's organization moves into the reformulation of the life of that community, shared decision-making becomes of even greater importance. The more difficult and demanding the decisions of an oppressed community become, the more it needs to arrive at those decisions through participatory democracy.

We see the Jewish community moving from a decision of what to do to the act of doing it. Nehemiah writes of the symbolic action the people took to validate their decision:

> "In view of all this, we are making a binding agreement, putting it in writing, and our leaders, our Levites and our priests are affixing their seals to it" (Neh. 9:38).

Once the people have decided together what they need to do in order to rebuild the life of the nation and of its city, they symbolize each person's participation in the implementation of that decision by publicly endorsing a binding agreement. It is as if the people, committed to the action they must undertake, ask "Where do we sign?"

The use of the symbolic as a way of gaining or affirming consensus is tremendously important in community organizing. Nehemiah knew the value of the symbolic, as indicated by this incident. In my church in Chicago—itself a congregation that felt its own powerlessness and vulnerability—the people developed a symbol that was visual, written, and sung. Through the use of our written symbol as a Confession of Faith, we reminded ourselves each Sunday of who we were to God and why God had placed us in that community. At each Communion service and on special occasions we sang the hymn our congregation had created. Our visual symbol adorned the face of our church bulletin and stationery, was present before the congregation each Sunday in the paraments sewn by church members, and flew from the church's flagpole each day as a reminder to both the community and ourselves of who we perceived ourselves to be. Evidence of the power of such a personalized symbol is the fact that this symbol is still in regular use by this congregation more than twenty years after the people created it.

How do people move beyond networking, community organizing, and issue orientation to the full empowerment of a community? A truly transformed community is born out of community celebration, reflection, participatory decision making, and intentional group action.

SURRENDER THE COMMUNITY TO THE PEOPLE

As the community empowering process nears its denouement, those who organized the process become less and less necessary to it. The people, having determined what must be done to build and sustain their newly emerging community, set about doing it. They are led by the people of the community who have naturally emerged as its leaders. The people, through the community's organization, are now discerning and identifying the pivotal issues and problems of the community, developing objectives and strategies for addressing those issues, and taking action to implement those decisions.

Some of those actions may be substantive in nature and in effort, but the people will be capable of taking on such long-term and intensive activity. They will even be able to deal with occasional failures without it influencing the way they feel about themselves, their community, or their organization. Most rewarding of all is that the people will set stricter requirements for the maintenance and development of their community than their leaders would dare set; these limits will be acceptable simply because it is the people who are setting them.

All of these signs of a community's maturation are evidenced in the closing chapters of the book of Nehemiah. Chapter 11 tells how the people carried out the commitments they had made to each other and before God in chapter 10. They identified new problems. The most notable was that, even with the voluntary effort approved earlier by the community (Neh. 10:32–39), the city of Jerusalem was not being adequately populated. Therefore, they came up with an ingenious measure:

> Now the leaders of the people settled in Jerusalem, and the rest of the people cast lots to bring one out of every ten to live in Jerusalem, the holy city, while the remaining nine were to stay in their own towns. The people commended all the men who volunteered to live in Jerusalem (Neh. 11:1–2).

The Jews took the ancient biblical injunction of the tithe (Lev. 27:30–33; Deut. 14:22–29) and applied it to people. Israel had formerly given a tenth of its produce and its money to the temple each year. Now, Israel would contribute a tenth of all its families to Jerusalem, in order to repopulate it.

It was a decision of the people. The people, therefore, gladly accepted the lot to move to Jerusalem. One-tenth of the nation's families gathered up their households, left the villages in which they had lived all their days, and moved their families into the city to establish a new life. This was massive disruption of a people, but the people did it willingly.

The tithe of humans was not the only sacrifice the people determined to make in order to rebuild the life of the nation and of Jerusalem. The stipulations this Jewish state developed to reformulate the life of the community (Neh. 10) proved inadequate to the task of dispelling gentile influence. So the people set a requirement which was awesome in its intensity and scope—a requirement Israel's leadership would never have dared institute. All Gentiles were to be excluded from Israel; they would have to leave (Neh. 12:27–13:3). This entailed a massive breakup of mixed marriages (Ezra 9:10–10:17). Every Jew married to a Gentile divorced the spouse; the spouse left the home and the country forever.

It was a radical action. It saved Judaism, however, and guaranteed the continued existence of the Jews. Through Nehemiah's organization, Ezra's reforms, and the people's enthusiastic self-determination, it was not necessary for Israel to be a state to maintain its identity. Israel had

228   City of God, City of Satan

become a people, centered around obedience to the Law of Moses. No matter how they would be scattered or what persecution they might face, the Jewish people would survive because their identity now lay in a never-changing law code and in their commitment to be "Jewish" together. The community had been unbelievably transformed!

What is the role of the church when it is time to surrender the community to its people? The church was integral to the community's organization, playing a pivotal role through networking, building coalitions, and identifying issues. It participated in reflection and action, dealt creatively with conflict, and participated in reformulating that community. But when the people of that community are ready to assume full responsibility for it and the community's organization, the church's role is to surrender any power or control it has held as a part of the organizing effort. The church's role is to become simply another participant in the organization, as an ongoing institution and living body in that community. The church's role is to continue to be the conscience of that organization, calling it to accountability. Part of its role is to stand side by side with the community on the issues, the actions, and the projects of that community organization as it seeks to maintain the power of the people for the good of all.

At the beginning of this chapter, I raised the question, "What are the marks of truly effective urban ministry?" I offered the following as marks:

- Are the systems of a city being confronted and offered real potential for change?

- Are the poor and exploited of the city provided the vehicles by which they can bring about change in their situation?

- Are the middle class and the powerful given the opportunity to join in common cause with the poor to confront the systems of the city and seek their transformation?

- Is there a spiritual transformation that is going on in that city, or are the changes only social? Are the lives both of that city's poor and its powerful being changed by God?

In the book of Nehemiah we can see how each standard was met. The systems were confronted and offered the opportunity to change. Sadly, they refused. The exploited then were provided the means to change their own situation. Happily, they fully accepted the responsibility. The powerful of Israel were given the opportunity to join with the people to seek the city's peace and prosperity. Even though they occasionally yielded to avarice and greed, they were willing to repent and to work side by side with the people to build a new community. Both individuals and the community underwent profound change as they restructured their entire life together and became a new people of God.

What about us? Is such ministry possible for us, or was it a onetime phenomenon? From my own ministry I know it is possible, for I have moved far enough along the continuum presented here that I can see intimations of what could be. Yes, it is possible. And yes, it is that full ministry into which God calls the urban church. For this is doing ministry God's way. It is a way open to all of us who name the Name.

Thus the book of Nehemiah draws to a close—centered not around tears (Neh. 1:4) but around the celebration of the birth of a people (Neh. 13:29–31). Nehemiah ends his work in Jerusalem, returning a second time to Susa, filled with joy. His book ends with the words:

Remember me, my God, for my happiness (Neh. 13:31 JB).

Happiness? Yes, happiness. For nothing fills one with greater joy than to be used by God to enable others—both the broken and the whole, the marginalized and the powerful—to discover their need for each other, to gain back their self-respect, to build a community together, and in so doing to become together what God had created them all to be! This is the work of God's people—the church—in the city.

PART III

SPIRITUAL DISCIPLINES:
POWER FOR MINISTRY

Chapter Ten

SPIRITUAL POWER:
SPIRITUAL FORMATION

It's not easy to walk in the rain,
And I walk with my eyes to the ground,
And I often ignore the rainbow above,
And the coming of the sun.

When I started on the journey I was so energetic
And I didn't know that it would be so slow.
Just a helping hand for neighbors
    And a smile to cheer the pilgrims
And the book to show us clearly where to go.
But so many fell behind, some didn't even know
About the journey we could take towards the sun,
And I find myself bewildered by the needs of those around,
    Struggling in the cold and rain.

There is beauty on the journey
    As the crippled and the poorest
Carry others' burdens too, to my surprise.
And I find we need each other
    As we struggle with the darkness
Often spurred by rays of light in clouded skies.
But the spirit of so many dies in all the gloom
And many others starve and fall along the way,
And I find myself in anger that the strongest will not share,
    Deafened to the cries of pain.

There have been times of heavy weather
    When I've thought of giving up
And questioned whether anyone has made it through.
But I stake my life on what I know of Jesus and his love
And see the rainbow as my sign that it is true.
And the power which comes from sharing all the power we have,
And the glimpse of peace and justice on the way

Is enough to make me lift my eyes and take another arm
　　Strong enough for one more day.

It's not easy to walk in the rain,
And I walk with my eyes to the ground,
And I often ignore the rainbow above,
And the coming of the sun.
And the coming of the sun.

　　　　　　　　　　　　　　　　—Ross Langmead[1]

In the previous nine chapters we have examined two basic themes: the city as the battleground between God and Satan and the vocation of Jesus Christ and the church as God's advance, his thrusting wedge into the city. We have looked at the city as God's creation, deeply loved by the Lord. But we have also seen the city as the abode of both personal and systemic evil dominated by demonic principalities and powers. No matter how severe the battle, it is God's intention to establish his kingdom there. God seeks to do this through Christ and the church.

Jesus came, we discovered, to release people, a city's systems, and the entire created order from the power of sin, death, and the law. He did so by taking upon himself all that evil could ever do; he thus freed us from evil's complex grasp. Therefore, the vocation to which the church is called is not to be the savior of the city (only Christ is that) but to be the body which exposes the lies the systems tell to keep the city in bondage and to be the advocate of the city given over to the kingdom of God. To this the church witnesses in its prayer, its presence, its proclamation, and its practice, as it works for the empowerment of the poor (the victims of the principalities), the liberation of the powerful (those seduced by the systems), and the reformulation of the city into a godly community (the kingdom of God).

We as the church must take quite seriously the biblical appraisal of the city as a battleground. For nearly half of the entire world (because half of the world will live in cities by C.E. 2000), the city is the primary locus of spiritual warfare.

The Christian and, consequently, the church are not called to be above this warfare, ignoring it as we seek to win individuals to Christ and try to build a church. Rather, by the very nature of the ministry to which we have been called, we are caught precisely in the middle of this warfare. The more effective our ministry is in the city, the more we will be focused on the battle between God and the powers of darkness seeking to conquer our city!

What this means is that the city pastor or Christian worker is not going to be above the noise, power, and evil of the city. Instead he or she is going to be caught up in the middle of it. That is reality, and it faces us with the greatest challenge of the urban Christian's life and ministry.

After a third of a century's experience in urban ministry, I am more convinced than ever that the greatest enemy of the urban Christian is not the city and its concentration of noise, power, and evil. Nor is it the church struggling to remain alive and vital, and in that struggle demanding all of its people's and pastor's energies. I am convinced that the greatest enemy of the urban Christian is the Christian himself or herself!

The battle of our city is a battle between God and Satan for the soul of our city. Precisely because it is spiritual warfare, because we Christians are the only ones who understand that warfare for what it is, and because we Christians are caught in the center of that warfare when we choose to minister responsibly in the city, the principalities and powers choose to attack us at our most vulnerable point. We urban Christians are most vulnerable in sustaining ourselves in ministry.

The most difficult task in urban ministry is to remain optimistic, creative, hopeful, and full of humor. Ministry demands that you give out constantly—and city ministry makes that demand relentlessly. But you cannot give out what you do not have. If you are not replenishing yourself in order to continue the spiritual warfare of the city, then you are exposing yourself to defeat, burnout, and spiritual exhaustion. After all, you can lead God's people only as far as you yourself have gone. If you have not paid attention to your soul's interior journey, you do not have the resources nor the experience either to sustain yourself or to lead your church in sustaining the battle with the Enemy.

I know whereof I speak, because I nearly became a casualty of the Enemy. I nearly became that casualty because I would not pay attention to my need for spiritual formation.

In 1971, my Chicago church and I were deeply involved in the development of ONE—the community organization about which I wrote in the previous chapter. Committed to the liberation and self-determination of the poor and exploited around our inner-city church, we had joined with leaders and pivotal groups in the neighborhood to create the organization which pulled all of us together to deal with our neighborhood's biggest problems. One of those problems was prostitution.

The people of our community, fed up with the blatant and powerful prostitution trade, took a number of strong, aggressive steps to stop it. Within a matter of weeks, the flood of customers to the houses of ill repute had declined to a trickle. It was then that the pimps and prostitutes decided to fight back.

The word came to our community organization that we—and the whole community—were about to discover how powerful the forces were with which we were doing battle. They announced to us that one of the community's leaders would be assassinated. The leader selected by them was me!

The community organization's leadership met to decide what to do. We made the decision that we would not be intimidated. We would continue our attack upon the prostitution trade. For the next twelve months, as I stepped into the pulpit of my church each Sunday, I never knew if I would live to finish that Sunday's sermon. As I climbed into my car, I never knew if it would explode in true Chicago fashion as I turned the ignition. As I walked the streets of my community to visit with its people, I never knew if that walk would be my last.

Those twelve months were hell for me! The spiritual warfare I went through is almost impossible to describe. Simply to go through the tasks of each day, never mind battling the primary issues of our poor neighborhood, became an almost insurmountable obstacle. In the midst of this emotional pain, I decided to renew my spiritual disciplines which I had been neglecting. Perhaps in prayer and in Scripture I could find strength to sustain me.

One day I took my journal from my bookcase. Over the years, I had written in that journal what God had been doing in my life. I opened my journal in order to write in it about the threat on my life—and I was shocked by what I saw. The previous entry had been written three years earlier! It had been three years since I had held personal devotions, three years since I had opened the Bible for anything other than sermon preparation, three years since I had allowed God to speak to me through the Bible's pages, three years since I had personally met with God.

So it was there, in the midst of the greatest spiritual and physical crisis of my life, that I realized I was spiritually bankrupt! I had not been nurturing my relationship with God. Now that my activist ministry was bringing me face-to-face with my own death, I did not have the spiritual depth to sustain me in that crisis. That was the beginning of my own struggle to develop the spiritual base I needed in order to be sustained in the warfare with my city's principalities and powers.

How do Christians sustain themselves in the spiritual warfare of the city? What is needed to enable us, as a city's committed Christians, to shape and sustain a church which will become God's Good News to our city? Out of my life-threatening crisis I discovered aspects of the Christian life that provide the primary power for sustaining city ministry. We will conclude our study of a biblical theology of the city by exploring these aspects over the next four chapters. They are:

1. Personal spiritual formation

2. Participation in community

3. Maintenance of a vision for the city

4. Faithfulness, rather than a search to be successful, in the practice of the Gospel

THE RHYTHM OF THE CHRISTIAN LIFE

The writer of Psalm 55 understands the evil within the city:

> I see violence and strife in the city.
> Day and night [the wicked] prowl about on its walls;
> malice and abuse are within it.
> Destructive forces are at work in the city;
> threats and lies never leave its streets (vv. 9–11).

The psalmist feels overwhelmed and inundated by the issues and problems of the city. In the face of this, he naturally desires to escape.

> Fear and trembling have beset me;
> horror has overwhelmed me.
> I said, "Oh, that I had the wings of a dove!
> I would fly away and be at rest—
> I would flee far away
> and stay in the desert;
> I would hurry to my place of shelter,
> far from the tempest and storm" (vv. 5–8).

How often we who are in city ministry feel just like the psalmist; we want to run away, to fly, to hide, to flee from all the tensions of city ministry and to be rid of its warfare. We cannot live our lives that way, however. Life consists of making hard choices and then abiding by those decisions. All the wishing for escape is not going to change that. So what is a city pastor or Christian to do?

> Cast your cares on the LORD
> and he will sustain you;
> he will never let the righteous fall (v. 22).

Here is the beginning of the rhythm of the Christian life: to go into the city, with its violence and its joys, its malice and its compassion. Such ministry demands all that a person can give. In such a context a person can feel overextended and burned out, wishing only to flee. But flight is not the solution. The solution is to cast one's cares upon the Lord! God's urban people are sustained as they, as individuals, move from the demands of the ministry to which they are called and into the bosom of God for support and refreshment. There, in relationship with God, one is spiritually formed and equipped to return to the demanding ministry of the city. Thus a person journeys outward into mission, then inward for spiritual sustenance, and once renewed, journeys outward once again, and once spent, travels inward once more. Journey inward, journey outward: the rhythm of the Christian life.

We can examine the rhythm of the Christian life by considering four propositions.[2]

1. We are not called by God to be committed to dealing with all the needs of the city, but to address only one pain of the world. A need does not constitute a call. The city is full of human pain—collapsing marriages, abused children, poverty, injustice, orphans, environmental pollution. Wherever we turn our heads, we, as sensitive Christians, are going to see intense human suffering. And as the whole body of Christians in the city, we are to be concerned about all its human need (see chapter 8).

We must trust God that he has created and has called his people in our city to address every one of these needs. We must trust that God's church—the body of Christ—will discover each of those needs it is to address. Our specific responsibility is to discover our particular call and the particular need in the city God wants us to address. That is the only need for which we can be responsible. This leads us to our second proposition.

2. The way we discover the human need to which we are called is not by dealing with that need and becoming absorbed in the effort, but by living the contemplative life. Our first tendency, when we realize that we are called to be responsible for engaging one primary need of our city, is to begin searching among all the city's problems to see what need tugs at our heart strings. Now it is possible that what might tug at our heart strings might be the need we are called to encounter. It is far more likely, however, that what will tug at our heart strings will be those needs in the world that are projections of hidden problems or issues within ourselves that we have never resolved. If those feelings are projections, we will not find God's call through that tug. The only way to discover God's call is not to look out, but to look in; we must begin to examine our own lives in Christ. As our fellowship with God deepens, the Lord will reveal the call. This brings us to the third proposition.

3. We discover God's call and begin acting upon it by reaching inward. There we discover ourselves, begin to love God, and build a Christian community. Each one of those elements of the inward journey is strategic to discovering God's call to us. *Discovering our inner selves* is strategic because only as we come to know our inner selves truly can we discover what causes us to act the way we do, what it is we project upon others, what are those weaknesses within us that need to become strengths, and what are those strengths that so dominate our personalities that they need to become comparatively weak.

Coming to know and love God is the second necessary element of our inward journey. As we come to know and love God through his Son, we understand more clearly the gifts of God's grace that liberate us, the demands God makes upon us as our Creator and ruler, and the possibilities that are open to us when we seek and follow God's will. Remarkably, we discover God and our inner selves the same way—by spending time in solitude before the Lord, by daily allowing the Scriptures to speak to the way we choose to live and prioritize our lives, by praying contemplatively, both aloud and meditatively, and by journaling. By following such disciplines, we cannot help but find ourselves growing both in self-understanding and in a deepening relationship with God.

The chance of hearing God's call simply by entering into ourselves and thereby discovering God, however, is slim, because such an introverted approach contains the danger that instead of discovering God, we would hear our own self-deception. An equal ingredient in hearing God's call is the *building of a Christian community*. God's call will come to us clearly when we practice the solitary disciplines of discovering God and ourselves, but only as a part of a supportive, loving community. It is as we journey together through the Christian experience with a small, sustaining group of fellow believers that we will be prepared to hear God's call to us. Such a group cannot be large; in the New Testament it is rarely over twelve people. It must be a group small enough to enter into that search for God's call with us and to care genuinely and deeply that everyone hears that call. As a result, the group must exemplify deep, godly love, which brings me to the fourth and final proposition.

4. *We more deeply grow in our relationship with God, self, and others by obeying our call to address a specific pain of the world.* As we enter into ourselves, as we fall increasingly in love with God, and as our support community deepens in its life together, God's call will come to us. As we begin to obey that call, we will find the portion of the body of Christ that is in the same mission as that to which we are called. These people will join with us and will enable us to live into that call. In this group, we can plan our strategy to deal with that issue or pain (this can be the coalition of a neighborhood or of a church described in the previous chapter). The group will call forth from all its members the unique and special gifts each one has to contribute to undertaking the common mission. As a part of that group, we move out in mission to the world.

At this point we discover that we are caught up in the most beautiful continuous spiral. Our journey to carry out our common mission to the world will bruise us, exhaust us, and try us deeply. We will then turn to Christ and we will find ourselves deeper in Scripture. We will want to be in prayer with God, we will cry on each other's shoulders, and the bonds of love will grow between us. In other words, by carrying out our call to a need of the world, we will be motivated to grow spiritually.

As we grow spiritually, we will find ourselves absorbed in that mission—that purpose for our lives for which God has created us. Consequently, our lives will take on a meaning and a joy that we never knew possible. We will have begun to follow God's strategy for the church that—if faithfully followed—can only result in transforming our city!

So the way out is in, and the way in is out. The way to reach outside ourselves is to reach within: discover our selves, love God, and build a

Christian community. The way to journey inward (to grow in our relationship with God, self, and others) is to journey outward and commit ourselves to a pain of our city: discovering the pain to which we are called, uncovering our gifts, and moving out in mission. This is the rhythm of the Christian life; this rhythm catches us up into increasingly effective ministry fueled by the way we continually foster our own spirituality.

SPIRITUAL FORMATION

St. Paul wrote to the Galatian Christians, "My children, I must go through the pain of giving birth to you all over again, until Christ is formed in you" (Gal. 4:19 JB). But how is Christ formed in us?

Luke tells a penetrating story of Jesus' encounter with two women:

> As Jesus and his disciples were on their way, he came to a village where a woman named Martha opened her home to him. She had a sister called Mary, who sat at the Lord's feet listening to what he said. But Martha was distracted by all the preparations that had to be made. She came to him and asked, "Lord, don't you care that my sister has left me to do the work by myself? Tell her to help me!"

> "Martha, Martha," the Lord answered, "you are worried and upset about many things, but only one thing is needed. Mary has chosen what is better, and it will not be taken away from her" (Luke 10:38–42).

This well-known story displays the compulsive pace of the frantic activist and the gentle and meditative pace of the contemplative, commending the introverted Mary for choosing "what is better." Mary recognized what seemed hidden to the activist Martha, that sitting at the Lord's feet and listening to him is of great importance. Without spending adequate time to foster our personal relationship with Christ, we become frantic disciples of the urgent.

The particular power of this story is that it moves us beyond the historical Mary and Martha to the recognition that both women are inside each of us. We hold within us a Martha who delights in action and issues and the challenge of urban life. But there is also within each of us a Mary who longs to sit at the Master's feet and learn from him.

Tragically for those of us influenced by Western culture, much in us works to silence our "Mary." We enjoy parish and community activism, but feel uncomfortable in the presence of the "still, small voice." Yet Jesus is saying that we will live rushed, urgent, and often trivialized lives unless we give permission to our "Mary" to take time to be in Christ's presence. It is only by nurturing our contemplative selves that we will discover peace with God, ourselves, and our ministry. It is only out of that presence that adequate power can be generated to enable us to be truly effective in the "Martha" work to which God has called us.

Christ, then, is formed in us through our calling forth of the contemplative that lies within each of us. But how do we nurture the "Mary" within, and thus cooperate with God in the work the Lord would do within our spirit? Paul suggests the way in his letter to the Christians in the city of Philippi:

> Therefore, my dear friends, as you have always obeyed . . . continue to work out your salvation with fear and trembling, for it is God who works in you to will and to act according to his good purpose (Phil. 2:12–13).

We are to "work out [our] salvation." We must work on our personal spiritual formation. Integral to that work is our practice of spiritual disciplines. The disciplines of the Christian life exist in order to enhance a Christian's personal relationship with God and to deepen one's internal self. The church has shaped the disciplines of the Christian life for nearly two thousand years for the purpose of enhancing a person's relationship with Christ. The disciplines have been tested and proven over the centuries, some to slip eventually into disuse and obscurity, and others to be proven by fire to be of help to a large body of Christians. We ignore to our own spiritual hurt the accumulated experience of the church. To live into those disciplines with which our soul most resonates will provide us with the spiritual means both to enhance our relationship with God and to turn us into effective and productive Christians in our cities. "For it is God who works in you"; we must trust God to do the work of spiritual formation within us.

Jesus, on the eve of his death, said to his disciples,

> I am the real vine, and my Father is the gardener. Every barren branch of mine he cuts away; and every fruiting branch he prunes, to make it more fruitful still. . . . Dwell in me, as I in you. No branch can bear fruit by itself, but only if it remains united with the vine; no more can you bear fruit, unless you remain united with me (John 15:1–2, 4 NEB).

Christ already dwells in us, Jesus is telling his disciples in this passage. This is his promise to us, based upon his saving work on Calvary; we have received it for our own lives by faith. It is already done. It is an accomplished relationship. Christ dwells in us. We can count on it. Now we are to dwell in Christ! "Dwell in me, as I dwell in you," Jesus is telling his disciples. "I am already at work in you," Jesus would instruct us. "Rest in that fact. Live into that reality. Rest in me and trust me." We do not need to live frantically and continually with the sense that we must be in control of everything. We can turn over the course of our lives to God—our work, our ministry, our relationships with others, our status with God—and let him take over. We can thus rest our lives in him.

This capacity to rest our lives and our ministry in Christ is the mark of the great saint. I saw this very clearly in Mother Teresa when I visited her in Calcutta in 1982. I wrote in my journal that night,

> She is truly a small, frail lady, her hands broad and gnarled with work, her feet misshapen. But there is a glow, a power, almost a luminosity about her. There is a gentleness and yet a firmness about her, an open acceptance of all and yet a high demand for all who would serve the poor. But what most stands out about her is her utter Christ-centeredness. Never have I heard the name of Christ more the center of a conversation than it was in that thirty minutes.

> I was particularly struck by: first, the total attention she gave us—as if nothing were as important to her as to hear our experiences and to share Jesus with us; second, her concern that we take time to be alone with Jesus in order to hear him say to us, "I love you"; third, her promise that she would pray that we grow in the likeness of Christ; and finally, her quietness, confidence, and utter tranquility. She so exhibited in herself—in her very selfhood—the kind of a Christian I have always wanted to be. But that kind of person comes to be only by being tempered by two opposable forces: first, the luxury of much time spent in solitude, prayer, and contemplation; second, the regular and intense engagement with the world, facing the Christ in his "distressing disguise," addressing the needs of the poor in body, mind, heart, and soul.[3]

Whether we are alone in prayer or are confronting the systems of the city, whether we are sharing in the community of faith or are ministering to "the least of these"—the poor and the hurting of the city—we can live into anything from this calm repose in Christ. God is utterly, utterly trustworthy. Because he is trustworthy, there is no need to depend upon anyone or anything but God himself. Not those elements upon which secular society depends: money, power, prestige, and group solidarity. Nor upon myself, nor others, not even the church. God is fully sufficient both to transform the city and to form Christ in me. For "it is God who works in you to will and to act according to his good purpose."

SPIRITUAL DISCIPLINES

Spiritual disciplines do not make a person more spiritual. The work that we do on our own spiritual formation we do simply to help us be more receptive to the work that Christ wants to do in us. It is God who does the work in and through us, and our trust in God that such work will be done is the cornerstone of our own spiritual formation. "Dwell in me, as I dwell in you."

Jesus described the process in his parable of the sower (Matt. 13:1–23). He described a sower broadcasting the seed on various types of soil and, consequently, getting various results. He was saying that our lives are like those soils. Sometimes we are hard and trampled-down soil and God's presence can take no root in us at all. Sometimes we are rocky ground; although God's Word does take root in us, it cannot grow, and so our relationship with the Lord soon withers. Sometimes we are thorn-infested ground, so that the cares and worries of life choke out of us any inclination to allow God to do his work in us. But, Jesus taught, we can also be fertile and tended ground which, upon receiving the Word, nourishes it so that it springs up into abundant harvest.

The task of spiritual disciplines is to turn, to enrich, and to make fecund the soil of our lives so that, as Christ does his work in us, we will be receptive people in whom God's presence can spring up into an abundant harvest. But what are some of the spiritual disciplines of the church that prepare us so that God can work more deeply in our lives? What are the disciplines that the church has discovered contribute to our spiritual formation?

Spiritual Autobiography

A good beginning point is to write a spiritual autobiography. Rewriting and updating that autobiography through the years enables the Christian to maintain a constant point of reflection, a basic part of the believer's search to understand better the work that God is doing in his or her life.

Paul wrote a good example of spiritual autobiography in his letter to the church in the city of Philippi:

[I was] circumcised on the eighth day, of the people of Israel, of the tribe of Benjamin, a Hebrew of the Hebrews; in regard to the law, a Pharisee; as for zeal, persecuting the church; as for legalistic righteousness, faultless.

But whatever was to my profit I now consider loss for the sake of Christ. What is more, I consider everything a loss compared to the surpassing greatness of knowing Christ Jesus my Lord, for whose sake I have lost all things. I consider them rubbish, that I may gain Christ and be found in him, not having a righteousness of my own that comes from the law, but that which is through faith in Christ—the righteousness that comes from God and is by faith. I want to know Christ and the power of his resurrection and the fellowship of sharing in his sufferings, becoming like him in his death, and so, somehow, to attain to the resurrection from the dead (Phil. 3:5–11).

As Paul recognized, the place for us to begin to perceive God's work in us is with our individual pasts. An essential characteristic of the growing Christian (magnificently displayed in Paul's statement above) is his or her ability to look at the past and perceive what God was doing there. This entails theologically and spiritually interpreting the activities, relationships, and commitments we each made both before and after becoming Christians.

There are several reasons why we should seek to interpret our pasts theologically and spiritually. First, it gives us a sense of identification—a recognition that we each are God's called, protected, loved persons, a part of God's chosen people. Second, it interprets the present for each of us, enabling us to formulate the commitments we need to make ("I want to know Christ"). Third, it opens us to the future and the work God still wants to do in and through us—because the God who could work miraculously in the past and profoundly in the present can do it again!

How does one go about writing a spiritual autobiography? Perhaps a place to start is with these questions:

1. Write down, briefly, the major events in your life.
2. Reflect on those events through these questions:
   a. How is your life different because of each of those events?
   b. What do you believe God was trying to do in your life through these events?
3. As you look at God at work in your past, what do you think, basically, God was trying to accomplish?
4. How do you see that same work going on in your life at present and possibly into the future?

Writing a spiritual autobiography opens the pathway for the other, ongoing spiritual disciplines.

Silence

Silence has been one of the most valuable disciplines for my own spiritual formation. Americans in particular are intimidated by silence, but it is one of the greatest gifts that God wants to give to us. God commands us, "Be still, and know that I am God" (Ps. 46:10). In the stillness we discover and enjoy the presence of God.

Contemporary society is one of great stress and frenetic activity. I am particularly struck by the noise of our cities. Christians have said to me on occasion, "God never speaks to me." Well, is it that God does not speak or that we are surrounded by so much noise, activity, and stress that we can not hear his "still, small voice"? For God does not come to us in the rage of a hurricane, the rumble of an earthquake, the roar of a great fire; God comes to us as "a gentle whisper" (1 Kings 19:11–12). We, and life around us, must be still enough so that we are able to hear God's whisper. One cannot know God unless one is still. One cannot be still unless one is silent. Silence is a primary means to becoming sensitive and receptive to God. And that can occur only as one is in solitude.

There is a profound difference between solitude and loneliness. A person chooses solitude, while loneliness is thrust upon him or her. Solitude is the practice of the presence of God—the intentional withdrawal from the hurry and the struggle of the day in order to let one's body, mind, and soul become centered in God the Father, Son, and Holy Spirit. It is the cultivation of peace—the purposeful withdrawal from the agenda of the day in order to give God the opportunity to meet with us individually. As one elderly Christian described it to me, "I just look at Jesus and he looks at me!"

I found the regular exercise of silence absolutely essential for me to cope with the high tension of my Detroit ministry. I would spend about one quarter of my daily devotional time in silence. But what was particularly special to me were the three or four silent retreats I would take each year. Once a quarter, I would go off to a Roman Catholic monastery or a Protestant retreat center where I would spend the week in silence. It was truly a time when "I just looked at Jesus and he looked at me." I would return from those weeks profoundly refreshed and ready once again to minister in the city.

Personally Relating to Scripture and Journaling

The Bible is a book of the heart and of the soul, as well as of the mind. Our tendency as Christians, however, is always to want to *study* the Bible. Just as the constant study of a poem can destroy the impact of that poem on us, so an exclusive emphasis on approaching the Bible intellectually can destroy it as God's Word to us.

There is another way of working with Scripture, a way that I have found makes the Bible come alive in my hands: to relate personally to the Scripture passage. Relational Bible Study is a means to live into the Bible, to use the Bible for deepening self-knowledge, building community with others, and relating personally to God.

I relate to the Bible devotionally in two ways. First, I spend a significant amount of time with one passage of Scripture, usually seven sessions (one week) on each chapter. Second, when I work with that Scripture, I first do an exegetical study. And then I begin to work with the Scripture by putting myself into it. For example, if I am studying the parable of the sower (which we discussed earlier in this chapter), I will ask myself the questions "What kind of soil have I been this past year: trampled, rocky, thorny, rich? Why have I selected that soil as representative of my life? In the light of the type of soil I have been, what do I need to ask of the Sower for myself?" I have discovered that, by living this way into Scripture, I have given it permission to deal with me in a profoundly personal way that cannot possibly occur when I am approaching it academically.

An exercise I find to be particularly supportive of such devotional work is journaling. Keeping a journal of your spiritual journey can be a profoundly enriching experience. Writing in that journal during your times of solitude and when you are living into Scripture, recording in that journal how God has revealed himself to you that day, and expressing in written word the struggles of your soul is a penetrating mechanism for enabling you to understand your spiritual journey. At the time, journaling provides the means for working with your soul that comes only through recording the insights and the process. Later on, it provides a record of what God has been doing in your life.

One of the most blessed events of each year for me is New Year's Eve, when I enter into silent retreat (I am not a party animal!) and read all of the journal entries for the year just ending. From the vantage point of year's end, I am always deeply moved to see how God has been at work in my life; I would not have the chance to come to this awareness if it were not for that daily record of my spiritual journey.

Prayer

Scripture and the history of the church stress the important place of prayer as a spiritual discipline. Scripture urges us to pray unceasingly (1 Thess. 5:17). Why is prayer this important to God and strategic to our spiritual formation?

The primary purpose for prayer, I believe, is based on the reality that our God is a personal God with whom we are meant to live in relationship. We can be intimate with God and God with us—just as we can with any person. Prayer is the nurturing medium of that relationship; it is the only activity that unites us to God "face-to-face." The only other intimate expression is service, for both prayer and service express God's relationship to us.

When I was in Calcutta to visit and work with Mother Teresa's Missionaries of Charity, I asked one of the sisters, "All of you seem so filled with joy in the midst of such depressing circumstances. Where do you get the power to carry on your ministry?"

"Oh," she replied, "we meet with Christ twice each day." When I asked her what she meant by that, she explained: "We greet Christ early each day in our morning prayers and then we meet with him all day long in the faces of the poor with whom we minister."

A chief purpose of prayer is to bring us into conformity with God's will. Our freedom allows us to act irresponsibly. Prayer corrects the misuse of that freedom, by increasing our sensitivity to God's desires and by raising our consciousness to those issues that break God's heart. By encountering Christ in prayer daily, we develop a oneness with God that enables us to see things God's way, to judge, act, and love his way. Prayer is thus a response to God's initiative—our response to God's longing to have us in a relationship with him.

How should we pray? An equally appropriate question is, "How should we carry on a conversation with our lover?" Obviously, there is no one appropriate way to carry on such a conversation. Sometimes we are tender, sometimes angry, sometimes joyful, sometimes playful, sometimes formal. All are appropriate modes for conversing with God. (Playful? Why not?)

I find it important to use a full spectrum of forms of prayer, both to be reflective of my mood and in order to keep interchange fresh and creative. When we use the word "prayer," we most often think of spoken prayers—prayers we give of adoration, confession, thanksgiving, supplication, and intercession. But prayer can also be silent; in fact, the practice of silence is prayer. For just as we speak to God through our spoken prayers, it is also important for us to be silent in order to provide the space for God to speak to us.

Structured, formal prayer is immensely helpful to me. A number of published resources are available to guide us in the use of the great prayers of the church. [4] To pray the Psalms is a particularly moving way of praying, as one connects oneself with God's people of over three thousand years. There is contemplative and meditative prayer, as one centers on an object filled with symbolic meaning (e.g., a cross or cup and paten), a passage of Scripture, or on reflection on the person of Christ or a cherished reality of the faith (e.g., God's love for the city). Journaling can be used as a form of praying; here it involves either writing prayers in the journal or keeping a record of the prayers one is lifting up to God.

I can become very preoccupied with whatever is concerning me at the moment and my wife, in desperation, will say to me, "Robert, talk to me!" One has to work at talking and at listening in a relationship. In the same way, one must work at his or her conversation with God. All these forms of prayer provide ways that we can do that work, so that our times of prayer remain vital and interesting to us as well as to God.

Finally, we who are urban pastors and city Christians need to remind ourselves that prayer by a person involved in urban ministry needs to be a particularly focused activity. If it is both to sustain our spiritual formation and to inform and embolden our ministry, our prayer must center not so much upon ourselves, our families, and our churches, but upon our city. In chapter 7, we explored some biblical injunctions regarding urban prayers. In brief, Scripture instructs us to pray for the economic, legal, political, and social well-being of our city and for individual relationships with God. Praying about the issues of our city, our community, and our neighborhood will have a transforming impact not only upon the social order but also upon our lives and our ministry in the city.

Spiritual Direction

A final discipline which enables us to grow in our relationship with Christ is spiritual direction. This discipline is little explored by Protestant and evangelical Christians, yet it is an ancient discipline of the church, modeled by our Lord and by St. Paul.

Spiritual direction is that process by which a more mature Christian walks with a brother or sister down the road of Christian experience. It is essentially a process of discipleship, as one helps the other in his or her Christian journey. It is critical to recognize that in effective spiritual direction, there is not a sense of superior Christian experience or knowledge on the part of the one giving the spiritual direction (in fact, to be effective, the director should have a spiritual director of his or her own). Rather, those who enter into such a relationship enter with the recognition that another can often see a person better than he or she can see him- or herself, and can therefore suggest wise directions in which the person needs to move in order to strengthen the personal relationship with God, with the inner self, and/or with the world.

If the idea of spiritual direction appeals to you, I suggest you select a spiritual director extremely carefully. It should be someone who has no other relationship with you (whether in the church, in your community, in your denomination, etc.), because that "other relationship" can influence the director's objective performance. Ideally, this person ought to have some experience either in spiritual direction or in discipleship building and should be under the authority of a spiritual director.

CONTEXTS FOR SPIRITUAL EXERCISES

There are several contexts for the practice of the disciplines of silence (which can include spiritual direction), personally relating to Scripture, journaling, and prayer. Unhappily, our varied church traditions have stressed one given context over the others. If the experience of the church over its two thousand years has taught us anything, however, it is the value of participating in all of these contexts.

Daily Devotional Time. A daily "quiet time" forms the foundation for practicing the disciplines of silence, personally relating to Scripture, journaling, and praying on behalf of the city. It is a particularly needful element to enrich one's spiritual life, to encourage one's heart (especially when the ministry becomes a burden), and to expand one's soul. Only by intentionally setting aside a portion of each day can a person sufficiently bear the troubles and tension of city ministry.

Psalm 5:3 extols the importance of meeting with God in the morning:

In the morning, O LORD, you hear my voice;
in the morning I lay my requests before you
and wait in expectation.

In the Psalms, the morning is regarded as the uniquely favored time by God for meeting with those who love him (cf. Ps. 17:15). This is so because we have not yet become caught up in the bustle and turmoil of the day; we are still quiet and at peace from the rest of the night. Thus, we are more in a frame of mind and spirit to come before the Lord.

Particularly intriguing is the line, "In the morning I lay my requests before you." The line could equally be translated "I hold myself in readiness for you" or "I offer my prayers to you" or "I present my sacrifice to you." In other words, the sense is one of God waiting expectantly to meet with us, and of us preparing ourselves to come before our God in fellowship and in adoration.

But where do we meet with God? We meet with God where he symbolically resides in our city:

But I, by your great mercy,
will come into your house;
in reverence will I bow down
toward your holy temple (Ps. 5:7).

In Jerusalem, of course, the place where God dwelt, the "house" in which God resided, was the temple. But where does God especially seem to live in your city? The psalmist suggests that it is in that place—a garden, a chapel, a special quiet or secluded place—that we go to meet him. There is wisdom in this, because I have found that my devotions take on special meaning when I pay attention to location and go to a place which seems "sacred" to me—a place pregnant with the presence of God.

What is the outcome of our going, early each morning, to God's abode to greet the new day with our Lord?

But let all who take refuge in you be glad;
let them ever sing for joy.
Spread your protection over them,
that those who love your name may rejoice in you (Ps. 5:11).

Those who meet with God in his holy place in the city each morning are those who "take refuge" in God, who psychologically live under a sense of God's protection, and who consequently take joy and experience exultation in being in God's presence. This is the importance of following the discipline of a daily quiet time.

I would make the practice of a daily devotional time the highest priority of your ministry. This can best be done by each day setting aside the same amount of time and the same time of the day for a quiet time.

Then make that time inviolable; I did that by having my church board inform the congregation that I was not to be disturbed before 9:30 A.M., even though I arrived at work at 8:30 A.M. That gave me a block of one hour each morning protected by a very watchful secretary who would let no phone call, person, or church issue near my door!

In order to have a balanced devotional time, I suggest giving equal blocks of time to centering down with silence, working with Scripture, journaling, and praying. While becoming centered, keep a note pad close by on which to write items you suddenly remember, so that you can then forget about them during your time with God. Live into Scripture by spending a great deal of time with a specific portion of the Bible, not moving on to the next chapter or topic until you sense that you have truly plumbed its depths. Approach the experience literally as a "time of quiet," an oasis in your day that gives you the opportunity to "be still and know that I am God."

Daily Study Time. If you are truly to be intentional about a quiet time in which you personally relate to Scripture, it is then also important that you set aside time for disciplined biblical research. This should not be done during your quiet time (otherwise the academic pursuit will gradually crowd out the act of living into Scripture). But you must allot time to maintain your skills in biblical exegesis and in exposition of the Word. When I was a pastor, I would allot two full mornings each week to do nothing but biblical research. I felt I owed it both to myself and to my congregation to do at least that much study.

Urban ministry is not for fuzzy thinkers. In order to be effective in urban ministry, it is vital to use one's head as well as one's heart and hands. It is biblical and theological reflection which informs the urban church and provides both direction and incentive to its mission priorities. I spent a year, for example, working with Paul's doctrine of the principalities and powers, and I integrated that study with another study I had done earlier in Deuteronomy on the biblical correlation between economics, politics, and religion. You have seen in this book the outcome of that work.

At the time I completed these studies, that continuing reflection had a profound impact on my perception both of the potential and the limitations of the political and economic forces within Detroit. For the first time, I saw theologically how those forces could be demonic or angelic in their influence on both the poor and the powerful. This, in turn, enabled me alternately to confront and woo those forces as I worked on housing and economic and community development with Detroit's poorest. I could approach these forces in a pragmatic rather than in a doctrinaire way because of the realistic social analysis that had come out of my biblical reflection.

Private Retreat. One of the tragedies both of the Protestant and the evangelical/fundamentalist movements has been the way we have ignored (or misused) the discipline of retreat. Until recently, we have been ignorant of retreat entirely. When we did discover it, we used it not for spiritual refreshment, but as a means to plan together intensively.

One critical context the urban Christian should practice should be the discipline of the private retreat. Precisely because the urban world is such a busy, noisy, and confused world, it is critical that Christians find a quiet place outside themselves as well as within themselves. Private retreat provides such a place.

I would recommend that every urban Christian include in his or her process of spiritual formation the act of going on private retreat. We can do this effectively only by withdrawing from the routine of everyday life. For a brief period (a weekend or several days during the week), get away from the city, go to a Roman Catholic or Orthodox monastery or a Protestant camp or retreat center and be alone. Enter into silence, and spend those few precious days in relaxation, in living into the silence (it truly becomes "golden"), and in leisurely practicing the four disciplines of silence, personally relating to Scripture, journaling, and prayer. A spiritual director might want to provide some guidance for the best use of your time at the retreat—particularly if it would be a new experience for you. If you are adventurous, you might even try the discipline of fasting!

I mentioned earlier in this chapter the three or four silent retreats I would take each year as a busy Detroit pastor and community organizer. In the retreats I took at a Roman Catholic monastery, I would rise before the sun and share with the Brothers in their pre-dawn worship. In so doing, I would feel intimately connected with the monastic tradition of the body of Christ which has worshiped this way for almost two thousand years. Having greeted the Lord at the beginning of a new day, I would spend the rest of the day in silence, in God's Word, in journaling, often in long and vigorous hikes through the nearby forest, and in relaxed conversational prayer. Finally, each day would end in the same chapel in silent meditation before the altar lighted by candles. No wonder I would return to Detroit eager to engage once more in the battle!

We have looked at a wide spectrum of the ways the urban Christian takes the journey inward; this is a process of continually getting in touch and staying in touch with one's own interior gladness. We have looked at some elements of spiritual formation—discovering one's inner self, of working on and resting our relationship with God. We have looked at several disciplines the Christian community has used over its two thousand years to enable people to participate more effectively in the rhythm of the Christian life. We have examined spiritual autobiographies, personal prayer, silence, relating to Scripture, journaling, spiritual direc-tion, personal retreat, a daily "quiet time," and the academic study of

Scripture. In the next chapter we will examine life in community, another element of spiritual sustenance.

The bottom line of spiritual formation, however, is for us to recognize that it is critical that we pay attention to feeding our own souls. We must not only have an adequate theology of spiritual formation and an understanding of its disciplines and contexts. We must recognize that spiritual formation is absolutely pivotal to our personal spiritual growth and our effectiveness in our urban ministry. We have to have it! And we need to be insistent in our pursuit of the support we feel we need from our church and from our brother and sister Christians in order that we might practice our own formation. If we need it, we need to be free to ask for it!

The author of the book of Acts describes the early church in this way:

> All the believers were one in heart and mind. No one claimed that any of his possessions was his own, but they shared everything they had. With great power the apostles continued to testify to the resurrection of the Lord Jesus, and much grace was with them all. There were no needy persons among them (4:32–34).

"There were no needy persons among [the Christians]." What was true of the first-century Christians needs to be true of the church today. There should be no physically nor spiritually needy among its people. It is appropriate—and in fact imperative—that every urban Christian ask the question "What is the spiritual support I need from my brothers and sisters in Christ, and where can I get that support?" Once the Christian has found the answer to that question, he or she needs to go after it unapologetically.

For we must "continue to work out [our] salvation with fear and trembling, for it is God who works in [us] to will and to act according to his good purpose" (Phil. 2:12–13).

THE END OF SPIRITUAL FORMATION:
THE JOURNEY OUTWARD

Spiritual formation is not an end in itself. It is a primary means to a far greater end. For the way out is in. The way in is out. We reach outside ourselves by first reaching in to discover ourselves in Christ, to foster our relationship with God and to build Christian community. From that growing base of spiritual formation, we reach out beyond ourselves to confront a pain of the city, and in so doing discover our call, uncover our gifts, and move out into God's mission for us.

We glorify God primarily through the service of humanity, by ministering to the least of these, Christ's brethren. The purpose for which we exist is to be personally, directly, and salvifically involved in ministering to and in the pain of the world. Our growth in our relationship with God, self, and others occurs to enable us to respond with greater depth to God's call to us to minister to the pain of the world. Our awareness of our vocation occurs only when our growing sense of our deep gladness in Christ connects with the deep hunger of the world!

When we looked at Isaiah 65:18–25 in chapter 8, we used it as a paradigm for the work or practice of the church in the city. We saw that God calls the church to be concerned about health care, infant mortality, longevity, stress, environmental pollution, adequate and fairly distributed housing, jobs for all at levels of skill that cause people to grow, economic development, legal systems that are just, relationship of all the city's people with God, and an entire city living at peace with one another.

So many needs. The church seems insignificant next to the enormity of the task given to it in the city. How can it responsibly address, with the Gospel, all the needs of the city? Paul provides us with the strategy that enables us to be fully responsive to the city.

> Just as each of us has one body with many members, and these members do not all have the same function, so in Christ we who are many form one body, and each member belongs to all the others. We have different gifts, according to the grace given us. If a man's gift is prophesying, let him use it in proportion to his faith. If it is serving, let him serve; if it is teaching, let him teach; if it is encouraging, let him encourage; if it is contributing to the needs of others, let him give generously; if it is leadership, let him govern diligently; if it is showing mercy, let him do it cheerfully (Rom. 12:4–8).

The church—the body of Christ—is called by God to address a holistic Gospel to the entire city, and this includes addressing all the city's needs (cf. Isa. 65). As we have discussed, however, it is not the responsibility of the Christian to address all the pain of humanity. Each is called by God to minister to one pain at a time. But the church, as the entire body of believers, is called to minister to all human need within all of society. It does this by equipping, encouraging, and preparing each of its members to recognize his or her specific call, to identify the others in that congregation who own the same call, and to pull these people together into a coalition to address that need together. The clergy of the church act to call forth, equip, and organize the laity so that they can identify and carry out their respective calls together.

As each mission coalition of the church, made up of all those called to a specific issue or need of the city, carries out its mission, then each issue will be addressed somewhere in the life of the body of Christ in that city. To be a faithful Christian in that context means to practice fully your call to a specific human need while trusting that each other human need will be addressed somewhere in that city by some other individual or group from the body of Christ. We are to trust the rest of the church to assume responsibility for those issues to which we are not called.

So it is that God has called each of us and all of us, as individuals and as the church, to minister in particular ways to the city's deep pain. God has provided for growth in our own self-understanding, in our relationship with him, and in our building of Christian community in order to prepare us spiritually for the mission set before us. He has gifted us, humbled us, and given us each other to enable us to move effectively into mission. And then . . . ?

> Then I heard the voice of the LORD saying, "Whom shall I send? And who will go for us?"
>
> And I said, "Here am I. Send me!" (Isa. 6:8)

Chapter Eleven

LIFE IN COMMUNITY

I had been invited to Melbourne, Australia, to deliver lectures in urban ministry. Within a week of my arrival, I concluded that the city pastors there needed to be teaching me. "Down under" I began discovering a whole way of "being church" that I had only rarely encountered elsewhere—and when I had encountered it, it had been only in third world city churches.

As I spent time in the inner-city churches of Melbourne and Sydney, I began to notice several common denominators that made these churches unbelievably dynamic. The first and most obvious was the spirit in the churches. Attending a worship service in any of these churches was profoundly celebrative: people rejoiced intensely in each other's company and worshiped God as one family. The people used music a great deal, including many songs written by members of the congregations (the lyrics of one such song began chapter 10). Whatever the tradition, worship seemed to focus around the sacrament of Holy Communion. There was an absence both of bulletins and a prescribed order of worship, which lent freedom and spontaneity to the worship. Children played a prominent role in the worship. In addition, it seemed that no one was "watching the clock."

A second common denominator among the churches was the inconsequential role programming seemed to play. Churches programmed—when they had to—but it seemed the exception, not the rule. Programming was done simply to accomplish what could not be done in any other way. And there were hardly any committees. It suddenly struck me, "Most first-world churches structure their lives around programming—and the price they pay for it is packed calendars, endless events, and burned-out Christians. These churches, on the other hand, build their lives around something other than programming—and as a result have discovered real freedom."

A third common denominator was the number and degree of community ministries. Even small churches were involved deeply in ministering to their communities, often in extremely costly ways. Churches of fewer than one hundred members operated drug-rehabilitation centers, emergency housing, legal aid clinics, and job-training and placement centers. Churches under three hundred members were not only involved in the rehabilitation of housing but also in the construction of new homes for the poor. All were involved in community organizations. "Where are they getting the money?" I asked myself.

I soon found out. They did not have full-time pastors. Very few of the churches I visited had pastors who worked exclusively for those churches. Almost all pastors had one or two additional jobs at which they earned their money; they were paid little or nothing by the churches they served. Yet most of the people tithed. Where did their money go? Not into salaries or operating expenses, but into mission!

A fourth common denominator was that few churches were pastored by only one member of the clergy. Even churches of one hundred members would have pastoral teams of three to six pastors (none of whom were getting paid much, either). These pastors would form a community within a Christian community, would support each other, worship, and work together. Ministry would be shared, with each pastor specializing in a particular portion of the work of the church. All would be involved in community ministry. All would take turns leading worship and preaching—and when not preaching, each would join his or her spouse and children to worship together as a family. The result? No one pastor felt the weight of a parish lying solely on his or her shoulders, all felt strongly supported, and burnout was minimal.

What was I experiencing? Life in community! I was experiencing— not in the occasional church, but in every church I visited—what it means for the church to be centered around community rather than programming, around life together rather than around the maintenance of an institution.

For these Christians, community was more than the sum of their relationships together. It was the base upon which they built their church life, their worship, and their willingness to serve each other and the hurting around their churches. Community was the foundation, motivator, and initiator for their ministries of compassion, action, intervention, and advocacy in their neighborhoods and cities.

When I saw such community, the question that kept coming to me was, "Am I seeing an example of the New Testament concept of community being acted out before my eyes? What are the biblical insights on the nature, extent, and influence community should play in the urban church?" And it dawned on me that there is a great source on this subject in Scripture—in those epistles Paul wrote to urban churches.

EPHESIANS: THE EPISTLE FOR THE CHURCH

It is suggested by many New Testament scholars that the book of Ephesians was written, not as a letter to the church in Ephesus, but as a tract to set forth systematically the heart of Pauline theology.[1] This tract, so it is believed by these scholars, headed up the assembled corpus of Paul's letters which filled one scroll and could be copied and distributed around the churches of the Roman empire. The book of Ephesians is meant, therefore, to be an introduction and summarization of Paul's theology, centered around his doctrine of the church. This gives the book a weight none of the letters would have, because rather than being responsive to a particular issue facing a given church, the book of Ephesians was an attempt to present systematically the heart of Paul's theology. As such, it is appropriate that we focus on this book as we study community.

Out of Chaos: The Church

Paul summarizes the book of Ephesians in a poem or hymn which occurs at its very beginning:

> [God] made known to us the mystery of his will according to his good pleasure, which he purposed in Christ, to be put into effect when the times will have reached their fulfillment—to bring all things in heaven and on earth together under one head, even Christ. In him we were also chosen, having been predestined according to the plan of him who works out everything in conformity with the purpose of his will, in order that we, who were the first to hope in Christ, might be for the praise of his glory (1:9–12).

Though the world seems to be sinking into chaos, Paul suggests, God has already acted to bring all of life together under Christ. The church is the foreshadowing of that new humanity, a sign and symbol of this new creation. It is the creation of God's new humanity (as exemplified in the church) which is God's primary work of grace; the individual and his or her salvation is an integral part of that larger work.

Therefore, the primary witness and work of the church in the city is not its proclamation, its practice, or its prayer, but its presence. It is to be a testimony to the city of the "New Jerusalem." The church is to be such a winsome symbol of community that people who live around that fellowship long to be a part of it!

The larger poem (Eph. 1:3–14) really is built upon a declaration of "every spiritual blessing in Christ" which Christ's body, the church, has received through him. These blessings are six in number:

- We are chosen (v. 4). God chose us, even before the world was created, to be holy and to live lives of love.

- We are adopted (vv. 5–6). Through Jesus Christ, we have been adopted by God as his children, in spite of our sins. God has done this simply because he loves us and because he chooses to do so.

- We are forgiven (vv. 7–8). Through Christ's death on the cross, God's grace has been showered on us through the miracle of forgiveness.

- We are a part of God's plan for the universe (vv. 9–10). God lets us know what he is doing through the ages, and lets us be a part of the out-working of that plan. He plans "to bring all things in heaven and on earth together under one head, even Christ"—to integrate and make whole a disintegrating world.

- We are claimed (vv. 11–12). God claims us as his own. Primarily targeted to the Jews, this blessing recognizes that God's predetermined plan has been at work since the beginning of time, slowly leading God's people to be "the first to hope in Christ."

- We are meant to be filled with the Spirit (vv. 13–14). The pagans, too, are meant to hear the Good News and believe it. The proof of this is the presence of the Holy Spirit in our midst.

What particularly strikes me about this entire passage is its corporate nature. Evangelicals interpret it as promises for the individual Christian. *But not a single noun or pronoun of the entire passage referring to the believers is singular.* Every reference is to the community of believers! What the writer is saying here is that these are promises made to the church; these are blessings given to the community of believers. Because those blessings are accorded the community, the individuals consequently receive them! These promises are intended for the whole church, and are the signs that this people is God's community of saints and not a collection of individuals "saved by grace."

The next paragraph of Ephesians 1 (vv. 15–23) follows inevitably from the spiritual blessings presented by Paul in verses 3–14. Paul prays that the Christians may have "the Spirit of wisdom and revelation" so that the "eyes of [their hearts] may be enlightened," so that they may see the nature of their call. They have been chosen, adopted, forgiven, called, claimed, and filled. For what purpose? So that they can see, understand, and participate in the great work God is doing for all humanity!

What has God accomplished in and through Christ? He has

> raised him from the dead and seated him at his right hand in the heavenly realms, far above all rule and authority, power and dominion, and every title that can be given, not only in the present age but also in the one to come. And God placed all things under his feet and appointed him to be head over everything for the church, which is his body, the fullness of him who fills everything in every way (vv. 20–23).

There are two assertions here. First, Christ becomes the integrating personality of a previously collapsing and chaotic universe. The rulers and authorities and powers and dominions no longer hold that role. Second, the church is Christ's body—at its very best, a physical manifestation of Christ on earth *today*, capturing his essence and fullness. The church, as the body of Christ, fills the universe with Christ's love.

All humanity lived lives separated from God, dominated by "the cravings of our sinful nature" and ruled by "the ruler of the kingdom of the air, the spirit who is now at work in those who are disobedient." "But," Paul continues in Ephesians 2,

> because of his great love for us, God, who is rich in mercy, made us alive with Christ even when we were dead in transgressions—it is by grace you have been saved. And God raised us up with Christ and seated us with him in the heavenly realms in Christ Jesus (vv. 4–6).

Out of this act of salvation, God began a miraculous work in each of our lives. God's grace began working in us, gradually reshaping and transforming us into his own people. Paul states it beautifully: "We are God's work of art, created in Christ Jesus to live the good life as from the beginning he had meant us to live it" (v. 10 JB).

But it is the other work Christ has done which captures Paul's greater attention and becomes the theme of this book: Christ's creation of community in the church.

Community: Precondition of Reconciliation

> But now in Christ Jesus you who once were far away have been brought near through the blood of Christ. For he himself is our peace, who has made the two one and has destroyed the barrier, the dividing wall of hostility, by abolishing in his flesh the law with its commandments and regulations. His purpose was to create in himself one new man out of the two, thus making peace, and in this one body to reconcile both of them to God through the cross, by which he put to death their hostility (vv. 13–16).

Here Paul states specifically the primary work Christ has done; he has so redeemed us and so destroyed the hostility between us that we are made into the new community. Redeemed humanity is not simply transformed individuals. It is a transformed community. Redemption's purpose is to create "one new man out of the two [alienated ones]." The evidence of authentic Christianity is community, in which the barriers that normally separate people have been overwhelmed and negated by the redeeming power of Christ.

Note the order laid out in verses 15–16 ("His purpose was to create . . ."). Today's individualistic Christianity would reverse this order. Paul states that Christ's act of redemption creates a community between two previously alienated people or groups. By restoring pre-Fall peace between them, Christ unites them into a new body—his body—the church. *That, in turn, fully reconciles them to God.* In other words, although receiving Christ as Savior is necessary to enable community to occur, conversion does not result in reconciliation with God. True reconciliation with God is not completed until one is reconciled with his or her neighbor and has begun to live in community with him or her. *Community is a necessary precondition of being fully reconciled to God!*

In Ephesians 3:1–13, Paul shares his personal call to apostolic ministry, and indicates why an outreach to pagans is primary to that ministry. He writes,

> Although I am less than the least of all God's people, this grace was given me: to preach to the Gentiles the unsearchable riches of Christ, and to make plain to everyone the administration of this mystery, which for ages past was kept hidden in God, who created all things (vv. 8–9).

How is the mystery of God's salvation to be dispersed? Through Paul? Only initially. Paul continues:

> [I am] to make plain to everyone the administration of this mystery, which for ages past was kept hidden in God, who created all things. His intent was that now, through the church, the manifold wisdom of God should be made known to the rulers and authorities in the heavenly realms, according to his eternal purpose which he accomplished in Christ Jesus our Lord (vv. 9–11).

God has chosen the church, his new community, through which to reveal his wisdom—his salvific work through Christ—not only to the people but to the systems and structures, the principalities and powers of the world!

It is out of the vocation to which the church is called that Paul prays for the life of the church. He records this prayer in Eph. 3:16–19. I always have interpreted it as Paul's prayer for us as individuals. The context does not allow that interpretation, however. The context of this prayer is the vocation of the church—not of the individual Christian. Paul states specifically that he is praying for the "family" of faith (vv. 14–15). Here he makes a play on the Greek words for "father" (*pater*) and "family" (*patria*) to indicate the social group descended from a common ancestor (or, in other words, "God's family," the church). Paul prays for the church:

> Out of his glorious riches . . . may [God] strengthen you with power through his Spirit in your inner being, so that Christ may dwell in your hearts through faith. And I pray that you, being rooted and established in love, may have power, together with all the saints, to grasp how wide and long and high and deep is the love of Christ, and to know

this love that surpasses knowledge—that you may be filled to the measure of all the fullness of God (vv. 16–19).

The vocation of the church is to be God's chosen revealer of his wisdom—his salvific work through Jesus Christ—for people, for systems and structures, and for the principalities and powers. In that vocation the church must demonstrate that salvific work through its own life in community and through its ministries of practice and proclamation. In the light of such a profound vocation, Paul prays for the life of the church, for its life is what must sustain it in such vocation.

What does Paul pray regarding the quality of the church's life? That the church may—

- Be empowered by the Holy Spirit
- Grow strong in its spiritual depths
- Be planted in Christ's love and be built on that love
- Grasp the full realities of life (to see with absolute clarity, to discern lie from truth)
- Be filled with the utter fullness of God

Only such a corporate life in Christ can sustain the church as it seeks to practice a vocation of the immensity assigned to it by Paul.

Ephesians 4:1 signals a change in focus in the book of Ephesians. Chapters 1–3 dealt with a theology of church as community. With the beginning of chapter 4, Ephesians shifts to consider the praxis of community; it will keep this focus through to the end of the book. It begins with Paul's words, "As a prisoner for the Lord, then, I urge you to live a life worthy of the calling you have received" (v. 1).

Our vocation or calling as the church is to be God's transformed community. The church is to be the sign, example, and communication (in word and deed) of God's salvific work through Christ among people, cities, nations, systems and structures, and principalities and powers. Now Paul tells the church, "Walk your talk!" We, both corporately and individually, are to live lives consistent with our vocation. We are to be, in our actions, our words, and our lives together, models of the community we claim to be!

Three Threats to the Church

In Ephesians 4, Paul introduces us to three threats to being church and indicates how we are to deal with those threats. He does not suggest that we avoid these threats, because we cannot. They are inevitable manifestations of the Enemy in any church seeking seriously to live in community. Rather than asking how we may avoid these threats, we need to ask how we may deal with them when they raise their ugly heads. As

Luther said, "You can't stop the birds from flying over your head. But you can stop them from building nests in your hair!"[2]

The three threats to the church's life in community noted in Ephesians 4 are (1) conflict between Christians (vv. 1–6), (2) diversity of gifts and services (vv. 7–13), and (3) heresy and unorthodox teaching (vv. 14–16). To these three threats the church should apply the principles of unity (vv. 1–6), peace (vv. 7–13), and purity (vv. 14–16).[3]

First, conflict between Christians (Eph. 4:1–6) threatens the church's life in community. Divisive conflict (as opposed to healthy conflict) undermines the church as it tries to live in community and exposes the talk of community as a lie. The answer to such divisiveness and conflict is unity based in the Spirit. Paul gives us insight into the nature of this unity:

1. It is a unity that must be *conscientiously practiced*. Paul writes, "Be completely humble and gentle; be patient, bearing with one another in love" (v.2). Being church requires us to be tolerant of one another, to be selfless, gentle, patient—not to take umbrage but to put up with what is irritating in each other. It is sort of like a marriage! A good marriage is one that can overlook what is irritating, bothersome, and petty in the other person in order to sustain the larger relationship. Being church requires the same thing.

2. It is a unity that must be *accentuated*. Paul writes, "Make every effort to keep the unity of the Spirit through the bond of peace" (v. 3). Tolerating each other and overlooking the annoying is not enough. One must also take affirmative action. We must seek to preserve our unity; we must work for our peace. It requires effort— intentional effort.

3. It is a unity that must be based on *affirmation of our common faith*. The apostle states, "There is one body and one Spirit—just as you were called to one hope when you were called—one Lord, one faith, one baptism; one God and Father of all, who is over all and through all and in all" (Eph. 4:4–6).

Once when I was involved in a church squabble, a church elder used this passage to bring unity and peace back to the body. It worked eloquently, I believe, because we all recognized instinctively the wisdom of these words—and the foolishness of our own. We are one because we are one in the Spirit, we confess one Lord, we have experienced a common salvation, and we are part of one community. Our differences are peripheral in comparison. So why accentuate the peripheral?

Second, diversity of gifts and service (Eph. 4:7–13) can threaten the church's life in community.[4] Paul writes,

But to each one of us grace has been given as Christ apportioned it. . . . It was he who gave some to be apostles, some to be prophets, some to be evangelists, and some to be pastors and teachers, to prepare God's people for works of service, so that the body of Christ may be built up until we all reach unity in the faith and in the knowledge of the Son of God and become mature, attaining to the whole measure of the fullness of Christ (vv. 7, 11–13).

Diversity does not have to mean division. In order for the church to function effectively both as a community and as an institution, Paul tells us, God has given a diversity of gifts to it. Some of these gifts are expressed in the "helping" functions of apostles, prophets, evangelists, pastors, and teachers (see chapter 8 for a fuller explanation of their functions). These functions make up a diversity of gifts. Behind such gifts is an even broader diversity of service.

The danger in this biblical principle for organizing the life of the church is that pride, jealousy, hunger for prestige, mistrust, resentment, and envy can come creeping in. Rather than celebrating and fully living into the ministry and gifts God has given us individually, it is easy to begin envying the gifts of others and their positions of respect and prestige in the church. When that dis-ease infects the entire life of a congregation, it can destroy that body through suspicion, resentment, and greed. How can one work against this destructive "green-eyed monster" in the church?

1. The *purpose* for the diversity of gifts must be stressed. All the gifts given to the body exist for only one purpose: to enable the community of faith—the entire community of faith—to undertake effectively its "works of service." Only in this way does the "body of Christ [get] built up," the "unity in the faith" get practiced, the knowledge of Christ become deepened, and the entire community become a mature community that is the actualized body of Christ.

2. *Recognition for the "lesser" works of service* must be stressed. Paul, recognizing the inherent danger in his principle of the diversity of gifts, asserts in a comparable passage,

   The eye cannot say to the hand, "I don't need you!" And the head cannot say to the feet, "I don't need you!" On the contrary, those parts of the body that seem to be weaker are indispensable, and the parts that we think are less honorable we treat with special honor. And the parts that are unpresentable are treated with special modesty, while our presentable parts need no special treatment. But God has combined the members of the body and has given greater honor to the parts that lacked it, so that there should be no division in the body, but that its parts should have equal concern for each other. If one part suffers, every part suffers with it; if one part is honored, every part rejoices with it (1 Cor. 12:21–26).

It is critical, Paul teaches in 1 Corinthians, that if you do not want to have dissent, jealousy, and bitterness in your church, you had better find

some effective way of bringing recognition to those people who are called
to the church's less prestigious tasks. People in such positions have every
bit as much need to be honored and recognized as do people in pivotal
positions—perhaps even more. If you do not have ways of helping them
to see how strategic they are to the life and work of the body, surely you
will encounter dissent.

> 3. The *peace* of the church must be stressed. The work of shalom—of
> working for the kingdom of God in the city—must be kept before
> the congregation. And the place of each church member's ministry
> and work in bringing about shalom must be addressed frequently.
> As well, the church must lift up its internal peace and the important
> contribution each member makes to the maintenance of that peace.
> Only in this way will the people keep their priorities straight and
> keep the diversity of gifts from becoming division, thus destroying
> that church's peace.

Third, heresy and unorthodox teaching (Eph. 4:14–16) threatens the
church's life in community. Paul writes,

> Then we will no longer be infants, tossed back and forth by the waves,
> and blown here and there by every wind of teaching and by the
> cunning and craftiness of men in their deceitful scheming (v. 14).

Paul uses several metaphors here. A church which does not practice
purity of doctrine and which is weak in its teaching ministry can be
likened to children who are led astray easily; they have no real
discernment. Or such a church can be likened to a boat, out of control on a
wild and storm-tossed sea; both lack control and a sure, steady hand at the
tiller. Or such a church can be likened to people watching a magician;
through his or her tricks and craftiness they can be deceived into believing
what is not so (which is the task of the magician—to make the impossible
believable).

Thus, surefooted belief, clarity, and conviction about the substance
of one's faith are as important as the peaceful use of the diversity of a
church's gifts and the practice of its unity. Without it, a church may be at
peace and in unity, but it will not be pure. It will lose its cutting edge.

I see this as the real problem of the church today: it lacks conviction
or common doctrine; it lacks commitment to commonly perceived and
endorsed perspectives about the faith. It is a church which has made the
sacrifice of its purity the price for maintaining its peace and unity. Thus it
is united only because of commonly accepted structures and liturgies. It is
at peace simply because no one wants to argue and thus disrupt a fragile
and painfully won armistice. But,

> Instead, speaking the truth in love, we will in all things grow up into
> him who is the Head, that is, Christ. From him the whole body, joined

and held together by every supporting ligament, grows and builds itself up in love, as each part does its work (Eph. 4:15–16).

The church grows "into Christ"—becoming, increasingly, his body, a community of faith relating to and responsible to each other and living under his authority—only as it lives both by "the truth" and "in love." In all its life, actions, worship, and teaching it must seek to live out the peace, unity, and purity of the church. Only by stressing, celebrating, and balancing all three can it really create the environment in which it can be, in deed and life as well as in theory, the community of faith.

No Community—No Christianity

If the Gospel is to do anything, it is to change lives. We are to become new creations in Christ. It is our life in community which will most sustain us as we live our new lives. Conversely, lack of community will erode what little faith we have. Without the faith and life of the whole church supporting our confessions of faith, we will be seduced into believing the lie and living our lives focused on self-interest. Without our practice of community, we will not experience authentic Christianity. It is to this reality that Ephesians 4:17–32 speaks. The first sentence presents the theme of this section:

> In particular, I want to urge you in the name of the Lord, not to go on living the aimless kind of life that pagans live (v. 17 JB).

Perhaps another word for *aimless* is the word *purposeless*. Life in Christ and in the community of faith brings purpose. But an aimless, uncentered life is what occurs outside of Christ and the community he creates; within his community others hold us accountable.

Paul first develops the extent of purposeless life (vv. 17–24). It includes intellectual dishonesty and faddish involvement, no sense of right and wrong, sexual fixation, licentiousness, and greed.

The task of Christians, rather, is to "put off your old self . . . to be made new in the attitude of your minds" (vv. 22–23), which manifests itself in behavior that builds community, is not self-oriented, and does not bring offense to the Gospel (vv. 25–32). Paul ends this exposition with the challenge, "Be kind and compassionate to one another, forgiving each other, just as in Christ God forgave you" (v. 32).

Paul then develops in Ephesians 5 and 6 the emphasis he introduced in chapter 4 on right behavior as strategic to building community. He now deals with sexual misconduct, greed, and salacious talk as those actions and attitudes that will both make Christianity a scandal and will destroy community. He then suggests how Christians ought to live in relationship to each other and before the world:

Be very careful, then, how you live—not as unwise but as wise, making the most of every opportunity, because the days are evil. Therefore do not be foolish, but understand what the Lord's will is. Do not get drunk on wine, which leads to debauchery. Instead, be filled with the Spirit. Speak to one another with psalms, hymns and spiritual songs. Sing and make music in your heart to the Lord, always giving thanks to God the Father for everything, in the name of our Lord Jesus Christ. Submit to one another out of reverence for Christ (Eph. 5:15–21).

Life in Christ and in the Christian community is also influenced by the morals of the home and the ethics of the business place. Ephesians 5:21–6:4 deals with two aspects of home life that are influenced, inevitably, by Christian community and lively relationship with God: marriage and child-raising. Likewise, the way employer (master) and employee (slave) treat each other and treat the business also witnesses to an authentic or unauthentic life in community. True responsibility and Christian love in marriage, parenting, and business must go far beyond what Roman or Jewish law demands, Paul says. Unlike what the laws dictate, you must always seek the justice of the weaker party and must extend yourself in love and compassion to him or her.

Except for the closing news and salutation (Eph. 6:21–24), the final section of Ephesians (6:10–20) deals with the spiritual warfare in which we are engaged as Christians. Paul reminds us that, in the final analysis, "Our struggle is not against flesh and blood, but against . . . the powers of this dark world and against the spiritual forces of evil in the heavenly realms" (v. 12). The only way to resist this power is to "put on the full armor of God" (v. 11). That armor, of course, is "truth," "righteousness" or integrity, "readiness," "faith," "salvation," "the word of God," and "prayer" (vv. 14–18).

When one reads this graphic passage, one envisions oneself as an individual Roman soldier, clothed in God's armor. That is not the context of this passage, however. It is important to realize that Paul is writing the book of Ephesians, not to individual Christians, but to all his churches. He is thinking in terms of girding an army, not just an individual soldier! It is the community of faith that has to confront the sovereignties and powers, and it is the community of faith that must live out the Christian life before the world. It is critically important to remember that Ephesians 6:10–20 is written to the church and not to individual Christians.

The book of Ephesians now draws to a close with Paul's final salutation. The apostle writes,

Tychicus, the dear brother and faithful servant in the Lord, will tell you everything, so that you also may know how I am and what I am doing. I am sending him to you for this very purpose, that you may know how we are, and that he may encourage you.

> Peace to the brothers, and love with faith from God the Father and the Lord Jesus Christ. Grace to all who love our Lord Jesus Christ with an undying love (Eph. 6:21–24).

Here we see the practical and pastoral side of Paul, doing what is needed (and what he desires to do) in order to build and maintain community. He is keeping his audience informed about himself and other Christians they know. He is asking for the people's prayers and, at the same time, reassuring them. And he presents God's blessings upon them.

This ending reminds us that theorizing about community is not enough, nor is theologizing (see chapters 1–3 of this book), nor is comprehensive implementation (chapters 4–9 of this book). There is also the daily, nitty-gritty work of maintaining community. Here in Ephesians we see that work in action. It is an important reminder of the concrete way in which community is finally proven to be an authentic force or a deception.

FURTHER INSIGHTS FROM PAUL

Ephesians is not the only book Paul wrote to urban churches about community. In each of his letters, he deals with the issues of community, but does so in the practical activities of each of those city churches. Here are a few highlights.

Determining Importance: Romans 12

> I urge you, brothers, in view of God's mercy, to offer your bodies as living sacrifices, holy and pleasing to God—which is your spiritual act of worship. Do not conform any longer to the pattern of this world, but be transformed by the renewing of your mind. Then you will be able to test and approve what God's will is—his good, pleasing and perfect will (vv. 1–2).

Do not live for the world's economic, political, and religious goals, Paul magnificently states. Do not measure yourself by the world's standards. Instead, think of yourself as a living sacrifice, offered to God. And live your life as if you are offered up to God; live your life in a manner that proclaims that your life is no longer your own, for you have been bought with a great price. Let your behavior be conformed to how God is transforming your mind and spirit, so that your actions and your lifestyle are in conformity with your reflections. When you do that, you will discover you are living your life in conformity to God's will for you.

This is the responsibility of the individual within the Christian community. But what should be the actual relationship between the individual and the community? Paul suggests a standard for determining that relationship.

> For by the grace given me I say to every one of you: Do not think of yourself more highly than you ought, but rather think of yourself with sober judgment, in accordance with the measure of faith God has given you (v. 3).

There is no place in the Christian community for egoism, Paul states. Each of us is not the center of the world; if we are committed Christians we are not even the center of our own worlds. We are not to exaggerate our own importance, for we are, first and foremost, a part—and only a part—of the body of Christ.

That is why the cult of personality today in the Christian movement is both very dangerous and seductive. With the advent of television coverage and the mass production of materials and media, the church focuses upon its primary leadership to a degree unknown in previous generations. But so to focus is seductive, because it draws us away from what should be our true focus: Christ, crucified, risen and living today through his entire body, the church. Rather than thinking of ourselves as being pivotal to God's kingdom, Paul instructs us to measure ourselves by "the measure [or standard] of faith God has given you" (v. 3). What is that standard?

> In Christ we who are many form one body, and each member belongs to all the others. We have different gifts, according to the grace given us (vv. 5–6).

The standard Paul gives us for structuring our life in community is the primacy of Christ's body. It is the body—its strength, maturation, and effectiveness—which is God's primary concern. We are to see ourselves both as an integral part of that body and, therefore, as belonging to and being accountable to each other. Each of us is gifted by God, not to be "showmen for Jesus," but to be of sustaining grace to the body. Those gifts have been given to each of us in order to guarantee that, among all of us, the body of Christ will be nurtured and equipped for, as well as capable of, undertaking effectively its mission.

Paul gives some examples of those gifts used to build up the body (vv. 6–8), rather than to advance the cause of the individual. He chooses prophesying (truth telling), administrating, teaching, preaching, using money in a biblically informed manner, organizing, and performing works of mercy. All these are examples of the tasks that must be done to strengthen and maintain the body of Christ, and each of us is gifted by God to play a strategic role in sustaining that body.

In the final verses of Romans 12, Paul gives some examples of Christian community at work. He outlines some of the ways Christians behave as the result of living in loving, intentional community. Christians *bless their persecutors*, not curse them. In community, people *rejoice with each other and mourn with each other*; they meet at the point of each other's joys and needs. They treat each other with equal kindness and *live in harmony* with each other. They are *committed to the poor*. They *avoid self-centeredness*, because that is the very antithesis of community and will destroy it. They intentionally *live high ideals* before the world and each other. And Christians attempt to *live at peace* with each other, seeking to avoid anger and the acting out of anger in wrathful acts. This is the style of life upon which community should be built.

Money and Christian Obligation: 2 Corinthians 8

In 2 Corinthians 8, Paul encourages the generosity of the Corinthian Christians toward the destitute Jerusalem church. He writes,

> At the present time your plenty will supply what they need, so that in turn their plenty will supply what you need. Then there will be equality, as it is written: "He who gathered much did not have too much, and he that gathered little did not have too little" (vv. 14–15).

The assumption behind that passage is that the Jerusalem church and the Acacian church are family. As family, they have a mutual responsibility toward each other. Their relationship creates the responsibility! Thus they meet each other's need in times of their respective leanness.

How to Feel About a Church: Philippians 1

> I thank my God every time I remember you. In all my prayers for all of you, I always pray with joy because of your partnership in the gospel from the first day until now, being confident of this, that he who began a good work in you will carry it on to completion until the day of Christ Jesus.
>
> It is right for me to feel this way about all of you, since I have you in my heart; for whether I am in chains or defending and confirming the gospel, all of you share in God's grace with me. God can testify how I long for all of you with the affection of Christ Jesus (vv. 3–8).

Paul loved this community! They were his joy. His every thought of them was a positive thought. Because this is a community with which he has fallen in love, Paul wants only the best for them.

Verse 6 ("He who began a good work in you will carry it on to completion") normally is used as a promise to the individual believer. The context of verses 1–8, however, insists that *you* is not a promise made to an individual, but to the church.

What Paul is stating here is that God is doing a good work in the Philippian church, a work God began in Christ and will complete at Christ's second coming. Paul goes on to state that his affection for the Philippians has come out of the ministry and the persecution he has shared with them. It has been out of their common discipleship that they have learned to trust and depend upon each other, and it is because of this common discipleship that the Philippian Christians have won a permanent place in Paul's heart. When Paul is absent from them, he longs to be with them, for he loves them very much. This is the active community of faith the church should be: a community not of theory and of theology, but of love and longing and fulfillment, matured by the good times and the hard times Christians have together, and based on Christ's common love for them all.

Demands Made by Life in Community: 1 Thessalonians 5

At first blush, 1 Thessalonians 5:12–22 appears to be a grocery list of demands and expectations Christians living in community have the right to anticipate from each other. But the organizing principle of this passage is found in verse 15 at the very heart of this section. It is as if Paul began laying out instructions and then, in the midst of the instructions, realized the essential principle that he was promulgating and gave it voice. He wrote, "Make sure that nobody pays back wrong for wrong, but always try to be kind to each other and to everyone else."

For the church to be community, each of its members needs to be other-directed. Each person's primary concern must be for the community itself, not the advocacy of his or her particular position or conviction. But what does it mean to be concerned primarily for what is best for each other and for the community? It is—

- To be considerate to those working in the community's midst
- To respect the community's teachers, and to have affection for them
- To be at peace with each other
- To minister to each other at the point of need ("Warn those who are idle, encourage the timid, help the weak, be patient with everyone" [1 Thess. 5:14])
- To be joyous at all times
- To pray constantly, giving thanks to God
- Not to suppress the Spirit or manifestations of the Spirit's work within the community (especially prophecy)
- To think before you do or say anything, in order to evaluate the consequences of such words or actions
- To hold on to the good and to avoid every form of evil!

Being Family to Each Other: Philemon

Onesimus, the unbelieving slave of the Christian Philemon, had run away from Philemon's estate in Ephesus to Rome where he met and was converted by the apostle Paul. But the relationship of that slave and his Christian owner was still not settled so Paul sent Onesimus back to Philemon bearing a short letter. Paul writes to Philemon:

> I am sending [Onesimus]—who is my very heart—back to you. . . . Perhaps the reason he was separated from you for a little while was that you might have him back for good—no longer a slave, but better than a slave, as a dear brother. He is very dear to me but even dearer to you, both as a man and as a brother in the Lord. So if you consider me a partner, welcome him as you would welcome me. If he has done you any wrong or owes you anything, charge it to me (vv. 12, 15–18).

Paul's argument for clemency for Onesimus is based on one essential premise: personal relationship with Jesus Christ makes us all family. We are all members of the same community, parts of the same body. Since we have one Lord and are consequently made one in Christ, there is no room for us to be alienated from each other, no matter how we offended each other before we became Christians. There is no room for social differences and legal obligations to stand between us, either—not even if we have aggrieved these obligations. Both obligations and their aggrievements have been done away with by the cross.

What this means for Philemon and Onesimus is that they are no longer simply master and slave, no matter what Roman law may say. Nor are they aggrieved owner and thieving runaway, so that the laws which provide punishment in theses circumstances are irrelevant. Philemon and Onesimus are now brothers—blood brothers at that, for both have been washed by their Elder Brother's blood. The only ground upon which they now come together is mutual forgiveness and acceptance, and full restoration to each other's favor. For they are of the same community of faith and they must live out that community before the world!

Paul has placed a heavy obligation on Philemon by asking him to receive Onesimus back into his household and grant him clemency. In verse 20, Paul shifts his argument from obligation to personal plea. He writes to Philemon, "I do wish, brother, that I may have some benefit from you in the Lord; refresh my heart in Christ."

Paul realized, of course, the difficult place in which he was putting Philemon, so he sought at the end of his little letter to encourage and uphold his brother in Christ. In that act of seeking to lighten the burden which he had no choice but to lay upon Philemon, Paul demonstrated an essential task of maintaining Christian community.

Community is not simply a lovely theological concept or an ideal about which the church should dream. Community is a living reality toward which the church works. The congregation—every member of it—counts on every other member to assume his or her role and take on the responsibility of contributing to the development and implementation of community in that parish. It is everyone's responsibility. It is only as each of us can be counted upon to assume our share (and even more than our share) in contributing to our church's implementation of community that we can put new heart into each other. Community is grace—given by God. It is also deed—responsibility assumed by each of us. Out of that wedding of grace and deed true community is created, becoming blessing and heart to all believers.

COMMUNITY AND THE KINGDOM OF GOD

Throughout this book, we have explored together God's intentions for the city: to actualize there the kingdom of God. He intends for the city's people and systems to live in justice and respect, to share equally the city's resources and to live in mutual relationship with God—in other words, to demonstrate what the Bible means by *shalom*. Jesus Christ provided entrance into that kingdom through his cross and resurrection, in the same way he provides for the release of the city's systems and people from the power of sin, death, and the law. The church has been placed by God in the city in order to expose to all in the city the lies that the systems tell to keep the city in bondage. The church is also placed in the city to be the advocate of the city given over to the kingdom of God. To this the church witnesses in its prayers, its presence, its proclamation, and its practice or work in the city. It seeks the empowerment of the poor, the liberation of the powerful, and the reformulation of the city into the kingdom of God.

The church will never fully accomplish these objectives, for only God will be able finally to bring in his kingdom. But the church is responsible to be faithful to its calling, and thus to be a sign of the kingdom by its life, work, and witness.

What Paul deeply appreciated, as he worked for the reconciliation of humanity in the great cities of the Roman empire, is that the church could never live into its vocation effectively or carry out its full-orbed ministry in the city unless it was first a true community of believers. Unless the believers were joined together as a community in the quality of their life together as well as in their rhetoric, they would not have the power even to begin to accomplish their mission. Being such a community, Paul insisted, had very practical implications to it. Being a body of unity, purity, and peace together would affect the expectations we would have of each other, the ways we would shape our marriages, our occupations, the personal ethics of our lives and the corporate ethics of the church, the way we would deal with money, and the level and extent of our commitment to each other. For without practicing authentic community in our church, we would not be fully reconciled to God. This absence of community would be a signal to the city that there was no authentic Christianity in that church.

The truth of this is obvious. The church is all that exists today of the kingdom of God! The church is the redeemed universe in miniature, a microcosm of human society as it is redeemed and thus is meant to be under God's rule. Its mission, then, is to sustain and to spread that "universe." It is called by God to witness to its faith to the whole world, both corporately and through each individual Christian. If it has not done that, it is a faithless church.

The primary means of witnessing, the final authentication of God's kingdom in the city, is the church's life together. For presence always speaks louder than either words or actions. If the church's life together is not a foretaste of the kingdom of God, then the church is an obstacle to the salvation of the city and not God's vehicle for salvation. Life in community is the ultimate test of the faithfulness or unfaithfulness of the church!

How can the city church be capable of filling such a demanding role? It cannot. It will always fall back into a divided, fighting, barrier-building, prideful conglomerate of individuals. That is why the church needs the Holy Spirit. God's gift to the church, the Holy Spirit, maintains it as the redeemed universe in miniature. The Holy Spirit can permeate and empower and undergird the church as it lives its life and seeks to do its mission in the city. The Spirit will undergird the church, however, only to that degree that the church will overcome its pride, be open to the Spirit's work in its midst, and accept the reality that even in its faithlessness it is accepted and loved by God. To this church, God has entrusted the responsibility of being in its life together the closest present reality to the kingdom of God.

SOME PRACTICAL CONSIDERATIONS

What do we do? We start! We start right where we are. We start with what we've got: the body of believers in our church, no matter what the condition of their work, witness, or life together. We start practicing community with these, our brothers and sisters in Christ, and we practice being church and practice being church until we get it right! Will we ever get it right? Never completely. But we can make it workable, to a certain degree. All that God asks out of us is that we try to be faithful to this heavenly vision.

In the previous chapter, we dealt with urban spiritual formation. The disciplines we examined for enabling our own spiritual formation were all individual disciplines. Besides such personal spiritual exercises, urban spiritual formation also needs to include participation in a nurturing community.

Christians are a corporate people, as we have seen clearly demonstrated in the apostle Paul's beliefs about community. Ours is not a faith practiced effectively in solitude. Individual spiritual disciplines are necessary for us to deepen our relationship with God and to gain greater insight into ourselves. If we are going to be equipped effectively to become Christ's servants in the city, however, we also need the support and sustenance of each other in the church. I would strongly suggest, therefore, that every Christian involved in urban ministry needs to find a nurturing Christian community in which he or she can participate and from which he or she can gain strength.

Nurturing communities come in all sizes and shapes. The most obvious form of such community is the local congregation itself, particularly if the church is small (such as the Australian inner-city churches I described at the beginning of this chapter). When a congregation exceeds fifty members, the church can create several nurturing communities. Nurturing communities can be found in other groupings, as well. House churches, neighborhood Bible studies, small support groups, groups oriented around a mission, groups centered around a particular cause, and clergy groups all can be strong nurturing groups for us. What all these groups, in all their diversity, have in common is that they are all primary groups (i.e., face-to-face groups) centered in Jesus Christ and existing in order to enable their members to serve him more effectively in the world.

What should one look for in a nurturing community? That question can best be answered, I believe, by asking and answering two preceding questions: "What do I need from my brother and sister Christians now?" and "How do I need to be enabled to serve Christ more effectively in my city?" To my mind, a good nurturing community is one which sustains and encourages each of its participants in his or her working relationship with God and self. It is an effective nurturing community when it enables its members increasingly to perceive God's call to them to serve him in specific ministries in the city, calls forth from each member the desire to exercise his or her gifts in those ministries, and provides the opportunities for its members to function more effectively in those ministries. The role of the nurturing community on its most basic level, therefore, is to encourage spiritual growth in its members in order to encourage their ministry in the city.

We had four types of nurturing communities at my church near Detroit. Most of our members involved in small groups were in "Support Groups." These were groups of church members who wanted to grow in their personal spirituality and in life in community, but who did not have a commitment to the same human needs. They gathered together to work relationally with Scripture, to pray together, to share and support each other in their respective concerns, and to hold each other accountable for self-selected spiritual disciplines.

"Task Forces" were the opposite of support groups. These were small groups of church members who came together around a common commitment to a particular human need, and who were willing to address that need together. Task Forces did not want to build as an intentional part of that group's life any support in individual or corporate spiritual formation. Examples of this kind of group were a Senior Citizens Awareness Task Force and a Task Force on the Cambodian Refugee Families which our church sponsored.

"Covenant Groups" were small groups of church members who were concerned about a particular human need and made a covenant with each other to study and to minister to that need for a designated period of time. During that time, the group would also commit itself to experiment in building an individual and corporate life together. An example of a covenant group was one on an Alternative Christian Life-Style, which supported its participants in living a simpler lifestyle while also working as a group on poverty and scarcity issues in Detroit.

A "Mission Group" was a small group of church members who believed themselves called together by God for the purpose of carrying out a mission to one specific human need, and who were therefore willing to work at their respective and corporate spiritual formation in order to enable them to be more effective in carrying out that discerned mission. One such mission group was one committed to the development of PIFU, about which I wrote in chapter 9.

The four types of groups would normally meet about twice a month, each meeting lasting about one and a half to two hours. Let me describe a typical meeting in a support, covenant, or mission group.[5]

Participants would gather in silence, as each person centered down for the evening's meeting. Following about a ten- to twenty-minute period of silence, participants would share around a designated passage of Scripture with which people had worked and journaled in their private quiet times over the preceding week(s). Out of that sharing would come discussion which would deal with the relationship of that Scripture passage to the lives of the group's participants.

Following that time of biblical reflection, the group would move to sharing directly out of their own lives. This could simply be an open time of sharing about that week (or two); the members might discuss the frustrations and joys they had encountered, or the serious problems they had faced. The group would be of support to each person as needed. The group could decide, instead, to deal with the perceiving of call (e.g., taking one person who would volunteer and really help that person to explore what caused him or her to weep over the city) or the evoking of gifts (i.e., the naming of the gifts of one group member).

Finally, the meeting would end with a time of worship and prayer. This time of worship would become increasingly specific as the group's previous work would be specific; for example, if the group had spent time evoking someone's gifts, perhaps the entire worship service would be spent consecrating those gifts to the service of God. With the close of worship, the group's meeting would end (except in the case of the mission and covenant groups, which would then go on to conducting the "business" of that group's mission).

The members of each group would be asked to set individual spiritual disciplines for themselves, and the group would hold them accountable. Some groups also developed spiritual direction, in which each member of the group was in spiritual direction from one member of the group and was spiritual director to another group member. Each group would have its corporate disciplines as well, which it would maintain by consensus.

It is through processes such as these that a congregation can develop nurturing communities within its fellowship. It is in nurturing communities like these that Christians can learn how to love God, each other, and their own inner selves, and thus grow in their relationships with Christ. The nurturing community can be the seedbed for the discovery of each Christian's calling. Each member's gifts can be evoked and he or she can both be sent forth and continuingly encouraged to carry out his or her vocation in the world. It is in small nurturing groups like this that Christians can live in community in the city, personal spiritual formation can be fostered, and the body of Christ can be formed in strength and vitality.

The Reverend Alan Marr, a pastor in one of the dynamic inner-city congregations in Melbourne, Australia, told me how his church came into being. He had been an associate pastor in a wealthy suburb of Melbourne. In that church, he had been part of a group exploring community together. Members developed deep, committed relationships. Responding to a report demonstrating the plight of Melbourne inner-city ministry, Alan became increasingly aware of God's call to him to move into a poor, working-class neighborhood on Melbourne's west side. It was his intent to found a new church by merging three very small neighborhood churches in that neighborhood.

That Saturday over breakfast, Alan shared with the members of the small nurturing community his decision to respond to this new call. The group fell silent. Finally, one member responded, "Well, tell me, when are *we* leaving?"

And "we" left. Families in that nurturing community sold their homes, moved from that east side suburb into that poor west side neighborhood, bought homes, settled down with their pastor, began entering into the life of that disadvantaged community, and became the backbone for the formation of that new, dynamic church built from those three small and no-longer-viable congregations. And why did these people follow their pastor into that working-class neighborhood? One told me quite simply: "Why, we're family, mate!"

When the day came for the formation of the Westgate Baptist Community from the three former churches, the new congregation gathered for worship. And these are the lyrics of the song they sang to celebrate their birth as a Christian community—a community called into being from three churches and from Melbourne's wealthy and poor from both east and west sides:

> What grace, to make us your people!
> What love, to call us your own!
> What power, to make us your body!
> What care! We're never alone
>   Because you have called us together.
> Oh, incredible love! We're in God's family.
>
> What pain we surely must give you!
> Such lives! We're covered in shame.
> How sad, we go to our corners.
> What stains we bring to your name
>   Because you have called us together.
> Oh, be patient we pray with all your family.
>
> Like slaves who flourish in service,
> Like jars with treasures untold,
> Like priests who pray for the people,
> Like sheep who sleep in the fold,
>   Because you have called us together.
> Oh, what various ways to see God's family.
>
> Father, your vision will lead us.
> Jesus, your love is the way.
> Spirit, creatively guide us.
> We'll meet to serve and to pray
>   Because you have called us together.
> Oh, Lord help us to learn to be God's family.
> Oh, what marvellous love to be God's family!
> Oh, incredible joy to be God's family![6]

Chapter Twelve

GOD'S VISION FOR THE CITY

To Jerusalem thy city return with compassion, O Lord, and dwell therein as thou hast promised. Rebuild thou thy city speedily in our days, O God, a structure everlasting. And the throne of David thy servant speedily establish there. Blessed art thou, O Lord, the builder of Jerusalem. Amen.　　　　　　　　　　—Ancient Jewish prayer[1]

In this section of this book, we are examining together the necessary power we need to undergird effective urban ministry. I suggested earlier that any pastor or church worker responsibly ministering in the city inevitably will be caught up in spiritual warfare. This is so because one cannot be effective in urban ministry without dealing with the systems and structures of the city, and the people who are either victims of or are seduced by those systems. To confront the systems at any level which promises change means that, unavoidably, one is confronting the principalities and powers of that city. That means spiritual warfare!

Essential to that spiritual warfare needs to be our recognition that the principalities and powers, sensing their exposure by and consequent vulnerability before the church, will attack us with all the forces at their disposal. The principalities will always choose to attack us at our most vulnerable point. That most vulnerable point for most urban Christians is our capacity to sustain ourselves in ministry. To remain optimistic, hopeful, and full of humor is the most difficult task in urban ministry. Thus the principalities will seek to make us feel overwhelmed, exhausted, and pessimistic about what the church actually can accomplish against the systems and structures. Once our hope has been destroyed, we have been destroyed!

I suggested that God has given us four basic ingredients to sustain us as we seek to make a difference in ministry in the city. We need to sustain those ingredients in our own lives. We have already examined two of those ingredients: personal spiritual formation and life in community. In this chapter, we will consider together the third ingredient: maintaining a vision for our city.[2]

For urban Christian workers or pastors to maintain hope and faith in their city ministry, they need to develop and tenaciously hold onto a vision for the city—a vision that is based on the biblical message that God and God's church will someday win!

The fullest description of the inevitable outcome of God's work in the city is found in the book of Revelation. In fact, I believe that the book of Revelation can best be understood when viewed from the vantage point of being an urban book. It is a book about doing ministry in the contemporary city in the light of a godly vision for the city. We will begin in this chapter to explore that book and its urban vision for present city ministry.

The book of Revelation is built around a single premise. Whereas throughout biblical history each city is seen as the abode of both God and Satan, in the book of Revelation the city is revealed to us as a city which is either the abode of God or the abode of Satan. In the book of Revelation, we are treated to the examination of two archetypal cities: Babylon—the city entirely given over to Satan; and the new Jerusalem—the city totally committed to God. The choice is made by both cities to be the abode either of Satan or God. The people and the systems of those cities make that choice as influenced by their principalities and powers. They *will* make a choice; it will be one or the other. No more will they hear: "How long will you waver between two opinions? If the Lord is God, follow him; but if [Satan] is God, follow him" (1 Kings 18:21). They will choose to be either the city of Satan or the city of God!

THE CITY OF SATAN

The author of Revelation first paints a picture of Babylon as the city of Satan (Rev. 17:1–19:10). Here we examine the eventual result of a city which has no redeeming value, a city given over to the wholehearted worship and pursuit of evil. The author initially shows us what caused the archetypal Babylon, the "great city, O Babylon, city of power" (Rev. 18:10) to become solely a city of Satan.

First, Babylon has become the city of Satan because she committed herself to the worship of another god.

> "Come, I will show you the punishment of the great prostitute, who sits on many waters. With her the kings of the earth committed adultery and the inhabitants of the earth were intoxicated with the wine of her adulteries" (Rev. 17:1–2).

> With a mighty voice [the angel] shouted,

"Fallen! Fallen is Babylon the Great!
  She has become a home for demons
and a haunt for every evil spirit,
  a haunt for every unclean and detestable bird.
For all the nations have drunk the maddening wine
  of her adulteries.
The kings of the earth committed adultery with her,
  and the merchants of the earth grew rich from her
    excessive luxuries" (Rev. 18:2–3).

"When the kings of the earth who committed adultery with [Babylon] and shared her luxury see the smoke of her burning, they will weep and mourn over her. Terrified at her torment, they will stand far off and cry:

  " 'Woe! Woe, O great city,
  O Babylon, city of power!
  In one hour your doom has come!' " (Rev. 18:9–10).

What is the adultery which Babylon has committed with the kings and nations of the world? What is the adultery in which all her people participated? Keeping in mind that Revelation is apocalyptic literature (i.e., writing marked by symbolic imagery and the expectation of an imminent cosmic catastrophe), *adultery* obviously does not mean illegitimate sexual intercourse. *Adultery* is used regularly by the Old Testament prophets as a pseudonym for *idolatry* (e.g., Jer. 3:8; 29:23; Ezek. 16:32; 23:37). Babylon's primary sin was idolatry.

Who is the god to whom Babylon gives herself with reckless and wanton abandon? It is the Roman emperor! Babylon has committed herself to the worship of the emperor and of the empire which he personifies. In order to maintain the empire, Rome had to make space within it for Hellenistic culture, the Oriental mystery religions, and Greek philosophy. These forces provided the psychological cement that held the empire together. Dependence on such movements to make the empire cohesive, however, was not enough because these elements did not center sufficient focus on Rome itself. Thus it was that the Romans were forced to invent a central focus for the empire: they established the worship of past emperors and the celebration of the divinity of the present ruler.

Emperor worship did supply the cement necessary to hold the Roman Empire together. You were free to hold to whatever philosophy you chose, to practice the culture of your people, to worship any gods you wished to worship—as long as you also worshiped the emperor. Emperor worship was required of all inhabitants of the Roman Empire except for the Jews (and Christianity was not perceived by the Romans as an extension of Judaism). Therefore, when a Christian refused to worship the emperor he or she committed treason against the state. Such Christians therefore invited upon themselves the persecution and wrath of Rome (this was why the official charge against the Christians was that they were "atheists"—that is, people who did not worship the emperor). Precisely because they refused to worship the emperor, church leaders like Polycarp, bishop of Smyrna, were put to death.[3]

The early Christians simply did not accommodate themselves to Rome and worship the emperor because to do so would be to act in an idolatrous manner. Emperor worship made a human being (the emperor) and a human institution (the Roman Empire) into a god. This was hubris of the most gross kind. But it was more than that. To make anything other than God god is the original sin—that which broke relationship with God in the first place, that which epitomized the sin of Satan which caused his ejection from paradise (Isa. 14:12–15), that which undermined all systems and structures of all the cities of the past (see chapter 2 of this book), and that which empowered the principalities and powers to capture the city's and nation's systems (see chapter 3 of this book). To worship the emperor was to deny God!

Therefore, for Babylon to commit herself solely to emperor worship was not only to bring about her spiritual disintegration, but also to cause the corruption of the people of her city, and the nations and kings around her. With her total and complete submission to emperor worship and idolatry, Babylon's interior spirituality had become irredeemably evil. Babylon had become the city of Satan first of all because she had committed herself to the worship of another god.

The second reason Babylon had become the city of Satan was that she had given herself to the unconditional exploitation of the world in order to foster her own economic security and luxury. The author of Revelation writes:

> The woman [Babylon] was dressed in purple and scarlet, and was glittering with gold, precious stones and pearls. She held a golden cup in her hand, filled with abominable things and the filth of her adulteries. This title was written on her forehead:
>
>
>
> MYSTERY
> BABYLON THE GREAT
> THE MOTHER OF PROSTITUTES
> AND OF THE ABOMINATIONS OF THE EARTH.
>
>
>
> (Rev. 17:4–5)

> "The merchants of the earth will weep and mourn over her because no one buys their cargoes any more—cargoes of gold, silver, precious stones and pearls; fine linen, purple, silk and scarlet cloth; every sort of citron wood, and articles of every kind made of ivory, costly wood, bronze, iron and marble; cargoes of cinnamon and spice, of incense, myrrh and frankincense, of wine and olive oil, of fine flour and wheat; cattle and sheep; horses and carriages; and bodies and souls of men.

"They will say, 'The fruit you longed for is gone from you. All your riches and splendor have vanished, never to be recovered.' The merchants who sold these things and gained their wealth from her will stand far off, terrified at her torment. They will weep and mourn and cry out:

> " 'Woe! Woe, O great city,
>   dressed in fine linen, purple and scarlet,
>   and glittering with gold, precious stones and pearls!
> In one hour such great wealth has been brought to ruin!'

"Every sea captain, and all who travel by ship, the sailors, and all who earn their living from the sea, will stand far off. When they see the smoke of her burning, they will exclaim, 'Was there ever a city like this great city?' They will throw dust on their heads, and with weeping and mourning cry out:

> " 'Woe! Woe, O great city,
>   where all who had ships on the sea
>   became rich through her wealth!
> In one hour she has been brought to ruin!' " (Rev. 18:11–19).

Babylon's demand for wealth, economic security, and luxury has brought the wealth of the world to her; it was brought through both her economic power and her military strength. The movement of all conceivable goods through her ports has greatly enriched the merchants, mariners, and kings of the world (and now you can understand why kings very willingly submitted to her adulteries). But this great, ongoing contribution to her luxurious refinements and economic security had to be done at the price of the economic well-being of the rest of the world. In essence, all the rest of the world had become the third world to Babylon; Babylon was enriched but the price was the destitution of the other countries and peoples of the world.

So in her commitment to another god than God, Babylon had—

- Seduced the peoples of the world

- Gotten all rulers to participate in this seduction (thus uniting the political and the religious systems of the world)

- Used the worship of her god as the means for her economic development (thus uniting the economic and religious systems of the world for her benefit)

To the author of Revelation, such grave misuse of the economic order was equal to the sin of idolatry. For Babylon's greed and lust for wealth and economic security raped the rest of the world, leaving it helpless and destitute, unable to cope either nationally or individually with the exigencies of life. The radical impoverishment of the world, both of its peoples and its natural resources, meant nothing to Babylon, as long as she could have her little niceties and obscene luxuries.

But the author of the book of Revelation gives us a third reason why Babylon has become the city of Satan. She has become so because of the radical misuse of her political power in order to oppress those people who represented a threat to her. The author of Revelation tells us:

> I saw that the woman was drunk with the blood of the saints, the blood of those who bore testimony to Jesus (Rev. 17:6).

> In [Babylon] was found the blood of prophets and of the saints, and of all who have been killed on the earth (Rev. 18:24).

There are two groups of people the text tells us were persecuted unto death by Babylon: the prophets and the saints. The saints, of course, are the Christians. The prophets are those in a city who call its leadership to accountability. These Scripture passages remind us that no government will tolerate being questioned at its very depths.

The prophets were questioning the intentional idolatry, the economic exploitation of the world for the accumulation of that city's luxury, and both the political suppression of dissidents and the oppression of all who would question the ethics and intentions of the city's government. The Christians questioned the policies which the economic, political, and religious systems of Babylon were using to deceive both themselves and their citizens; the Christians also proclaimed by their very lifestyle a way of life in total opposition to the one which the people and systems of the city had accepted as their own. The marriage of an economics of privilege and exploitation, a politics of oppression, and a religion of idolatrous control inevitably resulted in the martyrdom of the poor, the prophetic, and the spiritually liberated of the city. There was no longer any place for such in a city given over solely to Satan!

These were the forces that turned the city of Babylon into a city completely given over to Satan. What, then, was the inevitable result of such a city? The author of Revelation tells us:

> Then a mighty angel picked up a boulder the size of a large millstone and threw it into the sea, and said:

> "With such violence
> the great city of Babylon will be thrown down,
> never to be found again.
> The music of harpists and musicians, flute players and trumpeters,
> will never be heard in you again.
> No workman of any trade
> will ever be found in you again.
> The sound of a millstone
> will never be heard in you again.
> The light of a lamp

> will never shine in you again.
> The voice of bridegroom and bride
> will never be heard in you again.
> Your merchants were the world's great men.
> By your magic spell all the nations were led astray.
> In her was found the blood of prophets and of the saints,
> and of all who have been killed on the earth."

After this I heard what sounded like the roar of a great multitude in heaven shouting:

> "Hallelujah!
> Salvation and glory and power belong to our God,
> for true and just are his judgments.
> He has condemned the great prostitute
> who corrupted the earth by her adulteries.
> He has avenged on her the blood of his servants."

And again they shouted:

> "Hallelujah!
> The smoke from [Babylon] goes up for ever and ever."

The twenty-four elders and the four living creatures fell down and worshipped God, who was seated on the throne. And they cried, "Amen, Hallelujah!" (Rev. 18:21–19:4).

Babylon has become a city in which its systems and its people have given themselves solely ("soul-ly," as well) to religious idolatry (making the state into their god), economic injustice, and political oppression in which the demonic principalities and powers are now in full control. The consequence of total submission to the principalities and powers in the city's economic, political, and religious life is its total destruction. It has destroyed itself spiritually. Therefore its physical destruction is only a matter of time.

That destruction finally occurs. And "the smoke from [Babylon] goes up for ever and ever." The city is rejected by God and physically annihilated because it has given itself over fully to economic exploitation and privilege, political oppression of the weak and of the truth-tellers, and the selection of either its economic or its political order to serve as the center of its true and daily religion. Such seduction of its systems (and through the systems, the people) has led to the city's demonic domination by its principalities and powers, so that the interior spirituality of the city has become irredeemably evil. Such is the inevitable end of any city that allows itself to become the city of Satan!

THE CITY OF GOD

The other archetypal city presented in the book of Revelation is the new Jerusalem. This is the city which is totally dedicated to God: city as God has always intended city to be. It is described fully in Revelation 21:1–22:5. There is perhaps no greater description of the city of God than that which follows:

> Then I saw a new heaven and a new earth, for the first heaven and the first earth had passed away, and there was no longer any sea. I saw the Holy City, the new Jerusalem, coming down out of heaven from God, prepared as a bride beautifully dressed for her husband. And I heard a loud voice from the throne saying, "Now the dwelling of God is with men, and he will live with them. They will be his people, and God himself will be with them and be their God. He will wipe every tear from their eyes. There will be no more death or mourning or crying or pain, for the old order of things has passed away" (21:1–4).

Revelation 21:1–8 gives us the context for understanding the nature of God's city. First, the city of God exists only within the context of a new order. It comes about as "a new heaven and a new earth, for the first heaven and the first earth had passed away, and there was no longer any sea" (v. 1). It is built around a new physical environment and upon a new social order.

The reason for this assertion becomes clear in verse 2: "I saw the Holy City, the new Jerusalem, coming down out of heaven from God, prepared as a bride beautifully dressed for her husband." Both the image of a new environment and order and the image of an entire city being let down upon the earth exist in order to communicate this insight: the city of God will exist by God's actions, and not humanity's. The timing for when the cities of this earth become the city of God will depend upon God's activities, and not ours. We will not build the city of God. Our task, rather, is to faithfully practice our vocation as God's people in the city through the presence, prayer, practice, and proclamation of the church.

In verses 1–8 we see four outstanding characteristics of God's city:

1. God lives in the city among his people: "And I heard a loud voice from the throne saying, 'Now the dwelling of God is with men'" (v.3).

2. There will be no grief, pain, or death in God's city: "There will be no more death or mourning or crying or pain" (v. 4).

3. The city will be the place where the hunger and thirst that people have for relationship with God will be assuaged: "To him who is thirsty I will give to drink without cost from the spring of the water of life . . . and I will be his God and he will be my son" (vv. 6–7).

4. There will be no place in God's city for those who have rejected him
   and despised humanity: "But the cowardly, the unbelieving, the
   vile, the murderers, the sexually immoral, those who practice magic
   arts, the idolaters and all liars—their place will be in the fiery lake
   of burning sulfur" (v. 8).

The second way Revelation 21:1–8 gives us a context for understanding God's city is by showing us that the one who promises this city to us
and will accomplish its formation is the only true God, "the Alpha and the
Omega, the Beginning and the End" (v. 6). This is the God who stood
faithfully by his people from the call of the patriarch Abraham to leave the
city of Ur to the call of the church into the city of the new Jerusalem, from
the formation of Israel through Moses' confrontation of the principality of
Egypt to the church's confrontation of a "divine Roman emperor"
demanding worship, from the beginning of creation to the end of time.
This God causes to be what is caused to be, and thus will bring to pass the
city he has promised.

One of the most unique aspects of the book of Revelation is the detail
with which it describes the quality of life in the new Jerusalem. I believe it
is described in such detail to give us hope as we in urban ministry seek to
be faithful, though we are often overwhelmed.

The first emphasis on the quality of life in the new Jerusalem deals
with the size of the city. Revelation 21:9–17 includes elaborate measurements of the new Jerusalem. The measurements are quite extraordinary.

The city is a square: 12,000 *stadia* (v. 16), or 1,400 miles, (2,200
kilometers) to a side. That is an absolutely immense city that dwarfs even
the largest projected cities of the next several centuries. To give us a sense
of the immensity of the new Jerusalem, if that city were placed down upon
the globe today, it would stretch from London to New York, or from São
Paulo, Brazil, to LaPaz, Bolivia, or from Nairobi, Kenya, to Kinshasa,
Zaire, or from Calcutta to Delhi or from Bangkok to Taipei. Who can
imagine a city of that size?

Surprisingly, the walls are low in comparison to the size of the city.
Its walls are only 144 cubits high (v. 17); that is about 200 feet or about 65
meters high. That sounds high to modern ears, but not to the ancient
peoples. The walls of Babylon were 300 feet high and the walls around the
temple in Jerusalem were 180 feet high. Given either the size of the walls
of ancient cities or the relationship of wall-height to size of city, the walls
of the new Jerusalem are quite modest.

Why would such a gargantuan city have such low walls? Could it be
to suggest that God built the city this huge so that there is room for
absolutely everybody? And could the low walls be a way of suggesting
that God has no need to keep people out of his city or to defend it? Is the

city and its walls, therefore, a visual symbol of the inclusivity and peace of the kingdom of God?

God's city is meant to be a refuge for all of the world's believing immigrant population. In God's city, there are no slums, no squatter settlements, no *favellas* or barrios or *bustees!* There are no governmental policies to try to keep people out nor any economic standards which exclude the marginalized from effective participation in the marketplace. God has built the city for the whole world!

The city is not only immense, but also wealthy beyond imagination. The second emphasis on Jerusalem's quality of life is its wealth. The walls and city gates are described as gem-laden (Rev. 21:18–21) and the city's streets are paved with gold. What was precious in the former world is now so plentiful that it is used as common building material. Thus the city is described as a society in which all its people will live in plenty and security. All poverty will be gone, as well as all the exploitation and oppression which inevitably is generated by the maintenance of an unbalanced economy that favors the rich.

The third emphasis on the quality of life in God's city is most intriguing: "I did not see a temple in the city, because the Lord God Almighty and the Lamb are its temple" (Rev. 21:22). The city has no churches!

Why would there be no churches in a city whose creator and sustainer is God? Does God not want to be worshiped? Of course he does, but the Lord does not need churches to provide that function! The church is a foreshadowing of the kingdom of God, God's kingdom in miniature. But it is not to be taken for the kingdom itself. It was created to be transitional and temporary, the means by which God remains present in the city of humankind. It exists between the resurrection of Christ and Christ's return in glory. The church is unnecessary in the new Jerusalem where God can be directly present to his people.

"The Lord God Almighty and the Lamb are [the city's] temple." The center of the life of this city is God, and the center of the people's focus on God is worship. The life of the city—its economics, its political order, its housing, its religion—is centered in God, for this is the city of God.

It is obvious that the description of the city of God contained in Revelation 21 is dealing, once again, with the political, economic, and religious systems of the city. What makes this city different is that it is centered in God. This theme is not exhausted in verses 9–22; the description goes on. Consider these observations:

> The city does not need the sun or the moon to shine on it, for the glory of God gives it light, and the Lamb is its lamp. The nations will walk by its light, and the kings of the earth will bring their splendor into it (vv. 23–24).

The existence of the new Jerusalem will not mean that there are no other nations. There will be other countries and they will be governed politically. But all the nations will operate by the light of God, and rulers will govern under the authority of God. Jerusalem will be the center of all international affairs, and all governments of the world will live in peace and under the authority of God.

> On no day will its gates ever be shut, for there will be no night there (v. 25).

City gates in ancient times were shut for only one reason—protection from armies, thieves, or marauding gangs. For a city never to shut its gates would indicate only one thing to the ancient mind: there is nothing to fear because all crime is gone, justice for all prevails, and economic security is so accorded to all the people that none need fear robbery from anyone else.

Even the natural order will be under subjection, for "there will be no night there." Rather than tyrannizing humanity with its sickness and death-delivering power, or rather than having to be held in control through medication, surgery or therapy, the natural order will only benefit and enhance the life of people in the city. For "there will be no more death or mourning or crying or pain, for the old order of things has passed away" (v. 4). In Revelation 22 we read:

> Then the angel showed me the river of the water of life, as clear as crystal, flowing from the throne of God and of the Lamb down the middle of the great street of the city. On each side of the river stood the tree of life, bearing twelve crops of fruit, yielding its fruit every month. And the leaves of the tree are for the healing of the nations. No longer will there be any curse. The throne of God and of the Lamb will be in the city, and his servants will serve him. They will see his face, and his name will be on their foreheads. There will be no more night. They will not need the light of a lamp or the light of the sun, for the Lord God will give them light. And they will reign for ever and ever (vv. 1–5).

The river of the water of life and the tree of life bearing annually twelve crops of fruit are symbols for abundance and plenty. The author is sharing his vision of a rich abundance showered upon each resident of the city. The economy will benefit everyone.

The people of the city "will see [God's] face, and his name will be on their foreheads." Everyone will be in the most direct and intimate and continuing relationship with God possible. Direct relationship with God will not only mean a perfect worship of God. It will also mean that our work and activity in the city will be consecrated to God as each person works for the common good.

Finally, the political order, serving under God, will be both completely just and democratic. The vision of the river ends with an intriguing statement: "And they will reign for ever and ever." One would expect that the text would have said that God would reign forever. Instead it states that the people of this vast city—millions upon millions of people—will reign. In perfect submission to Christ, the people of that city will govern together as an integral part of a political system that is both democratic and just.

The indicators of what God intends the city of God to be like are quite obvious. This will be a city fully under God, a religious environment where all will be in relationship with God and thus in shalom with each other (Rev. 21:3, 6–8, 22; 22:3–4). God's city will also be one practicing an economics of plenty, equitable distribution, and security (Rev. 21:13–14, 18–21, 26–27; 22:1–2). This will include a transformation of the natural order so that death, illness, grief, and pain will be gone (Rev. 21:4, 25). Finally, the city will have a political order which is centered in God with room for everyone, a city whose political life will be completely just and in which everyone will play a part in the city's governance (thus it will be democratic; Rev. 21:24–25; 22:5). This will include a centralization of all international affairs in God's city as all governments of the world live in peace and under the authority of God (Rev. 21:24–25). This is as God intends his city to be.

In the new Jerusalem, where all live under the authority of God and the city exhibits the characteristics of the quality of life recorded above, what has become of that city's structures and systems? Obviously, they continue. The city is formed around its religious, economic, and political systems—just like the city of today. But these are transformed systems, transformed by being centered in God and in the Lamb.

And the principalities and powers that inhabit and control that city's systems? What happens to them? Given the frequent references to the angels of the new Jerusalem (Rev. 21:9, 15; 22:1, 6, 8–9, 16), one must recognize that the principalities and powers remain a part of the city's life. But God transforms the powers, for here they are in the service of God, and consequently, of the people of the city (Rev. 22:9). This perspective would certainly confirm other Scripture passages which we have examined earlier in this book that would indicate that the principalities would be redeemed and returned to their rightful role in the service of God and humanity in the city (Rom. 8:19–21; Phil. 2:10–11; Heb. 12:22). So the systems and the principalities of the city of God remain intact, but are freed from the corrupting power of Satan so that they might become the servants of the people and therefore the servants of God. They are able to become that which God intended them to be and created them to be in every city of the world.

THE VISION

The author of Revelation wrote this book in order to enable God's people to see what the city wholly given over to Satan and what the city given over to God both become, so that we might understand the eventual and inevitable outcome for both cities. Thus Revelation is meant both as warning and as encouragement: warning to those who would serve the cause of evil in the city, and encouragement to us who seek to live out the Gospel in an urban world.

Whenever we have dealt with this portion of Scripture in the urban workshops and consultations I have led, I have found it is important to have the participants work with certain questions that enable us to reflect on how the vision of the cities of Babylon and the new Jerusalem inform our own ministries. So let me share these questions with you. I would suggest, rather than quickly reading them through and completing this chapter, that you take some time to reflect on each question and to write your responses in your journal. For, prayerfully and intentionally answered, these questions can help you to look at your city and your ministry in a profoundly new way.

1. What are the forms of emperor worship to which you believe your city is tempted to succumb?

2. How does your city marry its economics, politics, and religion in order to worship its emperor? What are the results of this unholy marriage? Who in your city end up benefiting the most from this marriage? Who end up becoming its victims? Who end up being martyred?

3. What role(s) do you see the church as institution playing in this marriage? What role(s) do you see the people of God playing?

4. The vision of the new Jerusalem sets forth a definite quality of life for the city.

    a. If such a quality of life became the focus of your church's ministry to individuals, how would that affect your ministry?

    b. If such a quality of life became the focus of your church's ministry, how would that affect the ways your church would relate to your city's systems and structures?

    c. If such a quality of life became the focus of your church's ministry, how would that affect your perceptions of and the ways you would deal with your city's principalities and powers?

The vision of the new Jerusalem and the horror of the Satan-filled Babylon are given to the church in order to encourage us in our city ministries. We continue on in an unjust and uncaring world, sometimes wondering if the work we are doing is having any effect upon our city. For all our effort, our presence, our prayers, our words of proclamation, our deeds of mercy and justice, and our work for the liberation of the victims and the seduced of our city's systems seem to bear little fruit. And we cannot help but wonder whether it is worth it all.

The book of Revelation proclaims to us that what we do is worth it. We are among the faithful company of God's people who are waging war against the powers of darkness in our city—and we will win! God is at work in our city through us. Christ will continue to work through his people until that day when God will create that new city where there will be no more death or mourning or crying or pain, and the city will become the Holy City of our God. The kingdom of God for which we work in the city and upon which we focus our prayers really will arrive in all of its totality—someday!

> "Behold, I am coming soon! My reward is with me, and I will give to everyone according to what he has done. I am the Alpha and the Omega, the First and the Last, the Beginning and the End. Blessed are those who wash their robes, that they may have the right to the tree of life and may go through the gates into the city. . . . I, Jesus, have sent my angel to give you this testimony for the churches." . . .
>
> Amen. Come, Lord Jesus (Rev. 22:12–14, 16, 20).

Chapter Thirteen

AND HAVING DONE ALL, TO STAND: A FAITHFUL RESPONSE TO A FAITHFUL GOD

My denomination publishes annually a book of statistics on all its churches. That book contains such strategic information as how many members each church has, how many people joined each church in the previous year and how many were lost to that church, the enrollment in each church's Sunday school, the income of that church in the previous year, how much of that income was spent by that church on its own ministry, how much income went to the denomination and how much to other mission causes outside the denomination, and how much of the income was comprised of endowed or invested monies of that church.

I know of no instrument created by our denomination that gives city pastors a greater sense of failure and of little worth than this annual book of statistics, particularly since each pastor is obligated to fill out information forms for this book at the beginning of each new year. The whole process of completing the forms keeps driving home to the city pastor how "little" he or she has accomplished (according to denominational standards for success) the previous year.

What are those standards of success, subconsciously communicated to all pastors? Size of membership, success at attracting new people to the church, growth in church income, and how much of the income is going for approved denominational mission causes. On such statistics does your status in my denomination hang.

Now what is wrong with those measurements? Nothing—as long as they are contextualized. After all, those who created this annual book of statistics were not trying to send pastors on guilt trips. That consequence was far from their minds. What they were seeking was a simple way of maintaining accurate records on the denomination.

As I said, however, I know of no instrument that creates more guilt and sense of failure in my denomination than this instrument. That is because it favors any church located in a community of rapid growth and radically disfavors any church in a decaying, declining community. The first kind of community is found mostly in suburban areas of the United States, while the second is found primarily in inner cities.

While I was in seminary, I was assigned for two years to a church in suburban Chicago as a youth pastor. That community was going through profound growth, so that on a typical Sunday there would be about twenty first-time visitors in worship and about thirty-five returned visitors who were considering church membership. That church grew rapidly. It could not help but grow.

From that church, I went to an inner-city church in Milwaukee after my ordination. In the entire first year of my ministry there, we had a total of seven visitors to that church. How do you grow a church on that kind of response?

The situation has somewhat changed today in the United States, because the suburbs of our cities are not undergoing the rapid growth of thirty years ago. But the numbers in this annual book of statistics still communicate to the reader the strength and the growth of the suburban church and the apparent weakness and decline of the city church.

What would be the characteristics of statistics that would measure the success of city ministry? First, the intent of such statistics would have to change from seeking to measure numerical success to measuring faithfulness. The reason for such change is this: the church is not called by God to be successful; it is called to be faithful to its calling. That is a particularly important distinction to make for city ministry.

How can faithfulness be measured? Perhaps through statistics generated by questions like these: Are there nurture and support groups in the life of your congregation? How many church members participate in those groups? What is the percentage of worship attendance compared to the percentage of church membership (inner-city churches always have more of their members in church on a Sunday morning than suburban churches)? What is the percentage of church members involved in a ministry of that church, either to itself or to its community? What is the percentage of the congregation involved in adult Christian education which is geared to equip them for ministry? What is the average giving of the membership of that church (rather than asking for the total income)? How many ministries outside itself does the church maintain? How many members participate in those community ministries? Statistics like these measure the faithfulness of the church members and the pastor, because they indicate the real commitment of those people to the life and work of that body of believers in its community. For as I stated above, the church—the city church—has been called, not to success, but to faithfulness.

BEING FAITHFUL IN THE PRACTICE OF THE GOSPEL

Thus far in this section of this book, we have examined three of the critical ingredients that enable us, as urban pastors and workers, to sustain ourselves in demanding city ministry. We have explored how personal spiritual formation, life in community, and the maintenance of a vision for the city equips and strengthens us with hope and resolve. In this chapter, we will examine what I perceive as the other dimension of hope: the necessity for being faithful in the practice of the Gospel, rather than trying to be successful.

The cities of the new Jerusalem and Babylon the Great are not the only cities that appear in the book of Revelation. Seven other cities figure prominently in that Apocalypse; these are the churches in the seven dominant cities of Asia Minor. Those cities are not included by accident in this book that foretells the future. They are included because their churches are being offered the hope of God's eventual triumph even as they are being urged to be faithful in their everyday practice of the Gospel.

Both the audience and the purpose of the book of Revelation are given in Revelation 1:9–11:

> I, John, your brother and companion in the suffering and kingdom and patient endurance that are ours in Jesus, was on the island of Patmos because of the word of God and the testimony of Jesus. On the Lord's Day I was in the Spirit, and I heard behind me a loud voice like a trumpet, which said: 'Write on a scroll what you see and send it to the seven churches: to Ephesus, Smyrna, Pergamum, Thyatira, Sardis, Philadelphia and Laodicea."

John quickly affirms his relationship with his readers: "I [am] your brother and companion." He is their brother because they are all one in Christ, and it is their common salvation through Christ that unites them and upon which their fraternal relationship is built. John identifies with them in the persecution and difficulties under which they are all living (v. 9). He has shared in their sufferings, in their kingdom of persecution, and he has endured with them. So he is not only brother with them in Christ, but companion with them in their sufferings. It is out of their common fraternal relationship and their unity in persecution that John brings to them a word from the Lord.

It is important to recognize that the book of Revelation was not meant for the church at large; it was written to the seven churches in the strategic cities of Asia Minor: Ephesus, Smyrna, Pergamum, Thyatira, Sardis, Philadelphia, and Laodicea. It is a vision meant for God's people in seven pivotal cities. It is an urban vision for urban churches and urban Christians—John's brothers and sisters.

The message that John presents to them is a message of hope and encouragement in the midst of their persecution and suffering at the hand of Rome. The book of Revelation cannot be appreciated except as a letter of instruction and encouragement to urban churches regarding their life and mission in cities dominated by their persecutors and despisers!

MESSAGE TO SEVEN CHURCHES

The revelation John has for the seven churches is given in seven messages, one for each church, found in Revelation 2 and 3. Each message deals with the same issues; only the content of the message is different, reflecting the condition of each church. The eternal Gospel is contextualized for each situation, so that it is relevant to each city.

First, each message reveals an understanding of the history, the commerce, and the religious and political roles of that city in the empire.

Second, each message deals with the question, "How have you reacted to your city, as you have sought to minister in and to it?" Each message describes the effect the city has had on the church and/or the church has had on the city.

Third, each message affirms, exhorts, and makes promises to the church around the question, "What is it that I, the Lord God, want you to do?" Each message calls the church to faithfulness in ministry to that city.

Let's now examine each of the messages to the seven churches, because in them we may hear God's message to us and our church.[1]

To the Church in Ephesus

"To the angel of the church in Ephesus write:

These are the words of him who holds the seven stars in his right hand and walks among the seven golden lampstands: I know your deeds, your hard work and your perseverance. I know that you cannot tolerate wicked men, that you have tested those who claim to be apostles but are not, and have found them false. You have persevered and have endured hardships for my name, and have not grown weary.

Yet I hold this against you: You have forsaken your first love. Remember the height from which you have fallen! Repent and do the things you did at first. If you do not repent, I will come to you and remove your lampstand from its place. But you have this in your favor: You hate the practices of the Nicolaitans, which I also hate.

He who has an ear, let him hear what the Spirit says to the churches. To him who overcomes, I will give the right to eat from the tree of life, which is in the paradise of God" (Rev. 2:1–7).

First, note to whom the message is written. It is not written to the church itself, but "to the angel of the church in Ephesus." This is a pattern repeated in each of the letters, for the messages to all the churches in Asia Minor actually are presented to the angels of these churches. This is particularly significant in the light of our study of the principalities and powers and what we have presented in chapter 3 about the "brooding angel" over a city. Each church has its own angel as well, the author of Revelation assumes. And it is that angel who gives to that church its essential spiritual quality—either for good or evil. By addressing each message to the specific church's angel, John is indicating that God is dealing with the primary spiritual entity of that church, and that church had better deal with that entity, too!

We can learn some things about the city of Ephesus from this passage because it includes one direct and one oblique reference to the city. The direct reference is to the "Nicolaitans," a sect centered in Ephesus (we will examine the Nicolaitan cult later in this section). The oblique reference is in verse 1, in which the seven churches are referred to in terms of light· the "seven stars" and the "seven golden lampstands." The inscription on all the official seals, banners, and public buildings of Ephesus was the city's motto: *Lumen Asiae*—the "Light of Asia."

What do we know about Ephesus, and why did it call itself the "Light of Asia"? Ephesus was considered Asia's greatest and most strategic city. It had the greatest harbor in Asia, was the center of the Roman and pre-Roman Asian road network, and served as the political and economic gateway to Asia.

Ephesus was a free city, which meant that it was self-governing— not governed from Rome—and no Roman troops were permitted. It was also a judicial city, in which the Roman governor tried cases. It was the center of the worship of Artemis (Diana), whose worshipers formed one of the most important cults in the East, and was a center for many other religious cults (including the Nicolaitans). Finally, Ephesus was a metropolitan city, a "melting pot" of six different primary Greek and Asian tribal groups. So Ephesus rightly deserved the sobriquet, "Light of Asia." Ephesus was a shining light to the rest of the Roman world of what a Roman city ought to be like. It was an example for all metropolitan centers to follow.

How has the church been affected by being in this "lighthouse" to the Roman world? It is intriguing to note the words and phrases John uses to describe the life and work of the Ephesian church: *hard work, perseverance, you cannot tolerate, you have tested, endured hardships, have not grown weary*, and *you hate the practices of the Nicolaitans* [i.e., you reject heresy]. These are all defensive words, "hunkering-down" words, protective words. The church in Ephesus is being commended for surviving under attack!

What is pictured in this passage is a church under siege. The Ephesian church is being attacked from outside—by the "angel" of the city, confronted and tempted by the city's wealth, power, cosmopolitan nature, ethical and moral corruption, and religious persuasion. This church is not in danger of being seduced by the city, for she is defending herself against it.

The Ephesian church is also being attacked from within—by the Nicolaitans—a particularly insidious "Christian" cult. The Nicolaitans were the followers of a Christian leader named Nicolaus, who sought to minimize the differences between Roman society and the Christian faith. The Nicolaitans stressed that the Jewish Law was no longer formative for faith or ethics, that Christians were free to eat meat offered to idols, and that Christians need not practice the chastity and sexual regulations of the Law. Rather, the Christian was free to engage in both the feasts and the sexual promiscuity of the Romans, they taught, as well as to engage fully in Roman politics and their economic system. They believed that Christianity ought to be integrated into a culture, so that to be a good Christian and to be a good Roman were the same thing, for Christianity should endorse and bless the Roman system. The Nicolaitans were the most dangerous of heretics because, if they had succeeded in their attempt to dominate the church, the world would have changed the Gospel instead of the Gospel changing the world!

John points out how the Ephesian church has dealt with such internal and external erosion. It has worked hard; it has put up with a great deal. The Ephesian Christians have stood against wicked people and tested their leadership in order to separate authentic disciples from impostors. They have exposed those who were liars, have been patient or persevered in their struggle, and have ended up suffering much. For such determination, they are deeply commended by God.

"Yet I hold this against you: You have forsaken your first love" (v. 4). This, of course, is no light complaint. But why—given what this church has endured—is this such a serious complaint?

Those in the Ephesian church have developed a siege mentality, not only toward the city, but toward each other. They have maintained the purity of their church by resisting temptation and keeping themselves orthodox, but in their grim and tight-lipped determination, they have lost their love for God and their love for each other.

This is often the high price orthodoxy exacts. The church maintains its purity, but at a price to its peace and its unity. It sacrifices Christian community to the preservation of its orthodoxy.

The angel of the church in Ephesus is severely wounded. Because of the attacks coming from within and without, that church's spirituality of love has changed into a spirit of siege. To that degree, the Ephesian church has become truncated and demonically possessed!

What is it that God now wants the Ephesian church to do? How can it regain its lost love?

First, it must remember. "Remember the height from which you have fallen!" Recall your relationship with Christ and each other before you became absorbed in battling the pressures of this city and of the heretics in your midst. Realize the price you have paid in your absolutely necessary pursuit of orthodoxy and purity.

Second, it must repent. The word from God is quite terse: "Repent." Turn from your sin. Recognize the price you had to pay to win those battles. Accept personal responsibility for your failure. Confess your sin to God and to one another. Amend your ways and commit yourselves to rediscover your first love.

Third, it must act. "Do the things you did at first." Resolution and repentance alone are not enough. Action must follow reflection (as we have discovered throughout this book). Start all over again. Start treating your brother and sister Christians differently. Start spending quality time with God. Spend less energy defending the faith and more energy in celebrating the faith. Restore those broken relationships. Address those weaknesses. Heal those breaches. "You are already a church of purity," God in essence is saying to the Ephesian church. "Now become a church of love and unity."

Christ's message to the Ephesian church and its angel is not yet completed. For one final question must be asked: "What will happen if the Ephesian church ignores Christ's counsel and continues in its loveless orthodoxy?" Here is the answer:

> "If you do not repent, I will come to you and remove your lampstand from its place" (Rev. 2:5).

This is not a cruel or vindictive judgment. It is simply a statement of fact—this is the way life is. If the Ephesian church continues its course of loveless orthodoxy, two things will happen to it. First, increasingly it will become a highly judgmental church, constantly determining who is "in" and who is "out." The "in" group progressively will become a more rigidly defined and inevitably smaller group as it pushes out any persons voicing concern or raising questions about the group's wisdom. This group will make itself the final arbiter of truth.

Second, the church will, with its increasingly judgmental attitude, adopt a pattern of growing joylessness and lovelessness which will demand that people keep justifying themselves and proving themselves to those who sit in judgment.

The result will be that this church's "lampstand" will be taken "from its place." That church inevitably will cease to grow. It will become progressively introspective and thus increasingly irrelevant to and rejected by its city and insulated from it and from any other Christians not of like mind. Thus, as it declines, it will slip out of the place which it now holds among the seven churches of Asia, until it has declined to become the least of all the churches in its impact upon non-Christians and influence upon the body of Christ. This is the inevitable end of an unrepentant and loveless orthodoxy!

To what, then, is the Ephesian church called if it is to be a faithful church? It is called to the practice of love and unity. "To him who overcomes, I will give the right to eat from the tree of life, which is in the paradise of God" (v. 7).

To the Church in Smyrna

"To the angel of the church in Smyrna write:

These are the words of him who is the First and the Last, who died and came to life again. I know your afflictions and your poverty—yet you are rich! I know the slander of those who say they are Jews and are not, but are a synagogue of Satan. Do not be afraid of what you are about to suffer. I tell you, the devil will put some of you in prison to test you, and you will suffer persecution for ten days. Be faithful, even to the point of death, and I will give you the crown of life.

He who has an ear, let him hear what the Spirit says to the churches. He who overcomes will not be hurt at all by the second death" (Rev. 2:8–11).

Smyrna was the other great city in Asia Minor, competitive with Ephesus. It did not have the economic or political power of Ephesus, but it was a great trading city and "the fairest of the cities of Iona" (Lucian). What contributed to its beauty included (1) a constant west wind that kept the city cool and fresh; (2) a land-locked harbor in the city's heart, surrounded by rising hills upon which the city grew; and (3) the fact that it was one of the very few planned cities in the world and had great, broad streets, magnificent temples and planned architecture (the city, though founded in 1000 B.C.E., was destroyed in 600 B.C.E. and then rebuilt as a planned city in 200 B.C.E., continuing to today as modern Izmar). It had an extremely large, vocal, and economically powerful Jewish colony. Its most famous Christian was Polycarp, bishop of Smyrna, who was burned at the stake in that city on Saturday, 23 February C.E. 155. When begged by the police captain to deny Christ, make sacrifice to Caesar, and thus live, Polycarp replied, "Eighty and six years have I served him, and he has done me no wrong. How can I blaspheme my King who saved me?"

John's message to the church in Smyrna indicates that this is a church under persecution. He uses the words *affliction, poverty,* and *imprisonment* to describe the church's state. It, too, is a church under siege. This siege is not that which comes through the temptations and seductions of a city. This is an intentional committal on the part of community leaders to put that church to death!

The church is being persecuted: its people are living in extreme poverty; some of them have been imprisoned; some suffer persecution; all of the people have been slandered. John identifies the source of the trouble: "those who say they are Jews and are not, but are a synagogue of Satan." Smyrna had a large and economically strong Jewish colony, and it is that colony which is organized against the church (referring to people as "those who say they are Jews and are not" does not mean that they are not Jews, but that they are acting in ways that deny their Jewishness). It is this "synagogue of Satan" (or assembly of the Jewish colonists) which is behind the persecution, which is making slanderous statements about the Christians, raising fear and anger at them and thus motivating both the people and the state to persecute them. The church has a most formidable opponent in the Jewish colony in Smyrna.

What does God want the church of Smyrna to do in the face of such ominous persecution?

First, they are to keep their focus on Jesus. Christ is described in the message as "the First and the Last, who died and came to life again." Christ is the creator of the world and will survive the world, bringing about its end. The Jews could kill him but they could not stop him, for he was raised to life again. In his resurrection, Christ exposed the lie of persecution-power by conquering the worst that life could inflict, thereby freeing us for life in him. By keeping their focus on Jesus, the Christians in Smyrna would be able to maintain their resolve and commitment, because they would remember constantly that "the one who is in you is greater than the one who is in the world" (1 John 4:4).

Second, they are to stand firm and not allow themselves to fear about what they will continue to suffer. In essence, Jesus is saying to them: "Some of you will be placed in prison, some of you will suffer persecution. This is the inevitable outcome of the hatred which fills the hearts of the people in the 'synagogue of Satan.' You cannot stop that hatred. Nor can I change that which they are determined not to change. What you must do is to outlast them, to be faithful—even if it means death. Only in that way will this church and the Gospel survive in Smyrna. And you will receive 'the crown of [eternal] life.'"

If the church in Smyrna is to be a faithful church, it will suffer. "He who has an ear, let him hear what the Spirit says to the churches. He who overcomes will not be hurt at all by the second death" (Rev. 2:11).

To the Church in Pergamum

"To the angel of the church in Pergamum write:

These are the words of him who has the sharp, double-edged sword. I know where you live—where Satan has his throne. Yet you remain true to my name. You did not renounce your faith in me, even in the days of Antipas, my faithful witness, who was put to death in your city—where Satan lives.

> Nevertheless, I have a few things against you: You have people there who hold to the teaching of Balaam, who taught Balak to entice the Israelites to sin by eating food sacrificed to idols and by committing sexual immorality. Likewise you also have those who hold to the teaching of the Nicolaitans. Repent therefore! Otherwise, I will soon come to you and will fight against them with the sword of my mouth.
>
> He who has an ear, let him hear what the Spirit says to the churches. To him who overcomes, I will give some of the hidden manna. I will also give him a white stone with a new name written on it, known only to him who receives it" (Rev. 2:12–17).

Whereas Ephesus and Symrna were the economic and cultural "capitals" of Asia Minor, Pergamum was its political capital. It had been Asia Minor's capital city for nearly four hundred years. In 282 B.C.E., it had been made the capital of the Seleucid Empire, and remained such until 133 B.C.E. when it became the property of Rome. Rome then made Pergamum the capital of its province of Asia.

Pergamum was outstanding for many reasons. Its location was particularly commanding, situated on top of a steep rocky hill; it dominated the broad plain below it. Second, it had the most outstanding library in Asia (two hundred thousand parchment rolls), second only to the library in Alexandria; in fact, parchment was invented in Pergamum. Third, it was a religious center, especially of the worship of Zeus and Athene, and particularly of the god Asclepios—the god of healing whose temples were actually hospitals. Fourth, it was the administrative center and political capital of the Roman Empire in Asia.

This fourth item was especially important, and was the reason why John called it the city "where Satan has his throne." Because Pergamum was the administrative center and political capital of Roman Asia, it was the center of emperor worship in Asia. This was why John identified it as "where Satan lives"—because nothing was more Satanic to the mind of the early church than substituting Caesar for Christ as one's lord (see chapter 12).

Like the church in Smyrna, the church in Pergamum was a church under attack. Because it existed in the city where Satan had his throne, and because the church very decisively opposed emperor worship, Rome would have quickly perceived this church as an enemy. It is likely, therefore, that the attack the Pergamum church was under from the Roman authorities was severe.

This church's troubles did not come from the outside exclusively, however. It also had great troubles within, for the Nicolaitans and those "who hold to the teaching of Balaam" were there. We are already informed about the compromising perspective of the Nicolaitans. The Balaamites were probably a particular group of the Nicolaitan party which stressed participation in Roman worship (most likely, emperor worship) as well as participation in the Roman sexual practices. It was therefore a more liberal manifestation of the Nicolaitan perspective.

How did the Christians in Pergamum respond to dangers from without and within the church? The text makes it clear that they did not follow the course of the Ephesian church, which clung to the purity of the church. It is also clear that the church firmly resisted the threat of emperor worship (v. 13). Yet the church tolerated the presence of the Nicolaitans and Balaamites; that would mean that some of that church's members found these cults a suitable alternative amid the persecution.

What is it that John's message calls the church in Pergamum to do? One can sense that John wished for just a little more of the Ephesians' stiff backbone in this church. The church in Pergamum needed to continue to stand strong against emperor worship and not be tempted (like the Balaamites) to compromise with it in order to protect itself. The church needed to repent of the receptivity it had given to the Nicolaitans, and cast both them and the Balaamites out. It was to return to its spiritual origins by rediscovering the spirituality of the eucharistic sacrament ("the hidden manna") and thus renew its relationship with the Bread of Life, Christ.

Jesus promised that when the church had repented, driven off the heretics, and renewed its interior spirituality, then it would be given "a white stone with a new name written on it." Likely, this is a reference to the pagan custom, especially popular among children, of carrying a white stone with a god's name upon it as a good luck amulet. For the church to be given a white stone would be a reminder to the Christians that they are safe in life and in death because they "carry" the name of the only true God around inside them.

If it is to be a faithful church, then, the church of Pergamum is instructed that it must follow its calling to stand strong in its faith and to make vital its relationship with Christ. "He who has an ear, let him hear what the Spirit says to the churches. To him who overcomes, I will give some of the hidden manna. I will also give him a white stone with a new name written on it, known only to him who receives it" (v. 17).

To the Church in Thyatira

"To the angel of the church in Thyatira write:

These are the words of the Son of God, whose eyes are like blazing fire and whose feet are like burnished bronze. I know your deeds, your love and faith, your service and perseverance, and that you are now doing more than you did at first.

Nevertheless, I have this against you: You tolerate that woman Jezebel, who calls herself a prophetess. By her teaching she misleads my servants into sexual immorality and the eating of food sacrificed to idols. I have given her time to repent of her immorality, but she is unwilling. So I will cast her on a bed of suffering, and I will make those who commit adultery with her suffer intensely, unless they repent of her ways. I will strike her children dead. Then all the churches will know that I am he who searches hearts and minds, and I will repay each of you according to your deeds. Now I say to the rest of you in Thyatira, to you who do not hold to her teaching and have not learned Satan's so-called deep secrets (I will not impose any other burden on you): Only hold on to what you have until I come.

To him who overcomes and does my will to the end, I will give authority over the nations—

'He will rule them with an iron scepter;
    he will dash them to pieces like pottery'—

just as I have received authority from my Father. I will also give him the morning star. He who has an ear, let him hear what the Spirit says to the churches" (Rev. 2:18–29).

Thyatira was the least important of the seven cities to which John wrote in Revelation. Because it was so unimportant, we can retrieve little information about it. Thyatira was in a valley on the road to Pergamum and was created initially as a defense for Pergamum. Virtually indefensible, the military purpose of Thyatira simply was to delay an army several days while Pergamum prepared for a siege. No longer needed as a military outpost once the Roman empire ruled Asia Minor, Thyatira became a commercial center with a large number of guilds. Guilds about which we know were those established for people who worked with wool, leather, linen, bronze, outer garments, material dyeing, pottery, and baked goods, as well as those who traded slaves.

The guilds of ancient Roman society combined the legal and organizational power of today's labor unions with the economic power of trade associations, the social influence of clubs and voluntary associations, and the political power of special interest groups. Since each guild had its patron god, it had a religious dimension to it, as well.

The issue of participation in a guild posed a particular problem to early Christians. To refuse to join the guild in your field would be to sacrifice all prospect of commercial success—or even economic existence. You would be shut out of the market. But to join would compromise your faith seriously. To be a part of a guild would entail cooperation in all the economic decisions made by that cartel, to participate in the sacrifices made to the guild's god, and to participate in the common meals that were integral to each guild's protocol and decision-making process. These common meals were often occasions for drunken revelry and immorality, behavior expected of all guild participants. How could a Christian conscientiously be a part of such an economic system? Yet were Christians to abdicate the business world entirely?

The church in Thyatira apparently was thriving and prosperous. It was known through the city for doing good deeds and serving the needy. Its members were generous, and exhibited deep love and loyalty to each other (v. 19). Anyone looking at this church would be attracted by the quality of its life and its commitment to the needy. It would be a church whose Sunday services probably were packed and of which any person would be proud to be a member.

But "I have this against you: You tolerate that woman Jezebel" (v. 20). In the church in Thyatira was a very popular and persuasive woman who was apparently both a business woman and supposedly a Christian. She urged Christians not to cut themselves off from the political and economic life of their city, but instead to participate fully in the guilds. This included attending worship services of the guild's god, feasting at the common meals on the meat offered to that god, and even participating with joy in the guild's sexual adventures. Why? Because it was good for business!

Apparently the church heard her gladly. With its acceptance of Jezebel's ways, this church had become an accommodating fellowship to the business life of Thyatira. As well, many of Thyatira's leading citizens, led by Jezebel, had joined that church so that the church apparently was healthy, popular, and successful.

Such corruption of the church the Christ will not abide. So he declares through John that Jezebel will be cast down (v. 22), her businesses will fail (that is what v. 23, "I will strike her children dead" usually is considered to mean), those church members who were seduced by her compromising perspective and those citizens of Thyatira who joined the church because of her accommodating witness will be punished severely (v. 23). Only those who resisted Jezebel will escape the punishment; it is they who will possess "the morning star" (v. 28)—the Lord Jesus Christ—and so it will be they who will be saved.

To what, then, is the church in Thyatira called if it is to be a faithful church? It is called to reject its own popularity and the grounds upon which that popularity has been won, and to follow Christ. "To him who overcomes and does my will to the end, . . . I will . . . give him the morning star. He who has an ear, let him hear what the Spirit says to the churches" (vv. 26, 28–29).

To the Church in Sardis

"To the angel of the church in Sardis write:

These are the words of him who holds the seven spirits of God and the seven stars. I know your deeds; you have a reputation of being alive, but you are dead. Wake up! Strengthen what remains and is about to die, for I have not found your deeds complete in the sight of my God.

Remember, therefore, what you have received and heard; obey it, and repent. But if you do not wake up, I will come like a thief, and you will not know at what time I will come to you.

Yet you have a few people in Sardis who have not soiled their clothes. They will walk with me, dressed in white, for they are worthy. He who overcomes will, like them, be dressed in white. I will never blot out his name from the book of life, but will acknowledge his name before my Father and his angels. He who has an ear, let him hear what the Spirit says to the churches" (Rev. 3:1–6).

Sardis was almost a proverbial example of a city that was a contrast between past splendor and, at the time Revelation was written, present decay. It had been one of the greatest cities of the world seven centuries earlier, but by Roman times it was only a shadow of its former self.

Set upon a ridge fifteen hundred feet above the plains, with the ridge's sides smooth and precipitous, Sardis was considered impregnable. It had been the capital city of the Lydian empire. The people in Lydian Sardis panned gold from the river Pactolus and were the first to mint coins. The greatest of the Lydian kings who ruled from Sardis was Croesus (560–546 B.C.E.), whose name is synonymous with wealth.

Croesus declared war on Cyrus of Persia, was defeated in battle, and retreated to Sardis which was soon under Persian siege. There seemed to be no way to take the city, high on its unassailable rock. Then, one day, a Persian soldier saw a Sardian soldier lose his helmet over the battlement. To the Persian's disbelief, he watched the Sardian easily climb down the sheer rock cliff to retrieve his hat.

The Persian soldier checked and found a deep fissure which would allow a man to climb up and down. That night a party of Persian troops climbed up the fault, scaled the walls, found the battlements unguarded and the watches asleep, crept to the gates, and threw them open to admit the Persian army. And Sardis fell.

Amazingly, Sardis fell to the Seleucid army a second time two centuries later in the identical manner. When Christ commanded in this message to the church in Sardis, "Wake up!" it had a particularly relevant note for that city!

Although the church in Sardis had "a reputation of being alive" (v. 1), it was really quite dead. Sardis was a city where watchmen would sleep and posted soldiers would be absent from their battlements, where the people were soft, lazy, and comfortable, and the church had caught this infectious disease. This church was spiritually dead, unresponsive, and lethargic.

Intriguingly, the church of Sardis faced none of the overwhelming problems of the other churches in Asia. It faced no heresy from within its ranks. It was not persecuted by the Jews. It was untroubled by the Roman authorities. It did not even face the seduction that comes with popularity.

Any of the other churches gladly would have traded places with Sardis just to get some relief! But it was the Sardian church which was dead. It did not even have enough controversy to birth a heresy; the people did not hold strongly enough to their convictions to become a target of persecution. It was simply a dull church!

What does the risen Christ demand of the church in Sardis? It is very simple: "Wake up!" (v. 2). Christ asks the church to shake itself awake and take action before it dies from lethargy. And what must the church do to awaken itself? It must *remember* the Gospel it had received and experience once again its vitality. It must *repent* of its lethargic ways and recommit itself to a living Christianity. And it must *obey* the commands of the Gospel and begin living and acting with such conviction that persecution and theological debate could conceivably result (v. 3).

If the church does not act? "If you do not wake up, I will come like a thief, and you will not know at what time I will come to you" in judgment (v. 3).

There is hope for some in the church in Sardis. There are some with a glimmer of life in them (vv. 4–5)! If they respond and keep watch on the battlements of the Sardian church, they will not be wiped out of the Book of Life, but will have Christ confess them before God, and they will be honored in heaven ("dressed in white") for their faithfulness. They, at least, will be saved!

The Sardian church is called to "wake up" if it is to be a faithful church. It is called to work against a passive and non-demanding Christianity. "He who overcomes will . . . be dressed in white. I will never blot out his name from the book of life, but will acknowledge his name before my Father and his angels. He who has an ear, let him hear what the Spirit says to the churches" (vv. 5–6).

To the Church in Philadelphia

"To the angel of the church in Philadelphia write:

These are the words of him who is holy and true, who holds the key of David. What he opens no one can shut, and what he shuts no one can open. I know your deeds. See, I have placed before you an open door that no one can shut. I know that you have little strength, yet you have kept my word and have not denied my name. I will make those who are of the synagogue of Satan, who claim to be Jews though they are not, but are liars—I will make them come and fall down at your feet and acknowledge that I have loved you. Since you have kept my command to endure patiently, I will also keep you from the hour of trial that is going to come upon the whole world to test those who live on the earth.

I am coming soon. Hold on to what you have, so that no one will take your crown. Him who overcomes I will make a pillar in the temple of my God. Never again will he leave it. I will write on him the name of my God and the name of the city of my God, the new Jerusalem, which is coming down out of heaven from my God; and I will also write on him my new name. He who has an ear, let him hear what the Spirit says to the churches" (Rev. 3:7–13).

Philadelphia was a Greek city founded to be a missionary of Greek culture and language to Lydia and Phrygia. It was founded between 159 and 138 B.C.E. by colonists from Pergamum and was named Philadelphia ("brotherly love") because of the love the Seleucid king had for his brother. It is significant that the church is commended for its missionary activity as well—an "open door." Three centuries before, Philadelphia had been given an open door to spread Greek ideas in the lands beyond; here it has another great missionary opportunity—to carry to Asia the message of the love of Jesus Christ.

The message to the church in Philadelphia begins with a celebration of who Christ is. He is proclaimed as the Holy One, the one in whom lies all reality, and the one who "holds the key of David. What he opens no one can shut, and what he shuts no one can open" (v. 7). It is this vision of the opening and closing power of Christ which becomes the basic theme weaving through this message.

"I know your deeds. See, I have placed before you an open door that no one can shut. I know that you have little strength, yet you have kept my word and have not denied my name" (v. 8). The church in Philadelphia may be small and weak, but it has been faithful to Christ against overpowering odds. Because it has been faithful, Christ is now going to open to this church the door of missionary opportunity (v. 8). He can entrust these Christians with such a responsibility for they have proved faithful in the past, and will continue to be faithful. With this responsibility, they will proclaim the Gospel to Jew and Gentile alike, and see both peoples come to Christ (v. 9). The Christians will face persecution and conflict because of their work (v. 10), but Christ will keep them through such ordeals.

Then Christ reminds the Christians in Philadelphia, "I am coming soon" (v. 11). He is coming, and this news is to be encouragement to them in their ministry, comfort to the oppressed, and warning to those who ignore Christianity. And if the church in Philadelphia remains faithful to the open door of missionary opportunity given to them, Christ will richly reward them. They will be seen as pillars in the heavenly temple of God (v. 12). Jesus will write upon them the name of his God, the name of that eternal city—the new Jerusalem—which they will inherit, and his own name which will witness to their eternal service to him (v. 12). Such is the reward for the faithful labor of a faithful church.

The church in Philadelphia proved to be the most successful of all the seven churches. Over the centuries as Islam spread across Asia Minor, the church in Philadelphia stood firm. The city remained the last bastion of Asian Christianity, not falling before the Mohammedans until the fourteenth century. The church continues today and has a bishop and about a thousand believers. With the exception of Smyrna, the other churches are in ruins. But Philadelphia still holds aloft the banner of the Christian faith.

To what, then, is the church in Philadelphia called if it is to be a faithful church? It is called to proclaim, practice, and live out the Gospel in its city, to its region, and to the uttermost parts of the earth. "Him who overcomes I will make a pillar in the temple of my God. Never again will he leave it. I will write on him the name of my God and the name of the city of my God, . . . and I will also write on him my new name. He who has an ear, let him hear what the Spirit says to the churches" (vv. 12–13).

To the Church in Laodicea

"To the angel of the church in Laodicea write:

These are the words of the Amen, the faithful and true witness, the ruler of God's creation. I know your deeds, that you are neither cold nor hot. I wish you were either one or the other! So, because you are lukewarm—neither hot nor cold—I am about to spit you out of my mouth. You say, 'I am rich; I have acquired wealth and do not need a thing.' But you do not realize that you are wretched, pitiful, poor, blind and naked. I counsel you to buy from me gold refined in the fire, so you can become rich; and white clothes to wear, so you can cover your shameful nakedness; and salve to put on your eyes, so you can see.

Those whom I love I rebuke and discipline. So be earnest, and repent. Here I am! I stand at the door and knock. If anyone hears my voice and opens the door, I will come in and eat with him, and he with me.

To him who overcomes, I will give the right to sit with me on my throne, just as I overcame and sat down with my Father on his throne. He who has an ear, let him hear what the Spirit says to the churches" (Rev. 3:14–22).

Laodicea was founded in 250 B.C.E. by Antiochus of Syria. It was strategically located where three major roads converged. It was, consequently, one of the wealthiest cities in the Roman Empire. A measure of its economic power was the fact that, when it was destroyed by an earthquake in 61 C.E., the city's citizens rebuilt the entire city out of its public and their private coffers; they refused any financial assistance from Rome. In fact, one citizen donated a stadium and others donated other public buildings out of their own treasuries.

It is intriguing to trace the sources of Laodicea's prosperity, particularly in the light of Christ's criticism of the church there. The city's wealth came from three main sources. First, it was the center of the garment industry of Asia, specializing in raising black sheep which became the base for naturally black clothing. Second, it was Asia's primary banking center, specializing in buying and selling gold. Third, it was a medical center specializing in ophthalmology, and many in the city made a great deal of money from the sale of eye ointments and salves.

The church in Laodicea is the only one of the seven churches about which the risen Christ has nothing good to say. His words of condemnation are crude and vivid; they have captured the imagination of the church for two thousand years because one recognizes their profound truth:

> "I know your deeds, that you are neither cold nor hot. I wish you were either one or the other! So, because you are lukewarm—neither hot nor cold—I am about to spit you out of my mouth" (Rev. 3:15–16).

It would be a terrible thing to have someone say to you, "You are a nauseating Christian." But that is exactly what Jesus says of the Christians in the church of Laodicea. They make him want to vomit! Why? Because their Christianity is tepid, without conviction, indifferent. The risen Christ says to them, "I would rather you never had become Christians than to become the kind of Christians you are now!"

Why is this church without convictions and indifferent? There are three reasons, all integrally linked to the fortunes of its city.

First, at the time of this writing, Laodicea is a city of great wealth; it is the banking capital of Asia. The Christians have been seduced by money into perceiving themselves as rich. They do not realize that, instead of being wealthy and in need of no support, they are in reality "wretched, pitiful, poor, blind and naked" (v. 17). Well, they are about to be refined like gold in the fire, so that all their dross can be burned away (v. 18).

Second, Laodicea is the center of the garment industry of Asia. The Christians look at their rich clothes and think they have all anyone would need. In reality, they are naked before God and the rest of the church and need to have the integrity and insight to feel shame over that nakedness. Rather than clothing themselves with the black wool of Laodicea's sheep, these Christians need to clothe themselves in the white robes of righteousness (v. 18).

Third, Laodicea is a medical center specializing in ophthalmology and particularly in a highly curative eye salve. Yet, the church in Laodicea is spiritually blind. It needs to put spiritual eye salve on its corporate eyes so that it can begin to recognize its own blindness.

What must the spiritually impoverished, naked, and blind church in Laodicea do if it is not to be vomited away by Christ?

> "Those whom I love I rebuke and discipline. So be earnest, and repent. Here I am! I stand at the door and knock. If anyone hears my voice and

opens the door, I will go in and eat with him, and he with me" (Rev. 3:19–20).

The church must repent! It must get converted! It needs to recognize that it is Christian in name only, and receive Christ both as Lord and as Savior. And when those lukewarm, so-called Christians respond with an earnest commitment to Christ, they will discover that he is there, awaiting them. For he stands by the door of their church, ready to respond to their response. All they need to do is to undo the latch and swing wide the door, and he will enter into the life of their church, will break Communion bread with them, and will be at one with them.

To be a faithful church, the Laodicean Christians are called to repent of a conventional, indifferent Christianity, recognize their spiritual bankruptcy, and allow Christ to "remold them from within" (Rom. 12:2 PHILLIPS). "To him who overcomes, I will give the right to sit with me on my throne, just as I overcame and sat down with my Father on his throne. He who has an ear, let him hear what the Spirit says to the churches" (Rev. 3:21–22).

A FAITHFUL RESPONSE TO A FAITHFUL GOD

This study of the seven city churches in Asia Minor first shows us the close relationship between the effectiveness of a church and the nature of the city in which it lives. Some of these churches were seduced by their cities, in one way or another allowing the Gospel to conform to the world rather than becoming agents to enable the world to be transformed by the Gospel. In different ways, the churches in Pergamum, Thyatira, Sardis, and Laodicea allowed themselves to become "worldly" churches (i.e., churches which were seduced in some essential way by the systems or lifestyles of their cities).

Other churches resisted the siren call of their cities. They had other problems, even substantive internal problems. But each church saw that it was its responsibility to deal with its city or confront the city's systems or seek the city's transformation. What was true of all these churches—the churches in Ephesus, Smyrna, and Philadelphia—was that they assumed a pro-active role toward their cities, rather than a reactive role.

The essential response of these seven urban churches was to engage the interior spirituality of their cities. Some of them were seduced by the city's angel. Others confronted that angel. Still others sought to convert the city's angel. But whether seduced, confrontational, or evangelistic, the church could not avoid being influenced by and influencing the interior spirituality of its city. The city's angel was as powerful as was the angel of the church!

Second, we observe that all seven churches were called to be faithful to the Gospel. Success was not to be an acceptable motivation for any of them (not even the church in Philadelphia). But whereas all were called to be faithful, each would express faithfulness in a different way. To be faithful to Christ's call to them meant that—

- The church in Ephesus had to undertake the practice of love and unity.
- The church in Smyrna needed to be willing to suffer.
- The church in Pergamum had to stand strong in its faith and make vital its relationship with Christ.
- The church in Thyatira had to be willing to reject its own popularity and the grounds upon which that popularity had been won, and it had to be willing to follow an unpopular Christ.
- The church in Sardis had to "wake up" to its own passivity and seek a Christianity that was dynamic and full of conviction.
- The church in Philadelphia had to be willing to proclaim, practice, and live out the Gospel in an assertive manner in that city.
- The church in Laodicea had to humbly recognize its own spiritual bankruptcy, repent of a conventional, indifferent Christianity, and allow Christ to remold that church and its people from within.

Finally, it was the vision of the new Jerusalem which was to inform the faithfulness of each of the seven churches. If all the risen Christ wanted to do was to confront these churches with their respective issues and to call them to accountability and action, the book of Revelation would have ended with chapter 3. But the book continues: it presents a profound picture of the struggle between the powers of God and the powers of darkness for the soul of the world; it reveals what the city given over fully to Satan becomes (along with its inevitable fate); and it climaxes with the vision of the city as the city of God—the new Jerusalem—the realized kingdom of God.

Those seven churches were given this vision of the new Jerusalem both to inform them and to encourage them as they sought to be faithful to Jesus Christ in their individual cities. Since faithfulness was contextualized to each situation, it was the one, common vision that knit these churches together into one body of Christ. It was that vision which answered the question for all the churches, "Why should we be faithful?" It was not just to make God happy. It was not so they might somehow be doing what was right. They were to be faithful as an integral part of God's plan to bring about God's kingdom—not only in Asia Minor—but throughout the whole world. Those seven churches (as are all churches) were an integral part of the fulfillment of that plan. So, although the kingdom ultimately would come by God's action, each church was to perform its ministry as if the kingdom's coming depended upon the individual church's faithfulness.

What do we learn from this exploration of Revelation 2–3 about the faithfulness to which we are called in the city?

First, we realize that we cannot avoid interaction with our city's spirituality, and to seek to do so is, in reality, the height of unfaithfulness. We must deal directly with that spirituality, or it will seduce us.

We can be seduced in many ways. Like Thyatira, we can yield to the temptation to propound a popular and sanitized Christianity. Like Sardis, we can become lethargic in response to our city's primary issues. Like Pergamum, we can become so fixated on our internal problems that we lose sight of our responsibility toward the city. Or, like Laodicea, we can simply go about the business of running our church while ignoring the city, allowing its angel to blind us to the reality that the city is infiltrating and dominating our church. Thus, ignoring our obligations to the city while concentrating on maintaining our church becomes a sure way that the city's angel can seduce us into irrelevancy.

Or we can choose to interact with our city's spirituality. Like Ephesus and Smyrna, we can confront the city's angel at the point of our church's particular call. That may require us to suffer at the hands of the city (Smyrna) or it may press us into a different way of being church (as it did with Ephesus). Like Philadelphia, it might mean that we would seek the conversion of the city. But whether we are confronting, advocating the cause of the poor and weak, participating with the powerless in their struggle for self-determination, or proclaiming life- and system-transforming Good News to those who shape and who are seduced by the systems, faithful response to the Gospel calls us to deal with our city's spirituality. For only by dealing with the spiritual depths of our city—with its angel—will we participate in bringing about any permanent change in our city and in its people!

Second, we learn from this interaction with Revelation 2–3 that God's call to each of us in the city is to be faithful, not to be successful. This is not to say that success is not an option, but if it comes it is to be a result of faithfulness, not an objective of its own. Our objective must be to be faithful to the call God has given God's church in and to that city. If the faithful pursuit of that call leads to the church's success, praise God! But if that faithful pursuit leads to other results, we must be able to embrace that as well.

Faithfulness is not measured simply by following scriptural directives. Faithfulness must be contextualized. In the case of each of the seven churches, their faithfulness was determined by an exploration of the issues and needs of each city, the response of the church thus far to those issues, and, in the light of such analysis, an accurate perception of the next risky steps of faith into which God was calling each church. Faithfulness must always be contextualized. Contextualization occurs only when the church in the city is willing to look objectively at the systems of its city and look honestly at that church's response to those systems as well as its own interior life.

Third, we learn from this study of Revelation 2–3 that the faithfulness to which we are called as the city church is a faithfulness that must be informed by the vision of the new Jerusalem. We were introduced to that theme by using Jesus' nomenclature for it—the kingdom of God (chapter 4 of this book). And we recognized that it was that vision of God's kingdom that would give us purpose and direction, and would inform all that we would do and be as the church in the city. That became the case, as we explored together the redemptive work of Christ in the city, and the vocation and work of the church to which it has been called.

Now, in the book of Revelation, Jesus' vision of the kingdom comes to its climax. It comes to that fulfillment through the image of the new Jerusalem. Life is fulfilled for all humanity in a city. That is God's best intention for humankind. It is that vision which we are to keep before ourselves and into which we should live. Only by maintaining this vision can we faithfully seek to be God's church in our own city.

CITY OF GOD, CITY OF SATAN

We have now come to the close of this biblical exploration of the city. How can we conclude this time of new discovery together? I would like to end it with some closing words of St. Paul—words which have come to us several times during this study, words which are constantly relevant to those who seek to be the church in the city:

> Finally, be strong in the Lord and in his mighty power. Put on the full armor of God so that you can take your stand against the devil's schemes. For our struggle is not against flesh and blood, but against the rulers, against the authorities, against the powers of this dark world and against the spiritual forces of evil in the heavenly realms. Therefore put on the full armor of God, so that when the day of evil comes, you may be able to stand your ground, and after you have done everything, to stand (Eph. 6:10–13).

Together, we have looked at the Scripture on the city. We have discovered Scripture teaching us that the city is a great battleground between God and Satan, between the Lord of the universe and the Evil One who would destroy what God has created. We have studied both the dimensions of God's care for the city and the circumference of its evil, as it is expressed in the city's systems and principalities, as well as in its individuals. We have explored God's intentions for the city through the image of "the kingdom of God." We have discovered the comprehensive way in which God has acted through Christ to redeem the city, and the unique urban vocation and ministry to which the church is called.

We concluded our study by exploring the scriptural power which

God gives us in order both to sustain us and to enable us to be effective in our city ministry: personal spiritual formation, life in community, and maintenance of a vision of what God is doing to culminate reality in his city. But, in the final analysis, what God calls us most to do in our city is, in Paul's words, "to stand your ground, and after you have done everything, to stand."

God's call to you and me, as city Christians and as part of God's church in the city, is to be faithful—faithful to ourselves, faithful to our brother and sister Christians, faithful to our city's body of Christ, faithful to the poor, the powerless, and the lost of our city—and thus, faithful to God. And what does it mean to be faithful?

Early in this book, I shared an incident that happened in my first city ministry, an incident that revealed to me the ways the systems of a great city can conspire to destroy the soul of a beautiful young girl. A few weeks after that incident, I went to an old black pastor in that community—a pastor I had come to respect deeply. Overwhelmed by what had happened to that girl as well as by my own sense of incompetence and inability even to understand the problem, I went to this brother in Christ, a man perceptive with the wisdom of both age and experience. We talked long and hard that day. In that conversation, I began to see the city through black eyes, through eyes of powerlessness and poverty, and thus I received from him my first lessons in the ways of the systems of a city. I remain eternally grateful to him both for the wisdom and the compassion he showed to a confused, hurting brother that day.

As we approached the end of our conversation, I asked the question that kept coming to me with increasing insistency. "In the light of all we've talked about today, and all you've shared with me about the evil of this city, what keeps you going? What advice would you have for a young buck like me, just starting out in ministry in this city?"

That ancient pastor (I am sure he has long since gone on to his reward, for he was very old) sat in silence for the longest time, then reached out and took my hands, looked me in the eyes compassionately as if he could see all that I would go through in thirty years of city ministry, and responded, "Young brother, just keep on keeping on!"

"Just keep on keeping on." God asks nothing else of you!

NOTES

Chapter One: Our City: God's Creation

1. Rafael Salas, "Meeting the Challenge of Urban Explosion," *Indian Express,* Madras, India (5 April 1986).

2. "God and the City," in *The City—for God's Sake* (Monrovia, Calif.: Missions Advanced Research and Communications Center, 1987), videotape series.

3. Ibid.

4. Harley Schreck: research gathered from a number of sources, including United Nations urban data and the "World Population Data Sheet" of the Population Reference Bureau; research done for the Office of Urban Advance, World Vision International.

5. David B. Barrett, *World-Class Cities and World Evangelization* (Birmingham, Ala.: New Hope, 1986), 48–49.

6. Robert W. Fox, "The World's Urban Explosion," *National Geographic* 166, no. 2 (August 1984): 179–85.

7. Ibid.

8. *Stemming the Tide of Displacement* (N.p.: Coalition for the Homeless, 1986).

9. Patrick McAuslan, "Urban Land and Shelter for the Poor" (N.p.: 1985).

10. Research by Office of Urban Advance, World Vision International, on Bombay, India.

11. Gerald Luedtke and Associates, "People In Faith United Neighborhood Revitalization Plan" (Detroit, Mich.: PIFU, 1985).

12. Lester Brown and Jodi Jackson, "Assessing the Future of Urbanization," *State of the World* (N.p.: 1987 report).

13. Dominique Lapierre, *The City of Joy* (New York: Warner Books, 1985), 29–32.

14. The Population Institute, 110 Maryland Ave. NE, Washington, DC 20002.

15. Sir Leonard Woolley, *Excavations at Ur: A Record of Twelve Years' Work* (New York: Barnes & Noble, 1955).

16. Lewis Mumford, *The City in History* (New York: Harcourt, Brace, 1961), 62. Also see description of Babylon written by Herodotus, 77–78.

17. Ibid., 213.

18. Ibid., 218–20.

19. Rodolfo Aradeo Lanciani, *Ancient Rome in the Light of Recent Discoveries,* 8th ed. (Boston: n.p., 1892).

20. Mumford, *The City in History*, 259–60.

21. Ray Bakke, *The Urban Christian: Effective Ministry in Today's Urban World* (Downers Grove, Ill.: InterVarsity Press, 1987); Harvey Conn, *A Clarified Vision for Urban Mission* (Grand Rapids: Zondervan, 1987); David S. Lim, "The City in the Bible," *Evangelical Review of Theology* 12, no. 2, (April 1988); Albert Nolan, *Jesus Before Christianity* (Maryknoll, N.Y.: Orbis, 1978); Elizabeth O'Connor, *Call to Commitment* (New York: Harper & Row, 1963); Benjamin Tonna, *Gospel for the Cities* (Maryknoll, N.Y.: Orbis, 1981).

22. Millar Burrows, "Jerusalem," in *The Interpreter's Dictionary*, vol. 2 (Nashville: Abingdon, 1962), 843.

23. John Gray, "Shahar," and W. L. Reed, "Shalem,"in *The Interpreter's Dictionary*, 4:303. Also see Burrows, "Jerusalem."

24. Edwin M. Good, "Peace in the OT," in *The Interpreter's Dictionary*, 3:704–6. Also see Gray, "Shahar," and Reed, "Shalem."

Chapter Two: Our City as the Abode of Personal and Systemic Evil

1. Robert Linthicum, "Seduced by the City," *World Vision* (June–July 1989): 6.

2. Jack Finegan, *Light from the Ancient Past* (Princeton: Princeton University Press, 1946), 171–73.

3. Eugene H. Peterson, *Run with the Horses* (Downers Grove, Ill.: InterVarsity Press, 1983), 61–62.

Chapter Three: Our City as the Abode of Satanic Principalities and Powers

1. Debate by biblical critics surrounds the book of Ephesians regarding its origins and authorship. Some suggest it was not written to the church in Ephesus, since most early manuscripts omit the words "in Ephesus" from the greeting in verse 1: "To the saints in Ephesus." Some have suggested that the letter was intended as an encyclical, summarizing Paul's theology (and is therefore the most comprehensive of all his letters) and meant either to be circulated among all his churches or to be the introductory book in a collection of Paul's epistles following his death (see chapter 11 of this book). There is also debate over the authorship of Ephesians. Some contend that it was written by Paul, others suggest it was written by a disciple of Paul's following his death. Arguments against Pauline authorship center around the significant difference between the writing style exhibited in Ephesians and Paul's writing style in his other letters. It is my opinion that there is insufficient evidence to support the arguments of non-Pauline authorship of Ephesians. Therefore, throughout this book, I will refer to Paul as the author of Ephesians.

2. The Greek word *stoich* is best translated "elemental spirits" and refers to "astral divinities which control the spheres and are thus masters of human fate" (Francis W. Beare, "Introduction and Exegesis of Colossians," *The Interpreter's Bible* [Nashville: Abingdon, 1955]: 93.)

3. The Hebrew word *bene elohim*, which is translated in TEV as "god," is translated as "guardian angel" in MOFFATT and as "sons of God" in the RSV and JB. *Bene elohim*, when used elsewhere in Scripture (e.g., Job 1:6; Ps. 29:1; Ps. 82:1–2),

refs to "guardian angels." Some older translations depend on a variant reading
of the text and therefore translate the reference as "sons of Israel" (KJV); regrettably,
the NIV, used as the primary text for this book, chooses this variant reading. The
context makes it clear, however, that the author's argument in Deuteronomy 32:8–
9 is that God directly protects Israel whereas he has assigned only guardian angels
to protect the destiny of all other nations.

4. Mumford, *The City in History*, 320, 318.

Chapter Four: God's Intentions for the City

1. "Kingdom," *Webster's Ninth New Collegiate Dictionary* (Springfield, Mass.:
Merriam-Webster, 1987), 662.

2. The Grail, *The Psalms* (London: Collins, Fontana Books, 1963). In this
translation, Psalm 85 is numbered 84.

3. Compare, for example, the differences in translation (and therefore of
meaning) between the KJV (translated under the authority of a king), the present-
day NIV (a relatively cautious translation), and the JB in such passages as Leviticus
19:15; 1 Samuel 10:18–19; 26:24; Job 36:3; Psalms 4:1; 9:18; 18:20; 72:1–2; 85; 96:13;
Isaiah 1:21; 11:4–5; 26:9–10; 42:6–7, 21; 51; 62:1–2; Jeremiah 23:6; 33:16; Hosea
2:19; 10:12; and Zephaniah 2:3.

4. Roger Dowley, ed., *Towards the Recovery of a Lost Bequest* (London:
Evangelical Coalition for Urban Mission, n.d.).

5. Robert Linthicum, "Oh Calcutta" (a sermon preached at the Grosse
Pointe Woods Presbyterian Church, Grosse Pointe Woods, Michigan, on 13
February 1983, and published by Ministry of Money, Germantown, Md.), 4–5.

6. Robert Linthicum, *The People Who Turned the World Upside Down: Leader's
Guide* (Tucker, Ga.: Lay Renewal Publications, 1982), 59–61.

7. E.g., Ezekiel 17:22ff.; 31:1ff.; Daniel 4:10, 21.

8. Athol Gill, "From Down Under: Biblical Perspectives on Poverty and the
Poor" (Melbourne, Australia: Victorian Council of Christian Education, 1986), 9.

9. Claude C. Montefiore, "The Originality of Jesus," in *Contemporary
Thinking About Jesus*, ed. Thomas S. Kepler (New York: Abingdon, 1944), 385.

10. Colin Marchant, *Signs in the City* (London: Hodder & Stoughton, 1985),
114–15.

11. E. A. Speiser, "Genesis" in *The Anchor Bible* (Garden City, N.Y.:
Doubleday, 1964), 134: "*Yahweh paused in front of Abraham.* So the original text. But
the passage is listed among the rare instances of Masoretic interference known as
Tiqqune soferim 'scribal corrections,' whereby the text was changed to 'Abraham
paused before Yahweh,' for deferential reasons. The change is already witnessed
in LXX." Also Gerhard von Rad, *Genesis* (Philadelphia: Westminster Press, 1961),
206: "In v. 22 occurs one of the very few arbitrary changes which the postexilic
Jewish men of learning dared to make in the text (and which were of course
precisely noted): That Yahweh remained standing, as though waiting for Abraham, appeared to them as unworthy of Yahweh. Therefore they changed the
sentence so that Abraham remained standing before Yahweh. They sacrificed,
therefore, Yahweh's gesture of lingering, which contained a silent demand to
express itself, to their religious timidity."

12. Ibid.

Chapter Five: What Did Jesus Do for the City?

1. Caryl Micklem, *Contemporary Prayers for Public Worship* (London: SCM Press, 1967), 118.

2. The relationship between Luke 13:34–35 and 19:41–44 and Matthew 23:37–39 is a subject of debate among scholars. The gospel of Luke is generally considered to have at least two written sources, in its sharing common material with the gospel of Matthew (the "Q" source) and its having material that appears in no other gospel account (the "L" source). Because Luke 13:34–35 and Matt. 23:37–39 are similar, they are regarded as coming from the same "Q" source. But Luke 19:41–44 is unique in the Gospels, thus the "L" source.

The difficulty with the "Q" passages arises because of their location in their respective texts. The "Q" story is placed by Matthew after Palm Sunday, but by Luke before Palm Sunday. The reference to Jesus' coming to the city in Luke, therefore, would be a reference to his arrival on Palm Sunday; in Matthew, however, it could not be a reference to the Triumphal Entry but to the Second Coming. If Matthew's position is correct (and that is the most likely scenario), then it would have necessitated a second story in Luke (for Jesus to predict his second coming). Thus it is suggested by biblical scholars that the more comprehensive statement by Jesus given in Luke was divided by the author into the two statements that currently exist. But the difficulties of these passages cannot be resolved with certainty at this point.

Chapter Six: The Vocation of the Urban Church

1. It is debated among scholars whether Paul is referring solely to the Jewish legal and regulatory system or whether he is making reference to the entire "written code" that regulated all life—both Jewish and Gentile—in the Roman Empire. I have taken it to mean the latter, but holding the former would not detract in any way from the argument I present regarding this Scripture passage.

2. "Overrode"—JB; "did away"—TEV; "set aside"—RSV and NEB; "canceled"—NIV; "took it out of the way"—MLB.

Chapter Seven: The Presence and Prayer of the Church in the City

1. There is strong textual evidence to indicate that verses 8–9 do not belong in their present setting, but rather between verses 15 and 16. I have made this adjustment in the text, which heightens the clarity of this passage (e.g., see *Jerusalem Bible,* 1298–99).

2. Paul Boyer, *Urban Masses and Moral Order in America, 1820–1920* (Cambridge: Harvard University Press, 1978), 136.

3. Anne Keegan, "A Neighborhood Misses Jack and His Bike," *Chicago Tribune,* n.d., 1983. Copyright © 1983 by Chicago Tribune Company, all rights reserved. Used with permission.

Chapter Eight: The Practice and Proclamation of the Church in the City

1. I am indebted to Ray Bakke, director of Lausanne Urban Associates and president of International Urban Associates, for proposing Isaiah 65:18–25 as a paradigm for the work of the church in the city.

2. Statistics gathered by the Office of Urban Advance, World Vision International.

3. I have substituted the word *worship* for the word *fasting,* as given in the text. Fasting was a crucial element of Israelite worship, and I believe that in making the substitution I have maintained the author's intended impact.

4. William Skudlarek, "A Most Transparent Life: An Interview with Dom Helder Camara," *Sojourners* (December 1987): 19.

5. I have been unsuccessful in identifying the source for this statement, which is consistently attributed to D. L. Moody.

6. Much of this material has been taken from my article "Networking: Hope for the Church in the City," *Urban Mission* (January 1987): 35–36.

7. Some of the material contained in this section appeared in my article "Networking," 38–39.

Chapter Nine: Godly Ways for Community Ministries

1. The primary outline I have used for this study of Nehemiah is adapted from one developed by Kenneth Tollefson in his seminal article, "The Nehemiah Model for Christian Missions," *Missiology: An International Review* 15, no. 1 (January 1987): 31–55. The material that provides the substantive content for this study, however, comes out of my training and twenty-four years of experience in community organization.

2. Jacob M. Myers, "Ezra and Nehemiah," in *The Anchor Bible* (Garden City, N.Y.: Doubleday, 1965), 96.

3. Martin Buber, *Ten Rungs: Hasidic Sayings* (New York: Schocken Books, 1947), 84, 74.

4. Much of the material on networking in this chapter is taken from my article "Networking," *Urban Mission* (January 1987).

5. Skudlarek, "A Most Transparent Life."

6. Much of this material is taken from my article "Networking."

7. MARC Publications (919 W. Huntington Drive, Monrovia, CA 91016) has produced an hour-long video on networking as a part of the three-hour urban ministry video training program *The City—for God's Sake.* Printed materials on networking include my book *Empowering the Poor: Comunity Organizing Among the "Rag, Tag and Bobtail"* (Monrovia, Calif.: MARC Publications, 1991), chap. 4; my articles "Networking: Hope for the Church in the City," *Urban Mission* (January 1987); "Doing Effective Ministry in the City" and "Stephen Githumbi of Nairobi" and Mariano Avila, "Seek the Peace and Prosperity of the City," all in *Together* (April–June 1988): 1–2, 12–13; Ray Bakke, *The Urban Christian* (Downers Grove, Ill.: InterVarsity Press, 1987); Michael Eastman, *Ten Inner-City Churches* (London: MARC Publications, 1988); and Viv Grigg, *Companion to the Poor* (Monrovia, Calif.: MARC Publications, 1990).

World Vision publishes a newsletter, *Urban Advance,* three times a year. It deals primarily with networking and community organizing throughout the urban first and third worlds. There is no subscription charge. To receive *Urban Advance,* write the Office of Urban Advance, World Vision International, 919 W. Huntington Drive, Monrovia, CA 91016.

8. The "Congress on Urban Ministry," held every two years in Chicago, is an international event that features plenary sessions, seminars, and workshops on numerous urban ministry subjects and strategies. For information, write the Seminary Consortium for Urban Pastoral Education, 30 W. Chicago, Chicago, IL 60610.

In the United States, the Institute of the Church in Urban-Industrial Society (ICUIS) offers three to five courses each year in networking and community organizing. For information, write ICUIS, 5700 S. Woodlawn, Chicago, IL 60637.

In Great Britain and in Europe, the Evangelical Coalition for Urban Ministry also offers events and involvement in a UK-based urban network. For information, write ECUM, Lawrence Hall, Cumberland Rd., London E13 8NH, United Kingdom. In Australia, contact the School of World Mission, Whitly College, 271 Royal Parade, Parkville, Melbourne, Australia 3052. In Asia, Africa, Latin America and in Europe, the International Urban Associates and World Vision each offer six to ten urban consultations and workshops each year. To get a schedule of IUA consultation plans, contact Dr. Ray Bakke, International Urban Associates, 1043 W. Madison, Suite 200, Chicago, IL 60607 USA. To learn of World Vision's plans for urban workshops in any given year, contact either your nation's World Vision field office or the Rev. Ken Luscombe, Office of Urban Advance, World Vision International, 919 W. Huntington Drive, Monrovia, CA 91016 USA.

9. When I use the word *action,* I mean an activity the people take together that confronts the appropriate city structure to obtain for the people what they justly deserve. A *project* is an activity the people undertake to provide for themselves. Using the Nehemiah model, when the people built the wall of Jerusalem, they were engaging in a project. When they confronted Sanballet, Tobiah, and the Arabs (Neh. 4), they were engaging in an action.

10. Short-term workshops and training events on community organization are offered regularly by ICUIS (see note 8), the Organize Training Center, 1095 Market St., #419, San Francisco, CA 94103, and the Office of Urban Advance, World Vision International (see note 8). See my chapter "Uniquely Urban Strategies" in the book *Discipling the City,* ed. Roger S. Greenway (Grand Rapids: Baker, 1991); my articles "Community Organization: What Does It Have to Do with the Urban Church?" and "Urban Evangelism: Community Organization" and "What First World Christians Can Learn from the Third World Urban Church," all available from the Office of Urban Advance, World Vision International; and my book *Empowering the Poor.*

Books on community organization theory and practice that I particularly recommend are Saul Alinsky, *Reveille for Radicals* (New York: Random House, 1969); Kimberley Bobo, *Lives Matter: A Handbook for Christian Organizing* (Kansas City: Sheed and Ward, 1986); Robert C. Linthicum, *Empowering the Poor* (Monrovia, Calif.: MARC, 1991); Felipe E. Maglaya, *Organizing People for Power: A Manual for Organizers* (N.p.: Asia Committee for People's Organization, 1982; contained in Simpson's and Stockwell's workbook, below); Gregory F. Pierce, *Activism That Makes Sense: Congregations and Community Organization* (New York: Paulist Press, 1984); and Dick Simpson and Clinton Stockwell, *Congregations and Community Organizing* (Chicago, Ill.: ICUIS, 1987). I also recommend subscription to *The Organizer Mailing* (San Francisco: Organize Training Center), a periodic distribution of pivotal articles on community organization published in the previous quarter of the year.

11. Myers, "Ezra and Nehemiah," 100–101.

Chapter Ten: Spiritual Power: Spiritual Formation

1. Ross Langmead, "Pilgrim Song," on the record album *On the Road* (Spotswood, Vic., Australia: Ross Langmead), album copyright © 1987, song copyright © 1985), 8–11 of song book.

2. The development of the four propositions is taken from my book *The People Who Turned the World Upside Down: Leader's Guide,* 120–122.

3. Journal of Robert Linthicum, entry for 23 November 1982.

4. Prayer books I have found particularly helpful are the Episcopal *Book of Common Prayer; The Prayer of the Church: The New Roman Catholic Breviary* (London: Geoffrey Chapman, 1970); *Daily Prayer: The Worship of God* (Philadelphia: Westminster Press, 1987); Dom Helder Camara, *The Desert Is Fertile* (Maryknoll, N.Y.: Orbis Books, 1974); Bob and Michael Benson, *Disciplines for the Inner Life* (Waco, Tex.: Word, 1985); Clyde Manschreck, ed., *Prayers of the Reformers* (Philadelphia: Muhlenberg Press, 1958); and John Baillie, *A Diary of Private Prayer* (New York: Scribner's, 1949).

Chapter Eleven: Life in Community

1. Cf. Markus Barth, "Ephesians," in *The Anchor Bible* (Garden City, N.Y.: Doubleday, 1974), 53–59; E. G. Beare, *The Interpreter's Bible,* vol. 10 (Nashville: Abingdon, 1953), 604, 607; E. J. Goodspeed, *An Introduction to the New Testament* (N.p.: 1937), 222–39.

2. Source unknown.

3. In chapter 8 we looked at Ephesians 4–6 as a model for carrying out the practice and proclamation of the church in the city. Because the purpose of that study was to examine Paul's *strategy* for the church's ministry, these chapters were expounded differently from the way we will develop them in this chapter, where the emphasis is on the *vocation of the church as community.*

4. See note 3.

5. The small-group life of our Detroit-area church was deeply influenced by the mission-group formation of the Church of the Saviour in Washington, D.C. For information on the small-group life of this intentional and loving mission-centered community, write the Wellspring Mission Group of the Church of the Saviour, 11301 Neelsville Church Road, Germantown, MD 20874, or read Elizabeth O'Connor, *Call to Commitment* (New York: Harper & Row, 1963), or Gordon Cosby, *Handbook for Mission Groups* (Waco, Tex.: Word Books, 1976). Both books and other information on the church are available from the Church of the Saviour, 2025 Massachusetts Ave., NW, Washington, DC 20036, or from their Potter's House Bookstore.

6. Ross Langmead, "In God's Family," on the record album *On the Road,* 4–5 of song book.

Chapter Twelve: God's Vision for the City

1. Source unknown

2. Material in this chapter has been particularly influenced by the work of Henry Drummond, *The City Without a Church* (London: Hodder & Stoughton, 1893), and William Barclay, *The Revelation of John*, vol. 2, The Daily Study Bible Series (Philadelphia: Westminster Press, 1976).

3. "Martyrium Polycarpi," Secs. III, V–XVI.

Chapter Thirteen: And Having Done All, to Stand

1. Material in this chapter has been particularly influenced by the work of William Barclay, *The Revelation of John*, vol. 1, The Daily Study Bible Series (Philadelphia: Westminster Press, 1976), and R. K. Harrison, ed., *Major Cities of the Biblical World* (New York: Thomas Nelson, 1985).

BIBLIOGRAPHY

Bakke, Ray. Lecture in "God and the City." In *The City—for God's Sake*. Monrovia, Calif.: MARC Publications, 1986. Videotape series.

———. *The Urban Christian*. Downers Grove, Ill.: InterVarsity Press, 1987.

Barclay, William. *The Daily Study Bible Series*. 17 vols. Philadelphia: Westminster Press, 1976.

Bauman, Edward W. *Where Your Treasure Is*. Arlington, Va.: Bauman Bible Telecasts, 1980.

Brueggemann, Walter. "The Embarrassing Footnote." *Theology Today* 44, no. 1 (April 1987).

———. *The Prophetic Imagination*. Philadelphia: Fortress, 1978.

Bryant, David. "How Do You Pray for a City?" *Latin America Evangelist* (January–March 1989).

Burrows, Millar. "Jerusalem." In *The Interpreter's Dictionary*. Nashville: Abingdon, 1962.

Buttrick, George Arthur, ed. *The Interpreter's Bible*. 12 vols. Nashville: Abingdon, 1957.

Christian Faith and Economic Justice. New York: Office of the General Assembly, The Presbyterian Church USA, 1984.

Conn, Harvey. *A Clarified Vision for Urban Mission*. Grand Rapids: Zondervan, 1987.

Dogan, Mattei, and John D. Kasarda, eds. *A World of Giant Cities*. New Delhi: Sage Publications, 1988.

Drummond, Henry. *The City Without a Church*. London: Hodder & Stoughton, 1893.

Galilea, Segundo. *Following Jesus*. Maryknoll, N.Y.: Orbis, 1981.

Good, Edwin M. "Peace." In *The Interpreter's Dictionary*. Nashville: Abingdon, 1962.

Gray, John. "Shahar." In *The Interpreter's Dictionary*. Nashville: Abingdon, 1962.

Greenleaf, Robert K. *Servant Leadership*. New York: Paulist, 1977.

Greenway, Roger S. *Apostles to the City*. Grand Rapids: Baker, 1978.

———, ed. *Discipling the City*. Grand Rapids: Baker, 1991.

Grigg, Viv. *Companion to the Poor*. Monrovia, Calif.: MARC Publications, 1990.

Harrison, R. K., ed. *Major Cities of the Biblical World*. Nashville: Thomas Nelson, 1985.

Hawkins, Peter S., ed. *Civitas: Religious Interpretations of the City.* Atlanta, Ga.: Scholars Press, 1986.

Laymon, Charles M., ed. *Interpreter's Concise Commentary.* 8 vols. Nashville: Abingdon, 1983.

Linthicum, Robert C. "Doing Effective Ministry in the City." *Together* (April–June 1988).

———. *Empowering the Poor: Community Organizing Among the "Rag, Tag and Bobtail."* Monrovia, Calif.: MARC Publications, 1991.

———. "Networking: Hope for the Church in the City." *Urban Mission* (January 1987).

———. *The People's Bible Study.* 2 vols. Atlanta, Ga.: Institute of Church Renewal, 1980, 1982.

———. *The People Who Turned the World Upside Down.* Atlanta, Ga.: Institute of Church Renewal, 1982.

———. "Seduced by the City." *World Vision* (June–July 1989).

———. "Towards a Biblical Urban Theology." *Together* (April–June 1988).

Meeks, Wayne A. *The First Urban Christians: The Social World of the Apostle Paul.* New Haven, Conn.: Yale University Press, 1983.

Mumford, Lewis. *The City in History.* London: Harcourt, Brace, 1961.

Myers, Jacob M. "Ezra and Nehemiah." In *The Anchor Bible.* Garden City, N.Y.: Doubleday, 1965.

Nolan, Albert. *Jesus Before Christianity.* Maryknoll, N.Y.: Orbis, 1978.

North, C. R. "World." In *The Interpreter's Dictionary.* Nashville: Abingdon, 1962.

Nouwen, Henri J. M. *The Wounded Healer: Ministry in Contemporary Society.* Garden City, N.Y.: Doubleday, 1972.

Nyenhuis, Gerald. "Una Perspectiva Biblica de la Ciudad." Paper read at "Dia de Oracion y Reflexion por la Ciudad de Mexico," Mexico City, 19 September 1986.

O'Connor, Elizabeth. *Cry Pain, Cry Hope: Thresholds to Purpose.* Waco, Tex.: Word Books, 1987.

———. *Journey Inward, Journey Outward.* New York: Harper & Row, 1968.

Purves, Andrew. *The Search for Compassion.* Louisville: Westminster/John Knox Press, 1989.

Samuel, Vinay, and Chris Sugden. *Evangelism and the Poor.* Bangalore, India: Partnership in Mission—Asia, 1983.

Sider, Ronald, ed. *Cry Justice: The Bible on Hunger and Poverty.* New York: Paulist, 1980.

Tollefson, Kenneth. "The Nehemiah Model for Christian Missions." *Missiology: An International Review* 15, no. 1 (January 1987).

Tonna, Benjamin. *Gospel for the Cities.* Maryknoll, N.Y.: Orbis, 1981.

Wink, Walter. *Naming the Powers: The Language of Power in the New Testament.* Philadelphia: Fortress, 1984.

———. *Unmasking the Powers: The Invisible Forces That Determine Human Existence.* Philadelphia: Fortress, 1986.

SUBJECT INDEX

SCRIPTURE INDEX